MAKING THE GRADE
Grades 3–4

By the Staff of *SCORE!*

Simon & Schuster

**This series is dedicated to our *SCORE!* parents and children—
thank you for making these books possible.**

Published by
Kaplan Educational Centers and Simon & Schuster
1230 Avenue of the Americas
New York, NY 10020

President, *SCORE!*: Robert L. Waldron
Series Content and Development: Intentional Educations
Assessment Pull-Out Section Authors: Preeti Shah and Dr. Paul Glovinsky
Author of Chapter 4, "How Can I Help My Child Prepare for Standardized Tests?": Hannah Rubenstein
Educational Content Editor: Julie Landsman
Project Editor: Eileen Mager
Resources Section: Eileen Mager, Amy Arner Sgarro, Doreen Beauregard
Production Editor: Maude Spekes
Managing Editor: Dave Chipps
Executive Editor: Del Franz
Layout Design and Desktop Production: Krista Pfeiffer, Christopher Mattox
Desktop Publishing Manager: Michael Shevlin
Illustrations: Lorie Park and the Wild Goose Company

Special thanks to: Ruth Baygell, Jay Johnson, Kevin Rockmael, Ed Stanford, Barry Tonoff

Library of Congress Cataloging-in-Publication Data is available.

Manufactured in the United States of America
Published Simultaneously in Canada

Second Edition, October 1999

7 6 5 4 3 2 1

ISBN: 0-684-86896-2

CONTENTS

About Kaplan

Pull-Out Section: The Home Learning Quizzes

Foreword

Good grades can be encouraging and satisfying, and we at *SCORE!* are always pleased when the kids who attend our educational centers do well on their report cards. Even so, we want so much more for our children than straight A's. Many of us were honors students ourselves, so we know that "making the grade" is only the beginning. What we really want for our kids are good grades and everything that good grades are supposed to represent.

- We want our kids to master the key communication systems that make civilization possible: language (spoken and written), math, and music.

- We want them to build their critical thinking skills so that they can understand, appreciate, and improve their world.

- We want them to continually increase their knowledge, and to value learning as the key to a happy, successful life.

- We want them to always do their best, to persist when challenged, to be a force for good, and to help others whenever they can.

We know these are ambitious goals, but our children deserve no less. Our mission at *SCORE!* is to create great opportunities for learning and development for kids across the country. We've already helped thousands of children through programs in our centers, and we're eager to reach thousands more with this series of books designed for parents of first through eighth graders.

SIMPLE PRINCIPLES

We owe the remarkable success of *SCORE!* Educational Centers to a few simple principles, and we would like to highlight these points as you consider working with this book to create great Learning Adventures for your child.

Making the Grade

• We expect every child to succeed.

• We make it possible for every child to succeed.

• We reinforce each instance of success, no matter how small.

Such simple principles are easily understood, but understanding them is simply not enough. The purpose of this book is to help you put these principles into practice in order to support and enhance the academic development of your child. As a parent facing ever growing demands at work and at home, you need useful, practical answers now. We'd like to share what we've learned in our work with thousands of children across the country. We'd like to show you how to put these principles to work.

ASSESSING YOUR CHILD

Just as a good physician performs a thorough diagnosis before prescribing treatment, we recommend starting with a thorough assessment of your child's academic status. At *SCORE!*, we have learned that excellent grades don't always indicate academic excellence. As standards have eroded, more and more children get A's and B's in school. We often come across "straight-A students" whose actual skills lag behind national standards by a full grade level or more. And if your child's grades are poor, you will probably find it useful to improve your understanding of exactly what that means.

One helpful approach in assessing your child's skills is to ask yourself the following questions, especially as they relate to what you were capable of at your child's age:

1. How much is my child reading? At what level of difficulty?

2. Has my child mastered appropriate language arts skills, such as spelling, grammar, and syntax?

3. Does my child have the ability to express appropriately complex thoughts when speaking or writing?

4. Does my child demonstrate adequate mastery of all age-appropriate math skills, such as mastery of addition and subtraction facts, multiplication tables, division rules, etc.?

These questions are a good starting place and may give you new insights into your child's academic situation and how things have changed since you were a child. At the same time, the subjective assessment guidelines included in this book will help you to understand how your child is grasping school material, homework, and key concepts in language arts, math, and science. You will probably be surprised by the results, no matter what grades your child is earning at school!

WHAT'S GOING ON AT SCHOOL?

Teaching is a noble profession, and we have made the acquaintance of many fine teachers in the communities where our educational centers are located. Unfortunately, we have found a tremendous amount of disarray in those same teachers' school districts. No one seems to agree on what parents and students should expect of schools, and we are a long way from reaching a national consensus. In the meantime, many districts are striving to be all things to all people. Until we refocus our public and private institutions on excellence in learning, we can expect uneven results and knowledge gaps for children at every ability level, no matter how "good" the school district.

Parents will always need to monitor the situation at school and take responsibility for their children's learning. Even if your children attend the best school in the country—public or private—you should find out what your child should be learning at each grade level and match that against what your child actually learns. If knowledge gaps develop, you can work with your child's teacher to see that they are filled. Because class sizes are mostly too large and teachers are mostly overworked, parents need to take responsibility for this challenge. With the appropriate tools, you can catch and correct learning gaps before they become a problem.

ENCOURAGING YOUR CHILD TO LEARN AT HOME

There is so much you can do to enrich your child's opportunities for learning at home. This book is full of fun Learning Adventure activities you can do with your child that will help to build an understanding of key concepts in language arts, math, and science. Judging by our experience at *SCORE!*, the more kids understand, the more they enjoy learning. Each small experience of success reinforces confidence, brick by brick. As you help your child learn, please bear in mind the following observations drawn from experiences in our centers:

- Positive reinforcement is the key. Try to maintain a ratio of at least five positive remarks to every negative one. If you're not sure how you're doing, keep a tally for a day or two. The patterns you see may not be as positive as you would expect.

- All praise must be genuine. This is easy when children are doing well, but even when they are having difficulties you need to find something to honestly praise. For example: "That was a good try," "You got this part of it right," or "I'm proud of you for doing your best, even though it was hard."

- When a child gets stuck, giving the answer is usually not the most effective way to help. Try asking open-ended questions or rephrasing the problem, such as: "Maybe there's another way to do that," "I wonder what made you think of doing it that way," or "What would happen if you changed...?" (Questions that begin with "Why" should be avoided, since they will probably make your child feel defensive.)

- Remember to be patient and supportive. Children need to learn that hard work pays off.

FOR PARENTS OF UNUSUALLY BRIGHT CHILDREN

In the case of unusually bright children, you may need to seek out the kind of academic challenges they may not be getting in school. Gifted children are at risk of assuming that all learning is easy and boring. We often find that such children become extremely upset when faced with a challenge they cannot immediately conquer. When children face a difficult problem, they run the risk of making mistakes or being wrong, a prospect that can be quite scary for kids who depend on being right all of the time.

Consequently, a bright student can actually feel more threatened by a challenge than a weaker student would. We believe that it is healthier for children to come face to face with such challenges at an early age, because they can be taught that making mistakes is okay, that nobody is expected to be perfect all the time, and that hard work and perseverance are more important attributes than the ability to guess an answer right away.

We come across far too many children who have done very well in math through prealgebra, only to fail miserably as they begin algebra itself. Typically, such children rushed through their "boring" and "easy" math homework during the early years. As a result, they did not actually master the material. They also may not have learned patience and perseverance. The solution requires a complete review of math basics, followed by intensive encouragement to overcome angry outbursts and bad attitudes (these usually indicate significant fear of failure). We often are successful in getting such students back on track, but problems like this can be avoided entirely when they are addressed early on.

PARENTS ARE KEY

In many ways, especially as regards motivation, parents are not so very different from their children. At *SCORE!*, we often come across parents who need some encouragement. We are happy to offer it. In our experience, we have found that parents are uniquely suited to helping their children learn. Our simple principles apply to parents too, and you'll find lots of support in this book:

• We expect every parent to succeed.

• We help make it possible for every parent to succeed.

• We reinforce the success of each parent–child team.

We are doing our best to open new *SCORE!* centers across the country. Since we may not have arrived in your neighborhood yet, we invite you to look to the encouraging anecdotes, home learning resources, and useful hints throughout this book. We hope to share our discoveries with you and encourage your efforts to accelerate your children's learning.

THERE'S MORE TO LIFE THAN ACADEMIC EXCELLENCE

Most parents recognize that academic excellence is just one of many things they would like to ensure for their children. At *SCORE!*, we are committed to developing the whole child, and that is another key component of "making the grade." We emphasize:

• Academic skills and critical thinking

• Positive reinforcement to build confidence and a love of learning

• Extensive experience with setting and achieving goals

• Great role-model relationships with positive, admirable adults

SCORE! instructors are known as "Coaches," and for good reason. Great coaches instruct, lead, motivate, and serve as role models. Most importantly, they share responsibility for the performance of each team member. Likewise, our Coaches guide, inspire, and cheer on the children under their care and take ownership in the outcome. If there is one thing we at *SCORE!* have learned about children, it is that they rarely get too much positive attention from people who care about them. And every time we pay attention to a child, we get so much more than we give.

—From the Coaches at *SCORE!*

How Do You Foster Your Child's Interest in Learning?

In preparing this series, we surveyed scores of parents on this key question:

- "Even though I always buy my children books, we still continue to borrow books from the library because they have access to a better variety of books that interest her."
- "I've never forced reading. My oldest son had difficulty learning to read, and the struggle made him hate it. The thing that worked was to have him focus on reading sports books—that interested him. Now he avidly reads the sports section of newspapers, sports-related magazines, and sports-related nonfiction books."
- "I model good reading habits for my children by reading and belonging to a book group."
- "I put books and magazines in every bedroom and bathroom and in our living room so my daughter and I stay in the habit of reading."
- "Talk about the characters and discuss the stories that you've just read together."
- "We do many things together as a family. We give a lot of praise and positive feedback."
- "We keep the TV locked up. That thing only encroaches on learning."
- "No Nintendo! And no TV in the morning or until homework is done."
- "When her home workbooks are completed, we share them with her classroom teacher."
- "The most important thing we do is not give an immediate answer to homework questions. We try to use books, the computer, and other resources to discover the answers and information together."
- "Our fourth grader wasn't interested in reading his science book and doing science homework. Finally, my husband found out that he didn't understand what he was reading. We started reading the science book with him every day, and now he is very much interested in science."
- "We make homework low key, but non-negotiable—it's something that must get done."
- "We have a membership to a local museum that we all like to visit."
- "We take our children on many trips and outings. They cultivate their curiosities."
- "We like to expose our third-grade son to other people's lives and ideas, so we take him places."
- "I put my children in the environment of what I'd like them to learn so they experience it first-hand!"
- "Our daughter often bakes and prepares desserts with her dad."
- "We do a lot of experimenting when we cook with our children. We love to do science experiments in the kitchen together."
- "Sports are a great way for our kids to learn about life—cooperation, teamwork, leadership, goal-setting . . ."
- "Music—music lessons, attending concerts, involvement in children's symphonies and music groups—adds a great learning dimension to our kids' lives."
- "Walks are perfect learning experiences. You can really enjoy conversation and observation with your children."
- "We get together as a family for regular dinners."
- "We sit down together as a family and make a family mission statement."
- "I feel that parents should take all the little questions kids have seriously and answer them truthfully."

How to Use This Book

You want to do all you can to foster and support your child's successful progress through school—those important years in which learning and growing should reward the effort and enthusiasm your child invests.

The nature and amount of effort and enthusiasm children bring to their school work directly affect each child's educational rewards. But your child's effort and enthusiasm also depends significantly on the effort and enthusiasm you provide at home. You already knew that or you would not have purchased this book. What you want to know is how to best use this book to help fulfill your goal of promoting your child's enjoyment of learning and success at school.

The core of this book lies in Section III, where the "Learning Adventure" activities that you can do with your child show you ways to take advantage of time you spend together learning and developing valuable skills. The two sections that precede those activities provide a context that you will find valuable in observing and thinking about your child as he experiences his school years.

THE BIG PICTURE

Because being a parent sometimes feels like being entangled in an infinite web of questions, we focus *Making the Grade* around some very basic questions that all parents ponder as they worry about how best to contribute to their children's education.

Get Your Bearings—the Opening Sections

Section I—"What Should My Child Be Able to Do?"—focuses on your growing child, how he develops, how he learns, how schools look at his progress, and how a parent can fit into his educational world. Section II—"What's Being Covered in School?"—gives you a look at what schools are likely to be expecting your child to learn by the completion of his present grade.

Making the Grade

We have kept these opening sections as brief as possible; their purpose is to give you useful background and guidance for what you do with the Learning Adventure activities. We recommend that you read Section I in order to easily and quickly gain a useful perspective on factors that affect your child's learning and school experience. We expect you'll read this section initially and return to browse through it from time to time later on as you enjoy watching and participating in your child's learning.

We expect that you'll use Section II primarily for reference, to look up information about school expectations in specific areas of learning for your child at the appropriate grade level, and to review for yourself, as needed, specific school content that you may not have thought about for many years! To provide for convenient, quick access, we present each of the three content areas—Language Arts (which includes Reading), Math, and Science—separately. Each content area provides an outline of expectations for 3rd grade and then for 4th grade, followed by a sort of bird's-eye view of the content covered during those two years of schooling—descriptions or explanations of the concepts and skills listed in the two grade outlines.

If your child is presently in grade three, you can simply skip the grade four outline and save reading it for next year. If she is in grade four, there's no reason to read the grade three outline unless you're interested in seeing what she probably should have learned in the previous year. We expect parents to use Section II of the book in widely different ways. You may find reading through the content a fascinating trip down memory lane where you might discover new learnings that were not offered during your school years. Or you may simply dip into the content sections only when you feel a need to brush up on something. Maybe it's a spelling or punctuation rule (how to use apostrophes to show possession in plural nouns) or the meaning of a concept (like erosion), or both (the concept of perimeter and how it is calculated).

Know Your Way Around

Sprinkled throughout the book are sidebars and short features containing tips, strategies, stories, and advice from our *SCORE!* Coaches, teachers, and parents from around the United States. You'll also find the latest research to help you make your child's 3rd and 4th grade years true Learning Adventures. Look for these icons to help you know who is giving you information and why:

 Whenever you see the "house" icon, expect "learning at home" advice.

 The "blackboard strategy" icon offers thoughtful, sometimes inspiring tips and approaches for parents on learning and parenting.

 Parents and students have a lot to juggle every day! Our "juggler" icon signals practical "try this at home" tips and activities.

If it has anything to do with the Internet, computers, software programs, or learning technology, you'll find it under our "computer" icon.

 The "book" icon yields learning-related excerpts from recommended books and authors, as well as reading and other bookish matters.

 Finally, the *SCORE!* logo signals insights from *SCORE!'s* Coaches and stories from our national educational centers, intended to give you everyday insights you can use at home with your children.

The Heart of the Book—Learning Adventure Activities

The bulk of the book consists of learning activities and hundreds of "What's More" activity ideas geared specifically to the 3rd and 4th grade curricula and tailored for learning enjoyment at home. These are activities designed for parents to do with their children.

Time—Your Most Precious Resource. Money, property, and the best connections in the world cannot come closer to the value of time you spend with your child. We are convinced that the best way for parents to promote their children's educational success is for them to spend time with their children; the more time spent, the better the payoff! Our activities are offered as ways to help you focus that time on enjoyable learning.

Perhaps most often the time may involve your helping to get the Learning Adventure activity started and then taking a back seat, checking in, remaining interested, supportive, and inquisitive about what your child is learning. Several activities feature games you play together, where your involvement continues actively throughout the activity. Many activities can expand to include other family members or friends. You may be surprised by how many of the activities suggest valuable ways to use "down time" together, ways to take advantage of time you normally don't even realize you have available—driving time, waiting time, meal prep time, clean-up time.... You'll soon discover all kinds of time just awaiting your educational use. And most of these activities offer attractive alternatives to TV-viewing time.

In short, the core of this book contains ways parents and children can enjoy doing things together that contribute to school success. At the same time, they contribute to building a foundation of memories that secure your youngster's confidence in himself and in the parental support that encourages him to reach forward and learn more.

How to Use the Activities. You can use these Learning Adventures in any of a variety of ways—the rule is suit yourself, or more to the point, suit your child. There is no required order. (You can even jump into an activity from the next grade, or last grade, if it seems appealing to and appropriate for your child.) Select activities to build further upon strengths and interests you observe your child to have. Also select activities to assist your child where he may be having trouble or to augment work being done at school. Of course, you should also select activities simply because they appeal to you—they look like something you and your child can enjoy together.

Don't worry if you and your child do activities that "she doesn't really need" or that you've done before. Enjoyable repetition provides practice that reinforces and consolidates your child's learning. One of our authors recalls with special pleasure the endless games of Twenty Questions played with her family at Sunday supper and on almost any long car ride.

To provide an organizational structure and accommodate parents who wish to select activities according to subject area and grade, the activities are grouped accordingly. Thus, you can pick out a science activity related to any particular core area of the grade three curriculum. The "At a Glance" section of each activity will tell you which core area or areas the activity addresses, the main skills it promotes, the materials needed to carry it out, and approximately how much time it will take. The rest of the activity provides step-by-step instructions to help you do the activity. Of course, you can augment and adjust the steps as best suits you, your child, and your home environment. Each activity concludes with three or more suggestions of further activity ideas—the "What's More" sidebars—that you and your child can pursue.

Link Up with Learning. As you can see, choosing and carrying out activities should be linked to keeping in touch with what your child is doing at school and how she feels about it. Nothing beats talking with your child; in addition, use the strategies discussed in the essay in section I called "How Are Children Evaluated?" and in the Section IV questions under "The Parent-School Partnership," as well as the materials in our bonus pull-out section, "The Home Learning Quizzes," to help you assess what your child knows and can do, along with charting her progress and your own home learning knowledge and awareness.

More Support—Questions and Resources

The last section responds to the concerns most parents have and indicates where you can obtain further resources for promoting your child's educational development and pleasure.

We expect you'll browse among the questions out of curiosity, as well as consult them when particular questions or issues become important in your child's school life. We hope the resource listings will lead you to specific materials to contribute to activities you choose to do with your child, and give you avenues for enlarging your own learning.

Last, but Essential—The Home Learning Quizzes

Our book concludes with what we view as an invaluable tool for you and your child—your assessment materials. By using the strategies for learning about your child (and—surprise—probably a bit about yourself while you're at it), you will maximize the benefit (and pleasure) you and your child will experience.

Parents' Pages. The Parents' Home Learning Quiz enables you to teach yourself more and more about your child, how he learns, and what he is learning. As your child's learning coach, taking this quiz enables you to periodically assess your own knowledge and awareness of your child's learning process and progress, and discover more about how to maximize your child's education. You'll also be able to assess your own style of interaction with your child. Enjoy these new insights!

Your Child's Pages. The Kids' Home Learning Quizzes are meant to be fun "How much do I know?" questions taken right out of the grades three and four curriculum in language arts, math, and science.

Just like the popular BrainQuest™ series, these are sometimes easy, sometimes challenging at-grade-level questions for your child to tackle. Approach the quizzes like a game of trivia or one of the Learning Adventure activities: "See how many of these you can get right. . . ." Then congratulate your child on each right answer! There's no grading or scoring, just the good feeling of being able to have your child point out to you how much he knows.

While not a scientific tool to measure your child's grade-level abilities, the tougher problems and wrong answers will give you and your child good indications of where more learning needs to take place. (Or they may cover skills your child hasn't been taught yet in school.) Use outside resources and appropriate Learning Adventure activities from Section III to help practice and reinforce the skills. Can your child answer the quiz questions correctly after having more practice with the skills? And so the learning fun and quizzing continues . . . !

COMMUNICATE WITH *SCORE!*

And last but not least, we want to hear from you. We consider the parents who use our books to be invaluable resources. We want to hear your assessment of activities, your ideas, your success stories, and the questions that you want us to address in the future.

The "About Kaplan" pages at the back of the book give you a variety of ways to contact Kaplan and our *SCORE!* Educational Centers. Write, call, or e-mail us with your feedback and experiences. If you're online, subscribe to *SCORE! Edge,* our free electronic newsletter for parents and for students. Receive great home-learning advice, tips and contests, and plug into new language arts, math, and science activities. Subscribe to *SCORE! Edge* at www.ScoreLearning.com. Turn the *Making the Grade* experience into a lifetime of enjoyable learning for your family.

What Should My Child Be Able to Do?

CHAPTER 1

How Do Children Develop?

Children develop sporadically, surprisingly, rapidly, unexpectedly . . . . You can add just about any adverb you want, or any ten, and still not have the complete picture. Parenting can sometimes feel a lot like coping with cooking. Just as you've got the onions browning nicely, the rice boils over; while you're cleaning up that mess and cutting up the broccoli, the onions start to burn. It's just that children never stay the same. Their lives, their bodies, and their abilities are in continuous change. Sometimes the changes are steady and easily measured, and sometimes they are sudden and surprising. When it's not exhausting, it's exhilarating to be around children. In those moments when we surface for a breath above the sea of soccer, socks, and successes, we can appreciate what a privilege it is to witness the young human being in our care growing toward adulthood.

And as we fret about our own children, it is reassuring to remember that children throughout the world (along with their parents) are moving through the same developmental stages and have been doing so for countless generations.

Anxiety-Free Thinking About Your Child

We all have our worries about our children; are they too tall, too short, not enough of this, too much of that? Society, schools, grandparents and in-laws, and our own internal monitors all seem to be waiting to judge our children's performance (and ours as well). We've put some topics into this section to help you think about your child as the

PLENTY OF PATS

Sometimes just a pat on the back is motivation enough for your child in learning. Sometimes you pay a dollar for each good grade they receive. But I'd like my child to feel good about his grades with or without the dollar. It's important for any kid to internalize the motivation we can help give so that they feel good about themselves and their accomplishments.

I THINK I CAN . . .

The worst thing in the world is when a parent says in front of a child, "He can't do this," and the kid is standing there and hearing this negativity. One boy had a lot of basic skills he needed to work on. He and I started to work together to build his confidence. He was so determined to master spelling that he tackled it over and over again— it was almost too much. But after his mom said he couldn't do spelling, I pulled her aside and talked to her about *SCORE!*'s belief in "relentless positivity." I told her he can master spelling, he can do it if you believe in him, and his parents should coach him at home. Eventually, this boy's mother would cry at the end of every session because she was so amazed at what her child could do.

wonderful and unique person that she is, and to put to rest some of the anxiety you may feel.

There's no such thing as an average child. As you consider your child's development through the school years, it's helpful to remember that "average" is a statistical term and not the description of a person. The unit called *average* is arrived at by lumping together all of something and finding the mathematical mean. The average of anything is nothing more than the abstract quality of the middleness. Some aspect of each child's being may happen to fall on the mark called *average,* but it's unlikely. Each child is going to be more of this and less of that. Your child is a unique individual.

He got that from your side of the family! In the academic world, this topic is called "nature versus nurture." Much study has been devoted to this topic, but as far as this book's approach to parenting is concerned, there is no *versus* at all. Both elements, our own combination of genes and our environment, play their roles together in how we grow into adulthood.

For parents concerned with how development affects their children, however, the most significant differences among school age children are those of developmental timing, for instance, the more than six-year range between the earliest normal onset of puberty for girls and the latest beginnings for normal boys!

Some people with political agendas make endless efforts to prove that there are racially significant differences in intelligence. There is no valid scientific evidence to support the claim of genetic inferiority or superiority in intelligence. There is, however, extensive evidence that children with the loving support of their families and the society around them will do better in school.

Theories of Development

In earlier times, folks didn't think about human development much. There were occasional introspective geniuses (St. Augustine is one example) who left autobiographical records of their childhood and gave thought to education and development, but children were generally thought of as little adults who just got bigger and (most of the time) smarter.

The growth of science in the eighteenth and nineteenth centuries changed how we viewed ourselves. The knowledge and techniques of study learned from the natural sciences were applied to human beings, and the result was the growth of psychology and the study of human nature. Sigmund Freud, Erik Erikson, and Jean Piaget are the three most notable recent thinkers in this area. People may agree or disagree with their particular theories, but we all owe them a debt for stepping in to take a closer look at how the curious creatures we call humans develop.

The theorist who has had the most influence on education is a Swiss psychologist, Jean Piaget, who devoted much of his life to carefully examining how children think. Most contemporary western educational programs are built on aspects of his findings and theories. His observations of children led him to conjecture that our intellectual abilities increase through qualitatively different stages from infancy through adulthood. The infant who begins life by putting together only the simplest and most immediate or tangible facts grows through several intellectual stages into an adult capable of building and using powerful abstractions.

Seeing the Whole Child

No matter what particular theory of development rings truest to you, there is an important lesson to be learned from child psychologists, developmental specialists, and scientists of human behavior and learning like Piaget. This lesson is that thoughtful observation is the basis of understanding. In the case of the experts, it has led to understandings about large patterns of human nature. In the case of you, the parent, it is your understanding of an individual, your child.

All of us get caught up in the trap of comparing our child to other children (after all, Mozart was only three when he started to compose). Our parents probably did it to us and we know we shouldn't do it, but there we go again! One way to short-circuit this pointless exercise is to keep in mind that developmental age and chronological age are two different things!

THE OUTER LIMITS

Children really want boundaries. It's a major sign of caring on the part of a parent. Children usually feel a lot more comfortable knowing that there's a set of standards and rules that a family needs to abide by. "I love you and I want the best for you; I'm not setting up these rules because I'm mean and horrible!"

THINKING ABOUT DEVELOPMENT

Jerome Brunner, Robert Coles, Herbert Kohlberg, and Carol Gilligan are among the many contemporary specialists in different aspects of child development who are worth looking into. Their insights into the development of thinking, moral development, and valuing are fascinating. In this speculative field, there are no absolutes and lots of controversy and excitement. Check out their books and studies for a fascinating look at how children grow.

At any particular age, any three children can be at three very different stages of mental and physical development within a general range. Given our wildly different genetic makeups and the different timetables those genes set for our physical development (and don't forget to throw in the role that different environments play), there's really no accurate way to compare children on a point-by-point basis. The best that we can do is observe closely, try to understand, and do the best we can to support our children's own growth and development.

"I need new sneakers!"

First, let's talk about your child's physical growth and development. Human bodies don't grow at a sedately slow and steady pace. Different parts of us grow at different speeds and at different times. Our heads and the brains inside grow very rapidly until sometime between the ages of four and six and then continue to grow, but more slowly, until adolescence. Our height and weight increase tremendously from birth until around age three and then slow down until puberty when there is a second growth burst. Our lymphoidal tissue (the tonsils, adenoids, and parts of the intestines) grow quickly through about age ten and then taper off, still growing, but at a slower rate until maturity. Our reproductive organs grow very slowly until the onset of puberty and then grow rapidly. The muscles and our skeletal frame develop a little unevenly; feet, hands, and head reach adult size before the rest of us, and our legs lengthen before our trunk stretches out. (Hey, look! He's wearing high waters!) Kids outgrow their pants before they outgrow their shirts.

Quiet! Child Thinking

Mental development in children alternates between incremental growth and great leaps. Whereas the physical and emotional changes that our children experience can't be missed, mental growth can be less obvious. Ankles erupt out of pant legs, hairs sprout, doors slam, and last year's obsessions suddenly become little-kid stuff. Mental growth appears to be just as obvious at first. There is a clear, measurable increase in how much your kid knows.

Vocabulary grows (not always the words we want), skills increase, and children acquire more factual information. These are quantitative differences and they are substantial, but there are changes in your child's mental ability that are subtler and much more profound.

From Collecting Facts to Spinning Theories. Students of human development have come to realize that, as we mature, the very ways in which we do our thinking change. The differences between a toddler and an adult are much more than size of vocabulary and the accumulation of factual information.

Children start school being very specific, concrete thinkers. Their thinking is based on the manipulation of objects and immediate events and the relationships among them. In the later elementary and early middle school years, this kind of thinking is mixed with a more abstract ability. In this middle stage, they are able to generalize. They can consider a group of objects and think about them in terms of an abstraction that sums them all up. In late middle school and high school, they make a third transition. They become able to take generalizations and conjectures and think about them quite separately from real objects. They can theorize about tyranny, democracy, and relativity, and they can argue (and they do love to argue) about the general advantages and disadvantages of either of the first two or the philosophical fallout of the last.

Characteristic Questions. If you were to characterize children at different levels of mental development in a rough-and-ready way, you might separate them by the kinds of questions they ask. *What* is the question that belongs to the earlier years. *How* is the question for the middle school years. *Why* and *what if* are the questions of adolescence and beyond. Of course, these questions get asked at all ages, but the ability to fully understand them and appreciate the answers grows and unfolds as we mature intellectually.

There is no exact timetable for development. No one can say, "At half-past seven years of age your child will be able to do thus and such or think in this or that way." In fact,

THE GENESIS OF LEARNING

Learning begins in the first days of life. Scientists are now discovering how young children develop emotionally and intellectually from their first days, and, therefore, how important it is for parents to begin immediately talking, singing, even reading to their infants.
—from the *1997 State of the Union Address,* President Clinton

AFTER THE FALL

I wouldn't have had children if we didn't try to do the best job we could to make sure that they're secure, in an environment that's conducive to learning, and where they can flourish—but not to the point where we won't let our children take their own falls.

developmental specialists are very careful to make a distinction between developmental age (the age at which certain things generally happen) and chronological age (the actual age). Every child develops in her own way and at her own pace depending on environmental factors and her own genetic nature.

Looking at It Another Way. If children were squirrels, in grades two, three, and four, they'd be gathering and sorting nuts and enjoying the climb; they'd spend their next three years finding more trees of similar types and organizing nuts (while worrying, of course, about whether they were wearing the same thing as the other squirrels); and in grades six, seven, and eight, our squirrels would be planning storage facilities, worrying about how many nuts to set aside, and wondering how many they could eat right now because they're really hungry.

"Leave me alone!"

When it comes to emotional and social development, we also find varying rates of growth. You could speculate that this is nature's way of keeping parents on their toes. You get used to your child's behavior during a nice period of consolidation—life is going smoothly, your kid looks and acts the same from day to day (ignoring sudden external changes in fashion and hairstyle). Then, just when you were feeling relaxed, comfortable, and like maybe you were doing a good job as a parent, suddenly you're faced with a whole different person. It may be that the teddy bear gets demoted to a spot in the closet, or a certain food is only for babies, or you'll hear, "I'd never wear that" about yesterday's favorite garment. Whatever it is and at whatever the age, you scramble to quickly learn the habits and customs of what almost seems like a whole new species.

3rd and 4th Graders—A Snapshot

We've called this section a *snapshot*. It has to be a bit blurry, however, because the subject of the picture is always in motion! Development, whether physical, mental, or emotional, is a process. There is no moment where everything comes to rest and you can describe the static

ALL YOU NEED IS LOVE

Acceptance seems to matter most for children's overall adjustment and sense of self-worth: because they feel loved, they feel lovable.
—from *Beyond the Classroom*, Laurence Steinberg, Ph.D. (Simon & Schuster, 1996)

moment and the particular child and say that this is exactly how it is.

No snapshot can accurately catch the qualities of each child, because every child is unique. Within any group of children, there is an enormous range of development. Since children at any one chronological age stretch across the entire range of what is normal and appropriate for each particular stage of growth, we have tried to provide a general picture knowing that you will flesh out the portrait through observation of your own child's individual details.

At School. If the business of the primary grades is learning new skills, the business of the later elementary grades is mastering them. This transition occurs in grades three and four. The key word for 3rd and 4th graders is *competence*. They have the basics under their belts, are practicing them on a daily basis, are becoming good at using them in other areas of their school work, and are pretty proud of themselves.

By the end of grade four, most kids are well beyond the early struggles with deciphering words and are beginning to use reading both as a source of pleasure and as a tool for other subjects such as science and social studies. Mathematics and writing have much the same place in their curriculum. Skills are being both refined and added, as well as being used in other areas of school and life. These children are still very involved with factual knowledge. Memorizing geographical information, sports statistics, and the details of their life and times is a specialty and a pleasure.

Students in these grades tend to focus on the immediate present and on activities that have tangible results. Historical information is often interesting to them, but most do not yet have the abstract abilities that will allow them to deal with large generalizations about either the past or future. They prefer, and understand, the actions of rules, law (particularly

TYPICAL?

There are oftentimes two different kinds of parents. One is determined to get their child in line with the skills needed for a certain grade level. For instance, "By a certain grade, my son needs to learn to read well, or he has to have certain division and multiplication skills." And then there are the parents who are less interested in their children having attained certain skill levels but are more concerned with what skills their children do have. I tell parents that I'm not into gearing their child into being a "typical third grader" because there is no typical third grader—they're all over the spectrum. Students should be given the freedom to move ahead, catch up to their grade level, or whatever keeps them motivated and excited to learn.

Notice the little everyday successes your child has.

those that apply to their classrooms), and they aren't really ready to think about the underlying principles, with the exception of fairness. What is fair is an important factor in all their considerations.

Social and Emotional Concerns. These years reflect a period of relative emotional calm for children. There are the natural upsets, tensions about beginning homework, increased responsibilities at home and school, and worries about friendships and performance. For most kids, however, this period is the calm before the storms of adolescence. Friends are very important and usually are drawn from the same sex with groups and cliques forming and dissolving over short periods of time.

Making collections of all sorts is characteristic of this age; small collectibles, sports cards, and action figures are examples. Although any particular collection is usually of short duration, children manage to fill all available bureau tops and jacket pockets. In addition to being collected, these objects often become the basis for complicated trading and cataloging activities. Not surprisingly, mail order catalogs of everything from Halloween garb to sports equipment are the source of great pleasure for many. Childhood games and skills appeal to many children at this age and intense interest is generated by complex and rhythmic clapping games, four square, jumping rope, and the endless varieties of ball elimination games.

Physical Development. The velocity of growth for children (the rate at which they change physically) drops quickly between ages two and three. They do continue to grow, but at a slower rate until they reach the beginnings of puberty. Slower general growth seems to allow them time to become familiar with their bodies, and these years provide a generally more relaxed period of physical consolidation. This slower growth sometimes causes parents (or kids) anxiety and may lead to many extra pencil marks on whatever wall or door your family uses to record height. Perhaps, in general, this slower pace accounts for some of their emotional stability.

PENMANSHIP

Penmanship or handwriting is a subject undergoing serious reconsideration by contemporary educators. Technology has created profound changes in the emphasis on good penmanship in schools and even on the role of handwriting. In the late 1940s, students used to suffer through hours of dipping a scratchy steel-nibbed pen into an inkwell; today's '90s child is moving from a brief try at script into keyboarding. Expect lots of changes and some controversy in this realm (as in the realm of using a calculator versus knowing your number facts) over the next few years.

Boys almost never begin puberty during these years, but a small percentage of girls do. They may start their growth spurt and begin to develop secondary sexual characteristics. By the end of grade four, many girls may be thinking about what lies ahead, and it is important to deal sensitively with children who have already begun these changes.

A Group Portrait and a Last Thought

Imagine a 3rd grader, a 5th grader, and an 8th grader playing a game of Monopoly™. You see their obvious differences in size and physical maturity, and, by being observant, pick up on the less obvious differences in their interests and abilities. The 3rd grader is fascinated with all the houses and hotels, eager to get the right token, attentive to collecting and stacking the money and (although deeply interested in the rules and fairness) mightily concerned with winning. Meanwhile, the 5th grader loves to be the banker, is zealous about the rules and how they affect fair play, and makes quick moves without a lot of planning. And there's the 8th grader—knowing exactly the best property to own (and will argue with you about it), thinking in terms of strategy, and, although playing steadily and seriously for most of the game, occasionally exploding in tears or anger and remonstrating with the other players about being unloved and not respected.

It's almost as if they were playing three different games. In one way, they are. Although they are playing together, each child plays a game appropriate to that child's own developmental level. As they mature, they will pass through new stages and enter new versions of the game, just as we have done.

THE ART OF PARENTING

Our children are very artistic and social. We encourage them to draw things out and talk about them as much as possible. Our daughter wants the compliments and accolades. I pat her on the back and say, "That was so good," and I save everything she does in boxes.

ON MISTAKES ...

I feel like I'm a *SCORE!* success story, too. If I tell kids often enough, "This mistake is an opportunity to learn something, so you can go forward from it," then I also learn that I can build on any experience or craziness in my own life to make myself a better person. We help students take a proactive approach to when things hit the fan.

CHAPTER 2

How Do Children Learn?

Have you ever heard these comments before? "Kim is so good with her hands, but she just doesn't enjoy reading." "Jack remembers every little thing he reads, but he's not real well coordinated or good at sports."

DIFFERENT STROKES

Not every child understands from the same learning approach. There are several different approaches for each child. It's finding the way to teach the material to the child that's key for parents in helping their children learn. There are many ways to teach a concept, and parents will have to experiment with approaches and find one or more that work.

"Even when she was a baby, Julia could sing along with the radio, right on key." "Martin is a real people-person. He just knows how to get along with everyone, from the kids in his Scout troop to the cranky guy in the apartment upstairs."

For generation after generation, parents have been having those kinds of conversation about their kids. And although they weren't trained educators, these parents had made an important discovery: People learn in different ways!

Many Kinds of "Smarts"

It's not just kids. People in general have multiple intelligences—ways of perceiving, knowing, and understanding the world. Recently, experts have identified "seven kinds of smarts"—seven different types of intelligence. And, as people have always sensed, in most people, one or two or more of those intelligences are usually stronger than the others. That blend of traits makes each person unique. But the experts also point out that everyone can work on developing the other kinds of intelligences as well.

Your child's learning style—just like your own—makes it easier for him to learn and do certain kinds of things, from reading novels to doing gymnastics to playing the guitar. With your help, your child can also develop some of the

DON'T FREAK

I see all types of parents. Some are really strict and totally into the academic progress their children are making. Some parents really push their kids hard. I personally like to see parents allowing children to work at their own pace, knowing that the progress will happen without pressure. The parents who really monitor their kids so closely tend to freak out their kids a lot; if the kids miss even one problem on a lesson, it becomes a very stressful event.

FINDING THEIR OWN WAY

It was a real success for me as a parent to realize that my challenging son is not going to necessarily "like" school, but he can still succeed in school. I believe in supporting his school and his education as much as possible, while at the same time letting my son find his own way.

other ways of learning that will be useful both in school and in real life.

Learning Styles in School

Most traditional school courses, such as math or science or language arts, do draw on specific types of intelligence—mainly verbal, visual, and logical. In the classroom, skills in reading, writing, analyzing, computing, thinking critically, and learning from books are emphasized. The kid who is naturally strong in those kinds of intelligence may have an advantage in the classroom.

Modern textbooks, however, usually try to give teachers suggestions for activities and approaches that will help children who have other styles of learning. And, as the experts note, children (with the help of their parents) can also work to strengthen the specific learning styles that are emphasized in school. That is what many of the activities described in this book are designed to help you accomplish with your child.

Seven Ways of Learning

How does *your* child learn? Look for the characteristics described here and apply them to what you've already noticed about your child. What are her strengths? Her weaknesses? What types of intelligence are stronger in your child? What types need encouragement?

Take note of some of the general approaches mentioned here to encourage the development of each kind of intelligence. Then look through the specific Learning Adventure activities described in Section III of *Making the Grade*. These will help you work with your child to strengthen the kinds of intelligences that are needed to be successful in school, while still keeping the unique blend of traits that make up your child's personality.

Verbal/Linguistic. If your child is strong in this kind of intelligence, he may have started to talk early and in complete sentences. Probably he learned to read early and easily, too, and has a wider vocabulary than many kids his age. He likes books, puns, word games, and puzzles and probably enjoys writing. He may have more trouble taking in spoken information, such as from a lecture, than he does, for instance, in reading printed directions. This is the kid "whose nose is always in a book," who may ignore the scenery during a car ride and read a book instead.

Verbal/linguistic intelligence is one of the ways of learning that is very important in many school courses. You can encourage your child's verbal/linguistic intelligence by making reading and its associations fun and pleasurable. Many kids who are good readers and writers learned by imitating their parents, so show that you enjoy reading.

Make reading material—books and magazines—easily available at home. Encourage trips to the library and take an interest in the books your child likes. (You may be surprised to find how enjoyable some so-called kids' books can be.) For younger children, storytelling, poetry, and reading aloud are especially important.

Logical/Mathematical. Logical/mathematical intelligence goes beyond being "good at math." Perhaps your child has a good dose of this kind of smarts. Strength in this type of intelligence includes thinking in clear, logical ways and liking to analyze problems and situations. These kids are good at finding patterns and sequences, and they may frequently point out logical flaws in other people's actions. They are curious about new ideas and developments in science and may enjoy "brainteasers" that demand logical solutions. They can reason their way to solutions and think abstractly.

Most kids who are strong in this type of intelligence like science and most kinds of math. You can encourage logical/mathematical intelligence by giving your child a chance to use these skills outside school. Learn about science by star watching or hiking in the woods. Build

VERBAL VARIETY

Parents can tell their children that they're soon going to be a "published author!" Kids love to write stories, type them up, add a byline and artwork—and parents can collect writings that they've done over the year and make it a fun home project to bind them together. And there are so many writing games that parents can use at home. There are travel games related to poetry, reports, and stories, and many other games kids can play with to help build a more powerful vocabulary and comfort with the language.

Help your kid think of multiplication and division as games!

"what if" experiments, math computation, or logical problems into everyday situations. For instance, ask your child to figure out (with mental math) the comparative price per ounce of two different brands of breakfast cereal in the supermarket. Or when you are buying gas, ask, "Can you figure out how many miles per gallon we got with that last tank of gas?"

Visual/Spatial. This intelligence includes both artistic vision—sensitivity to color and imagery—and a sense of space and spatial relationships. These kids often like to draw and doodle and they have a good visual imagination. If your child is strong in this kind of intelligence, she may enjoy jigsaw puzzles. She's likely to be good with maps and location and can probably find her way around unfamiliar places. In math, she'll probably think geometry is fun, but may have more trouble with algebra, which is more symbolic and abstract.

Encourage visual/spatial intelligence by supplying your child with tools and materials: a camera or camcorder, drawing and painting equipment, and well-illustrated books. A younger child will enjoy manipulatives and design blocks. Give your child a taste of good art and design, not just by visiting art museums and galleries but also by looking at buildings and surroundings, and sharing an interest in good architecture, furnishings, cars, gardens, and houses.

Body/Kinesthetic. People as varied as athletes, inventors, and dancers have this type of "hands-on" intelligence. They are aware and confident of their own movements and physical self and are generally well coordinated. This characteristic also makes them restless—this is the kid who "can't sit still for a minute."

Since action and activity are so important to this kind of kid, parents need to make sure these kids have a chance to do what they are good at. A kid like this is likely to want to spend time actively outdoors or to work at handicrafts and activities such as pottery or woodworking. He may be interested in sports, hiking, dance, or gymnastics. Remember that this is a kid who learns best by doing—by practicing an

KEEP MOVING!

We do not allow a lot of sitting-around time at home. We stress "do something." As a family, we go to the beach, we go on hikes, we go for walks, we go to bookstores, we go to the library, we go to the pool and do swimming together.

We spend a lot of family time together, especially on the weekends. That's the way we foster a learning atmosphere for our child.

activity rather than just watching or reading about it. Children who are not strong in this kind of intelligence can be encouraged to develop their physical skills and abilities.

Musical/Rhythmic. Your child's musical/rhythmic intelligence can show itself in different ways and to different degrees. Even very young children show a good sense of rhythm and an ability to sing along or imitate a song they have just heard. They may hum to themselves, tap out rhythms, or make up their own songs and tunes.

In many schools today, music and art programs have been eliminated or cut back because of budget cuts. You can make up for this problem to some extent at home. No matter what her musical ability or formal training, you can help your child enjoy and appreciate different kinds of music through tapes, CDs, radio and TV, and live concerts or performances.

If your school system offers instruction on musical instruments, you'll be doing your child a favor by enrolling her. Music as recreation can bring immense pleasure to people throughout their lives, even if they do not have the skill or inclination to perform professionally. Real involvement in music has even been shown to enhance acquisition of traditionally academic skills such as mathematics, literature, and writing.

Interpersonal. Interpersonal intelligence includes "people skills," the ability to get along, communicate, and work together. While hard to quantify, these skills are usually quite obvious. Your child may be the one who almost always gets along with others, whether in school or at play. He likes to be involved in social activities or group sports and is often a leader or the center of a group of friends.

If your child is strong in this type of intelligence, you will not have to work at encouraging him to be active and sociable. In fact, you may have to work to keep him from becoming overscheduled. He may need to develop the ability to enjoy his own company and solitude. For a shyer, less outgoing child, one who has less of this kind of intelligence, it is important to encourage and support social activities while not pushing too hard.

ARTSY IN THE A.M.

When my son was younger, part of my morning routine with him was to get up, put on some fun music, and color and paint with him. He still loves to do it.

GOALIES

My husband and I love Score@Kaplan from the standpoint that they give kids goals. It's not just this fun place where kids go and play on the computer. They learn, but it gives them an educational, fun format where they can reach and attain goals and be commended. Kids love that! Kids love to be patted on the back. They like being told, "That was great! Good job. Look how hard you worked." They might not be getting this praise somewhere else, and if they're not, what a great experience for them to get it here. Our daughters love it, and they tell us, "I'm almost to my goal!" "I got a Score card!" "I've got 25 Score cards and I'm going to get a gold one." This has been a healthy, good, fun experience for our girls.

"MY BOOK"

Give your children the tools to succeed. My mother bought me a blank journal. It said "My Book" on the outside of it, and every day I wrote a poem in it. This was like a little assignment that my mother and I did together each day. A year later, I had a full book of poems that I can't imagine having done on my own without my mother's encouragement. But she gave me the tools to express myself to do it.

Intrapersonal. While interpersonal intelligence looks outward, intrapersonal intelligence looks inward. Children strong in this kind of intelligence are likely to be thoughtful, and they are generally more aware of their feelings and emotions than children for whom this is not a strong intelligence. Not necessarily a loner, this child is probably self-reliant and independent and enjoys solitude and her own company. She is likely to have a firm idea about what she believes and what her goals are. She is self-directed and will explore ideas on her own.

Keeping a journal is one way for your child to develop intrapersonal intelligence and self-awareness. A child who is already strong in this type of intelligence may need encouragement to reach out to new friends and join in group activities.

Playing to Your Strengths

Your child is a unique blend of different intelligences—and so are you. Your own interests and ways of learning will inevitably have an influence on the kinds of activities that you can and want to do with your kid. Not surprisingly, it will probably be easiest to encourage the kinds of activities and approaches that you yourself are most comfortable with.

After you've analyzed your child's different kinds of smarts, take a look at your own. You may want to make a checklist for both of you.

• What are the areas in which each of you are strong?
• Do your strongest learning styles differ much?
• Do you share weaker learning styles?
• Or do your areas of weakness and strength complement one another?
• Which are the kinds of smarts that are the easiest for you to work on with your child?
• Which kinds are the hardest?

"We're so different!" After thinking about the seven kinds of smarts, you may come up with this conclusion. One of the challenges parents face in helping their kids do better in school occurs when there are differences in their learning styles. Just because you and your child belong to the same family, you aren't necessarily alike in interests or learning styles. If you have more than one child, chances are that they're not exactly alike, either.

Before you can cope with these differences, you have to recognize them. Think of things you've noticed in everyday life—you love sports, your kid thinks they're boring. Your kid is a whiz at math; you can't balance your checkbook without a calculator. You work on a dozen different handcraft projects; your kid would rather read.

Paradoxically, it can be hardest to help your child develop the kinds of smarts that you already have. For instance, if you're very verbal and a great reader, it's easy to become impatient and critical with a child who isn't. You may find it hard (even frustrating) to understand just why this stuff is hard for her.

On the other hand, you have an advantage because you like and appreciate books and reading or the constant discoveries of science. Here you have an opportunity to pass on some of that appreciation to your child. It just may take a little more patience. And remember, she may never be the book lover or science whiz that you are. But you can be a terrific role model.

"That's not what the book says." Another pitfall of being skilled or knowledgeable in a certain area or way of learning is that you may try to explain things to your middle-school child in college-level terms. If you're an engineer or accountant, for instance, your math skills and knowledge are much greater than what your child needs to know—for now, at least. A too-rich explanation could make things harder for him.

When trying to help, check out what kinds of solutions or answers the textbook or homework assignment is actually asking for. Give your child just the help that's needed. Think back to when you were first learning these facts and

THE BIG TEN

There are at least ten different strategies for your child to use to solve math, word, and other homework problems (from *The Problem Solver* by Shirley Hoogeboom and Judy Goodnow). Every parent should know them and teach them to their children— they're not necessarily going to be covered in school!

1. Act out or use objects.
2. Make a picture or a diagram.
3. Use or make a table.
4. Make an organized list.
5. Guess and check.
6. Use or look for a pattern.
7. Work backwards.
8. Use logical reasoning.
9. Make it simpler.
10. Brainstorm.

MAKE MUSIC

Relaxation induced by specific music leaves the mind alert and able to concentrate. The music found most conducive to this state is baroque music, like that of Bach, Handel, Pachelbel, and Vivaldi . . . . Most baroque music is timed at 60 beats per minute, which is the same as an average resting heart rate.
— from *Quantum Learning* by Bobbi DePorter (Dell, 1992)

processes. Then use the Learning Adventure activities in Section III to work on the skills he needs to know this year.

Learning Together. On the other hand, through family ties and influence, you and your child probably have some similar learning styles, along with similar areas in which you're both less comfortable. You may both be good musicians and athletes, not so good at verbal or visual skills. As a result, you may both have to work in areas of less strength, rather than avoiding them.

Maybe mathematical/logical intelligence isn't your strongest area—or your child's, either. But as you help your child to make the grade, you may find yourself developing new kinds of smarts yourself. As you work through activities in math and science together, for instance, you'll find that both of you are building new skills and strengths.

CHAPTER 3

How Are Children Evaluated?

From the moment of birth, we start measuring and sizing up our kids. At first we have only their physical characteristics (birth weight and length are just the beginning) to work with, but right away we begin to compare them to some norm. How is my child doing compared to others? We keep asking ourselves this question. As kids begin to walk and talk and learn—the hundreds of little skills they do before entering school—the comparisons fly. All through the toddler and preschool years, we watch, we read, we talk, and we wonder, Is my kid doing okay? Before we know it, our baby is off to school and this evaluating stuff goes big time. When schools judge how well your child is doing, the process is called *assessment*.

Assessment Is . . .

Few topics on the school reform agenda have generated as much discussion and scrutiny as assessment has—after all, how well your child is doing has been at the core of the school experience since the beginning of time, hasn't it?

Simply put, assessment is the systematic and purposeful method of looking at where students are and where they should be going in their classroom and in their school system. The measurements are made about all development aspects of your child—emotional, social, cognitive, physical, and intellectual. The results can be used for several purposes:

THE PRICE OF LEARNING

America's schools spend more per pupil then virtually any of the countries that routinely trounce us in international scholastic comparisons.
—*Beyond the Classroom,* Laurence Steinberg, Ph.D. (Simon & Schuster, 1996)

KEEPING THE FAITH

I have a video of Mary Lou Retton, the Olympic gymnast, working out before the 1984 games. She was doing a switch from the parallel bars, and she was doing a very tough move. She missed it 20 times in a row. She got back up and kept trying. That's physically and mentally exhausting to do, but she kept getting up and trying again. She got it on the twenty-first try, and went on to big achievements in her sport. Parents need to help children be patient and persevere. And parents need to have faith, to give their children the space to fail and encourage them to keep trying and learning until they finally understand.

- To tell you and your child how she is doing
- To give teachers information to plan what and how to teach your child
- To provide school districts with the data they need to see how well they are doing their teaching job

Changes Underway

Along with the many current efforts to make schools more relevant to kids, educators are making some big changes in how they assess kids. They are:

- Moving away from something that teachers do to students towards more of a partnership between teachers, students, and their parents
- Moving away from a single letter grade on a quarterly report card towards a more continual process involving a series of tests, observations, and work samples
- Moving away from single events treated separately from the learning process ("Stop what you are learning and take this test . . . .") to an activity that is interwoven into the lesson plans

As a parent, you need an understanding of these kinds of assessment. Here's a closer look at some of the old and the new ways schools are evaluating children's educational growth.

Traditional Assessment

Remember the joys of this kind of testing! You'll recall that it:

- Is mostly paper-and-pencil based
- Is given formally—every child has to do the same thing at the same time
- Usually involves a multiple-choice format that emphasizes memorizing facts
- Is almost always subject specific (ah, those weekly spelling tests, reading pop quizzes, and history unit tests)
- Involves comparison of a child's progress to that of other students

- Is based on what a child is able to remember at the time of the test
- Often is required by the district or state (as in the case of a standardized test like the California Achievement Test, or CAT)

You'll learn more about the traditional assessment tool of **standardized tests** in the next chapter, in which the test prep experts at Kaplan discuss the different types of standardized tests and how you can help your child prepare for them. You can even see which tests your child will be taking at different grade levels, from Kaplan's new state-by-state listings of standardized test requirements.

Alternative Assessment

A wide variety of other ways of evaluating students' progress is now available. Alternative (as opposed to traditional) assessment is more of a process than a single event. It puts the emphasis on your child's progress over time rather than on individual test scores. Alternative assessment:

- Is an ongoing picture of the work a child does in a variety of contexts
- Is focused on a child's work compared to his own previous work
- Is meant to show how kids apply what they know, not just facts they memorize
- Is able to show progress not just in single subjects but also in interdisciplinary projects (where subject matters, like reading in social studies, are combined)
- Is often conducted informally, through observation or conversation
- Is commonly referred to as *portfolio assessment*, since the notes and work samples are usually kept in a manila folder

Here's a look at some of the specific types of portfolio assessment. Notice how these methods typically include much more information than what a child writes on paper.

ON TESTS . . .

Remember that all tests have their limitations. They are not perfect measures of what your child can or cannot do. They are at best one entry in the overall picture of your son or daughter.

Some tests may not measure just what we think they do. For example, in an assignment to copy spelling words from the blackboard, we may learn this about students:

- How well they can print
- How well they can copy
- How long they can sit still
- How quickly they can work
- How willing they are to do work that may seem meaningless to them

---

"Not everything that counts can be counted and not everything that can be counted counts." —*Albert Einstein*

achievement test—an objective exam, often given to groups of students at a time, that measures educationally relevant skills in subjects such as spelling or math

diagnostic test—an in-depth evaluation of a specific skill area in order to identify specific learning needs of an individual student

norms—performance standards that are established by a reference group and that describe average or typical performance

percentile—the percentage of people in the testing sample whose scores were below a given score

raw score—the number of items that are answered correctly

standardized test—a form of measurement that has been normed against a specific population; an individual's score is then compared to the norm group's performance

Performance Tasks. These are assignments (whether student-initiated or teacher-planned) that are designed to measure your child's skill in a certain area; for example, being able to write a persuasive essay or to follow written directions to build a specific kind of birdhouse. Looking at the entire process rather than just the end result takes into account each child's individual learning style.

Observation. By paying attention to how students approach a problem, interact with other students, or use their free time, teachers and parents can build the complete picture of your child's success in learning. Teachers may take notes in checklist form or in more of a narrative, anecdotal fashion.

Self-Evaluation. When children are encouraged to make thoughtful evaluations of their own work, they begin to accept responsibility for their own learning—a key element in their educational growth.

What's a Parent to Do!

The ways you can help your child succeed in school are changing, too. It used to be that test scores and grades were sent home without much explanation. But now it's increasingly possible for parents to talk with teachers about what certain grades and scores mean. In these discussions, you can also contribute to your child's success in schoolwork by helping the teacher get the big picture of the your child. These are opportunities for you to offer unique information about your child's likes, dislikes, and way of doing things that are important for the teacher to know.

Supporting Your Child in the Assessment Process
Do you remember how your folks reacted to your report cards? Your attitudes about test taking and report cards send a message to your kids that can help or hinder their school progress. You can help your child by:

- Not being overly anxious about scores or grades
- Not judging your child on the basis of a single score
- Using mistakes as a focus of discussion rather than reasons to punish

• Using all modes of reports as opportunities for discussion (along with praise and encouragement)

Staying in touch with teachers about your child builds partnerships for the benefit of your child. These partnerships are important to help your child get the best education possible.

How You Can Use Assessment

Assessment is not for schools and teachers alone—you and your child should get involved too! *Making the Grade* includes a bonus pull-out section containing home learning quizzes for parents and kids, because the whole point of assessment is to use it as a learning tool. Our parents' quiz provides strategies for you to use to learn about how your child is doing—what he knows and can do, what is difficult for him, what helps him progress, and so forth. It also provides a way for you to discover what you know about home learning and how aware you are of your child's progress, growth, and habits. Use the quiz to help you choose appropriate home learning resources and Section III activities to fill in your child's knowledge gaps. But, above all, use the home learning quizzes to have fun with your child and develop a "big picture" of your child's progress. Self-assessment is important to everyone's learning, and so the pull-out section encourages you and your child to see what you already know and explore some new ground.

YOU'VE COME A LONG WAY

When kids are behind in a subject, they're not often fully aware of how far behind they are. They may have started out being a year behind and then maybe work up to only three months behind, but in their mind, they're still way behind. They don't realize they've made a lot of progress. Parents can help out so much just by encouraging students and pointing out how far their child's hard work is carrying them.

CHAPTER 4

How Can I Help My Child Prepare for Standardized Tests?

Standardized tests...the term conjures up images of impersonal classrooms, hard bucket seats, and the fast-moving hands of a looming black clock. What could be more fun? Well, all we can say is that it's got to be better than this, because as a school-aged student of the new millennium, your child will be taking quite a number of these tests.

Fortunately, contemporary educators, teachers and test makers alike, are a dedicated and sensitive lot. They've chosen their profession because they like children and want to help them thrive. Most are quite creative in their teaching methods.

As dedicated as these educators are, your child will benefit enormously from your thoughtful participation in the test-taking process. You can help your child prepare for standardized tests in a variety of ways, from attending to the basics (getting enough sleep and eating well before the test), to helping him become a "test-wise" test taker. But first, just what is a standardized test?

What is a Standardized Test?

Standardized tests provide a common measure of student performance. A standardized test contains the same set of

ASK THE TEACHER

- Are the test results consistent with my child's performance in the classroom?
- What do the test results mean about my child's skills and abilities?
- Are any changes anticipated in my child's educational program?
- What can I do at home to strengthen my child's skills?
—"What Should Parents Know About Standardized Testing in Schools," by Carolyn B. Bagin and Lawrence M. Rudner. Published by ERIC. Accessed online at www.accesseric.org/resources/parent/testing.html.

questions and is given under the same conditions to different groups of people. The answers are scored in the same manner. Standardized tests are designed by commercial publishers or state committees, or by a combination of the two. These tests use as their foundation the curriculum your child is studying.

What Kind of Standardized Tests Will My Child Take?
The standardized tests your child will take are usually of two general types. One is called the *norm-referenced test*. Norm-referenced tests measure your child's skills and knowledge against a representative sample, or "norm," of other children. That sample may be drawn anywhere, from the third graders in local Hebrew day schools to the national population of third graders. Tests in this category include the Terra Nova, the Stanford Achievement Test, and the Iowa Test of Basic Skills.

The other test type is called a *criterion-referenced test*. Criterion-referenced tests also measure your child's skills and knowledge, but rather than gauge little Leopold's skills against other children, criterion-referenced tests assess his grade-level mastery. Most criterion-referenced tests are developed by state-appointed committees, who define the number and types of questions that should be answered correctly to demonstrate this mastery.

While norm-referenced tests remain the most commonly administered of standardized tests, criterion-referenced tests are gaining ground in many states, as politicians and educators at the state level want to know how strong or weak the teaching (and learning) is at their schools. Most states have adopted initiatives set forth in the *Goals 2000: Educate America Act*. This federal legislation, passed in 1994, calls for content and performance standards in the core disciplines. Criterion-referenced tests are meant to chart this progress within the various individual districts. Norm-referenced tests usually align themselves with national standards.

As you can see in the state-by-state listings starting on page 44, some states, such as Connecticut, mandate only that

CHILDREN WITH SPECIAL NEEDS

Children with special needs can arrange to take standardized tests under conditions conducive to them. They might take the test as if it were a regular in-class test, alone, or perhaps at home. Time and other requirements may be altered depending on the child's individual needs.

None of this will be possible, however, if your child has not been officially diagnosed by the school's Individualized Education Program (IEP) as having a learning disability. In other words, you may not simply decide that your child is learning disabled and request special testing conditions. Your child must first receive a battery of tests by the IEP, which then decides, along with your child's teachers (including any special education professionals assigned to him or her), upon an official evaluation.

students take the state's own criterion-referenced test, such as the Connecticut Mastery Test. (Individual school districts, however, may administer other tests as they see fit.) Other states, such as Idaho, rely on the nationally administered, norm-referenced Iowa Test of Basic Skills (ITBS). A quick glance at the chart reveals that many states are moving towards a combination of state-developed criterion-referenced tests and nationally administered norm-referenced tests.

What's New and Different About Standardized Tests?
The standardized tests you might remember from your own school days—norm-referenced tests that were largely, if not exclusively, multiple-choice—are changing their stripes. While today's tests continue to contain ample numbers of multiple choice items, they also rely on several types of open-ended questions (see sidebar), writing exercises, and other higher-order thinking activities. The belief is that these testing formats offer a more accurate assessment of students' knowledge and skills.

Today's standardized tests are actually more difficult than those of previous years. Rather than focusing on the memorization of rules and procedures, the newer generation of tests require your child to use her critical-thinking skills and to write more. In the math portion of some tests, she'll be asked to explain how she arrived at her answers. In the language arts portions, she'll find a type of open-ended item called a constructed response question, which might ask her to explain an author's statement, or perhaps diagram an article's main event and supporting details.

Many tests now include extensive sections on written communication, including prewriting, composing, and editing exercises. These *performance assessments*, increasingly favored by educators, require students to demonstrate their knowledge and skills, including the process by which they solve problems. For example, your child may be asked to spend 45 minutes writing a story based on a short "prompt" or scenario. Or he will use prewriting skills, such as identifying general references and using dictionary skills.

OPEN-ENDED QUESTIONS

In the testing world, open-ended questions include constructed response, short answer, and extended response questions. *Constructed response* questions ask students to respond with a sentence, phrase, or bulleted list to a variety of material—from identifying the main idea in a passage to responding to questions about spelling and grammar. *Short answer* questions ask students to respond with a written paragraph, while *extended response* questions may take your child up to 45 minutes to complete in essay form.

IMMEDIATE ACADEMIC ASSISTANCE

If your child does poorly on one or more sections of a standardized test, don't panic. A focused effort will be made to solve the problem relatively quickly. First, we'll work with you to identify the roots of your child's difficulties, which can often be attributed to two things: skill gaps and lack of confidence.

Once we assess the extent of the skill gaps, we'll be able to tailor your child's curriculum to her specific needs. Personalized instruction in reading, language arts, and math will restore your child's self-confidence as she learns at her own pace, excited about succeeding time and again in a previously weak subject area.

You can help your child prepare for these performance-based activities by asking the teacher to explain what types of items appear on the test. Once you know this, you can engage your child in activities that encourage problem solving and creativity.

How Do Schools Use Standardized Tests?

Schools (and related institutions and agencies) use standardized tests for a variety of purposes. Beyond measuring how well or poorly students perform, schools—or, more precisely, the agencies that govern them—use these tests to measure how well the school itself is performing. State assessment agencies use standardized tests to compare scores among towns, districts, and individual schools. Increasingly, as you've probably heard, poorly performing schools are feeling the heat to raise scores; administrators usually do this by changing their curriculum.

As a parent, you should be concerned not only with your child's scores, but also with her school's. How does the school rank in comparison with others in your district? In neighboring towns? With other states? Has the school's test scores improved or declined in recent years? How much of your child's curriculum is driven by standardized tests? Too much? Not enough? If you have concerns about these or other issues, talk to your school administrators. For detailed information, you may also want to contact your state's office of assessment.

Most important of all is how the school will use your child's individual scores. Increasingly, schools are using standardized tests as diagnostic tools to pinpoint students' strengths and weaknesses. Students needing extra help may receive tutoring both during the regular school day and after hours. Generally, this is a good thing, although there are instances when a child may feel burdened and/or stigmatized by participating in special after-school or even summer programs. Help of the same sort is available through private centers like *SCORE!* Educational Centers, an educational subsidiary of Kaplan.

Precisely because your teacher may use your child's test score diagnostically, it is vital that you be informed about the school's test-score policies. Are their any specific consequences for your child's score? Make sure you discuss your child's strengths and weaknesses so that you can work with her not only in preparation for a specific test but throughout the school year.

How Long Do These Tests Take?

Perhaps the last test you took was the SAT (the Scholastic Aptitude Test). All you can recall is sitting in a sea of strangers, wrestling with an endless stream of mind-numbing, multiple-choice items. Not exactly what you'd wish for your child, especially one who has barely graduated from the playground. You might have heard that your child will be tested for five days running. Not to worry; the test could run for up to a week (or longer), but the longest block is usually no more than about 50 minutes. While it's no picnic, most children are certainly able to cope with these blocks of time, especially if they're prepared. So be sure to find out how long each test segment will be and then discuss this with your child.

Classroom Preparation

Schools vary considerably in how they prepare students for standardized tests. The majority spend at least some time on them, alerting students to upcoming tests, discussing test formats, timing, and so forth. Some schools teach test readiness skills while others don't. Critics charge that certain school districts, especially those serving poorer children, come perilously close to "teaching to the test"—devoting virtually all class time to test-related drills.

Research confirms that test-taking skills improve performance, and that a lack of such skills prevents students from achieving valid test results. Certain students become easily confused under pressure and fail to understand directions during the test. The younger the child, the more likely this is to occur. But all children (and adults) who lack

WHAT IS CRITICAL THINKING?

Critical thinking is the ability to evaluate ideas on the basis of sound reasoning. Critical thinkers:

- Evaluate evidence
- Analyze assumptions and biases
- Identify faulty logic and contradictions in arguments
- Consider multiple perspectives
- Summarize and judge facts for themselves

You can spur your child's critical thinking by asking him questions such as these:

- Why do you think that?
- Explain your reasoning.
- Can you support your statement? How did the author support hers?
- What else could the author (problem, idea) mean?

YOUR LEGAL RIGHTS TO TEST TAKING

Several precedents and laws define legal rights related to taking tests in school:

- Under the Family Education Rights and Privacy Act of 1974, also known as the Buckley Amendment, you have a right to examine your child's academic records. If these records contain test scores, you have a right to see those scores.
- Your child has a right to due process. For example, your child must get adequate time to prepare for a test.
- Your child has a right to fair and equitable treatment. Schools cannot, for example, have different test score requirements based on gender or race.
- Schools are not, however, necessarily liable for tests and test results being misused. The best way you can protect your child from misuse of testing is to be knowledgeable about the appropriate uses of various types of tests.

—"What Should Parents Know About Standardized Testing in Schools," by Carolyn B. Bagin and Lawrence M. Rudner. Published by ERIC. Accessed online at www.accesseric.org/resources/parent/testing.html.

test-taking savvy are at a disadvantage. To ensure that your child is adequately prepared to take tests—that he or she is "testwise"—be certain to ask the teacher the following:

- How will my child be prepared for the test? Does the school administer practice tests?
- Are the different question formats described and explained?
- Are specific directions, such as "all of the above," "as is," and so forth, explained?
- Does the teacher review time requirements and describe how students can pace themselves? (TIP: Some students spend too much time on the first part of the test or on the most difficult questions, leaving too little time for other items.)
- If there are separate answer sheets ("bubble sheets"), do the students receive practice filling these in?
- What can I do to help?

Sample Test Items

Look over the following test questions to get an idea of what your child may be asked to do on a standardized test. Notice how your child's skills will usually be assessed in context, stressing the functional use of language, mathematics, science, and social science.

These test items are similar to some of those found in the Stanford Achievement Test (Stanford 9), a norm-referenced test used in several states. Check out Kaplan's state-by-state listing of standardized test requirements at the end of this chapter to see which tests your child will be taking and which subjects she'll be tested in.

Reading Vocabulary Question

You should make a <u>right</u> turn at the next stop sign.

In which sentence does the word <u>right</u> mean the same thing as in the sentence above?

(a) You have no <u>right</u> to punish me!
(b) Is this the <u>right</u> answer to question number 12?
(c) Jake broke his <u>right</u> arm last summer.
(d) Mom says that it's not <u>right</u> to tell a lie.

Spelling Question

Read the sentences below. Decide if one of the underlined words is spelled wrong or if there is no mistake.

    (a) She was <u>hideing</u> behind a tree.
    (b) I think you've had <u>enough</u> ice cream.
    (c) My brother <u>cried</u> when he lost his toy.
    (d) No mistake

Language Question

Read the sentence below. If the underlined words contain a mistake in punctuation, capitalization, or word usage, choose the answer that is the best way to write the underlined section of the sentence. If there is no mistake, choose *Correct as is*.

I'm glad you'll be in <u>Mrs Brown's</u> math class with me.

    (a) Mrs Browns
    (b) Mrs. Brown's
    (c) Mrs Browns'
    (d) Correct as is

Mathematics: Problem Solving Question

Mr. Connors bought 10 plants for his garden. All of the plants were different prices. The least expensive plant cost $6, and the most expensive plant cost $10. Which is the most reasonable estimate of how much money Mr. Connors spent on all of the plants?

    (a) $50
    (b) $80
    (c) $100
    (d) $120

AIM HIGH

Research suggests that there are differences between high- and low-achieving students. For example, high-achieving students:

- Are more likely to have positive self-esteem and greater self-confidence in their abilities
- Do not feel intimidated by tests and feel well prepared for all types of tests
- Are more persistent with regard to their schoolwork and doing well on tests
- Are more likely to use appropriate strategies when taking tests
- Are more "testwise"

    —Preparing Your Elementary Students To Take Standardized Tests (Chicago Board of Education, 1999)

NUTRITION AND STRESS: THE DO'S AND DON'TS

Do eat:
- Fruits and vegetables
- Protein such as fish, poultry, beans, and legumes (like lentils)
- Whole grains such as whole wheat bread, pastas, and brown rice

Don't eat:
- Refined sugar and high-fat snacks (simple carbohydrates like sugar make stress worse and fatty foods lower your immunity)
- Salty foods (they can deplete potassium, which your child needs for nerve functions)

Mathematics: Procedures Question

There are 204 windows in the school building. Mr. Nasta cleaned 112 of those windows yesterday. How many windows does he still have to clean?

(a) 88
(b) 92
(c) 112
(d) 16
(e) Answer is not here

Science Question

It takes 24 hours for the Earth to make one complete turn. If the Earth turned more quickly, each day would be:

(a) shorter
(b) brighter
(c) longer
(d) hotter

Social Science Question

In the early 1900's, many people came to the United States from places such as Ireland, Italy, and Russia. How did they usually travel to the United States?

(a) by train
(b) by airplane
(c) by covered wagon
(d) by ship

Managing Test Anxiety

Test anxiety is extremely common, for children and adults alike. In fact, feeling nervous before a test is perfectly normal. Your goal for your child should not be to rid him of nervousness entirely but to help him channel it constructively. Channeled properly, nervousness boosts performance.

In their concern about testing, some parents convey their own anxiety to their child. Try not to do this! As one industry expert puts it, "The more positive the approach to the test, the more accurate the data is." So if everyone involved—parents, teachers, and other administrators—conveys a positive attitude, your child stands a better chance of producing a score that truly reflects his knowledge and skills. Don't put so much emphasis on scoring well that he feels unduly pressured. Take a positive approach, one that emphasizes the fun and value of learning for learning's sake. Work with your child throughout the year, a little at a time. You can accelerate your efforts somewhat in the weeks before a test, but consistency throughout the school year will serve him better.

Like the rest of us, children fear most what they don't know and can't control. Children need to be prepared psychologically for standardized testing. The more you can prepare them for what will take place, the less anxious they will feel and the more they will be able to channel their nervousness constructively. Make sure they know what will take place. Ask the teacher to clarify each of the following questions, and then go over them with your child. Knowing the answers will cut down on confusion during the actual testing situation, allowing her to focus on the test itself:

- What kind of test is it?
- Where and when will the test be given?
- How is the test timed?
- Are questions permitted during testing?
- Can students go back and work on previous sections of the test if they finish a section early?
- Should students guess on questions they do not know?
- What should students do when they finish but others are still working?[1]

Generally speaking, it doesn't help to tell children who are anxious to "just relax" or "think about something else." If, however, you can help them to focus on the specific test-taking strategies outlined in this chapter, chances are that

[1] Phillips, Art. *Test Taking Skills for Primary Grades.* A SORD project. March 1983. Southern Oregon Research and Develpment Committee (SORD).

KEEPING IT STRAIGHT

Some children have difficulty keeping their place on the test page or answer sheet. The results can be incorrectly marked answers. Teach your child to fold the test booklets and answer sheets so that only one page of each is showing. And remind him to check the page number of the test booklet every time he turns the page. This way, if two pages get stuck together when turning, the results won't be disastrous.

—*Teaching Test-Taking Skills: Helping Students Show What They Know,* by Thomas E. Scruggs and Margo A. Mastropieri. (Brookline Books, 1995)

rather than feeling overwhelmed by such global thoughts as "I'm gonna fail," they will feel in control and empowered. As teaching experts Nell Ducke and Ron Richart put it, for maximum performance, your child's test-taking demeanor should be "serious, confident, and strategic."

Test Taking Strategies

Standardized tests measure your child's knowledge in reading/language arts (reading comprehension, spelling and word usage, and written expression) math, and, sometimes, in the content areas taught in school, such as science and social studies. Understanding the curriculum and helping your child grasp important material is the single most important way you can help her score well on standardized tests.

Having said this, it is also true that a lack of test-taking skills can harm even the highest-achieving students. Here are some general strategies every test taker should know. Review these carefully with your child. They should become part of her background knowledge, as easily retrievable as the characters from her favorite novel.

Rule Number One: Answer the Questions You Know First.

The best test takers skip (temporarily) difficult material in search of the easier items. As they do, they mark the ones that require extra time and thought. This strategy buys time and builds confidence so they can handle the tough stuff later.

Your child should know that the test will include items that will be difficult even for the best students. He should also know that most tests do not get progressively harder. Many, though not all tests, are designed according to the "easy-hard-easy" model. So mulling over questions that are difficult at the expense of answering those you know is a poor strategy. Instead, the test-wise student builds his sense of mastery by tackling what he knows first.

DIVIDE AND CONQUER

At the beginning of a test, students should quickly compute how much time they have for each question. So if there are 60 items and one hour is allocated, test takers should answer, on average, no less than one question per minute. Of course, given that the questions will vary in difficulty, some questions will take less time and others more. And ideally, it's good to have time left over at the end of a test so that you can check your answers and return to those items that gave you the most difficulty. But using this method will help your child keep on track. To make it easier, she can divide the total time period into four equal periods. Thus after 15 minutes she can take note of how many items she has answered. If she's only checked off four, she'll know to adjust her speed accordingly.

—*Teaching Test-Taking Skills: Helping Students Show What They Know*, by Thomas E Scruggs and Margo A. Mastropieri (Brookline Books, 1995)

This strategy will only work if your child correctly identifies those items to which he must return. Be sure to remind him to put a big circle around the number of any question he skips. When he goes back, these questions will be easy to locate.

Rule Number Two: Answer All of the Questions.

Nearly all of the tests your child is likely to take are designed to allow ample time to answer all questions. Since children with the greatest number of right answers score highest, each question counts. So as a rule, it's a good idea to answer all of the questions.

There is the occasional "speeded test," designed to assess students on the basis of how many questions they can answer in the time allotted. In this case, of course, they should answer as many questions as possible, but not expect to answer them all.

Since most tests contain items designed to stymie all but the very best students, answering all the questions relies on two key test-taking strategies: *elimination* and *guessing*.

Rule Number Three: When in Doubt, Eliminate.

Oftentimes, children will have some knowledge of the information being tested. Savvy test takers use this information to eliminate less likely choices. Elimination helps narrow the possibilities, thereby increasing the odds that the test taker won't skip the question altogether or rely on random guessing.

If unsure of an answer, counsel your child to choose the one she thinks is best. Eliminate the most obvious poor choice(s) first, followed by those that are less obvious. She should then select among the remaining items, asking herself which one seems most reasonable.

Rule Number Four: Make Educated Guesses.

Closely allied to the elimination strategy is making educated guesses. This strategy recognizes that all test takers have their strengths and weaknesses, and that most tests include a certain percentage of items that most students will not be able to answer.

STANFORD ACHIEVEMENT TEST

The math portion of the Stanford Achievement Test includes test items assessing three content areas. These include:

Number Concepts

These questions ask students to demonstrate their knowledge of arithmetic procedures and properties of number systems.

Patterns and Relationships

These questions measure students' ability to recognize and extend patterns as well as demonstrate their understanding of the quantitative, geometric, or logical relationships between variables, data sets, or elements of sequence.

Concepts of Shape and Space

These questions ask students with to use and develop principles of measurement and geometric properties.

EENIE, MEENIE, . . .

TIP: If two multiple-choice items are similar, except for one or two words, choose one of these answers.

The test taker who makes educated guesses plows through with a "can do" attitude. Rather than reacting with an "I just don't know" and giving up, these students take things one step further, searching for what they might possibly know after all. This is especially effective with multiple choice items, since the answer does lie in front of them, and they have a one-in-four chance of getting it right even if they guess at random. But rather than rely on random guessing, your child should consider the following:

- What do I already know?
- What does my logical reasoning tell me?
- What key terms can I identify that might jar my thinking?
- What do I think the answer should be? Can I find an answer that most closely matches this?

Note that some tests, such as the Iowa Test of Basic Skills (ITBS) and the Illinois Goal Assessment Program (IGAP), actually penalize students for not guessing. Obviously, if taking these tests, your child should always guess.

Rule Number Five: Read the Entire Question.
Sometimes a child will decide he knows the answer to a question before he's through reading it. Students should read all questions through to the end, even if they think they know the answer. A better answer may occur to them if they carefully consider each option.

Rule Number Six: Manage Your Time.
Time is of the essence on standardized tests. Precisely because this is so, some test takers tend to get quite anxious about it. Merely knowing there are strict time limits can paralyze some kids, or at least considerably slow them down. Others may react by unnecessarily rushing through items, not giving themselves enough time to competently comprehend and respond to a question.

Obviously, the greater your child's anxiety about a test, the more likely he will be to fumble time-wise. This is just one more reason to stress the positive during the test-taking period.

Your child's teacher may or may not discuss time management with your child. Either way, a review never hurts. Ask the teacher how the test will be timed and discuss this with your child. As noted, most standardized tests are designed to allow students enough time to finish the test, but not to dawdle. A minority are "speeded tests," which measure how many items your child answers correctly in a given time period.

Regardless of the test type, keeping track of time and pacing yourself is key. And savvy test takers always use any remaining time to recheck the answers and review any hard questions they may be uncertain about.

Preparing for Reading/Language Arts Tests

The reading/language arts sections of most standardized tests assess your child in reading comprehension, spelling and word usage, and written expression. Many, if not most, also include listening and study skills subtests (assessing your child's familiarity with and ability to use reference works such as dictionaries, encyclopedias, almanacs, and so forth). All of these sections contain a mix of multiple-choice and open-ended items.

Reading Comprehension

The reading comprehension sections of nearly all standardized tests follow a similar format. Students are asked to read a passage and then respond to a series of questions, both multiple choice and open-ended. The trend today is towards increasingly lengthy and more demanding passages— or "meaningful chunks," as described in one such test.

The new generation of standardized tests are looking for everything from simple recall of information to the more sophisticated skills of interpretation, critical evaluation, and personal reflection and response. Your child may be asked to explain why an event in a story occurred, for example, and how the story differed from something that occurred in his own experience. He may be asked to agree or disagree with the author's point of view, or to compare the article or story to another he has read.

GIFTED AND TALENTED

Many studies suggest that early stimulation of a child's brain and body can enhance general intelligence. When the child's natural curiosity is encouraged and fostered, and learning is made fun, intelligence is enhanced.
—*The Parent's Answer Book* by Gerald Deskin, Ph.D. and Greg Steckler, M.A. (Fairview Press, 1995)

KEEP A LOG

Have your child keep a "Web log" whenever he goes online. This will get him to analyze what he's seeing instead of just mindlessly surfing. Reporting his Web whereabouts will also discourage him from going to inappropriate sites.

Establish a Family Book Club. You can help your child to do well in reading comprehension by encouraging her to read a variety of materials, both fiction and nonfiction. Encourage her to practice reading at a higher level of difficulty, so she is prepared for the rigor of the test. Most important of all, schedule time to discuss what she's read. Ask her to identify the central idea, purpose, or theme of the work. Can she describe important characters, settings, relationships, events, and details? Can she summarize the work? What techniques does the author use? What's the author's point of view?

Students who perform well on this portion of the language arts test tend to be year-round readers. They are comfortable with sustained reading and take pleasure in it. They also can stand apart from the material they read and apply a critical stance. According to the National Center for Education Statistics' Reading Report Card for the Nation and States, students who have home discussions about their studies at least weekly have higher average reading scores than those who do so less frequently. So go for it!

Writing Assessments

As noted earlier, some tests now include direct assessments of writing. This timed subtest (usually 45 minutes) requires students to respond to a brief prompt by writing a story. Your child may also be asked to critique and revise a written passage for punctuation, capitalization, and correct word usage.

A prompt used on a recent Connecticut Mastery Test went as follows:

> Imagine that one day you try a new kind of breakfast cereal. After eating it you find yourself getting smaller and smaller. Write a story about what happens to you as you become smaller.

Children who scored well on this assignment produced detailed and colorful stories with elaborate details and clear organization.

Grab the Quill. As in reading, skillful writing is a matter of practice. Encourage your child to write stories, fleshing out characters and spicing things up with lots of detail. Make it fun by "publishing" her stories when she's finished. Gather the family together for a special reading.

Preparing for Math Tests

The math component of today's standardized tests reflect the growing belief that in addition to rote learning, test items should elicit critical thinking. And, as elsewhere, the all-multiple choice format is no longer seen as adequate to fulfill this function. So in addition to straightforward questions that test computation skills and arithmetic procedures, your child is also likely to encounter test questions requiring him to actually demonstrate his reasoning and problem-solving ability. Some questions might ask him to draw a geometric figure, or perhaps construct a graph from information provided in a table. Others may require him to explain in writing how he arrived at the answer.

This shift from an emphasis on simply "getting the numbers right" to demonstrating conceptual understanding and problem solving in a real world context reflects the National Council of Teachers of Mathematics (NCTM) recommendations on curriculum and standards. The NCTM's recommendations, which, in a nutshell, strive to make mathematics meaningful, have been widely adopted nationwide, both in the classroom and on standardized tests.

Chances are high that your child will be tested on the following:

- Numeration (numbers and counting)
- Computation with whole numbers, fractions, decimals, and percents (including addition, subtraction, multiplication, and division)
- Ability to estimate and round numbers
- Ability to interpret (and sometimes construct) tables, graphs, and charts
- Simple probability questions

MATH LANGUAGE

Lots of kids (and adults) have trouble making sense out of those long, confusing word problems. this is because you have to figure out the *equation* before you can even start to calculate the answer.

Try having your child invent her own word problem. When designing the problem, be sure to include all the information necessary to solve it. Work with your child to write out a complete solution to the problem.

- Measurement and geometry (two- and three-dimensional shapes, area, volume, and units of measure)
- Problem solving (solving word problems, estimation, spatial reasoning, recognizing patterns)
- Money and time (recognizing and computing units of money and time)

For an overview of your child's math curriculum, we suggest you review chapters 8 and 9 in this book (3rd and 4th grade math). To score well on the math test, he should be comfortable with this material. For further practice, engage in the learning adventures suggested in chapters 14 and 15.

Think Mathematically in Everyday Situations. Given the real world application of many test items, encourage your child to think mathematically in everyday situations. Play games with money, in which you line up different kinds of coins and then ask her to add them up. Ask her what time it will be when a three-and-a-half hour movie will end. Practice rounding numbers so that she becomes familiar with the process. When you go to a store together, show her the price of an item that costs $1.99 (or $2.95, or $3.99, etcetera). Ask her to estimate how much four such items would cost.

Review the commonly used math terms, such as *sum, difference, product, quotient,* and *set.* A surprising number of students get stumped by these terms and don't progress beyond them. Review mathematical symbols, such as greater than (>) and less than (<). Practice reading charts and graphs so that your child becomes at ease with them.

Be Proactive. Given the variety of question types involved, it's important that, if at all possible, your child be exposed to practice items. This way, she won't be stumped by the novelty of the question types and will be able to focus instead on solving them. Ask the teacher if students will take practice tests. How much time will be spent on practice items? If you are not satisfied with the answer you receive, you can always contact the test publisher (if a nationally administered norm-referenced test) or the state assessment office (if a state-administered, criterion- referenced test). In

HOMEWORK HELPER

In the learning process, your child will eventually encounter some high-level processes that may be quite difficult. Acknowledge that you may have at one time done schoolwork like this, but you don't quite remember how it goes. Then ask your child to explain what she already knows—get her to teach you about what she already knows.

some cases you will be able to receive sample items from older tests, which you can then review with your child.

Finally, many tests require students to use a ruler and a calculator during certain portions of the test. To ensure that your child arrives prepared, be sure to find out well ahead of time whether he should bring these items with him.

The Basics of Body and Soul

You've heard the line about the "best laid plans." Too often we hear about kids who scramble in late on the day of the test. They may be harried because they went to the wrong room. Halfway through the test they're dizzy from hunger. The room is cold and they have no sweater, and so spend valuable time shivering instead of strategizing. Each of these scenarios is easily avoidable with a little planning.

Get Them to the Church On Time. Nothing will throw a child off more quickly than a poor start. Avoid this unnecessary pitfall by knowing when and where the test will be and by making certain your child gets there, and on time.

Burn off Steam. Encourage your child to exercise regularly before the test. A well-conditioned body lowers stress levels and increases performance. Beware, however, that she doesn't exert herself so much that she's fatigued on the day of the test.

Get Some Beauty Rest. Make sure that your child gets a good night's sleep before the test. The more rested she is, the more likely she will be to bring all her powers to bear on the test.

Dress Comfortably. The best way to dress for a test is in loose layers, with sweater over shirt and so forth. This way, your child will be prepared no matter what the temperature of the room.

Eat a Hearty Breakfast. Your child should eat a nutritionally sound breakfast on the day of the test. He should also be well hydrated.

TROUBLING

One-fourth of the students we surveyed said their family "never" did anything together for fun, and only 30 percent said their parents spend some time talking with them each day.
—*Beyond the Classroom,* by Laurence Steinberg, Ph.D. (Simon & Schuster, 1996)

STANDARDIZED TEST REQUIREMENTS BY STATE

In addition to those state-mandated tests listed below, many individual districts offer additional tests as needed. Contact your child's school administrators for more information.

STATE	TEST	GRADES	SUBJECTS	TIME OF YEAR GIVEN
Alabama	Stanford Achievement Test (Stanford 9)	3–11		Spring
Alaska	California Achievement Test	4, 7	English language arts, math	Spring
Arizona	Stanford Achievement Test (Stanford 9)	2–11		Spring
Arkansas	Stanford Achievement Test (Stanford 9)	5, 7, 10	math, reading/language arts, social studies, science	Fall
	Arkansas Criterion-Referenced Test	4, 8	math, English, reading, writing	Spring
California	Stanford Achievement Test (Stanford 9)	2–11	reading, language arts, math	Spring
	Statewide standards-based assessment being developed			
Colorado	Colorado Student Assessment Program	3 4, 7 5, 8 10	reading reading, writing math, science math, reading, writing	Spring Spring Fall Spring 2001
Connecticut	Connecticut Mastery Test	4, 6, 8		Fall
	Connecticut Academic Performance Test	10		Spring
Delaware	Delaware Student Testing Program	3, 5, 8, 10 8, 11 4, 6	English language arts, math science, social studies	Spring Fall/Spring Spring 2000
District of Columbia	Stanford Achievement Test (Stanford 9)	1–11	math, reading	Fall/Spring
Florida	Florida Comprehensive Achievement Test (FCAT)	4, 8, 10 3, 5, 6, 7, 9 5, 8, 10 3, 4, 6, 7, 9 4, 8, 10	reading reading (multiple-choice) math math (multiple-choice only) writing	Spring
	Stanford Achievement Test (Stanford 9)	3–10	reading comprehension, math problem-solving (multiple-choice only)	

How Can I Help My Child Prepare for Standardized Tests?

STATE	TEST	GRADES	SUBJECTS	TIME OF YEAR GIVEN
Georgia	Georgia Kindergarten Assessment Program	kindergarten	reading, math	Spring
	Iowa Test of Basic Skills (ITBS)	3, 5, 8		
	criterion-referenced tests being developed	3, 5, 7	English language arts, reading	
	writing assessments	3, 5, 8		
Hawaii	Stanford Achievement Test (Stanford 9)	3, 5, 7, 9	math, reading	Spring
	Hawaii State Test of Essential Competencies (HSTEC)	10		
Idaho	Iowa Test of Basic Skills (ITBS)	3–11		Fall
Illinois	Illinois Standards Achievement Test (ISAT)	3, 5, 8, 10 4, 7, 11	reading, writing, math science, social science	Winter Winter
	Prairie State Achievement Test (in development)			Spring 2000
Indiana	Indiana Statewide Testing for Educational Progress (ISTEP)	3, 6, 8, 10	reading/language arts, math	Fall
Iowa	no statewide assessment program			
Kansas	Kansas Assessments (state-developed, standards-based)	3, 7, 10 5, 8, 10 4, 7, 10 5, 8, 11	reading writing, science math social studies	Fall/Spring
Kentucky	Commonwealth Accountability Testing System (CATS)	4, 5, 7, 8, 10, 11, 12	reading, writing, math, science, social studies, humanities, practical living/vocational	Spring
	TerraNova/Comprehensive Test of Basic Skills (CTBS)	3, 6, 9		

Making the Grade

STATE	TEST	GRADES	SUBJECTS	TIME OF YEAR GIVEN
Louisiana	Louisiana Educational Assessment Program (LEAP)	4, 8	English, math, science, social studies	Spring
	Iowa Test of Basic Skills (ITBS)	3, 5, 6, 7, 9		
	Graduation Exit Exam	10, 11	English, math, science, social studies, writing	
Maine	Maine Educational Assessment	4, 8, 11	English language arts, math, science/technology, social studies, health/phys. ed., visual/performing arts, career preparation, languages	Spring
Maryland	Maryland School Performance Assessment Program (MSPAP)	3, 5, 8	reading, math, English language arts, science, social studies	Spring
	Maryland High School Assessments	9	English, algebra or geometry, government	
Massa-chusetts	Massachusetts Comprehensive Assessment System	4, 8, 10 3, 4, 7, 10 4, 6, 8, 10 5, 8, 10	writing reading math science/technology, history, social science	Spring
Michigan	Michigan Educational Assessment Program (MEAP)	4, 7 5, 8	math, reading science, writing, social studies	Winter
Minnesota	Minnesota Comprehensive Assessment Program	3 5 10 11	reading, math reading, writing, math reading, writing math	Spring
Mississippi	Iowa Test of Basic Skills (ITBS)	4–8	English language arts, math	Fall
	Tests of Achievement (TAP)	9	English language arts, math	
	Functional Literacy Exam	11	reading, math, written communication	
	Subject Area Tests	9–12	algebra, U.S. history, biology	
Missouri	Missouri Assessment Program (MAP)	4, 8, 10 3, 7, 11 3, 7, 10 4, 8, 11 5 5, 9	math communication arts science social studies fine arts health/phys. ed.	Spring Spring Spring Spring 2000 Spring 2001 Spring 2001

STATE	TEST	GRADES	SUBJECTS	TIME OF YEAR GIVEN
Montana	districts choose from among commercially prepared tests, i.e., Iowa Test of Basic Skills (ITBS), TerraNova/ Comprehensive Test of Basic Skills (CTBS), Stanford Achievement Test (Stanford 9)	4, 8, 11	reading, language arts, math, science, social studies	Spring
Nebraska	No statewide assessment program			
Nevada	TerraNova/Comprehensive Test of Basic Skills (CTBS)	4, 8, 10	reading, writing, math	Fall
New Hampshire	New Hampshire Educational Improvement and Assessment Program (NHEIAP)	3 6, 10	English language arts, math English language arts, math, science, social studies	Spring
New Jersey	Elementary School Proficiency Test (ESPA)	4		Spring
	Grade 8 Proficiency Test (GEPA)	8	math, language arts	
	High School Proficiency Assessment (HSPA) being developed			
New Mexico	New Mexico Achievement Assessment	4, 6, 8	math, science, English language arts	Spring
	Reading Assessment	1, 2	reading	
	Writing Assessment	4, 6	writing	
	High School Competency Test	10–12		
New York	State Assessments	4, 8 5, 8	English language arts, math, science social studies	Spring Spring 2000
	Regents Exam	11 10	English math global history/geography, U.S. history/government, science	Spring Spring being phased in for 2003

Making the Grade

STATE	TEST	GRADES	SUBJECTS	TIME OF YEAR GIVEN
North Carolina	End of Grade Tests	3–8	reading, math (multiple-choice only)	Spring
	Open-Ended Assessments	4, 8	reading, math (written out/problem solving)	
	Writing Assessment	4, 7	writing	
	Tests of Computer Skills	8	computer skills	
	Competency Tests	10	reading, math	
	High School Comprehensive Test	10	English language arts, math	
North Dakota	TerraNova/Comprehensive Test of Basic Skills (CTBS5) and Test of Cognitive Skills (TCS2)	4, 6, 8, 10	reading, vocabulary, language mechanics, math, spelling, science, social studies	Spring
Ohio	Ohio Proficiency Test	4, 6, 9, 12	reading, writing, math, science, citizenship	Spring
Oklahoma	Iowa Test of Basic Skills (ITBS)	3, 7		Spring
	Oklahoma Core Curriculum Tests	5, 8, 11	math, science, reading, history/government, writing, geography, arts	
Oregon	State-developed criterion-referenced tests	5, 8, 10 3, 5, 8, 10	science, social science reading and literature, writing, math	Spring
Pennsylvania	Pennsylvania System of School Assessment (PSSA)	5, 8, 11 6, 9 11 5, 8, 11	reading writing writing math	Spring Fall Spring Spring
Rhode Island	Metropolitan Achievement Test (MAT)	4, 8		
	Rhode Island Writing Test	3, 7, 10	writing	
	New Standards Reference Exams	4, 8, 10 4, 8	math English language arts	
	Health Education Assessment	5, 9		

How Can I Help My Child Prepare for Standardized Tests?

STATE	TEST	GRADES	SUBJECTS	TIME OF YEAR GIVEN
South Carolina	Cognitive Skills Assessment Battery	1, 2	general knowledge	Fall
	Palmetto Achievement Challenge Tests (PACT)	3–8	language arts, math science	Spring
	PACT Exit Exam	10	reading/English language arts, math, science, social studies	Spring
South Dakota	Stanford Achievement Test (Stanford 9)	2, 4, 8, 11	reading, math, science, language arts, social studies	Spring
	Open-Ended Writing Assessment	5, 9	writing	Fall
	Otis-Lennon School Ability Test (OLSAT)	4, 8		
Tennessee	TerraNova/Comprehensive Test of Basic Skills (CTBS), Complete Battery Plus	3–8 4, 7, 11	English language arts, math, science, social studies writing	Spring
	Tennessee Comprehensive Assessment Program (TCAP)	9	English language arts, math	
Texas	Texas Assessment of Academic Skills (TAAS)	3–8, 10 4, 8, 10 8	reading, math writing social studies, science	throughout year
	National Assessment of Educational Progress (NAEP)	4, 8	math, science	Spring 2000
Utah	Stanford Achievement Test (Stanford 9)	5, 8, 11		
Vermont	Vermont Development Reading Assessment	2	early reading	Spring
	New Standards Reference Exams	4, 8, 10	math, English language	
	Vermont Science Assessment	6, 11	arts	
	Local districts choose a norm-referenced test (optional)	5, 9, 11	science	

Making the Grade

STATE	TEST	GRADES	SUBJECTS	TIME OF YEAR GIVEN
Virginia	Stanford Achievement Test (Stanford 9)	4, 6, 9	English language arts, math; science and social studies optional	
	Virginia Standards of Learning Test (SOL)	3	English, math, science, social studies	
		5, 8	English, math, science, social studies, computer technology	
Washington	Iowa Test of Basic Skills (ITBS)	3, 6	English language arts, math	Spring
	Iowa Test of Educational Development (ITED)	9	English language arts, math	Spring
	Washington Assessment of Student Learning (WASL)	4, 7, 10	English language arts, math	Spring
West Virginia	Metropolitan Readiness Test	kindergarten		Spring
	Stanford Achievement Test (Stanford 9)	311	English language arts, spelling, math, science, social sciences	
	West Virginia Writing Assessment	4, 7, 10	writing	
Wisconsin	TerraNova/Comprehensive Test of Basic Skills (CTBS)	4, 8, 10	math, science, English, language arts, social studies, writing	Spring
	Wisconsin Reading Comprehension Test	3	reading	
Wyoming	Wyoming Comprehensive Assessment System	4, 8, 11	math, language arts	Spring

CHAPTER 5

How Else Can I Affect My Child's Success?

Parents are the single most important factor in a child's educational success from the earliest months through the school years. Our shoes may be scuffed, our wallets thin, and our gasoline tanks running on empty,

FOLLOW THE LEADER

Parents who are not able to take advantage of opportunities to participate in their child's school life, or, worse, who let these opportunities slip by, send a message: that although we say that school is important, we don't have the time to get involved in it. In many such households, the child concludes that he or she doesn't have the time or energy to be very involved in school, either.

—*Beyond the Classroom*, Laurence Steinberg, Ph.D. (Simon & Schuster, 1996)

but it is our effort, energy, and support that make the difference.

We all look back on that time when our toddler first held up a bug or a blade of grass and proudly named it for us. We cherish being a part of that moment of learning and hold on to the hope that every moment of learning in our children's lives will be as exciting and as important.

Children make those first discoveries both for themselves and for the loving adults around them. Your presence, your pride, your support, and your enthusiasm were an essential part of that moment and will continue to be a part of their learning moments for as long as they live with you. As children mature, enter school, and continue up through the higher grades, the intensity of their learning experiences changes and their public expectations of us change (try gurgling excitedly over your 13 year old's mastery of the square root), but our basic role remains the same.

Spend Learning Time Together

We may do more supporting and less teaching once our children hit school, but there are many opportunities for support that have nothing to do with textbooks or classroom lessons. These are the times when you and your

PARENTS COUNT!

Parents are educators too. By the time your children enter school, you will have taught them more than they will learn during their entire school experience!

MOM ON A SOAPBOX

My biggest advice to parents is don't rely on a school to be the sole educator of your child. If learning is important to you, you have to be involved and you have to help your child. You cannot expect someone else to do it. You have to take the initiative, and that might be to plug them into another outside resource to help foster a love of learning.

child can build a wonderful relationship around learning together.

One parent may discover a local garden club's edible-plant walk to take with his seven-year-old botanist. Another may share her skills with carving tools and linoleum blocks with her son. Others are willing to join a teenager under the car. All are engaged in learning with their children. These are the parents and children who are joined in a learning process that transcends the ordinary routines of living together.

Parents Can

We are sometimes intimidated by schools and schooling. This happens most frequently in later years when the more advanced mathematics, language, or science curriculum can leave us scrambling for reference books as we try to help our struggling young chemists or geographers. It can also happen in earlier years, particularly if our children have problems with specific skills like reading and if the school is using teaching techniques different from the ones used when we were in school.

At such times, it's important to keep in mind that no one person and no single institution can possibly provide all of the care, support, and expertise that are required to educate a young human being. We, as parents, may not have the pedagogical skills or knowledge to teach a particular subject, but we are the primary support team, the cheerleaders, the enforcers, and, when necessary, the champions of our young students. As you read this book, you will also find that there are many ways to supplement and support your child's education that require only our energy and enthusiasm for learning (of course, knowing how hard parents already work, that is a big *only*).

Provide the Taste of Success

Good educators (good managers, successful politicians, and great generals as well) all know that success breeds success and that nobody thrives or learns in situations in which there is frequent failure. To learn well, we all need to build on successful experiences.

Learning should be tailored so that children can taste success. A fact, a skill, or a concept successfully acquired will stick—and contribute to *more* learning. This doesn't mean that learning won't be work. Learning, as we all know, often takes lots of work. Stumbles, guesses, and trials occur all along the way. These are part of the process and part of the learning. When something becomes too full of stumbles and sulks and tears, however, it's time to take a break.

A break is also a good idea when there are tears of frustration over a homework assignment. If your child is stumped and it's appropriate for you to help, lead him back to a simpler level. Try to break the present task into smaller steps. If the steps lead to small, recognizable successes, the original, frustrating task can be easily accomplished.

If you are working with your child and using the activities in this book, avoid situations in which defeat and disappointment seem likely. This is not always easy to do, but learning to read your child's reactions will help you know when to halt an unsuccessful attempt. While you pause, consider the child and the task, and then rethink the task. Can you break it into smaller units or subtasks? Can you try teaching in a different way? Or should you abandon it and try something totally different?

Providing tastes of success is like carefully laying a new course of bricks in a wall. If you have crumbly bricks and lumpy mortar, there'll be trouble higher up. When each brick is even and snug and the mortar satisfyingly set, you have laid the perfect foundation for a new course.

Learn to Listen

Good listening skills are necessary for learning, but they are equally (or perhaps even more) necessary for teaching.

The First Level of Listening. There's an old educational maxim, "He who does the talking, does the learning." Talking requires putting your thoughts together. The more your child talks about something that she's learning, the more putting together—learning—she does. This is a simple

HOME COOKIN'

Parents can show kids how learning basic skills applies to everyday life. Use the tools you have around the home, and have a lot of fun too. Do projects with your children. Focus on one child or all siblings. Turn measuring food ingredients into the lesson of the day. Split a recipe in half or double it. Whoa—there's a huge math lesson going on there! Do it. Use the measuring cups. Use the flour and the sugar. Break some things, make some mistakes along the way. Have fun. What do you have at the end of the "lesson"? Chocolate chip cookies, and the kids get to brag about how they got to make them. My mom's not the best cook in the world, but we really had fun cooking together.

CAVEGIRL

One mother told me that her daughter was really amazing at math and phonics, but she hadn't opened her mouth in school the whole year. This was a big issue for her and the teacher. I told her that at Score@Kaplan we really interact with the children, and her mother said she didn't think that could really happen. I told the girl to raise her hand and say "I'm done," because when you do, you'll get a Score incentive card, which children can use to redeem for prizes or gifts. The mom was so surprised she even opened her mouth.

The mom called me a few nights later. Her teacher freaked out because the next day in class the girl raised her hand and said, "I have a question." The teacher thought, Oh my god, Lazarus has come out of the cave, because she never spoke up before. That's what's going on at Score. We're teaching life things here, beyond what you learn in a textbook. We're teaching kids how to be people.

and extremely useful thought, but it's very easy to forget, even for the most experienced teachers.

If *you* are quiet enough, you'll get the thrill of watching those miraculous moments when your child's learning takes place. The sound of the penny dropping can be the most important (and satisfying) sound in the world.

The Second Level of Listening. This level of listening is a bit harder. It requires you to be both quiet and as completely aware as possible of everything about your child. We use this skill unconsciously in conversations with our friends. We are sensitive to their facial expressions, read their body language, and monitor the tone of their voices. With your child, make this a more conscious process. Deliberately watch her face as an exercise is being written. Notice the enthusiastic posture (or discouraged or bored slump) as your child talks to herself during a hands-on activity. Pay attention to changes in behavior. These and many other subtle signals will help you determine how well, or how poorly, a particular educational activity is going.

Learn Something Yourself

We know a parent who began learning Hebrew at the same time as his child was learning to read. His child was having a struggle. Because this parent had to learn a new alphabet from scratch as well as how to read right to left, he was especially sympathetic with and supportive of his child's struggles.

Learning something new yourself has two other benefits (besides having a good time learning ballroom dancing or car maintenance or whatever). The first is that it makes you an observer of how your own learning process works, and that *always* makes you a better teacher. The second is that you are providing your child with an excellent model.

Remember Your Own Learning

Everyone who engages in teaching touches a lot of old hot buttons. There were subjects you loved, subjects you hated, teachers who helped you, and teachers you just couldn't please. These are useful memories, but they are primarily useful to you as an adult engaged in education. They can help you think about what works or doesn't work, but they can also bog you down while you're working with your child. As much as possible, keep your memories to yourself while you are working with your child at the homework table or using the activities in this book.

This is not an iron rule, though—nothing in education should be ironclad. If an old feeling or experience makes helpful sense at the moment, share it. All children are curious about their parents' lives as children, and you should share whatever you feel comfortable about sharing. Usually, however, it's better to do it at some other time.

Finding More Educational Resources

Beyond this book lies a whole world of educational opportunities. Like most parents, you are probably the phone book, resource manager, librarian, transportation officer, executive secretary, and personal assistant in your child's education right now. Here are a few ideas of resources to make your job more rewarding and easier.

Use the institutions around you. Almost all areas of our country are within range of a college, university, research field station, or county extension service. Such institutions often sponsor a variety of public educational events staffed by young, eager graduate students or professionals who are happy and proud to show and talk about what they do. Call them up and find out what they have to offer and get on their mailing lists.

Meet interesting neighbors. Ham radio operators, retired people with exotic hobbies, the guy who raises parakeets or poodles for sale, and many others like them live somewhere nearby. They are usually happy to share their stories and skills with interested families.

Plug into the Web. It can be confusing and it can be maddening, but the possibilities of finding facts, books, articles, connection resources, and you name it are so great that tuning into the hum of information on the World Wide

YOUR ROLE

I'd say a parents' role in a child's education should be to offer encouragement. Congratulate. Help. Be there. Show an interest in what they're doing. Even if their work is not perfect, you can encourage them to do their best.

HOW PLACES WORK

Factories, farms, greenhouses, fire stations—any place of business—can be a learning site for your child. Call these businesses up and see if they can handle family or small group tours.

LEADER OF THE PACK

Use your child's friends to help out with home learning projects and keep everything fun and exciting. Sometimes older siblings can be great role models to younger children. I wanted my older sister to read to me all the time; have older brothers and sisters read to younger children. Parents need to encourage this kind of positive experience in the family.

TOOL TIME

Teach your children how to use a dictionary, encyclopedia, or different kinds of software reference tools. Many kids don't know how to look up the meaning of a word because no one's helped them or shown them how. You don't learn some of these skills until late in school, so it's a big headstart if your children learn at home first.

Web is worth the effort. Having your own computer helps, but it isn't necessary. Libraries all over the country now offer access to the Internet as a resource and will be happy to help you search.

Make your own connections. Everyone seems to work harder and have less time these days. This is very isolating for parents who have the added responsibility of child rearing. You can be sure, however, that there are lots of people out there just like you. Use your PTA, visits to the park, church, or synagogue, membership in organizations, and contacts with other places where you meet adults with children to raise issues about children and education. This connecting can be as simple as finding enough interested families to organize a modern dance class or as complicated (and important) as galvanizing parents to take action against a program cutback in the local schools.

Contact home-schooling groups. Home schoolers have taken on the whole burden of their children's education and usually have done extensive research into the educational opportunities in the communities around them. Subscribe to any publications they produce and talk with them about what they've found useful.

Check out professional and trade associations. Many of these groups have extensive educational and public relations resources that you can use to supplement hobbies or educational activities. Offerings range from posters and booklets to some quite sophisticated educational materials. Many libraries have indexed directories for professional and trade groups. You and your child could spend a pleasant time browsing through one of them looking for areas of interest together (and you'll be amazed at the variety).

Use the library with your child. Libraries not only offer special programs for families, they are increasingly defining themselves as community information and resource centers. Their bulletin boards reflect this and will guide you to unsuspected educational opportunities ranging from reading programs and book clubs, to arts and crafts classes, to author readings. And, of course, take advantage of the professional skills of the children's librarian.

Finally, don't forget your mother! Members of your extended family make wonderful resources. We often overlook the richness of wisdom and experience available in our own immediate circle. An aunt who crochets, a cousin who loves to do woodworking, or a grandparent who cooks some special food all have skills to share. Older relatives may have personal experiences like military service, life in another country, or skills in an occupation that no longer exists that they would be happy to share for oral history projects.

Making the Most of Small Moments

Teaching moments exist all around you. It's easier with younger children because their defenses aren't up and they ask great questions. But, in fact, older children are as curious and eager to explore if you open up situations. An example might be stopping by the road to read a notice board about an area of reclaimed prairie and then researching this at home. Budgeting for throwing a party is a natural. And minilessons don't have to be complicated. A game of "subway-stop bingo" (looking for all the letters of the alphabet on a subway station map) can change a tedious wait into a language arts lesson.

Remember—You Do Make a Difference

Whether you work on the Learning Adventure activities in this book, share your child's enthusiasm for all the right answers she got on the Kids' Home Learning Quizzes, zealously support your children's homework efforts, seek out exciting field trips, drive your child to an enrichment program, or do all of these, your support makes a big difference in your child's educational success. Everything you do, no matter how small a beginning, encourages and strengthens her learning. Thanks for making the effort.

MAKE IT REAL

One boy in our center was not expected to walk or talk after a severe accident. He had a great recovery, but still has a bad vision problem and needs to sit very close to a computer screen. I told his mother that I had a good friend who also had poor vision and hearing problems, and he got accepted to a top college. He had to sit in the front row of class and tape lectures and use his laptop to record what he heard, but he adapted just fine to higher education. And I told this boy's mom that he could go to college— Berkeley, for instance, has an extension service for students who have challenging physical problems—and just to be aware of the opportunities out there. She started crying. "Nobody ever talked to me before about my son going to college. Nobody has ever made that a reality." If children under any conditions are given a taste of success, like moving forward in their skill levels, it's a good thing. Then it's not a matter of *if* the child is going to college, but which college to attend.

What's Being Covered in School?

CHAPTER 6

What's My Child Studying in Language Arts?

Reading, writing, speaking, and listening form the basis of language arts instruction in elementary school during the first few years. Many schools have begun to include viewing—that is, the processing of visual information such as graphics, illustrations, videos, TV—as part of the curriculum as well. Since all these means of communication are the key tools for success in today's world, you are wise to have decided to play an active role in helping your child succeed with them early on.

These are all dynamic fields, constantly changing in both content and emphasis. Remember when being a literate person meant simply being able to read a book and write legibly? Today the definition of literacy has expanded to include our interaction with information we view and hear from many sources: radio and television, audio tapes and videotapes, word processing, and the Internet. Though each may seem to be a separate skill (Look, Mom, I can read!), they are very much interrelated.

- Each has thinking at its core.
- Each is a matter of processing input and constructing a meaningful response.

As a result, language arts instruction in grades three and four has a lot to do with the thoughtful application of basic literacy skills and rules being learned in order to communicate effectively.

TOGETHERNESS

It's often difficult to create a great home environment for learning. No child wants to disappoint a parent. Parents are the most important people in a child's life. To fail in front of parents is often devastating. It's best to see parents feel comfortable about making mistakes in front of their children, and to be laughing about it and make it less of a competitive atmosphere. When both parents and children can learn together, that's the recipe for success.

READ AND READ AND READ

How do my husband and I foster our child's interest in learning at home? We read and we read and we read. We never turn down reading to him and we never turn down buying a book. That's one of the biggest things that we do together.

YOU CAN DO IT!

I heard something on National Public Radio that somebody finished a longitudinal study of children through college, and the biggest determiner of success is not IQ level, it's how well parents motivate their kids. This is an area that I as a parent would like to learn more about!

It is very common for children's language abilities to vary across the skill areas—your child might read up a storm, but shy away from any written assignment; or she might find reading tough, yet shine in any activity involving oral presentation. Keep in mind the need to accentuate the positive (as the old song goes), even as you work on helping your child strengthen areas that may come less easily. Remember too, that especially in developing language arts skills, children's growth is often sporadic—periods of doldrums suddenly illuminated by spurts of spectacular achievement. Take it patiently as it comes, nurture it, and await the thrill of the blossoming.

The outlines that follow provide a general overview of skills that are likely to be introduced and taught in your child's 3rd or 4th grade.

Ten Core Areas in Language Arts. The following ten core areas form the basis of most language arts programs in grades three and four:

1. Reading Comprehension Strategies
2. Decoding and Phonics
3. Vocabulary Strategies
4. Written Expression (composition, writing process)
5. Grammar and Usage
6. Mechanics (capitalization, punctuation, handwriting)
7. Spelling
8. Listening, Speaking, and Viewing Skills
9. Study Skills and Information Resources
10. Appreciating Literature and Language

Approaches to Language Arts Teaching. Though the basic elements of language arts teaching (reading, writing, speaking, listening) remain constant through your child's school years, the variations of actual how and when of instruction are as numerous as the number of elementary classrooms. Variations in instruction are due to factors such as the teacher's passions and preferences, the school district's standards and testing programs, and the school's access to equipment. The following instructional approaches that you may read about or hear about in teacher conferences can have a great deal of effect on how and when language arts instruction is carried out in your child's class.

Learning Centers Many elementary classrooms feature areas defined by their physical arrangement and contents in order to stimulate interest in and focus attention on specific activities for learning. In the case of a language arts center, there might be rug mats and comfortable pillows, and bookshelves to encourage reading; cassette players and tapes; pictures and other things the children can use as story starters; a computer and printer for word processing; maybe even a VCR. Children's time in learning centers is usually self-directed.

Curriculum Integration In an integrated language arts program, the ideas that come from reading a story become catalysts for speaking, listening, writing, and further reading. These communication skills are introduced, mastered, and applied within the context of other school subjects—science, social studies, literature.

Phonics, Basal Readers, and Whole-Language Instruction Using phonics, your child learns to read by sounding out individual letters, using letter combinations to sound out words, then using words to make sentences.

Basal reading programs teach reading in a sequential, skill-oriented structure, with many specific lessons and workbook pages, each tied to certain skills in the sequence.

Whole-language instruction involves children in a holistic approach to developing language skills; children learn to read, write, speak, and listen through the use of actual books (usually by recognized authors). Their language arts activities are tied to purposeful goals, often self-defined, rather than worksheets.

The Writing Process Much research has been done recently on the steps that writers take when they write. For the teaching of writing, that process has been subdivided into five general phases or steps:

"I HATE READING!"

I worked with a boy who had attention deficit disorder. He was just going into third grade when he first came to our *SCORE!* Center. Early in the program we found out that he really hated to read. He would run around, fidget, and do things other than read.

Day by day, he saw that he was doing better and better. Eventually, he finished three months of academic progress in reading and reached his first goal level. You could see the excitement in his face—when he finished his goal, all the coaches and kids in the center recognized him for his achievement. We all watched him shoot his baskets and receive his *SCORE!* cards and see him put his name up on *SCORE!* Mountain. After that, he was excited about reading and wanted to do his silver goal (six months of academic progress) in reading. After another month, he kept doing more reading and admitted, "I like reading. I love to read."

THAT COMPUTES!

My child and I are on America Online™. She has a few girls that she's contacted through the American Girl Web site, and she's been pen pals with them. She writes letters to them every day, and I've noticed that her spelling has improved so much—she really wants to do a good job communicating with her friends. I've encouraged her to do these great things online. She also has a cousin in Fresno, and they e-mail back and forth with each other via computer.

COOL IDEA

Kids need better vocabularies these days. "Cool, neat, big, small . . ." are used too often in student writing, so parents should encourage children to expand and grow their knowledge of new words. Parents should always have a dictionary and a thesaurus on hand, and teach children how to research and use these tools.

- Prewriting
- Writing (drafting)
- Revising
- Editing
- Postwriting/publishing

The amount of time and attention devoted to each stage varies from phase to phase and from writer to writer, but attention to this process helps kids (all of us for that matter—you too!) become more fluent, happier writers.

Using Technology Perhaps nothing varies as much in classrooms across the country as the amount of access teachers and their students have to equipment such as computers, modems, VCRs, TVs, and the like. Some schools aren't able to get the hardware; others have it, but scheduling becomes a burden to already overloaded teachers. During the school day, it has become increasingly likely that your 3rd or 4th grader may be engaged in any of the following technology-based activities:

- Use a computer for word processing, perhaps even have a keyboarding class
- Use a computer for exchanging letters with an electronic pen pal
- Use a software program for working on spelling, grammar, or vocabulary development
- Use a computer for reading CD-ROM storybooks (stories that are spoken and enhanced by sounds and animation)
- Use a VCR for viewing videos related to language arts activities
- Listen to books on tape or in other audio presentations
- Watch TV programs with an educational focus

What's Taught in Grade Three?

The 3rd grade is often seen as the end of the primary school years—the years in which the foundations for later learning are laid. By the end of grade three, you can expect your child to be reasonably confident with reading and writing and to see those skills as tools she will use for lifelong learning.

In this grade, you're likely to see a wide range of reading materials come home with your child as she begins to work with literature that includes stories from different cultures, from newspapers and magazines, and in other literary forms such as poetry and nonfiction pieces. Your child will start to do story analysis by identifying setting, characters, and plot in stories. She will extend her study and research skills to include identifying parts of a book, using the dictionary, thesaurus, encyclopedia, and maps.

In the writing arena, your child will begin to write in a wide variety of contexts: journals, friendly letters, stories, poems. While inventive spelling may still be viewed as okay for journal writing and creative efforts, weekly spelling word lists are likely to be commonplace and figure in your child's homework. In grade three, children begin to learn the revision phase in the process of writing. They learn to spice up their writing by using antonyms, synonyms, compound words, different tenses, prefixes, and suffixes. They use punctuation to help add meaning to their writing.

Grade three is where children are typically expected to master the switch from print to cursive writing (as well as get an introduction to keyboarding). In terms of the oral aspects of language, your child will get a lot of practice in telling and retelling stories, sharing information informally with the class, participating in focused discussion groups, and reading aloud to learn about speaking with expression.

Core Area 1: Reading Comprehension Strategies
• Draw conclusions by using details and facts from a story
• Predict the ending to a story
• Describe the cause and effect of an event
• Tell the main idea and give some supporting details
• Summarize a story

Core Area 2: Decoding and Phonics
• Make syllable generalizations
• Read words with all vowel sounds
• Read words with beginning and ending consonant blends
• Read compound words

DEAR DIARY . . .

For our *SCORE!* writing classes, we have children keep a journal at home. This is a great activity parents and children can do together. We come up with a lot of fun questions and we really play it up—we give an envelope to each kid just before they go home. "Now you can't peek. Open this up ten minutes before you go to bed, and spend that ten minutes writing about what's in the envelope." Even though the journal writing is private, most kids were excited to read what they wrote the night before. Parents can make up questions to help kids write a journal entry, and they can make a game of it for their children. Write down things like, "What would you do if you were three inches tall?" or "If your family turned into animals, what would life be like?" You can do questions geared to any grade level. Just get children to write and enjoy writing for themselves, something they can do privately for entertainment. It ties in with their self-esteem too, allowing them to write out their feelings on paper. This joy of writing will help psych them up for English classes!

Making the Grade

ON THE GO

We have a lot of computer programs and books and magazines around the house. We have *Boy's Life* because our son is in scouts. We do Girl Scouts. We do piano lessons. It's all stuff that takes a lot of time! Fortunately, I don't work outside the home, so I can do a lot of running around. I'm a Brownie leader and a Cub Scout leader. We encourage our children every moment we're together.

DRIVEBY LEARNING

We do our spelling words in the car each morning on the way to school. We sing, and I want them to have a happy experience on the way to school. Not stressed about anything. Just fun.

Core Area 3: Vocabulary Strategies
- Identify and use homonyms
- Use synonyms and antonyms
- Identify and use common idioms
- Define words with more than one meaning from the context
- Use similes, metaphors, and onomatopoeia
- Identify simple prefixes and suffixes and their meanings
- Define and use compound words in sentences

Core Area 4: Written Expression (composition, writing process)
- Compose a paragraph of at least four events in time order
- Write in various categories such as a mystery, a journal, and friendly letters
- Use prewriting, writing, and revision phases of the writing process

Core Area 5: Grammar and Usage
- Identify and write declarative, interrogative, and exclamatory sentences
- Identify and correct sentence fragments and run-ons
- Identify simple subject and predicate in sentences
- Substitute proper nouns for nouns
- Substitute pronouns for nouns
- Use correct subject/verb agreement
- Use correct present and past tenses of verbs
- Use adjectives to add color to a description
- Use adverbs correctly

Core Area 6: Mechanics (capitalization, punctuation, handwriting)
- Use good graphics: margins, spacing, indenting, overall neatness
- Shift from print to cursive handwriting
- Use correct punctuation for sentences
- Use comma to separate words in a series
- Put quotation marks around single direct quotation
- Use correct capitalization for sentences and proper nouns
- Use correct contractions
- Use correct possessives for singular and plural nouns
- Use basic abbreviations correctly

Core Area 7: Spelling
- Spell words with beginning and ending blends
- Spell words with silent final letters
- Spell words with various vowel combinations
- Spell compound words correctly
- Learn assigned spelling words

Core Area 8: Listening, Speaking, and Viewing Skills
- Listen to a news report for presentation for specific details and facts
- Listen to a passage being read and identify the type of writing
- Retell a story using accurate sequence of action
- Conduct an interview using original questions
- Give an oral review of a book, television program, or piece of software
- Read a poem with appropriate feeling
- Tell some of the differences and similarities between print and nonprint media
- Watch a video or TV program to obtain specific information
- Watch a video or TV program and identify the type of presentation it is

Core Area 9: Study Skills and Information Resources
- Alphabetize words and topics to use reference books
- Follow a sequence of written or oral directions
- Identify parts of a book: title, table of contents, index, and bibliography
- Use guide words, pronunciation key, multiple-meanings list in a dictionary
- Identify cities, states, and capitals on a map
- Interpret simple charts and graphs

Core Area 10: Appreciating Literature and Language
- Identify various types of literature: play, poem, fable, nonfiction, and biography
- Make connections between one's own life and various reading selections
- Recognize cultural perspectives and customs in literary selections
- Understand the roles of author and illustrator
- Distinguish fact from fiction

REMEMBER YOUR READING

My child absolutely loved her teacher, but I was trying to understand why my daughter wasn't coming home with her reading homework. Finally the teacher said, "Listen, your child has to learn this responsibility at some point in time." I felt, great, now I've got something constructive to grasp, and I told my daughter that she *had* to bring home her reading. I told her I don't care what it takes, but every night before you get in the car, you're going to have your reading folder. If it takes fifteen more minutes and I have to sit in the car and wait for you to go get it, so be it.

NOW SHE GETS IT

Before *SCORE!*, my daughter was frustrated with school. She had a tutor to help her in reading comprehension, but it just didn't help. She couldn't comprehend paragraphs that she was reading, and she didn't take the time to really understand the material. The way Score sets up the learning, it makes it fun and exciting for her— she finally gets it and she can understand things. I notice that in the car, she'll want to know what certain words mean, whereas it was a bother to her before because she was just too tired to try to figure it out. Now she wants to.

What's Taught in Grade Four?

As they begin the intermediate school years, children in grade four become reasonably confident and independent learners. They can read for both information and for enjoyment. Their reading includes a wide range of literature types such as folktales, historical fiction, science fiction, and short stories. Phonics, which had been important in the first three school years, typically disappears as a separate core area.

Students can write for a variety of purposes and are able to revise a composition, including incorporating responses from peers. Their spoken language skills can usually carry them successfully through discussions, oral reports, explanations, and play reading. They become comfortable using most research and study facilities in the library.

Students during these years receive lots of practice in creating various sentence types and building meaningful paragraphs that are well punctuated and free of spelling errors. On handwritten assignments, cursive will generally be expected, while using a word processor to complete a written assignment (perhaps at home if not also at school) has become acceptable in schools. Oral aspects of language—listening and speaking—continue to be practiced through focused discussions, oral reading, and formal speeches. Some teachers in grade four begin to introduce discussions about the impact of language on learning.

Core Area 1: Reading Comprehension Strategies
• Identify the author's purpose
• Make, confirm, and revise predictions
• Identify topic
• Distinguish fact from opinion
• Make generalizations from information presented
• Follow directions

Core Area 2: Decoding and Phonics

Core Area 3: Vocabulary Strategies
• Use figurative language
• Make analogies
• Extend knowledge of prefixes and suffixes

- Use context in learning and recognizing words
- Interpret common idioms

Core Area 4: Written Expression (composition, writing process)
- Write personal narratives, descriptions, informal letters, and poems
- Use all five steps of the writing process
- Compose a paragraph with a topic sentence and supporting details
- Vary sentence structure
- Write dialogue

Core Area 5: Grammar and Usage
- Combine sentences with comma and conjunction
- Use *good, bad,* and *well* correctly
- Use future verb tense
- Use personal pronouns
- Identify compound subjects
- Use comparative adjectives
- Use helping verbs
- Combine predicates
- Identify and use negative words correctly

Core Area 6: Mechanics (capitalization, punctuation, handwriting)
- Write legibly and use good graphics: margins, spacing, indenting, and overall neatness
- Capitalize correctly
- Use commas in series and compound sentences
- Use apostrophe to show possession
- Use abbreviations for titles and initials

Core Area 7: Spelling
- Master assigned spelling words
- Learn rules related to spelling 4th-grade vocabulary words
- Use apostrophe in contractions
- Recognize and spell homophones correctly

HOW AM I DOING?

SCORE! uses an amazing, adaptable computer tool that offers individualized curriculum for each child. But that's only half of what we have to offer—the other half is the Score coaches, quite frankly. We get to know each kid and what motivates them. We let them know on a very personal level that we know they can do it—we're totally behind them and we're there for them.

A parent is the person who needs to make learning—and all of life—exciting for children.

CRAFTY M.B.A.

I started designing jewelry because I never had the time to do anything creative. I did all these earrings and necklaces and loved all these colors, and my son enjoyed doing necklaces with me. My friends looked at me like I was out of my mind—you spent time together doing crafts, and you're a parent with an M.B.A.? They thought crafts were a big waste of time. But activities like this encourage creativity and perseverance, and my children enjoy them.

Core Area 8: Listening, Speaking, and Viewing Skills
• Listen to oral presentation and identify point of view
• Introduce someone as a speaker
• Make presentation to classmates
• Speak with appropriate loudness, clarity, speed, and phrasing
• Apply comprehension strategies in listening activities

Core Area 9: Study Skills and Information Resources
• Use pronunciation and parts of speech guidance in dictionaries
• Use line graphs and tables to get information
• Take simple notes in outline form
• Skim and scan for information
• Choose appropriate resource for type of research
• Find information in an encyclopedia

Core Area 10: Appreciating Literature and Language
• Tell whether writer intended to entertain, inform, or persuade
• Identify various writing genres including fables, poetry, and drama
• Describe characters from a story
• Identify use of dialect, point of view, and imagery

CHAPTER 7

What Language Arts Content Should I Review?

Children come to school already knowing a lot about language, and they've learned much of it without formal instruction, haven't they? The school's goal then is to give them skills to continue their growth and exploration—without dampening their enthusiasm. That's the art of fostering learning, of course.

Use the following skill areas as a review for yourself—and then go for it! Think of as many ways to talk, listen, watch, and write with your child as you can each day. After all, how do we learn to ride a bike? By actually riding, not by just reading the manual.

Core Area 1: Reading Comprehension

Like a child who is no longer worried about losing her balance on her bike and can now enjoy the journey, most 3rd and 4th graders who can read without difficulty enjoy the reading experience. There are many ways to think about and analyze reading materials. Here are several skills that your youngster will be using.

Draw Conclusions. After reading a passage, your child should be able to talk about or answer questions about what happened in the passage, using the details available to figure it out, or to draw conclusions. For example, if the story mentions that a boy is blowing out eight candles on a cake, your child could conclude that the boy is eight years old.

Make, Confirm, and Revise Predictions. One popular reading technique for this age group is to stop the story just

HOOKED ON BOOKS

We buy books. My daughter spends a lot of time reading books. We talk about books. We go over newspaper articles together. We go to the library. Now the librarian is hooked up to the Internet, and my daughter gets to look up certain kinds of books on the Net. She loves ice skating, so she tries to find every book on ice skating or certain subjects for school.

I'M NO GOOD

Countless kids have come to *SCORE!* hating a particular subject in school, and they've left their Score experience looking forward to doing more of that subject in school. My favorite stories are those of kids who say "I can't do math" or "I'm no good at reading" and you see the improvement—courtesy of Score, their own hard work, and their parents' encouragement—on each report card.

TIME TO READ

Parents have to spend quality time with their children. They always have to read to their children and make the reading time together very enjoyable. We all sit together as a family and we make the reading time fun and dramatic. We also make a big deal about new vocabulary words that we come across. We also provide workbooks for our children to use, and sometimes we share them with their teachers to show their progress.

short of the ending. Children then have to predict what will happen. Readers this age can learn to use word clues, descriptive statements, and draw on their own experiences in order to predict action and endings accurately.

Identify Cause and Effect. Almost every action we take causes another action to happen. In reading, kids can use the question *why* to identify a cause, and the question *what happened as a result* to identify the effect. As your child advances in reading, she can begin to identify multiple causes and effects, too.

Tell the Main Idea. A paragraph is a group of related sentences that tell about one thing called the topic. The main idea in a paragraph is a general statement about the topic. Kids should know that the main idea is sometimes contained in a single sentence and sometimes needs to be pulled together from information in several sentences.

Give a Summary. If your child is able to state the main idea of a passage and briefly tell a few important points about it—in other words, summarize—then you have a good indication that she has understood what she read.

Identify the Author's Purpose. This means thinking about why the author wrote a certain piece and what impact he was hoping to make on the reader. If your child is able to identify these motivations in her reading material, she may find some new motivations in her own writing.

Identify the Topic. Much of the reading and language arts instruction in elementary schools is theme based; that is, all reading, writing, speaking, and listening activities are related to and connected by a single category, topic, or idea—like friendship, pets, or your community. Readers at this level should be able to identify the topic of their reading material and point to some details that support the choice they made.

Distinguish Fact from Opinion. Here's a strategy that applies a lot to our daily living. Many of our actions are based on information we read or get from other people. Making decisions based on an opinion as if it were fact can put us in a little hot water. While reading, kids should know that a fact is a statement that can be proven to be true; it can be checked by looking in resource materials or speaking with certain people. A fact is something that's true no matter who writes or says it. An opinion, on the other hand, is a statement that tells what someone thinks or feels. It does vary by who writes or says it.

Make Generalizations. Making generalizations involves being able to make a broad statement about the information learned by reading. To make a generalization, your child must think about the information and ideas in a passage and decide how they are related in a general way. Looking for words like *many*, *most*, *all*, or *none* in a passage are clues to what the general point or idea might be.

Core Area 2: Phonics and Decoding

By the end of third grade, kids have received all the formal phonics instruction they are going to get from most schools. However, many teachers will periodically have review sessions for kids that may include the following skill areas:

Make Syllable Generalizations. One way to read words is to divide the word into parts. A syllable is a word or word part that has a vowel sound. When a word has two consonants between two vowels—like the word *buzzer*—the word is divided between the two consonants. When this happens, the vowel in the first syllable is more often short, like the *a* in *matter*, than long like the *a* in *made*.

Read Words with Various Vowel Sounds. Kids have mastered short and long vowel sounds by this time but might benefit from a review of some of the many unique sounds that vowels make when they are with other letters such as *or* in *storm*; *or* in *work*; *oi* in *boil*; and *oy* in *boy*.

Read Words with Beginning and Ending Consonant Blends. Another area of review for third graders has to do with reading words with letter combinations such as *bl, cl, tr, wh, str,* and *thr* at the beginning of words and *nt, ng,* and *gth* at the end of words.

WONDERFUL WORDS

Of TOUGH and BOUGH and COUGH
    and DOUGH.
Others may stumble, but not you,
On HICCOUGH, THOROUGH, LAUGH
    and THROUGH.
Well done! And now you wish, perhaps,
To learn of less familiar traps.

Beware of HEARD, a dreadful word
That looks like BEARD and sounds
    like BIRD.
And DEAD—it's said like BED, not BEAD.
For goodness sake, don't call it DEED!
Watch out for MEAT and GREAT
    and THREAT.
They rhyme with SUITE and STRAIGHT
    and DEBT.

A MOTH is not a MOTH in MOTHER,
Nor BOTH in BOTHER, BROTH in
    BROTHER,
And HERE is not a match for THERE,
Nor DEAR and FEAR for PEAR and BEAR.
And then there's DOSE and ROSE
    and LOSE—
Just look them up—and GOOSE
    and CHOOSE.
And CORK and WORK and CARD
    and WARD.
And FONT and FRONT and WORD
    and SWORD.
And DO and GO, then THWART and CART.
Come, come, I've hardly made a start.

A dreadful language? Man alive,
I'd mastered it when I was five!

—Anonymous

ate, eight
buy, bye, by
dear, deer
guessed, guest
hear, here
hour, our
knew, new
one, won
read, red
their, there, they're
to, two, too
weak, week

BUYING TIME

The biggest shortage of educational resources in any home is time. I'm happy with all of our material resources: TV, computers, books, etc. But the biggest shortage we have is time. If someone could find a way to package and sell it, I'd buy it—like I'd buy clean air if I could!

Core Area 3: Vocabulary

Kids of eight or nine begin to find the power of words (and their ability to wield it) somewhat fascinating. In their lives outside school, as they sit in front of the TV or computer game or with friends, kids constantly add to their vocabularies, effortlessly and often joyfully. Your child may be less enthusiastic about the more formal vocabulary development strategies that you are likely to see in assignments throughout the year, but they too can be fun.

Identify Homophones. These are the pairs of words that sound alike but are spelled differently and have different meanings. You might remember learning them as *homonyms.* From a vocabulary standpoint, kids need to be able to match the meaning of the word they want to use (or are reading) with the correct spelling. They can use context clues (that is, the meaning of the words based on the rest of the sentence) to help decide which *one* (or is it *won?*) of a *pair* (or is it *pare?*) of homophones to use. Some dictionaries give homophone listings, *too* (or *to?*)

Use Synonyms and Antonyms. As kids write more and more during their school years, and the process of writing—sentence construction, spelling, punctuation—gets more automatic, they begin to be able to turn their attention to the use of a wider range of vocabulary words. Using a variety of words by working with synonyms, words that mean the same or almost the same thing, and antonyms—words that mean the opposite thing—almost always make writing more interesting to read. In the middle elementary grades, kids learn that many dictionaries list synonyms and antonyms along with definitions.

Use Context to Define Multiple Meaning Words. When you save your kitten from falling out of a tree, does it mean you put it in the bank? Your quick answer, "No," means that you realize the word *save* has more than one meaning. Figuring out which definition of *save* to use has a lot to do with what the rest of the words in the sentence mean—called the *context.* When you read a sentence that tells about falling out of a tree, you probably think of danger, and so you know "to rescue" is the needed meaning for *save*, not "to keep from wasting or spending." Kids in grades three and four can be expected to use context clues frequently to help in their reading and writing.

Use Figurative Language. Sometimes writers use figurative language, that is, words or phrases that do not mean exactly what they say. The recognition and use of literary devices such as metaphors, similes, and onomatopoeia is another skill that represents a child's growing level of sophistication in reading and writing. Being able to understand these techniques can mean getting greater enjoyment from reading the work of others as well as from reading your own writing. Here's a quick review of techniques that 3rd and 4th graders might see and use.

• *Similes* compare two unlike things using the words *like* or *as*. Here are a couple examples:

My science teacher has a voice like a tuba.
Our baby rabbit is as light as a feather.

• *Metaphors* compare things without using the words *like* or *as*. Writers use metaphors to look at an object or idea in a new way. Try these out:

The trees on the hillside were a colorful, patchwork quilt on the sunny autumn day.
Soaked from head to toe, the soldier struggled just to put one lead weight in front of another as he marched.

• *Alliteration* and *onomatopoeia* are two techniques that use the sound of words for their effect. You probably remember alliteration, because it's fun. It involves the use of repeated initial letter sounds to achieve a certain rhythm or musical quality in a sentence or paragraph. Onomatopoeia describes words whose sounds when pronounced help express their meanings. (This technique is definitely easier and more fun to do than it is to say or spell!) Check out which is alliteration and which is onomatopoeia in these two examples:

A cricket chirped cheerily in the chimney of the church.

NO TO NEGATIVITY

Some parents lob a couple of negative comments at their children when they drop them off at our center, and it drives me crazy. You see it when kids come in—they're afraid to come in and make mistakes; they're afraid to do anything. These are the kids who are acting up or not concentrating. They're afraid to even try because they're going to get the negative feedback again. Score@Kaplan talks about "relentless positivity" or positive coaching, and you can see the difference it makes with kids. If a child is acting up, we turn it around by saying, "Okay, how can we make this better, how can we get through this, how can we learn this?" And if kids say, "I'm stupid," we say, "No, you're not." We constantly give them good feedback. We hope that parents will, too.

The drip, drop, drop, drop of the leaky faucet kept Joe awake all night.

Use Prefixes and Suffixes. Understanding the word parts that we call *prefixes* and *suffixes* and how they work enables readers to understand the meaning of words they may be seeing for the first time.

- *Prefixes* are word parts that are added to the beginning of a base word and that add meaning to the word. *Re-* is a prefix that means *again*; so *write* becomes *rewrite*, which means to write again. Oh yes, *pre-* is a prefix too.

- *Suffixes* are word parts that are added to the end of a base word and that add meaning to the word. The suffix *-ful* means *full of* or *having*. *Help* becomes *helpful* which, predictably, means to be full of help.

Use Compound Words. Sometimes two words are put together to make a single word, called a *compound word*. Your 3rd or 4th grader should be able to tell the meaning of a compound word by looking at the words that make up the compound.

After the rain stops and the sun comes out, there is a colorful bow in the sky called a rainbow.
Rain + bow = rainbow.

Dictionaries vary in their specifications about writing compound words as one word (*database*), two words (*data base*) or with a hyphen (*data-base*). You can check with your child's teacher about local preferences.

Recognize and Use Analogies. When you compare things and present it as in the example below, you are making an *analogy*. Being able to see the relationship between the compared items shows a deeper understanding of the word meanings.

Spider is to spinning a web as family is to building a house.

ROLE MODEL DAD

When I was growing up, I used to ask my dad, "Dad, what does this word mean?" and he always replied, "Look it up! Look it up!" That wasn't fun. I wish it would have been something we could have done together. "Well let's go look that up together, son." It would have been a good learning experience for both of us. Most children will love the attention.

Raising kids takes so much time, and sometimes society is overly harsh with parents. It's a rough job—you work, then you go home…it's a gnarly thing! Parenting takes a lot of time and patience. But developing this attitude of "let's do this together" with your child will make a big difference. "Let's explore this together," and this sets the example with children. My dad is now 67, and I see where he's still trying to learn, and what a great role model he is now for me!

Core Area 4: Written Expression

In these grades kids begin to see themselves as authors. They may still need support in the mechanics of writing, but they now see writing as a means of both expression *and* communication. They can use written language to achieve a goal: I want to write to a company and get their catalog.

Use the Steps of the Writing Process. This series of five steps helps writers (new and experienced alike!) to produce quality writing. They are now commonly taught throughout the country's classrooms and grades.

- Prewriting means preparing to write by thinking about what you want or need to do, deciding on a topic or finding resources for an assigned topic, and making notes.
- Writing a first draft means starting to get information down on paper without worry about spelling, grammar, or punctuation for the moment. The focus is on getting the ideas in logical order and providing supporting details.
- Revising means rereading what you wrote and letting others read it and make comments about the content of it. Then you decide how and where you want to make the changes in order for it to be a better composition.
- Proofreading means doing a careful review of your work specifically to check details of spelling, punctuation, grammar, and usage.
- Publishing means making a final copy of a composition and showing it to others.

Write in Various Categories. With the skills that most 3rd and 4th graders have, the doors now open to a wide and wonderful range of writing possibilities. You might see your child come home with any number of composition assignments. Or if she has to write something of her own choosing, you could go over this list of the kinds of writing with her:

DO IT AS A FAMILY

We've got a crazy lifestyle. I admit that my kids have done their homework in the car, en route to places. But my thing is, as long as we're together, it doesn't matter where we're at. I know there are certain areas and conditions where it would be better for them to do their homework, but right now, we have to do what we do, and we do it as a family. If I can't help one child with schoolwork, then my husband helps out while I'm with the other child. We do a lot of back and forth and we let the girls interact with each other. Sometimes we throw out a topic, like one child has to write a creative writing story. So we brainstorm together. Our younger child can brainstorm right along with our older one. Once we were all looking together for pictures in magazines of objects that began with the letter *v*. Homework is important, it has to get done, and we do it together.

Parents should keep the learning challenging, but not forceful.

WRITING TOOL

Explore *Write Source 2000: A Guide to Writing, Thinking, and Learning.* This is a clever school and home resource for "writers and students of all ages," written and compiled by Patrick Sebranek, Verne Meyer, and Dave Kemper (D.C. Heath & Co.), available at bookstores or by calling (800) 235-3565 (then press 5). *Write Source 2000* covers everything from managing time, writing letters, spelling, and types of sentences to facts about the world, maps, atlas material, and other resources to use for writing. And it has tons of writing ideas and story starters.

- Journal
- Written instructions
- Story or description
- Friendly letter or invitation
- Research report
- Poem
- News story
- Fairy tale or fable

Anything that motivates your child to write is a good place to start.

Write a Topic Sentence. The topic sentence in a paragraph contains the controlling idea of that paragraph; it tells the reader what the paragraph is about. The other sentences develop the idea expressed by the topic sentence. Here's an example of what a 3rd grader might write:

> Norway is a beautiful country. It has big blue mountains, with fresh streams running through them down to its deep fjords. Pretty farms dot the steep hillsides above the fjords.

In the above paragraph, *Norway is a beautiful country* is the topic sentence. The other details about mountains, streams, fjords, etcetera, are supporting pieces of information.

Write a Paragraph with Four Elements in Logical Order. A paragraph is a series of sentences developing one topic. The details of the topic can be presented in chronological order (time), spatial order (place), or order of importance. Starting with a numbered list can help your child organize her information logically.

Vary Sentence Structure. As she continues to write for a variety of purposes and in a variety of styles, your 3rd or 4th grader should become more and more aware of the impact her writing can and does have on her readers. One of the things she can do to increase readers' interest and enjoyment is to use a variety of sentences—statements, questions, exclamations, and commands—in her composition.

Core Area 5: Grammar and Usage

Here comes the nitty-gritty of everyone's written and spoken language. Kids have been introduced to dozens of rules by this time and now are expected to really begin using them in purposeful ways to communicate their ideas.

Sentence Types. In your everyday conversations, you probably communicate a lot without using complete sentences. You might say:

No more ice cream for me!
Over there.

Your meaning is clear to your listener when it is part of a conversation. In written English, however, you must generally use a complete sentence in order for it to make sense to the reader. A complete sentence is a group of words that expresses a complete thought. Look at these examples:

The crowd outside the building (not a sentence)
The crowd outside the building rushed into the rock concert. (sentence)
The crowd is outside the building. (sentence)

My favorite television program (not a sentence)
I got home just in time to watch my favorite television program. (sentence)
Do you know my favorite television program? (sentence)

Sentences fall into four categories, each with a different purpose; that is, you use them for different reasons:

• A *statement* (or declarative sentence) is a sentence that tells something. It ends with a period.

Ellen is a good athlete.

• A *question* (or interrogative sentence) is a sentence that asks something. It ends with a question mark.

What sport is she best at?

SPOONFUL OF SUGAR

There are many ways for parents to involve their kids in everyday learning experiences. It can be as obvious as playing an educational game or as real life as cooking with your child. Take a recipe for eight people, and you have four in the family, so how would you cut down the ingredients and measurements? It's all in how you present something. If it's fun, a "spelling game" can be no different from the spelling "work" in school or other curriculum, but kids will get excited over fun games.

- A *command* (or imperative sentence) is a sentence that tells someone to do something. It ends with a period or an exclamation point.

  Have a good time at the game!

- An *exclamation* (or exclamatory sentence) is a sentence that shows strong feeling. It ends with an exclamation point.

  I am so glad that the team made it to the play-offs!

Sentence Fragments and Run-Ons. If a group of words does not express a complete thought, it is called a *fragment*. Here are some examples:

  popcorn and drinks
  talking in his sleep

These groups of words can become sentences only when other words are added to make the thoughts complete:

  I sell popcorn and drinks at the theater.
  Randy is talking in his sleep again.

If a sentence contains more than a single thought and doesn't contain the right punctuation, it is called a *run-on sentence*. Look at the following run-on sentences:

  Where are Gadget and Gizmo those cats won't come when I call them.
  Last summer we went to California, this summer we plan to go to Maine.

Run-ons can be made into two separate sentences or into a compound sentence using a conjunction like *and* or *but*.

  Where are Gadget and Gizmo? Those cats won't come when I call them.
  Last summer we went to California, but this summer we plan to go to Maine.

Subject and Predicate. All complete sentences have two parts: a subject and a predicate. The *subject* is the part of the

ACTION!

There are parents who try to work with their kids at home, and they read to their kids and they make an effort to point out numbers, but we recommend that parents encourage kids to be more active—children can read to the parent, children can sound out the words themselves, and children can add the different prices at the store.

sentence that tells whom or what the sentence is about, and usually comes at the beginning of the sentence. Simple subjects have one word and complete subjects have more than one. Look at the italicized words in the sentences below. You can always find the subject of a sentence by asking whom or what is the sentence about.

Shelly walked to the playground.
Some young children were in the sandbox.

The *predicate* is the part of the sentence that tells what the subject does. Simple predicates have one word, and complete predicates have more than one.

Everyone who exercises *sweats.* (simple)
The twins *sleep in bunk beds.* (complete)

Parts of Speech. We use words to communicate with and we use different words to achieve different purposes. The way the word is used determines the part of speech that it is. Kids this age study nouns, verbs, adjectives, adverbs, pronouns, prepositions, and conjunctions.

• *Nouns* are probably the most commonly used part of speech. A noun names a person, place, or thing. *Girl, library,* and *boat* are nouns. When a specific person, place, or thing is named, it is called a *proper noun. Sarah, Hillside Public Library,* and *Queen Elizabeth II* are proper nouns. The main word in a subject is often a noun.

• *Pronouns* take the place of nouns and allow us to avoid repeating a noun over and over. In the case below, using the pronoun *it* rather than saying wallet twice makes the sentence read better, right?

Sam looked into his wallet and saw that it was empty.

• *Verbs* are most often the action words in sentences. They tell what the people or things in a sentence do. *Kicks, laughed,* and *think* are all examples of *action verbs.* Another kind of verb does not show action. These verbs involve our state of being, that is, the use of the verb *to be.* This

LEARN A NEW LINGO

Parents should start kids young with learning a foreign language. Try to find programs in your community that don't just work out of textbooks, conjugating verbs and turning language into something bone dry. At *SCORE!*, we set up something like an acting class—and Spanish comes alive with props, games, repetition, and singing. After only a week of this exposure, it's amazing the vocabulary words kids can pick up and the excitement they have for a new language.

HOME TUTORING

Sometimes my children come home from school and complain that they didn't learn anything that day. So I try to motivate them and help them by acting as a tutor. I don't know if I'm doing the right thing by doing that, but it does help my child work up to her level, to her potential.

PUSH IT

Parents who are hardcore about their children's success may find that their children are going to have problems getting to the top academically. But the parents who allow their children to make mistakes will find their children are going to make that extra jump in school or in life. Those kids who have to be perfect all the time are going to have a sense of stasis about them, but the ones who are really excelling are the ones who are pushing it. They make mistakes and they move on. The kids who are the movers and achievers are the ones who make mistakes and learn something and push it a little bit. Succeeding in school and life is not about "getting it perfect."

includes the verbs *am, is, are, was,* and *were.*

Dianne was tired last night.
I am sleepy now.
Who is still tired?

• *Adjectives* are the words that describe nouns. They can make language a little more interesting to read or hear and give us more detail about the subject. Which of the following sentences do you like better? The italicized words in the second sentence are all adjectives.

The firefighters sprayed water on the flames.
The *exhausted* firefighters sprayed *cool* water on the *hot, raging* flames.

• The words *a, an,* and *the* are special kinds of adjectives called *articles.* You use *a* before nouns that begin with consonant sounds and *an* before nouns that begin with vowel sounds.

• *Adverbs* are words that describe verbs and adjectives. They tell you something about how the action happened and most often end in *-ly.*

The wind blew fiercely through the trees.
Billy's clothes barely fit him anymore.
The children worked well.

They also adjust the meaning of adjectives.

My new puppy is very frisky.
A barely conscious man looked up from his bed.

Subject–Verb Agreement. You may have heard someone say something like, "He don't know the answer." Do you know why it sounds funny to you? It has to do with using forms of words that are mismatched. The word that matches *he* is *doesn't,* right? The word *don't* matches *you, they,* and *we,* but not *he* or *she* or *it.* They agree in number, like *doorbell rings, cat purrs,* or *lightning strikes.* When a word refers to more than one, it is plural in number and requires a different verb ending to match it, like *doorbells ring, cats purr,* or *lots of lightning bolts strike*.

> My brother knows the answer. (singular)
> My brothers know the answer. (plural)
> One girl rides the bus. (singular)
> Many girls ride the bus to school. (plural)

Helping Verbs and Verb Tenses. Verbs tell not only what action is happening but when the action happens.

> Alison runs to catch up with her brother. (present tense)
> The horses run to the other side of the pasture. (present tense)
> Mrs. Wood is the job supervisor. (present tense)
> Heather steered the car into the parking space. (past tense)
> Tom unplugged the computer before opening the lid. (past tense)
> My grandfather was a good cook. (past tense)

Words such as *have* and *has*—called *helping verbs*—help other verbs to show action in the past.

> I have sung in a choir before.
> Jaime has read many of the books on the best sellers list.

Using Negative Words. Here's a trouble spot for many writers: using the correct verb form in sentences with *no, nothing*, and *none*. When they are used, the verb of the sentence should usually not be negative.

> It doesn't make no difference to me. (incorrect)
> It makes no difference to me. (correct)
> The rescue squad haven't found nothing after two days of searching. (incorrect)
> The rescue squad has found nothing. (correct)
> We looked for a seat in the crowded theater, but there wasn't none. (incorrect)
> We looked for a seat, but there was none. (correct)

These errors are called *double negatives*—you can see why— and are to be avoided in writing. Some people used to think

BORN FREE

It's a good goal to build autonomy and independence in your child as a learner. You can't start too young. Little babies sometimes reach out for a cup, and sometimes parents will automatically put the cup in their hands. But some parents will say, "What's that? It's a cup . . . c-c-c-cup!" and then they'll give it to them after inserting that little bit of learning. With older children and math, for example, parents don't always have to know the answer. We can help our children look it up or seek out resources to help us get to the answer. With independence in learning as our goal for children, we don't have to know all the answers and feed them to our children. Instead, we're there to support and guide our children through the learning process. Give children the space to develop independence and flourish, sometimes backing off and allowing them to learn, make mistakes, discover, and grow.

that the more negatives you put in a sentence, the more emphasis you gave it: Thomas does not never do no homework. Think about that for a second. Can you figure out whether or not Thomas does homework?

Core Area 6: Mechanics

In this area, kids are expected to continue to apply rules they have learned to their own writing. They need to be making thoughtful choices about words, sentences, and punctuation in order to achieve a desired impact or result.

Overall Presentation. This means using good graphics, including page setup, neatness, and legible handwriting. With the advent of computers and word processing, some of these issues may seem less relevant to you or your child, but try to find out what your child's teacher's expectations are for how papers look when turned in. Much of 3rd and 4th grade work is still done by hand, and your child needs to be aware of the following:

- Margins should be present on all four sides of the written work.
- The child's name should have prominent position.
- The work's title should be clearly presented and capitalized.
- New paragraphs must be consistently indented.
- Spelling errors should be at a minimum.
- Handwriting should be legible print or, starting usually in grade four, cursive.

Capitalization. By 3rd grade, kids are aware of several key places to use capital letters when writing:

- The first letter of the first word in every sentence

  Everyone at the school assembly enjoyed Mr. Blair's jokes.

- Proper nouns like people's names, book titles, product names

  Aunt Helen drove her Toyota across the George Washington Bridge into New Jersey with her dog, Pepper, in the backseat.

GET PSYCHED!

Many parents feel that learning should be a reward in and of itself. You must learn in order to get knowledge. Many students, by virtue of having lived for several years, get great presents or other materialistic things for studying from their parents. Which reward method is best to help motivate students to learn? If a kid is really struggling, it's good to reward solid effort with rewards that aren't goals in and of themselves. Parents have to be careful in this materialistic society so that the rewards don't detract from kids getting psyched about learning.

Tales of a Fourth-Grade Nothing by Judy Blume is Sally's favorite book.

- Names of months, days, and holidays

Easter is always on a Sunday, but it can be in either March or April.

Punctuation. At this point, kids are also aware that certain punctuation marks are needed at the end of every sentence. The punctuation varies by type of sentence:

- Periods go at the end of every statement and some commands.
- Question marks go at the end of every question.
- Exclamation points go at the end of exclamations and sometimes commands.
- Commas are punctuation marks that help give sentences clearer meaning. It helps the reader know where to pause. One of the more common uses for a comma is in a series of words. Consider the following sentence.

Mary Ann and Ginger are sisters.

How many girls are we talking about there? Just two? Watch what a difference a comma can make.

Mary, Ann, and Ginger are sisters.

Now we know there are three girls. The comma made an important impact on the meaning of that sentence.

A lot of kids actually use too many commas, as if they automatically put one in every time they pause their pencil. If your child is guilty of this comma craze, you might take a moment to go over some of the guidelines with her.

- Quotation marks show the reader the exact words that someone said. Kids this age should know when they see quotation marks in writing that someone is talking. They may be alerted to the fact that quotation marks are often preceded by the words *said, replied, asked,* and *added.*

REWARDS

Good behavior and good results, like an A in school, don't have to be rewarded with material things like ice cream cones. Positive talk from a parent is often a strong reinforcer, and children are hungry for the recognition. The memories that last are usually tied in to the nonmaterial rewards. "I remember when I tried really hard to learn something, and I did it, and my mom told me she was really proud of me!"

CAST YOUR NETS

Parents can use other parents as models to help them bring effective learning into the home. Take examples from others. Use what you have on hand, and create a network of resources you can use. You might find some amazing tips that will help you.

Most students don't learn how to use notecards in school for making book reports and research, and it's something that really kills them in school later on. Even though they're doing outlines in school, something's still not clicking mentally for them. Learning about notecards is something fun that parents and kids can do together, and it beats having to wait until the night before a report is due and having parents put the whole report together.

Have your child plan ahead and help budget time for making reports. Teach her to use notecards to jot down notes and quotes as she does her reading. Help her label notecards and show her how to lay them out on the floor and play around with them to organize the outline. Some students really get the hang of this skill in high school, but it's much better to start earlier!

Bill said, "I always take my water bottle when I ride."

Your youngster can now also begin to use quotation marks in her own writing when she is using someone's actual speech. She may also begin to notice that capital letters and commas are important when using quotations in writing.

Apostrophes. When two words are put together and shortened into one word, it is called a *contraction*. An apostrophe is used in place of the letters taken out. Many contractions come from combining a verb and the word *not*.

- *does not* becomes *doesn't*
- *cannot* becomes *can't*
- *are not* becomes *aren't*
- *do not* becomes *don't*
- *is not* becomes *isn't*
- *will not* becomes *won't* (Isn't it just like the English language to throw a curve like that!)

Apostrophes are also used to show possession. Take a singular noun, for example, add an apostrophe and an *s*, and you have made a *possessive noun*.

The store's window display was beautiful.
Nancy's cat has six toes on one paw.

If you start with a plural noun, one that ends in *s* already, and add an apostrophe, you have a *plural possessive*.

All the boys' parents were involved in the meeting.
Please be sure to clean out all the cats' dishes on Saturday.

Using Common Abbreviations. Most of the time we can spell out words when writing, but sometimes there are shortened ways to spell words—*abbreviations*. The ones that your 3rd or 4th grader will come across most often are

- Days of the week and months of the year (Mon., Jan.)
- Names and titles (Mr., Capt., Ms.)

She will be using them in writing charts and schedules for herself and the class and for writing letters.

Core Area 7: Spelling

The English Language certainly poses a challenge in terms of learning rules for correct spelling. And, of course, you probably remember that there seem to be many exceptions to each rule as there are words that fit the rule. Helping your child to stick with it and feel confident in using the available resources is a valuable contribution.

Weekly Word Lists. Weekly spelling tests are pretty routine in grades three and four. The lists may come from a traditional spelling book or from a variety of other places (the science book, a play they are doing, literature). The headings below cover specific categories of study you're likely to see as part of your child's homework assignments.

Homophones. These pairs (or sometimes triplets) of words that sound the same but are spelled differently and have different meanings may have been called homonyms when you were in school. Labels aside, at some point during your kid's education you will probably find yourself contributing to the longest list of homophones ever written. Homophones can be tricky for kids when they write, so it's good to help your young writer remember *which/witch one/won* to *use/yews*!

Apostrophes. Though mentioned under Mechanics (above), apostrophes need attention here as important elements of spelling. They appear in contractions such as *they're* (*they are*) and possessives like *baby's*. Teachers will take points off or count the spelling as incorrect when apostrophes are missing where they are needed (or present when they should not be). Many kids see them as extraneous marks rather than parts of a correctly spelled word. This is a good point to reinforce with your child.

Compound Words. As their vocabularies expand, kids can begin to put their word knowledge to use to improve their written expression as well. Using more and more compound words—words that have the meanings of the shorter words that form them—is something that you can encourage your child to do.

POCKET PAL

Ask at your bookstore for one of those great little, pocket-sized speller's books. American Heritage's is called *Word Book II*. The whole family will be glad you brought one of these home.

A READING ARMY

We must do more to help all our children read. Forty percent of our 8-year-olds cannot read on their own. That's why we have just launched the America Reads initiative—to build a citizen army of 1 million volunteer tutors to make sure every child can read independently by the end of the 3rd grade. We will use thousands of AmeriCorps volunteers to mobilize this citizen army. We want at least 100,000 college students to help. And tonight, I am pleased that 60 college presidents have answered my call, pledging that thousands of their work study students will serve for one year as reading tutors.
—from the *1997 State of the Union Address*, President Clinton

DIGGING DEEPER

The things that your child learns in school could send him to the library or to the Internet every day after school—he might be able to learn something new in school each day and have fun looking into it more. That's a great activity for you and your child to do together.

More Advanced Rules. At this age, kids often feel like they know it all when it comes to spelling. But in this age when new words enter the language almost every day, spelling correctly is not a static target. Is anything really? Guess it felt like it was back when we were in school.... Anyway, it is likely that your child will be studying some words in the following categories:

- Beginning and ending consonant clusters and blends: *br, cr, dr, nt, ng*
- Silent consonants: *knot, wrap, match*
- Vowel + *r* combinations: *dark, hair, winter, first, our, ear*

Core Area 8: Listening, Speaking, Viewing

In the same way that specific strategies have been outlined for teaching and learning reading and writing skills, there is a specific approach to the other key elements of communication. Listening, speaking, and viewing skills, though not based on the written word, can be practiced and acquired through careful planning and evaluation.

Apply Comprehension Strategies to Listening. This ability can be a challenging one for folks of any age since it generally means sitting still and concentrating on what's being said. Auditory learners (kids who understand and remember best what they hear) may seem to have the advantage here, but if that's not your child, take heart. He (like most of us) can train himself to learn through listening purposefully: for the topic, the main idea, and important details. If your child learns to look at the speaker and ask questions, he will increase his listening comprehension.

Interview and Introduce Someone. This is a brief but valuable exercise that focuses on listening and speaking skills. As an interviewer, your child needs to first formulate questions that will uncover interesting information about the interviewee. Then he needs to sort through it all and retain the details needed to make a concise introduction.

Make a Variety of Oral Presentations. In much the same way that readers adjust their rate, approach, and effort to meet the style of the reading material, kids need to learn to make adjustments in their speech rate, intonation, even body language when making oral presentations.

Evaluating the type of material to be presented and planning the correct approach are skills that 3rd and 4th graders work on. Oral reports can be a little less formal than written ones, but they need to have the same type of organization and logical conclusion.

Compare and Contrast Print and Nonprint Media. Remember the saying, "A picture is worth a thousand words"? There are many ways of communicating besides the printed or spoken word—and we have so many to choose from now, including photos, drawings, video, animations, dance, pantomime, web sites, computer software, and music. Each has its own kind of communicative impact. Sometimes you plan the impact, but you can't or don't anticipate the effect. Schools help children begin to understand how different modes of communication work. They will explore strength areas, advantages, and disadvantages of the various media types, and your child can begin learning to make educated choices about how to use them.

Apply Comprehension Strategies to Viewing Activities. It's hard to pick up a newspaper or magazine without seeing a reference to couch potatoes or to an act of copycat violence from a TV show or movie. We all know what an impact TV has on our lives, and many of us are concerned about it. More and more schools are beginning to include skill training for kids to evaluate what they see on TV. A top priority is getting them to realize that they need to watch different shows for different purposes—how you watch and listen to the news is different from how you watch cartoons (or it should be, anyway!). It is likely that your child is seeing much more information than she is reading, so being able to make sense of it and evaluate it are important skills.

Core Area 9: Study Skills

Learning how to organize your own study style in terms of time, space, and approach can be a lifelong endeavor. Good

ACT UP

Confidence in Communication was a hugely successful *SCORE!* class for elementary school students. The class was packed. So many parents wanted it because they felt their children were really shy and didn't stand up for themselves in school. They didn't raise their hand enough in class, so they felt this would be a big motivator for them. We did great self-esteem activities, voice stuff, acting, and role playing.

Acting classes are great for parents to enroll their children in, especially if they're worried about their children sticking up for themselves in the classroom. Acting ties in well with confidence and good communication skills. There are a lot of good books on acting, but it's better to sign up for a live workshop experience.

study styles constantly change, and they constantly reward. It is never too soon to help a kid get focused for organized study. What catches many kids by surprise is that studying skills have to be learned along with all the content stuff.

In fact, unless your kid is superbright (or superlucky), she is going to have to become familiar, even comfortable with, many of the following skills areas if she wants to do well in school. Connecting them with everyday experiences, not just homework, helps with the motivational factors.

Using a Dictionary. Your child will need to be able to alphabetize words and have a general sense about how words being studied are spelled in order to use a dictionary comfortably. Once in there, she can be expected to use:

- Guide words to quickly locate a needed word on a page
- Pronunciation key to help with saying the word
- Multiple meaning listing to see if it is the word she wants to use after all
- Parts of speech guide to make sure she is using the word correctly in a sentence

Follow Sequence of Directions. Being able to read (or listen) and perform a task with accuracy is at the core of school success. Written and oral directions are given to children dozens of times during the course of a school day. Two, three, or sometimes even more steps or directives are presented to kids at this level and they are expected to follow through independently. It is in this arena that teachers and parents can find out rather quickly about a child's auditory memory (remembering what they hear) and reading comprehension (understanding what they read). Slow readers may seem uncooperative or inept for not completing things, when in fact they just couldn't make sense of what was on the written page. Other students may not remember any more than one direction given out loud even though they are strong readers.

Use Parts of a Book. Your child can make maximum use of his study time if he is able to get to the needed

TUBE TIME

Television itself is not a "bad device," but I'm not a big fan of most television for children. Parents can help children by monitoring what they watch. There's a lot of great programming, like from PBS or National Geographic—educational television can be a very productive use of time. It's fun and sneaky because children like TV in and of itself, so when they're watching something educational, it's not as if they're purposely being sat down to "learn."

information quickly. At this age, he can be expected to use a book title, table of contents, and an index to help decide if a particular book will be helpful to him or not.

Choose Appropriate Resources. Today's students have many more resources to choose from for doing research than you did. In fact, a prominent feature of the current Information Age is access to thousands of documents and libraries of information via the Internet. Libraries remain a treasure chest of research materials, and many also have access to online information.

Knowing where to search for information is a very valuable skill, never more so than today. Encyclopedias, atlases, online databases, nonfiction books, and other publications all may be resources your 3rd and 4th grader uses for different purposes during the school year.

Read Graphs and Maps. These resources present information to us in a visual way, and there are special skills related to using them.

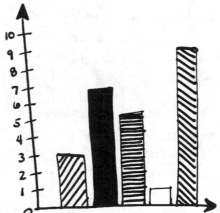

- *Graphs* are drawings that compare different amounts of things. *Bar graphs* use vertical or horizontal bars to stand for numbers and often appear in expository writings such as in magazines.

- *Maps* are drawings that depict the location of places. A *globe* is a special kind of map—it's round, not flat—and shows the whole earth. *Symbols* are used to represent different features of the area shown—roads are usually depicted by lines and cities are shown by names next to dots. The *map legend* tells you what the symbols mean. The *compass rose* on a map indicates each of the four directions—north (N), south (S), east (E), and west (W).

STUDY BUDDIES

In *SCORE!*'s Study Skills class, we teach children general study skills, note taking, organization, report writing, and projects. We teach them right away how to go home and set up their study areas. They need to have a dictionary and thesaurus on the desk or table and a writing resource book to help them in school projects.

TAKE A HIKE

Parents have to allow for some fun time with their children, despite the demands of household chores and homework. Fun time and learning have to happen together. Make learning exciting. Instead of saying "Between 5:00 and 5:30, we're going to study spelling," take a walk with your child and go over spelling words along the way.

Skim and Scan for Information. Another skill related to efficient study is being able to read through material quickly to see if it is the resource you need or to find the piece of information you are looking for. This skill has a little to do with overall reading ability; it can be learned and becomes increasingly useful as your child moves through school (and beyond).

Take Simple Notes. Kids at this level should be able to listen to a story or lecture, or read some material and take simple notes about the important parts of what they heard or read. They need to write just enough words to help them remember so that they can use the information accurately in a report. It gets tricky, of course, to tell a 3rd or 4th grader that it is okay to use only phrases and not to think so much about spelling or punctuation for note taking, when on that very day she may have been practicing writing complete thoughts, with punctuation, for sentences. As in so many other situations in life, children learn that there are different processes for different purposes.

Core Area 10: Appreciating Literature

Reading—what can we say that is worthy of it? For children, it should be a pleasure as well as a tool. What can match it? It knows no seasonal limit; it doesn't require much money (none, in fact, if you use your library); it's portable; it requires no one but yourself, though it can be enjoyed with others; it puts pictures in your head; it gives you fresh ideas and new ways to think about old ones; it offers information; and on and on. The more your child reads, the better.

Read and Identify Different Types of Literature. During the 3rd and 4th grade, your youngster should be reading from a wide range of genres (types) including fables, letters, nonfiction, poetry, short stories, journals, periodicals, and content area books. The importance of reading as a model for writing is a connection that 3rd and 4th graders begin to make for themselves.

Make Connections with One's Own Life. Personalizing reading becomes a very real experience for kids during these school years. They learn that reading materials can offer them information, entertainment, motivation, and even emotional support. They come to realize that although reading can be an enjoyable solitary venture, there is pleasure to be gained from sharing what they read in discussions with others. Drawing on personal experience to relate to something in a story creates a strong connection that can be a powerful motivater to kids, not just to keep reading, but to probe its meaning.

Identify the Use of Literary Techniques. Students continue to encounter new examples on the lengthy list of different writing styles and literary techniques. Being able to understand and interpret both the actual words and the meaning behind them are skills that come from directed practice in a classroom setting and from the personal experience of reading. Here are two in particular that are introduced in third and fourth grades:

- *Dialect* is the particular way in which the people living in an area speak. It may contain slang and informal words and differ from the standard written language your child is learning. But it can be a powerful tool for making a written piece sound authentic.

- *Imagery* is the use of words that create mental pictures (images) that help the reader understand the subject the writer is describing. They can be words that help your child see, feel, hear, smell, and even taste what she reads.

Describe Characters. Characters are an important part of any story. What characters are like and what they do affects the plot (the events that happen in a story). Having your child describe a character gives her great practice in the use of adjectives (nearsighted, stingy, foolish, optimistic), and describing how characters behave lends itself to practice with adverbs (bravely, stubbornly). Finding a character that grabs our interest (seems like us, or intrigues, amuses, or

RELATE TO READING

When my granddaughter was very young, we used to read in bed. I would explain every detail about the story. She would ask many questions. The books are our friends. The characters are our cousins.

Summer reading programs in libraries are great incentives for kids.

PROUD HERITAGE

My husband and I are from India. We have a festival of lights called Deepawali, and it means "a row of lights." It celebrates an actual historic event 5,000 years ago. We set up a tradition where we invite over fifty people to our house and celebrate in a real authentic way. That's something our children look forward to. There are also community organizations that we try to attend as often as possible to give our children a sense of heritage. My parents visit me almost once in two years, and we visit India too.

worries us) keeps us reading—and the same will be true for your child.

Recognize Cultural Perspectives and Customs. Most reading and language arts programs in elementary schools provide literature selections by authors from all over the world and from different time periods; it is an important way for kids to learn about cultural backgrounds, experiences, emotions, and ideas different from their own.

Since it is a rare occasion for kids to experience other cultures firsthand, literature in almost every form—essays, short stories, biographies, plays, poems—can become the vehicle for understanding and enjoyment.

Distinguish Fact from Fiction. Strategic readers evaluate fact and nonfact by deciding whether information can be proven true or false. A fact is something that cannot be successfully disputed. For example, George Washington was the first president of the United States. Look it up and there he'll be—number one on the list. Nonfacts about George Washington—information that cannot be proven and may have been made up—include the story about his chopping down the cherry tree and saying, "I cannot tell a lie."

The ability to distinguish fact from nonfact is an important one for kids to develop since they are part of the Information Age in which accessing primary historical documents is only a mouse click away from many other, less significant documents (like essays by a local cybernaut). Children learn that just because something can be read (or heard) does not make it true, and does not make it a fact. Then there are all those made-for-TV movies based (however loosely) on real-life events. Kids benefit from discussions about what they are reading (or seeing and hearing). By exposing your child to a wide range of reading and viewing materials and, most importantly, talking about them, you and your child's teachers are helping him develop the critical analysis skills he needs.

CHAPTER 8

What's My Child Studying in Math?

The elementary math curriculum is designed around the essential math concepts and skills that are the foundation of all math. In grades three and four, students learn from many of the same topic areas that they studied in earlier grades. Math is a fascinating sequence of content building blocks.

NEW ATTITUDE

We had a few parents at our center who would go ballistic when their children made mistakes. "Gosh, Jimmy, it's 5 times 5 . . . you've got to know what's 5 times 5!" Parents have to give their children the space to learn. If a child doesn't know 5 times 5, it's not an apocalyptic event. This is a chance for children to learn and for parents to lovingly encourage and reinforce.

Take a deep breath if your child doesn't know the answer to a question, maybe something she's getting wrong in her homework. Then look at what your child doesn't know and use it as a goal to move towards.

Eight Core Math Areas. The following eight core subject areas form the basis of most schools' elementary math curriculum:

1. Numeration (numbers and counting)
2. Computation (addition, subtraction, multiplication, and division)
3. Money and Time (units of money, money calculations, clocks, and calendars)
4. Geometry and Measurement (two- and three-dimensional shapes, area, volume, and units of measure)
5. Fractions and Decimals
6. Graphing (bar graphs, pie charts)
7. Statistics and Probability
8. Problem Solving (solving word problems, estimation, spatial reasoning, recognizing patterns, experimenting and inventing new strategies, and other analytical skills)

Innovations in Math Content. In addition to the standard topics such as adding, subtracting, multiplying, and dividing, some districts emphasize problem-solving and critical thinking skills. Students develop number sense and mathematical thinking by using problem-solving techniques

TAKING THE TIME

When I was growing up, I could do my homework by myself. Maybe it's just the way modern technology has gone crazy, but our oldest daughter (going into third grade) needs some help with her homework, just to make sure she's on the right track. You have to be willing to sit down at the table with them and spend some time. You can pay the bills before they go to bed, but they need to have somebody making sure that they get the idea that homework needs to be done in a timely fashion and you can do other things later. Help give kids the idea that you are interested about what they're studying, and help give kids something to share from their homework experience.

such as estimation, observing patterns, working in groups, and communicating their solutions. They may solve extended word problems that make use of many problem-solving techniques, and some may collect data about their world to put their skills to use and to introduce the concepts of probability and statistics. For example, students may collect data about their foot sizes by measuring their feet and graphing the data.

Other innovations in the math curriculum are the use of manipulatives and use of student portfolios. Since children learn in different ways, math educators have developed materials and alternative strategies to help students learn. Many third graders use blocks, counters, cubes, rods, string buttons, and other objects to count, calculate, and estimate. Students may use board games and card games to learn new concepts and to practice skills. In addition, some teachers urge students to write and reflect on what they have learned and the strategies they used to solve problems. Teachers collect the work of each child in a folder or portfolio.

What's Taught in Grade Three?

The teaching of math in grades three and four is all about multiplication, division, fractions, and decimals. Of course, a well-rounded curriculum includes topics from the eight core areas, but the primary emphasis is on these four topics.

In grade three, your child will learn the basic multiplication facts, that is, the times table up to nine times nine. These fundamental facts are essential to success in multiplying and dividing as well as in all subsequent math. Much of the teaching of multiplication and division relies on these basic facts and place value. Your child will likely multiply two- and three-digit numbers by one-digit numbers in third grade. Although division is introduced in third grade, students typically do not do complicated divisions until fourth grade.

Another key topic in third grade is fractions. Your third grader will learn the meaning of fractions and see fractions as parts of a whole. In addition, your child will learn about equivalent fractions. Students in grade three usually compare fractions and learn the relationship between fractions and decimals.

In grade three, students develop and strengthen their skills in other core areas. They build and extend their knowledge of numbers, addition and subtraction, money, geometry, and fractions. Your third grader will take advantage of her mastery of earlier mathematical concepts to learn new skills. For example, your child will use her understanding of place value to learn numbers greater than 1,000. In addition, she'll learn new topics by discovering the connections that relate that topic to what she already knows. For example, she may learn that multiplication is just repeated addition (e.g., 3 × 3 is the same as 3 + 3 + 3).

Many schools also emphasize problem solving, estimation, and critical thinking skills in this grade. Many third graders do a great deal of estimating to strengthen their number sense and to learn how to scrutinize answers they compute either by hand or with a calculator. For example, students may learn to round to the nearest ten and hundred and estimate the answers to addition and subtraction problems.

The following outline represents the content of the typical third grade math curriculum. Since each district designs its program of study to meet the needs of the local community, this summary may not describe your child's math curriculum precisely. These topics are organized according to the core areas of this elementary math curriculum. For descriptions of the topics and skills, refer to the section titled "3rd and 4th Grade Math Content."

Core Area 1: Numeration
- Read and write four-digit numbers (thousands)
- Read and write five-digit numbers and six-digit numbers (tens and hundreds of thousands)
- Write numbers in standard and expanded form
- Compare and order thousands
- Count thousands by twos, fives, and tens
- Round to the nearest ten or hundred

Core Area 2: Computation
- Add thousands
- Subtract using regrouping more than once
- Learn multiplication facts up to 9
- Multiply by a one-digit number

BIG-TIME LEARNING

SCORE! emphasizes learning as an "event." For instance, "We learned the times tables today," and boom—we have a learning event! We hear many children say, "This is division, and I can't do division," and they categorize what they're not comfortable with. We help teach kids that they can "do division," and it's a revelation to them. It becomes this event for kids. "Oh wow, I just did division. I just did the 100-yard dash in under 10 seconds!"

Learning moments between parents and children should become learning events. "We're going to work on 5 times 5," and make it an event. Then when your child masters 5 times 5, it's like it's up on a billboard for kids: "This is what I can do!" When a kid can say, "I can tell time," that should become an event too. And so on and so on.

- Multiply by multiples of 10 and 100
- Learn that division is the opposite of multiplication
- Divide by a one-digit number
- Divide by multiples of 10 and 100

Core Area 3: Money and Time
- Add and subtract money
- Tell time to the minute

Core Area 4: Geometry and Measurement
- Learn about perimeter, area, and volume
- Study the transformations of a figure
- Learn angles and rights angles

Core Area 5: Fractions and Decimals
- Learn the meaning of fractions
- Recognize equivalent fractions
- Compare fractions
- Use fractions in word problems
- Learn about decimals and their relationship to fractions
- Learn decimal place value to tenths and hundredths

Core Area 6: Graphing
- Read line graphs and bar graphs

Core Area 7: Statistics and Probability
- Calculate averages

Core Area 8: Problem Solving
- Estimate addition and subtraction
- Solve word problems involving fractions, money, and decimals
- Calculate area and volume using tiles and cubes

What's Taught in Grade Four?

Grade four math is all about decimals and division. Grade four is the year that your child will learn all about decimals. Students typically read and write decimals, and they add and subtract decimals up to hundredths. The other primary skill taught in this grade is division. Students in grade four typically learn how to multiply using two- and three-digit

NOT ALL BAD

My son is quite challenged in math. He's not bad in math, actually—he got an A! He just lacks confidence. Hands-on experience is probably better than other forms of learning for him. When he was young, we counted out M&Ms, and we played with sticks that were different measurements.

MATERIAL BOY

My child is an only child and certainly wants for nothing. I worry about rewards for his doing good work and the overemphasis we sometimes put on material things.

numbers and then use those skills in learning to divide using two-digit divisors.

In fourth grade, students also develop and strengthen their skills in other core areas. They build and extend their knowledge of numbers, multiplication, division, geometry, and fractions. Fourth graders take advantage of their mastery of earlier mathematical concepts to learn new skills. For example, fourth graders use their understanding of place value in learning about decimals. In addition, students learn new topics by discovering the connections that relate that topic to what they already know. For example, they may learn that to multiply two-digit numbers they can use the same techniques they used to multiply by one-digit numbers.

Many schools also emphasize problem solving, estimation, and critical thinking skills in grades three and four. Many fourth graders do a great deal of estimating to strengthen their number sense and critical thinking skills. For example, students may learn to round large numbers and estimate the quotients in several ways.

The following outline represents the content of the typical fourth grade math curriculum. Since each district designs its program of study to meet the needs of the local community, this summary may not describe your child's math curriculum precisely. The topics are organized here according to these eight core areas of the elementary math curriculum. For descriptions of the topics and skills, refer to the next chapter.

Core Area 1: Numeration
• Read and write up to nine-digit numbers (hundred million)
• Compare and order numbers up to hundreds of thousands
• Count by hundreds
• Round to the nearest thousand

LIFETIME OF LEARNING

A *SCORE!* Coach is a pretty special person. We've all done pretty amazing things with our lives. But to be expected to know everything, like the material our children learn in our centers—particularly some of the math!—is asking way too much of anybody. But we know the importance of saying to children whenever we're stumped, "Hey, let's try to figure this one out together."

I'm happy to tell that to parents too. Parents should tell their kids, "I don't know everything. That's what learning is all about. We learn every day." Parents should remind kids that learning happens every day, and it continues to happen once we leave school. You probably learn even more outside of school because you've got your basics down. Build your child's confidence NOW to prepare her for a lifetime of learning.

My son is the kind who won't let me teach him anything. He has to figure it out for himself, then he tells me.

MATH MAGIC

The beauty of *SCORE!* is the interaction the children have with their Coaches. One of the people I've met at *SCORE!* who affected the way I look at life is a girl who had a great deal of difficulty with her self-confidence. She was challenged in school, she was used to making mistakes, and she had a big problem with numbers. Reading a number like 13,627 would be the end of the world for her. Every once in a while we would go to the back of the room and I would write out consecutive random numbers. I would start out with the 100's and I would say, "What's this number?" She made a lot of mistakes at first, but we stuck with it, then we moved on to the 1,000's. Then she was up to the millions a couple of months later!

Rather than just the math skills, she realized that we really liked her, we thought she was smart, and we knew she could really do the work. It was a small victory for her to read an ad and see that a car costs $25,327, and it was exciting to see a nice young lady who made many mistakes want to correct those mistakes and reach her goal.

Core Area 2: Computation
• Add and subtract up to five-digit numbers
• Multiply by two-digit numbers
• Multiply by three-digit numbers
• Divide by two-digit numbers
• Estimate quotients by rounding
• Adjusting quotients

Core Area 3: Money and Time
• Multiply money
• Work problems involving time

Core Area 4: Geometry and Measurement
• Study quadrilaterals, parallelograms, and rhombuses
• Classify plane figures and identify common properties
• Identify and draw perpendicular and parallel lines
• Identify congruent and similar figures
• Learn about circles

Core Area 5: Fractions and Decimals
• Add and subtract fractions with common denominators
• Write and compare mixed fractions
• Write and compare decimals up to hundredths
• Add and subtract decimals up to hundredths

Core Area 6: Graphing (bar graphs, pie charts)
• Draw number lines
• Draw line graphs and plot points

Core Area 7: Statistics and Probability
• Introduce the idea of probability
• Learn about experimental and theoretical trials
• Find some elementary probabilities
• Learn about counting and tree diagrams

Core Area 8: Problem solving
• Estimate length in inches, feet, yards, and miles
• Estimate other measurements
• Perform computations with measurements
• Solve word problems

CHAPTER 9

What Math Content Should I Review?

In this section, you can find descriptions of each concept and skill in the outlines of 3rd and 4th grade math. The concepts and skills for both grades are organized together according to core area. You can use this section as a reference to review concepts and skills. For example, both multiplying by one-digit numbers (a 3rd grade skill) and multiplying by two-digit numbers (a 4th grade skill) can be found under the head "Core Area 2: Computation."

READY, WILLING, ABLE

We try to tell kids that they CAN do something new. Kids might have to make mistakes when they see new things, but they can learn in the process. With perfectionistic kids, we tell them they can do this; they see new things all the time. Many parents see money and tell me, "My kids can't count money," and I say, "Let's step back and talk about this." I try to show them their child's scores in math and convince them that their child is ready to count money. It's a new thing, and maybe the parent needs to work at home with the child to help reinforce the learning.

Core Area 1: Numeration

Numeration is a word for the system of numbers that we use. This core area is devoted to learning about numbers and comparing and rounding numbers.

Read and write four-digit numbers (thousands). Four-digit numbers include 5,249, which is read "five thousand two hundred forty-nine." For this number, 5 is in the thousands' place, 2 is in the hundreds' place, 4 is in the tens' place and 9 is in the ones' place. The value of a number depends upon the number of places it has. For example, 900 is vastly different from 9,000—especially if we're talking about your credit card balance!

Read and write five-digit numbers and six-digit numbers (tens and hundreds of thousands). Numbers between 10,000 and 999,999 are in this category. For example, one such number is 83,979 which is read "eighty-three thousand nine hundred seventy-nine."

Making the Grade

CLIMB EVERY MOUNTAIN

The goal program is my favorite part of *SCORE!*, and I always talk it up with parents. We sit down with kids for the first time and work with them to set an academic goal. We steer them toward challenges. First it might be doing math lessons. They might not love math, but they set some goals and accomplish them. Then they know they can do math and they might pick math for their next goal program. That is such a rewarding experience to share with their parents!

Read and write up to nine-digit numbers (hundreds of millions). The gigantic budget deficits that the U.S. government has been ringing up fall into this category. For example, in 1992, the government was swimming in $290,203,000 of red ink. Read it and weep: "two hundred ninety million, two hundred three thousand dollars."

Write numbers in standard and expanded form. The number 4,592 is in standard form. In expanded form, it is 4,000 + 500 + 90 + 2.

Compare and order thousands. To compare two numbers, compare the values of each place value starting from the left. For example, 4,567 > 2,364, because the 4 in 4,567 is greater than the 2 in 2,364. The symbol > means "greater than."

Compare and order numbers up to hundreds of thousands. Use the same method to compare these larger numbers. You just have more numbers to deal with. For example, 834,959 > 830,880 because the 4 in the thousands' place of 834,959 is greater than the 0 in the thousands' place of 830,880.

Count thousands by twos, fives, and tens. To count by twos, just add 2 to each number. For example, 1,800, 1,802, 1,804, 1,806, etcetera. To count by fives, add 5 to each number: 1,800, 1,805, 1,810, etcetera. To count by tens . . . well, you get the idea.

Count by hundreds. Add 100 to each number: 11,800, 11,900, 12,000, 12,100, etcetera.

Round to the nearest ten or hundred. To round to the nearest 10, use the nearest multiple of 10. For example, 7,448 is rounded (up) to 7,450. To round to the nearest 100, use the nearest multiple of 100. For example, 7,448 is rounded (down) to 7,400. If the number you want to round is equally close to the numbers above and below it, always round to the larger number. So, 7,450 rounded to the nearest 100 is rounded (up) to 7,500.

Round to the nearest thousand. Use the same method, but now you use the nearest thousand. For example, 7,488 is rounded (down) to 7,000. Note that when you round a number, you may round up or down depending on which number is closer.

Core Area 2: Computation

Computation refers to addition, subtraction, multiplication, and division. This core area also uses estimation to help perform the calculations and to check answers to calculations.

Add thousands. To add thousands, add the numbers in the same place (column). If the sum is greater than ten, carry the tens' digit of the sum to the next row. For example, to add 3,064 + 6,228, the sum of the ones' column is 4 + 8 = 12. Carry the tens' digit of the sum (that is, 1).

$$
\begin{array}{r}
{}^{(1)} \\
3,064 \\
+6,228 \\
\hline
9,292
\end{array}
$$
Carry the tens' digit of the sum to the tens' column.

The sum 3,064 + 6,228 = 9,292.

Subtract using regrouping more than once. *Regrouping* is a fancy term for borrowing a 1 from the next larger place. You remember how to subtract 5,781 − 235 by borrowing 10 from the tens' place in 5,781. Then, you rewrite the 1 as 11 and subtract 11 − 5.

$$
\begin{array}{r}
{}^{(7)(1)} \\
5,781 \\
-\ 235 \\
\hline
5,546
\end{array}
$$
Think of the ones' digit as 11 by borrowing from the tens' place.

Thus, 5,781 − 235 = 5,546.

Add and subtract up to five-digit numbers. The methods for adding and subtracting are the same; just the numbers are bigger. For example, to add 10,415 + 22,924,

LITTLE EXTRAS

We got our daughter an assignment book last year so that she could do a little extra schoolwork to turn in. This was something that wasn't on her school supply list, so now she knows that we think this is important, and she knows that Mom and Dad are helping her out.

Making the Grade

ALL OVER THE PLACE

At *SCORE!*, I had a family with a pair of girls, both of whom were diagnosed with an illness when they were young. They were both behind in school and had speech problems. Their mother advised me not to pay attention to their educational grade level. "I'm only interested in their skill levels." She told me she was proud of whatever progress they could make, and that's what's important.

Parents should ask themselves what kind of goals they can set with their children and what kind of skills they should have, and that can be incorporated into their overall academic goals. And keep making new goals all the time. Some fourth graders can work on fifth grade math, for instance. Parents should realize that kids are all over the place academically and are always at different skill levels— not necessarily at their grade levels either.

the sum of the hundreds' place is 13. Carry the tens' place of the sum (that is, 1) to the next column.

$$\begin{array}{r} (1) \\ 10,415 \\ + \underline{22,924} \\ 33,339 \end{array}$$

For some additions (or subtractions), you may have to carry (or regroup) several times.

Learn multiplication facts up to 9. Quick, what's 8 times 9? These multiplication facts provide a solid understanding of numbers and are essential problem-solving tools. If necessary, use a calculator to check your multiplication facts.

Multiply by a one-digit number. To multiply 718 by 4, you multiply each digit in 718 by 4. If one of these products is greater than 10, carry the tens' place of the product to the next column. For example, in the ones' column, the product is $8 \times 4 = 32$. Carry the tens' digit (that is, 3) to the next column.

$$\begin{array}{r} (3) \\ 718 \\ \times \underline{4} \\ 2,872 \end{array}$$

Carry the 3 because the product of the ones' columns is 32.

Multiply by multiples of 10 and 100. To multiply by a multiple of 10 or 100, you consider the multiplier in terms of groups of 10 or 100. For example, to multiply 34×40:

- Think of 40 as 4 tens
- Then, the product $34 \times 40 = 34 \times 4$ tens $= 136$ tens or $136 \times 10 = 1,360$

Multiply by two-digit numbers. Multiply two numbers 23×57 by placing one on top of the other as shown below.

- Multiply 23 by the ones' place of 57: $23 \times 7 = 161$ (see the first row under the horizontal rule).
- Since the five is in the tens' place, it represents 5 tens or

50. Multiply 23 × 50 = 1,150 (see the second row under the horizontal rule).

- Add the two rows.

$$
\begin{array}{r}
23 \\
\times\ 57 \\
\hline
161 \\
\underline{1,150} \\
1,311
\end{array}
$$

Thus, 23 × 57 = 161 + 1,150 = 1,311.

Multiply by three-digit numbers. We can use the same process to multiply three-digit numbers. To multiply 646 × 312, follow these steps:

- Multiply 646 by 2 and write the product directly under the rule.
- Next, multiply 646 by 10 (1 ten) and write the product under the first result.
- Now, multiply 646 by 300 (3 hundreds) and write the product under the previous two results.
- Add the three rows.

$$
\begin{array}{r}
646 \\
\times\ 312 \\
\hline
1,292 \\
6,460 \\
\underline{193,800} \\
201,552
\end{array}
$$

The answer is 201,552.

Learn that division is the opposite of multiplication. Division is the opposite of multiplication; it reverses the process of multiplication. For example:

- Starting with 2 and multiplying it by 8 produces 16.
- Dividing 16 by 8 gives you 2, the starting point.
- Thus, 16 ÷ 8 = 2 because 2 × 8 = 16.

IT ALL ADDS UP

There are small success stories every day in a *SCORE!* Center—teaching children how to do multiplication, or borrow and carry numbers in addition or subtraction, or there's something that's been frustrating for them in school, and then all of a sudden a light goes on.

CREATING PARTNERSHIPS

Single parents who are employed outside the home, parents who live far from the school, and fathers are less involved, on average, at the school building, unless the school organizes opportunities for families to volunteer at various times and in various places to support the school and their children.
—Joyce L. Epstein, Johns Hopkins University

CHALLENGE AND SUPPORT

The Carnegie Task Force on Learning in the Primary Grades (September 1996) says children's long-term learning and development depend a lot on what happens between ages three and ten. "With the right combination of challenge and support from parents, educators, and the community, virtually every child, by the end of fourth grade, can be reading, writing, and doing math and science at levels now achieved by only a few," says the 23-member panel of leaders in child development, education, business, government, and media.

POOR EXPECTATIONS

Compared with other countries, our schools expect relatively little from students. Our school day is not especially long, and most of it— about 60 percent, according to national studies—is spent in nonacademic activities, including study halls, ancillary classes, and break times.
—*Beyond the Classroom*, Laurence Steinberg, Ph.D. (Simon & Schuster, 1996)

Divide by a one-digit number. To divide a number by a single-digit number (a number between 1 and 9), use the fact that division is the opposite of multiplication. For example, to calculate $45 \div 9$, ask yourself what number multiplied by 9 gives 45. The answer is 5. (See—your 3rd grade teacher was right! These multiplication facts really are useful.)

Divide by multiples of 10 and 100. To divide by a multiple of 100, think of the numbers in terms of groups of 100 and use your handy multiplication facts. For example, to divide 3,600 by 400, think of the numbers as 36 hundred divided by 4 hundred, which is the same as $36 \div 4$. The answer is 9.

Divide by two-digit numbers. Suppose you need to divide 912 by 24. Follow these steps.

- Since the divisor 24 has two digits, we try to divide it into 91, the first two digits of 918.
- Dividing 91 by 24, you see that 3 is the largest multiple of 24 that is less than 91. We write 3 above the horizontal rule above the tens' place.
- Since $3 \times 24 = 72$, you write 72 under 91 and subtract. The answer is 19.
- Now, you write the remaining digit in 912, which is 2, next to 19 to produce the number 192 and divide again by 24.
- The answer is 8, which you write above the rule next to the 3. So you've found that $912 \div 24 = 38$.

Estimate quotients by rounding. Estimating quotients will help figure out what the answer to a division problem should be.

- To estimate the quotient $389 \div 8$, you can round 389 to 400 and divide $400 \div 8 = 50$. Thus, $389 \div 8$ is about 50.
- Suppose you need to divide $1,971 \div 38$. Since 38 is not a convenient divisor, let's round 38 to 40. Now, although 40 does not go into 1,971 without a remainder, it does go into 2,000. Round 1,971 to 2,000 and divide $2,000 \div 40 = 50$. Thus, $1,971 \div 38$ is approximately 50.

Adjusting quotients. You can use rounding to perform a division. Suppose you need to find $335 \div 46$. Since 46 doesn't divide 335 evenly, you can try rounding 46 to 50 and 335 to 300. Thus,

$$300 \div 50 = 6$$

You try 6 as a quotient and get $6 \times 46 = 276$, but when you subtract, you get a remainder of 59, and $59 > 46$. Since the remainder is greater than the divisor, the quotient is too small. You then adjust the quotient to 7 and find that $7 \times 46 = 332$. Thus, $335 \div 46 = 7$ with a remainder of 3.

Core Area 3: Money and Time

Working with money, adding and subtracting money, and multiplying amounts of money by whole numbers prefigure decimals, which students begin to learn about in grade four.

Add and subtract money. Adding and subtracting money is important to making change. Add and subtract money as you would add and subtract whole numbers. Make sure the decimal points of the numbers are aligned.

Multiply money. Multiplying $0.25 by a whole number suggests decimal multiplication, which occurs in grade five. To multiply $0.25 by 5, multiply as you would multiply whole numbers, add the dollar sign, and insert the decimal point to the left of the second place from the left. Adding 5 quarters together is a concrete way to explain this multiplication to your child.

Tell time to the minute. "The big hand is on the four...." By the end of grade three, your child should be able to accurately read a clock. Recall that the numbers on a clock represent intervals of five minutes, and the small marks between the numbers indicate one-minute intervals.

Work problems involving time. Remember those troublesome bus or train timetables? Well, that's what these problems involve. You can make up your own problems

SISTER ACT

I remember two special sisters who were in an unpleasant family situation, a sticky divorce in which they got shuffled back and forth between their mom and dad. One of them had a hard time lifting her head up. She mumbled hello and she was far behind in math. Her younger sister was outgoing, dyslexic, and really having a hard time in reading. After a few months of going to *SCORE!*, the younger girl started to read in the car—she never read voluntarily before in her life. Now she reads all the time on her own! The older sister didn't want any help in math, and it took a while to convince her to use scratch paper. Finally, she started using it to do her math problems at home and at school. And she set goals for herself at Score and brought her math grades from almost a D to almost an A!

Making the Grade

PLUG INTO THE POSITIVE

Getting my child into the habit of sitting down with his homework and actually doing it was a nightmare. It was a struggle, and it came to the point where we had to keep going and keep plugging away with him. Now our child has great study habits.

Parents need to stick with a positive goal and keep going. Build up a reward system with your child because whatever it takes, you need the positive reinforcement that works with your child to develop those positive study habits. And it's easier to plug them into the positive habit earlier in life than later.

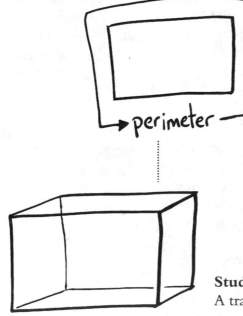

A three-dimensional figure

about the time it takes to go to school or to grandma's house. To solve problems like these, recall that:

- There are 24 hours in a day.
- There are 60 minutes in a hour.
- There are 60 seconds in a minute.

Take extra care with problems that involve switching time from A.M. to P.M. or vice versa. One way to solve a problem that switches time from A.M. to P.M. (that is, morning to afternoon) is to first find how much time it is to noon and then add that time to the hour in the A.M.

Core Area 4: Geometry and Measurement

Geometry in grades three and four involves plane figures (two-dimensional figures such as rectangles) and solid figures such as cubes. Geometry is now considered an essential part of elementary math. Help your child master the essential ideas of the perimeter and area of a plane figure and the volume of a solid figure.

Learn about perimeter, area, and volume.

- The *perimeter* of a plane figure, such as a rectangle, is the distance around the figure. To calculate the perimeter, add the lengths of the sides.
- The *area* of a plane figure such as triangle or a square is the amount of surface the figure has. Area is measured in square units and is usually calculated by multiplying two measurements.
- The *volume* of a three-dimensional figure (see representation at left) such as a cube is the amount of space inside the figure. Volume is measured in cubic units and is usually calculated by multiplying three measurements.

Study the transformation of a figure.

A transformation of a plane figure changes its position or orientation without changing its shape or size.

Following are the transformations of a plane figure that are commonly studied.

- A *reflection* (or *flip*) flips a figure over from one side of a point, line, or plane to the other so that it is the same distance from the point, line, or plane and its orientation does not change. This is like flipping a pancake from one end of a griddle to the opposite end.

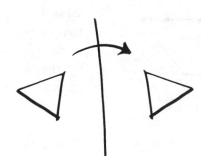

The reflection of a plane figure about a line

- A *rotation* (or *turn*) rotates a figure about a fixed point like spinning a pinwheel.
- A *translation* (or *glide*) slides a figure across a plane without changing the figure's shape or size. Think of a puck sliding across the ice.
- A *dilation* stretches or shrinks a figure equally in all directions in such a way the its shape remains the same. Only its size changes. Those fun-house mirrors that distort your height or weight do not produce dilations. These mirrors change your shape and size.

A dilation of a plane figure

Learn angles and right angles.
An *angle* is formed by two lines meeting at a point. For example, two edges of a sheet of paper that meet in a corner form an angle. The meeting point is called the *vertex* and the two lines are called *rays*. A *right angle* is formed when the lines meet to form the corner of a square or rectangle.

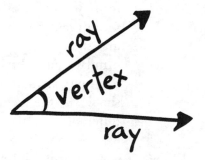

A vertex with two rays

Study quadrilaterals, parallel-ograms, and rhombuses.
- A *quadrilateral* is any plane figure having 4 sides. A quadrilateral has 4 vertices and 2 diagonals.
- A *parallelogram* is a quadrilateral with 2 pairs of parallel sides. Rectangles and squares are special kinds of parallelograms.
- A *rhombus* is a parallelogram with 4 equal sides.

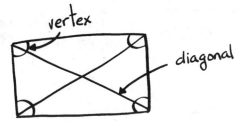

A quadrilateral with vertices and diagonals labeled

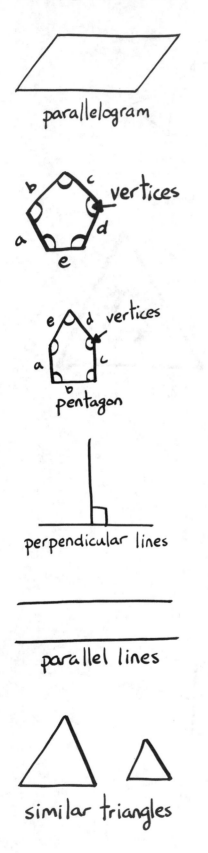

parallelogram

vertices

pentagon

perpendicular lines

parallel lines

similar triangles

Classify plane figures and identify common properties. Plane figures vary widely. Any closed figure formed by line segments is a *polygon*. Polygons are classified by the number of sides and vertices. The following table shows the number of sides and vertices of some polygons.

Polygon	Number of Sides	Number of Vertices
Triangle	3	3
Quadrilateral	4	4
Pentagon	5	5
Hexagon	6	6
Octagon	8	8
Decagon	10	10
Dodecagon	12	12

Identify and draw perpendicular and parallel lines. Perpendicular lines meet to form a right angle. Parallel lines never meet.

Identify congruent and similar figures.
- Congruent figures are identical; they have the same shape and size.
- Similar figures have different sizes but the same shape. For example, an automobile in a photograph has the same shape as the actual automobile. Only their sizes are different.

Learn about circles. A circle is a figure having a round shape like the edge of a round dish. Every point on the circle is the same distance from the center of the circle.

- The line between two points on the circle that contains its center is called a *diameter*.
- The line between the center and a point on the circle is called a *radius*.

There are many diameters and radii of a circle.

Core Area 5: Fractions and Decimals

Understanding the concept of a whole and its division into equal parts is an essential ingredient in understanding fractions and decimals. Explore these concepts with your child and practice the skills.

Learn the meaning of fractions. A *fraction* is a number that represents a part of a whole. Third graders learn about fractions by dividing things into parts and describing each part with a fraction. The next time you have pizza or a birthday cake, think fractions. Practice using fractions to describe various parts of a pizza or cake.

- The top number in a fraction is called the *numerator*.
- The bottom number in a fraction is called the *denominator*.

Recognize equivalent fractions. Fractions that are equal are called *equivalent fractions*. For example, the fractions 1/2, 3/6, and 4/8 are equivalent because they each are half of the whole.

Compare fractions. You compare fractions by determining which is the larger part of the whole. For example, 7/8 is greater than 1/2 because 7/8 is 1/8 less than the entire whole but 1/2 is far less. To compare fractions, first find an equivalent fraction for each fraction such that the equivalent fractions have the same denominator. The fraction with the greater numerator is greater.

Use fractions in word problems. When you have word problems involving parts, think fractions. Ask your child why fractions should be used to solve the problem. What clues and facts suggest the use of fractions? Using fractions to solve problems in the real world demonstrates the importance of fractions.

Add and subtract fractions with common denominators. When fractions have the same denominators, add or subtract the fractions by adding or subtracting their numerators:

HAND-RAISING EXPERIENCE

There's a girl in our Center who is very shy and her academic work level was just average; now it's much improved. She came in with her new math book from school the other day, just after school started, and she was very excited. She opened up her book and pointed out how she's done this material in *SCORE!* already and she knows how to do this and this and this. When her teacher asked, "Does anybody know how to do this?" she got to raise her hand. She was really excited about getting her brand new math book, and it wasn't all new to her.

$$\frac{5}{7} - \frac{3}{7} = \frac{2}{7}$$

Write and compare mixed fractions. A *mixed fraction* is a whole number combined with a fraction, such as 1 3/4. A mixed number is a number between two whole numbers. For example, 1 3/4 is between 1 and 2. To compare two mixed numbers, compare the whole parts and, if necessary, compare the fractional parts. For example, 2 2/3 is greater than 1 9/10 because 2 is greater than 1.

Learn about decimals and their relationship to fractions. The decimal 0.1 is another way of writing 1/10. A decimal is any number that uses the places to the right of the decimal point. For example, the number 2.7 is a decimal.

Learn decimal place value to the tenths and hundredths.
- The first place to the right of the decimal point is called the *tenths' place*. The decimal 2.7 is read, "two and seven tenths."
- The second place to the right of the decimal point is called the *hundredths' place*. For example, 0.01 is called *one hundredth* and is the same as 1/100. The number 3.85 is read, "three and eighty-five hundredths."

Write and compare decimals up to one hundredths. To compare decimals, compare the whole number parts first, and if necessary, compare the decimal part. For example, 5.71 is greater than 5.55 because 71 (the decimal part of 5.71) is greater than 55 (the decimal part of 5.55).

Core Area 6: Graphing

Graphs are an effective way to organize and depict data. Students at an early age begin to learn how graphs represent data. The shape of a graph, its highs, lows, and the way it increases and decreases provide a great deal of information about changes in the data.

BIG PICTURE

The U.S. Department of Education's Office of Educational Research and Improvement is going to spend the next 15 years researching many goals, including:

- Strengthening schools
- Strengthening the teaching force
- Supporting schools in preparing culturally diverse populations for American economic, social, and civic life
- Improving teaching, curriculum, assessment, and student learning
- Promoting learning in informal settings (families, private companies, libraries, sports)

Read line graphs and bar graphs. You know those connect-the-dots puzzles that create a picture when you finish? Well, the same principle is at work in line graphs. A *line graph* is a collection of points connected by lines. A *bar graph* contains vertical or sometimes horizontal bars that show the amount of each item. The amount is read by looking at the height of each bar.

Draw number lines. First, draw a horizontal line and make vertical marks at equal intervals along the line. Label the first mark on the left either 0 or a number of your choice. The other marks represent increments of the sum of a constant number (usually 1).

Draw line graphs and plot points. Draw two number lines (called the *horizontal axis* and the *vertical axis*) perpendicular to each other as shown below. Points on the graph are written (x, y). Plot a point by moving x units along the horizontal axis, moving y units straight up, and then drawing a dot.

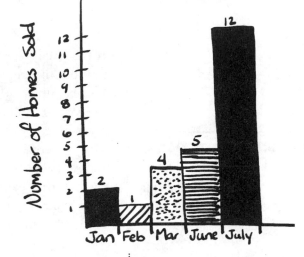

Core Area 7: Statistics and Probability

Statistics and probability are the tools used to analyze problems in our world. They are used to take surveys of attitudes on smoking and to find the chances of winning the lottery. Frequently students choose the kinds of issues they wish to investigate. Since many topics for study are problems that students wish to learn

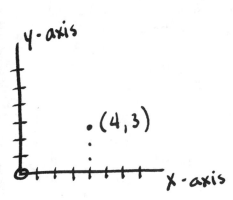

about, they become involved and interested in learning the concepts.

Calculate averages. The *average* of a group of numbers is the sum of the numbers divided by the number of items in the group. For example, here is how you figure the average of 4, 12, 5, 7, and 22.

$$\text{average} = \frac{4 + 12 + 5 + 7 + 22}{5} = \frac{50}{5} = 10$$

Introduce the idea of probability. A *probability* is a number that represents the chances that an event will occur. For example, weather forecasters say the probability of rain today is 6 out of 10 (0.6). Fourth graders learn about probability by choosing green and yellow balls out of a hat. They discover that if there are a lot more green balls than yellow balls, then the chances of choosing a yellow ball are small. Other examples of probability include the chances of your child's winning the school raffle or your chances of being chosen for jury duty.

Learn about experimental and theoretical trials. A *trial* is one occurrence of an event, such as flipping a coin and its coming up heads. *Experimental trials* are the results of a series of coin flips. Theoretical trials are a description in theory of what should happen if you flip a coin several times. For example, say you flip a coin 100 times and get 49 heads. Those flips are some experimental trials. Since the chances of getting heads is 1/2, then the theoretical trials for flipping a coin 100 times should be 50 (1/2 of 100). In most cases of a fair game of chance or coin tossing, the experimental trials should be close to the theoretical trials. If they are not, then you'd better call the sheriff!

Find some elementary probabilities. Students at this level find the probabilities of doing things like flipping coins, rolling a die, and choosing balls from a hat. To find the probability of a specific event, such as rolling a die and getting 6, count the number of ways you can get that result and divide that number by the number of all possible outcomes of the game. For example, since there is one way

TROUBLING STATISTICS

The Parents' Resource Institute for Drug Education just released some disturbing research:

• Students are much more likely to get warnings about drug abuse from their teachers than their parents. Kids, unfortunately, aren't heeding their advice—drug use is on the rise.

• The percent who say their parents talk to them "a lot" about the dangers of drugs has dropped from 40.3 percent in 1990–91 to 26.6 percent in 1995–96.

• "Our data reveals that seven out of ten parents are essentially sitting on the sidelines as teen drug use spirals out of control."
—Douglas Hall,
PRIDE's Executive Director

of rolling a 6 (specific result) and there are six possible outcomes of rolling a die (numbers 1–6), then the probability of rolling a 6 is 1/6.

Learn about counting and tree diagrams. Students learn how to count the number of occurrences of some events, such as flipping a coin 3 times. A *tree diagram* shows the 2 possible outcomes of flipping a coin (head and tail) for the 3 coin flips.

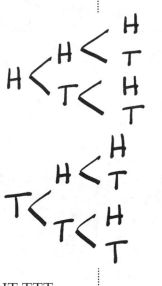

At each possible result, that is, each head or tail, draw a "branch" that indicates head and another "branch" that indicates tail. The diagram shows that for three coin flips, there are eight possible outcomes:

HHH, HHT, HTH, HTT, TTH, THH, HHT, TTT

where H means head and T means tail.

Core Area 8: Problem Solving

Problem solving in math consists of a set of strategies for tackling word problems in an organized way and includes the following characteristics:

- Understanding and exploring the problem
- Thinking creatively and trying many approaches to the problem
- Persevering until the problem is solved or a new approach is discovered
- Answering the question and explaining how the problem was solved

As your child solves a problem successfully, she will gain confidence in her problem-solving abilities and will develop her thinking and reasoning skills. Problem solving is a key part of elementary math that improves student achievement and helps students build self-confidence.

Estimate addition and subtraction. Estimating improves students' number skills and helps them develop

COUNT WITH YOUR KIDS

Begin to explain measurements and allow your children to sort shapes and colors. Let your children help sort laundry, measure ingredients for a recipe, count or sort money, or pick out shapes in books. Early experience with counting, sorting, and numbers builds early math skills. By being positive, playing math games, and connecting math to the real world, your children will see the importance of math in everyday life.
—The National PTA®

Making the Grade

MONEY TALKS

Money for education does make a difference, researchers have concluded. An April 1994 study published in *Educational Researcher* indicates that the relationship between school resources and student achievement may be stronger than originally thought, and that earlier research showing little relationship between school expenditures and student outcomes may have been flawed.... The effect of certain resources on student achievement (such as per pupil expenditure and teacher experience) is substantially positive.
—American Educational Research Association

their reasoning, judgment, and decision-making skills. Estimation is useful:

- For checking whether a computation is correct
- When an exact answer is impossible
- When an exact answer is not necessary

Of the many ways of estimating addition and subtraction, two of the most common are rounding and front-end estimation.

- Rounding: Estimate by rounding the two numbers and adding or subtracting the rounded numbers.
- Front-end estimation: Estimate using front-end estimation by adding or subtracting the first digit of each number (the front end) and putting zeroes in the other place values. For example, to estimate $737 - 453$, subtract $7 - 4 = 3$ and then write two zeros after the 3 to get 300 as an estimate.

Estimate length in inches, feet, yards, and miles. Estimating lengths is another way to develop number sense. Children typically measure and estimate the measurements of objects in their environment. These activities often are exploratory investigations that develop skills in estimation, problem solving, and concept development. For example, students can estimate measurements using familiar things whose measurements they know, such as their hand or their forearm. Or, your child may prefer to measure using nonstandard measuring units. Help her evaluate her estimates to make her a better problem solver.

Estimate other measurements. Students apply the same estimation strategies to estimate weight and capacity. Knowing the capacity of a glass can be used to estimate the capacity of a fish bowl.

Perform computations with measurements. Students multiply and divide measurements to convert to different units. For example, to convert from meters to centimeters, multiply by 100. Help your child use estimation techniques and other problem-solving methods to estimate complex computations and evaluate their answers.

Solve word problems. Solving word problems is an art that requires patience and persistence.

- Encourage you child to think clearly and logically, and suggest that he ask many questions.
- Listen to your child to see if he understands the problem.
- Encourage your child to explain his thinking.
- Ask "what if" questions to explore the problem and extend your child's understanding.
- Encourage your child to try different strategies to solve the problem.
- Help your child persevere, encourage him to be flexible, and praise him for taking risks and trying new approaches.

Solve problems involving fractions, money, and decimals. Use many of the strategies listed above to solve these problems. Also use pieces of paper to represent fractions, coins and bills for money, and strips of paper divided into 10 parts to represent decimals.

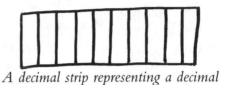

A decimal strip representing a decimal

Have your child explore the problem using these items and ask "what if" questions to help him gain an appreciation for the problem.

Calculate area and volume using tiles and cubes. Using a square tile to represent a square unit, cover the area of the figure with the tiles to estimate the area. To estimate volume, fill a solid figure with equally sized cubes representing a cubic unit.

New Ways of Teaching Math

Sometimes, parents discover that their children's math is being taught in a new way, a way they worry they won't understand. Teachers seem to place less emphasis on addition and multiplication, and they are teaching math in unusual ways. Students don't have math homework as much as their parents were accustomed to. What's going on here?

CHOICE PRODUCTS

A number of math software products "made the grade" with *Newsweek* magazine. Here are some of their "Editor's Choice" titles:
- *Go West* (Edunetics Ltd.) includes some practical budgeting and planning experience for kids
- *Math Heads* (Theatrix Interactive) is a virtual TV Land filled with math fun and attitude
- *Mega Math Blaster* (Davidson & Associates) is an arcade-style romp that teaches math concepts while blasting through a colorful universe
- *Mighty Math Number Heroes* (Edmark) combines entertainment with geometry, fractions, probability, and computation.
- *Chessmaster 5000* (Mindscape) teaches critical thinking, problem solving, and key math skills.

ENJOY IT

Our *SCORE!* experience has been very good. The program gives my older child the ability to learn without an adult seemingly standing over her. She seems to be more willing to take a chance at something new without the fear of being wrong (she is somewhat of a perfectionist). Even my five-year-old son likes the computers and getting rewards. His ability to sit through a computer session versus book reading is so much greater that learning is more fun for him. At any age, that is the real goal of learning. Learning should be enjoyable.

A Response to Problems. In recent years, innovative math programs have been written in response to the serious problems in math education. Clearly, in many schools, the success rate in math has not been high. Test scores are lower, and students have trouble learning and using arithmetic facts.

In study after study, students have shown that they are not interested in math and have not been engaged by the subject matter. Many are frustrated and have difficulty understanding the purpose of the math facts. What's going wrong here?

Researchers have learned that:

- Standard teaching methods do not always reach all students. Children learn in many different ways. The memorization of arithmetic facts does not compute for students whose learning styles do not fit this approach.
- Learning arithmetic facts does not ensure that students can solve problems. Knowing how to begin to solve a problem and which operations are appropriate for the problem requires a level of understanding different from and beyond the number facts.
- Memorization of math facts does not stimulate the creativity that is necessary to be a good problem solver. Students have difficulty applying arithmetic facts flexibly in different situations.

Many new programs to deal with these issues have been developed, based on the recommendations that math professionals have come up with.

Characteristics of a Strong Math Program. The new methods of teaching math are centered around problem solving. What, you may ask, does that mean and how does it relate to good old addition and subtraction? It means that problem solving is a set of strategies for describing and solving a problem in ways that are meaningful to a child. A good problem solver studies a problem by:

- Talking about it with others

- Using reasoning skills to explain and justify their thinking
- Making graphs or drawings that describe the problem
- Trying a variety of approaches to attempt to solve the problem
- Using concrete objects to represent numbers

Students investigate extended problems involving things within their world. For example, they estimate the time it takes to get to school or distances in their neighborhood. By solving real problems, they learn that math is important and is used frequently in life. In addition, they come to appreciate that math is more than just number facts. Just as reading is more than learning the meaning of each word, math is more than reciting arithmetic facts.

Talking with others. Usually students work in small groups to explore a problem. Each group member brings his own information and talents that others may or may not possess. As students share their ideas and ways of thinking, they develop their mathematical vocabulary and explain the relevant math in their own words. Teachers assist them by asking questions and modeling other exploration strategies to promote investigating and describing the problem.

Use reasoning skills. Students are encouraged to question and to elaborate on suggestions made by others. Teachers ask students to explain how they came up with the answer, why the solution worked, and how the solution is similar to other related problems. Students are encouraged to recognize patterns and relationships so that they learn that solutions may be used in numerous contexts.

Making pictures. One important way to express mathematical ideas is with a picture. For example, students represent the heights of classmates using a bar graph. The number of children who are a certain height is shown by a bar on the graph. Graphs and other drawings are important ways in which data is organized and information in a problem is

WHAT'S THE PROBLEM?

There are many exciting innovations going on in mathematics and the way it's being taught right now! This is something that parents should know: *You should no longer tell children how to do math problems.* Rather than say, "This is how you borrow" or "This is how you multiply" or "You go through these steps and this is how you get the answer," have your children articulate for themselves over and over again "What is the question and how do I solve the problem?"

It's exciting for kids to get together to work on a problem, explaining what the problem is and how they can tackle it. There will be many different ways that kids use to come up with the answer, and it's fascinating for them to see how everyone thought differently in the problem-solving process. It's also valuable to articulate the process—that's the real moment of learning, where it all starts to gel for them. Math can be fun and creative!

Limit passive entertainment for your child!

NO CHEATING!

My daughter and I don't really sit down specifically and try to do things like math cards with each other. We tried that and it didn't work for us. We'll do real-life things instead. For example, we go to the store and add up things together. I tell her we have only five dollars, so what should we get, and she'll add up our purchases. I let her hand the money to the store clerk, and she knows how much money she should get back—she's even corrected a few people when they have shortchanged her!

PATIENCE IS A VIRTUE

The hardest parents for me to deal with are the ones who stand behind their children saying, "What?! Don't you know what you're doing? 2 + 1 = 3!" And if the parents weren't standing over them, the kids would just type in 3, but they get nervous and upset and don't respond well. At *SCORE!*, we try to create a very positive environment. We can't tell a parent how to parent. What we can do, however, is set a good example by how we treat their kids in our Centers.

represented (such as the dimensions of a rug). Organizing information visually promotes clearer thinking and helps students get started.

Trying different approaches. Teachers encourage students to take risks and explore different ways to solve a problem. Unlike what we learned, there is no right way to solve a problem. Some might solve a problem using blocks, and others might solve it by drawing a picture or pacing it out.

Using objects. Children in their early years are tactile beings. They effectively express and work with mathematical ideas using objects. At age 2, they learned about numbers by counting their fingers. At age 6, they practiced addition by grouping objects.

Manipulatives. are specialized objects that teachers use to teach math. Following are some common ones.

- Unifix cubes are interlocking cubes that connect in one direction. These cubes are used for counting, addition, subtraction, and many other kinds of work with numbers.
- Pattern blocks are colorful, geometric shapes that usually are triangles, squares, trapezoids, and hexagons. These are useful for studying geometry, exploring patterns, and working with fractions.
- Snap cubes that connect on all six sides are used to explore three-dimensional figures.
- A hundreds board is a square grid showing the numbers from 1 to 100. This is useful for addition and multiplication, skip counting, and learning about patterns in the number system.

If your child is having trouble learning math facts using paper and pencil, you too can use manipulatives to practice. Ask your child's teacher which manipulative would be appropriate to teach the skill. Refer to the Resources section for companies that sell these items. Usually the manipulative kit comes with complete instructions on how to use them.

How Parents Can Help. Having some information about the purposes of the program is not enough. We're all familiar with the experience of trying to help our children and being told, "But that's not how my teacher does it!" To provide your child with support and assistance, first and foremost, approach this endeavor with a sense of adventure and curiosity. Fostering an inquisitive attitude will help your child see the value and excitement of doing math. In addition, we recommend the following:

- Always read the letters and other notices sent home.
- Do math homework along with your child.
- Have your child teach you how it is done.
- Go to math night at your child's school.
- Talk to your child's teacher.
- Talk to the math curriculum coordinator.
- Read the sources listed in this book's Resources section.
- Enjoy the Learning Adventure activities in this book.

These new math programs are best understood by doing them. Take every opportunity to participate in workshops and to do activities with your child, so that you can share the sense of accomplishment that comes with becoming a skillful problem solver.

SO PROUD OF YOU

Kids who always get things right on the first time may not know the excitement of having failed or made mistakes at first before they finally get it right. Success feels so great, and parents need to reinforce how great their children's hard-won successes are. "I'm so proud of you for working through that. It was tough, but you did it!"

NEW AND IMPROVED

In some schools now, we have the "new-new math," and the difference between that and what they've taught in the past is more of a problem-solving approach. Rather than focusing on memorizing math facts, like multiplication tables, they might take all the kids out to the playground and have them figure out the area of the soccer field or how much grass they'd need to purchase to lay sod down in a certain area. In many schools, there's more of a focus on the logical and problem-solving approach than ever before. I think, however, that critical math skills are just as important for kids to have.

CHAPTER 10

What's My Child Studying in Science?

If the question is, What are our children being taught in science classes? the short answer is, Not anywhere near enough. Science education in American schools is spotty and erratic. This is both surprising and discouraging for parents in a country that is seen as a world leader in scientific thinking and technological innovation.

Some schools excel at science education and others, at the dismal end of the spectrum, lump science in with the extras. Although most schools fall between these extremes, we feel that being vaguely in the middle is not good enough. If there is one area in which parents can make an enormous difference in helping their children make the grade, it is in science education.

Young scientists need physical experiences. The most important thing you can do for your child is to restore science to its roots in the world of physical exploration. "Project 2061" is a massive study of science teaching that was begun in 1989 by the American Academy for the Advancement of Science in collaboration with some of the best science teachers in the country. It is still in progress. In their report *BENCHMARKS for Science Literacy* they say, "For students in the early grades, the emphasis should overwhelmingly be on gaining experience with natural and social phenomena and on enjoying science." Our science activities sections will help you accomplish this goal.

Elementary educators who are comfortable with science are enthusiastic about incorporating physical exploration and

WEIRD SCIENCE!

Science students sometimes come up with "quirky" explanations. Here are a few, courtesy of *Popular Science* magazine (© 1996 Times Mirror Magazines, Inc.):

• Three kinds of blood vessels are arteries, vanes, and caterpillars.

• The moon is a planet just like Earth, only it is even deader.

• The pistol of a flower is its only protection against insects.

• A fossil is an extinct animal. The older it is, the more extinct it is.

• The purpose of the skeleton is something to hitch meat to.

TRY THIS AT HOME

The more freedom we give children to explore, the more they learn. One of our coaches set up something innovative for the kids in our chemistry classes. Instead of providing a lab for them, he taught them the five steps of scientific thinking and then gave them the chemistry lesson plan. He said this end result is what you want to look for, he handed the lessons over to the kids, and they went for it! For about an hour and a half, they explored and worked super hard and afterwards, they presented their findings.

REAL LIFE

You have to know your kids and their interests very well. When our SCORE! program sets goals, we relate them to something they know and feel passionately about. When your kids are not passionate about something they're learning, it's your challenge to help them with a real-world application for what they're studying so they will start to get more excited.

experimentation into their busy days. They do a great job. Unfortunately, others who are less comfortable with science themselves, or are in less well-equipped schools, rely on stories, readings from textbooks, and paperwork to satisfy their system's requirements. Large differences between individual classrooms, schools, and even states means that there is much for you to do. You can be alert and outspoken about your particular school's situation, and you can do a lot as a parent to encourage, supplement, and expand your child's curiosity about the world.

Helping with science is easy and pleasurable. There's no need to force your child to spend time memorizing science vocabulary and abstract descriptions of science concepts. This is actually a waste of time. Advanced ideas and obscure terms sound impressive, but they are beyond the conceptual ability of most children at this age and are more appropriate for high school or college students.

The memorization of advanced material confuses and frustrates more often than it illuminates, and the time spent on rote learning takes time away from useful physical experiences. Learning how lipoproteins move through cells is a task for the older biology student. It is a task that is much easier when a student has spent time in the elementary years experimenting with mixtures of oil and water. That student will bring a living image and concrete experience to the more abstract task.

Parents are sometimes intimidated by the rapid and complex advances in contemporary science. But the doing of science, the actual work of learning and achieving, has its base in simple, enjoyable, physical exploration. E. O. Wilson is a Nobel Prize-winning entomologist. One of his greatest pleasures is to get back to the Costa Rican rain forest where he can wander the dense trails with a small jeweler's eyepiece in search of new and interesting ants. That is what science is really all about.

Our Curriculum Outlines. We have combined what is currently taught in our better schools with what scientists and science educators generally agree should be at the heart of the best science learning in order to provide you with a picture of the kinds of learning that your child should be experiencing in the 3rd and 4th grades.

You will find that most of the topics and skills listed here are at least touched upon in all schools. But in each particular child's case, how thoroughly and usefully they are presented depends on the efforts and commitments of individual teachers and school systems.

Newer Curriculum Models. Some American schools have begun to adopt what is called the *integrated unit curriculum* in their elementary and middle school classes. In this type of curriculum, a central unit of study is built around a single topic or theme, and much of the classroom work revolves around it.

A typical example of an integrated unit might be "From Sheep to Shirt." In this particular unit, a student's science lessons would focus on the characteristics of the animals and plants providing material for fabrics; the properties of plants used for dyeing fabrics; the chemistry of dyeing; and the technology of weaving and clothing manufacture. You won't find such exact topics in this chapter. However, integrated units are usually thoroughly researched and prepared and they will incorporate most of the concepts and skills you'll find here.

What's Taught in Grade Three?

In grade three, simple writing tasks are usually incorporated into classroom science activities. This is one of the things that distinguishes 3rd grade science from science that is done in grades one and two.

The following six core subject areas represent the principle topics in science during the elementary years. Science is really all of a piece—it's the study of the totality of the natural world. Curricular divisions like these are used to

MAKIN' MUD PIES

I worked for a developmental psychologist for two years as a nanny to her children. She taught me a lot about parenting and good views on what to do with kids. The best thing she did with her kids was to encourage them to explore everything. Even at a very young age, if they wanted to go outside and sit naked in the mud and play around or go on nature hikes, she encouraged them to do a lot on their own and go out and explore their environment. When they were done, she'd hose them off and bring them into the house! It worked. At first I thought this was a really weird parenting style. These children now have a natural affinity for learning, and they seem to pick things up so quickly because they've always been taught to explore and ask questions.

I think one of the best learning experiences my child has is just exploring outside.

Making the Grade

THE SCIENCE CYCLE

Use the Learning Cycle when doing science with your kids. Coined in the 1960s by the Science Curriculum Improvement Study, the Learning Cycle has three stages:

- **Explore**—First do some exploring with your child by doing hands-on activities, uncluttered by vocabulary and such.

- **Explain**—Then you can explain the concept, connecting it to the hands-on experiences your child just had.

- **Apply**—Most children don't fully understand the concept at this point, so they need to apply the concept in new hands-on situations.
—The Wild Goose Co.

help teachers and evaluators organize the subject matter to be covered.

Core Area 1: Life Science
- Distinction between living and nonliving things
- Animals: insects are usually considered, with an emphasis on the life cycle (tadpoles, meal worms, and small classroom animals are often used)
- Plants: germination and growth, effects of different conditions such as soil quality and light; inventories and studies of plants in the local environment
- Microscopic life such as that found in pond water
- Skeletons and bones: from different animals, different bone structures, bones in the human body
- Essentials of life: basic needs and processes that living organisms have in common such as respiration, food, elimination, and reproduction
- Web of life: interdependence of organisms, effects of pollution, and how we can help our environment

Core Area 2: Physical Science
- Properties of matter: studies of materials in the student's environment; differences between pure materials and materials that are combinations of other materials; characteristics of easily studied materials such as iron, wood, and stone
- Forms of energy: static electricity and simple electrical circuits using bulbs and batteries
- Position and motion of objects: how different objects move by themselves and in relation to one another, use of rubber bands, magnets, and other forms of force, vibration of strings in simple musical instruments

Core Area 3: Earth and Space
- Geological structures of our planet and the processes that create them; volcanoes, deserts, deltas, mountains, and rivers
- Physical properties and characteristics of earth materials such as sands, soils, and rocks
- Dynamic physical aspects of our planet's surface, consideration of the water cycle, the sky, clouds, and weather

- Our star, the sun, as a source of heat
- Our relationship to the sun, night and day, the moon and planets, seasonal cycles

Core Area 4: Technology

- Basic computer skills
- Uses of technology
- Famous inventors and scientists
- Distinctions between natural and human produced objects
- Using tools and materials to make objects that solve simple problems
- Identifying recyclable and nonrecyclable materials

Core Area 5: Health

- Considerations of different kinds of disease: communicable, noncommunicable, chronic
- Inside the body and out: circulatory system, respiration, skin (sun exposure, itchy plants)
- Substances that can harm the body: dangers of smoking, alcohol, and drugs; pollution and toxic substances in local environment such as drain cleaners, bleach, and paint
- The food we eat: what is healthy and what is not

Core Area 6: Inquiry Skills

- Observing and describing: objects and events, characteristics and properties, similarities, and differences
- Investigation: planning simple experiments with familiar objects and nonhazardous materials—trying them out and discussing results
- Description: developing and expanding the concepts and words for texture, hardness, color, size, and smell, and different measurement systems
- Categorization: materials and the properties of materials, such as listing the characteristics of living and nonliving things, the characteristics of mammals and insects, or the properties of different minerals
- Tool use: becoming skilled with the tools of observation, measuring dimensions with rulers and tapes, weighing with balances, practice with the terms and tools for measuring
- Record keeping/reporting: using notes, graphs, discussion, and charts

RIDING THE SCIENCE CYCLE

Use the Learning Cycle to help do fun science stuff at home! Here's a real-life example:

- **Explore**—Give your child a microscope and have him start looking at pond water, human skin, onion skin, or anything that can be called an organism and has a definite cell structure he can see under the microscope. Don't tell your child about cells and then have him look for cells in the organisms. Just have him describe what he sees and compare one thing with another.

- **Explain**—Focus on the similarities between the organisms, and sooner or later, your child will latch on to the similarities in structure. Then you're ready to introduce the word *cells* and explain that all life forms contain these little chunks.

- **Apply**—Modify the "explore" phase of the activity. For example, instead of looking at a piece of onion skin under the microscope and describing what he sees, have him look at a completely different organism and draw a picture of the cells in it.
—The Wild Goose Co.

Making the Grade

LET KIDS INVESTIGATE

The National Science Standards strongly recommend that adults get kids involved in their own science projects so they can get a feel for what real science is all about. So you announce, "Today we're going to begin working on a science project. You can investigate anything you want. Get started figuring out what kind of question you'd like to answer with a scientific investigation." Kids get worried by this—it seems that doing their own investigations is intimidating. They think they'll have to do a lot of background reading in an encyclopedia in order to come up to speed on some unsolved problem in genetic engineering and then come up with a cure for cancer and the common cold. They have a view of what science is, and it usually has little to do with their everyday lives. What can you do to get kids involved? Let them know that almost any kind of question can be addressed—and not necessarily answered—with a scientific investigation.
—The Wild Goose Co.

What's Taught in Grade Four?

Fourth-grade science is usually a continuation and elaboration of themes and topics developed in 3rd grade. It is preparation for the greater depth and complexity in science study that will begin in the 5th grade.

Core Area 1: Life Science
- Human, plant, and animal interdependence; ecology
- Animal behavior: life cycles and ways of life that differentiate animal species
- The single cell as a building block and the smallest self-reproducing unit
- Plant study: how generations can differ, beginnings of concepts that will lead to the study of genetics

Core Area 2: Physical Science
- Considerations of heat: heat's effect on materials, events that produce heat, and heat transfer
- Energy: electricity, energy sources; combustion, movement of air and water, solar, and geothermal; the exchange of energy
- Interaction of solids and fluids
- Properties of motion, pendulums
- Further study of properties and ways to classify materials, both natural and human made

Core Area 3: Earth and Space
- Processes that change the earth's surface, erosion, glaciers, and the movement of the earth's surface
- Formation of rocks
- Characteristics of different rocks
- Water cycle
- Greater detail about the solar system, the sun as a source of energy, both heat and light

Core Area 4: Technology
- Continuing study of computer use and how a computer works, concept of programming instructions, limitations of computers
- Using plans and simple tools to build machines and structures to solve simple problems

- Distinction between science (asking how and why about natural objects and events) and technology (asking how and why about solutions to human problems)
- How machines shape materials to our purposes

Core Area 5: Health
- More detailed look at human body systems, nervous system, growth and development
- The affects of different substances on the body's systems
- The body's defenses against disease (skin, digestive system, immune system), immunity and vaccination, genetic disease
- Learning to read food labels

Core Area 6: Inquiry Skills
- Extending measuring skills, more rigorous use of tools such as the balance, thermometers, and rulers
- Observing with tools that change the scale of observation, such as binoculars, microscopes, and magnifying glasses
- Continuing to develop methods and vocabulary for classification and description
- Planning and executing investigations
- Considering whether something can be investigated through direct observation or not
- Beginning to apply multiple lines of investigation to solve problems

LIST YOUR QUESTIONS

We recommend that parents and teachers help kids realize what kinds of things they can investigate in science projects by having kids list questions they have whenever the questions come up. Start with a poster or bulletin board on which you list any kinds of questions about the natural world (including humans), whether the questions come up over everyday things or during homework or lessons in science, math, art, or whatever.
—The Wild Goose Co.

CHAPTER 11

What Science Content Should I Review?

As reflected in the "What's My Child Studying in Science?" chapter, science teaching in the elementary years is usually built around five core content areas and a core skills area. In this section, you can find discussion of most of the content generally covered in grades three and four in each core area. Because of the great variations found in the teaching of science to younger children, however, there are likely to be differences in emphasis regarding how some of the topics are discussed here and how they are handled in your child's school.

You'll also find that some variations in science education are particular to one region or another. Students in the Pacific Northwest, for instance, may spend more time learning about volcanoes and the movements of the earth's surface than children elsewhere in the country. Or students in parts of the northeast, where rabies has become a serious health concern, might find an emphasis on learning about rabies included in the health core, while children in the middle west have more exposure to learning about precautions to be taken for tornadoes.

Science Is Fun—Really!

As parents, we are sometimes intimidated by science. Does science seem to bristle with obscure vocabulary, incomprehensible formulas, and complicated concepts? We can feel at a loss when it comes to helping our children with their homework as we hastily scribble vaguely remembered diagrams of the solar system to remind ourselves of where Mercury or Neptune fit.

DON'T BUY THE HYPE

A word to parents: Don't be overwhelmed by the hype. It's hard to pick up a newspaper or magazine these days without reading something about how technology is going to transform everything from shopping at the mall to performing brain surgery. While there's no question that computers are slowly becoming a valuable tool in the classroom, they are just a tool—like books or paper or pencils. And they're useless without good software and teachers who know how to make the most of the material.
—from *Newsweek's Computers & the Family* (Fall/Winter 1996)

ENVIROLINK

You and your child can spend some time surfing the World Wide Web for cool science sites. There are many great ones that will give you and your child hours of fun sci experience. For instance, look into Envirolink for their environmental library, articles from *OneWorld* magazine, and teacher lesson plans on great science projects: http://www.envirolink.org

Much of this discomfort is the result of the inadequate science teaching that we may have received. But most important to recognize is that teaching has nothing whatsoever to do with the pleasantly messy and exciting process of exploring the natural world—the process that is the heart of science and that children in some fortunate classrooms have the pleasure of experiencing today in school.

Exploration Instead of Explanation. All science depends on the use of our senses. (You remember the five senses—science depends on seeing, touching, smelling, hearing, and tasting.) The explorations that take place in the sandbox are identical in spirit to those that occur in the laboratory. (Gee, when it's wet, it's better for building! When it's sloppy wet, it makes better dribble ornaments; when it's damp wet, it packs better; when it's dry, it just crumbles.)

Of course, the level of abstract thinking of the practicing scientist is different from that of the young sandbox engineer, but the basic human impulse to fiddle around with something and wonder "Why?" or "What will happen if...?" is the same. Good teaching has begun to reflect this understanding of science; and the emphasis, especially for younger children, has shifted from frustrating recitals of poorly understood facts to actual explorations of the physical objects and events that generate scientific learning.

Core Area 1: Life Science

Life science is the study of things that are living or were once living. In the elementary grades, this area of study is as broad as a child's world, everything from ants to giant sequoias is up for grabs, and—as in all the areas of science study—for younger children, the emphasis is on the grabbing. The reason for this is simple. Physical exploration lays the intellectual groundwork for all higher science learning. The desire to satisfy one's curiosity and the skills required to reach this satisfaction will always serve the goals of science. Children who spend their science time doing science instead of memorizing it will come out way ahead.

Nowhere else has this been more dramatically illustrated than within the field of biology. College students in the late 1950s and early 1960s had to unlearn much of their textbook high school and college biology when the discovery of the role of DNA and RNA revolutionized the life sciences. Much of today's scientific dogma will just as surely be revised or rewritten.

Living and Nonliving Things. Categorization—the ability to sort information into coherent and understandable units such as the distinction between living and nonliving things—is essential to science and a favorite activity for children. It becomes crucial in the later elementary years. Making definitions and distinctions sharpens intellectual skills. What is alive and what isn't alive? Is a fossil a living thing because it used to be living? What about the woody interior of a tree trunk, or a board, or paper; are these alive? The study of the life sciences often begins with classroom deliberations on this question of what is to be categorized as living.

Microscopic Life. Can something so small be alive? A powerful magnifying glass or a low power microscope opens up a world of plants and animals so small that they are imperceptible—until you look! A drop of pond water, a fish tank, or the water from a flower vase can open a universe of speculation. What are those wiggly things? What do they eat? Do they eat at all?

Rotifers, amoebas, and hydras are among the creatures that flourish just below the threshold of our vision, along with jungles of blue-green algae. Algae are simple, primitive plants. When they grow densely, they form stringy clumps big enough to be pronounced gross by most people because of their less-than-appealing, slimy look. Under magnification, however, they exhibit their lovely symmetry and color.

SPACE TO LEARN

SCORE! gives children space to learn. Not only can they raise their hand and get our immediate attention, but if they want us to back off so they can work on their lessons, we can do that too. It's great when that happens with their learning at home, too.

THE SCIENTIFIC METHOD
PART ONE

Here's a version of the Scientific Method that is fun and clear for parents to share with their children. The first three (out of six) points appear below; the next sidebar contains the other three.

Think of an Idea: The first thing you need to do is think of an idea. It may be something you want to explain or do in an experiment or something you just want to study. The best way to get started is to adapt an existing experiment in a way that's unique to you. Ask a question that needs an experiment to get an answer.

Research Your Topic: Find out what's already known about the topic. See what you can add to the general body of knowledge. It's a good idea to take some notes.

Plan Your Experiment: This part of the Scientific Method is called the *procedure*. You make a game plan of when, where, how, what, and why you're going to do what it is that you're going to do and what you need to do it.

Animal Study. Insects, such as butterflies or mealworms, or small amphibians like frogs, make good subjects for science study because they are easily kept (equally important in classrooms and homes) and have a short life span, which enables us to see them mature.

Like most insects, the butterfly transforms several times during its life cycle. It hatches from its egg as the larva (the caterpillar) changes into the pupa (hidden away in its cocoon), then finally becomes the familiar adult. Being able to observe birth, growth, change, and death establishes a comparative base for the time when human growth and development are studied in later grades.

Third and fourth graders aren't the only ones who profit from spending time with insects like this. Much of the exploratory work done in modern genetics uses the fruit fly, an insect whose life span is measured in weeks and that anyone who has ever accidentally left a banana out has encountered. Geneticist Dr. Michael Rose began his extensive study of aging by wondering what would happen if he saved in his lab only the eggs of the fruit flies that lived the longest. He bred generation after generation of these long-lived flies. Each time he allowed only the eggs of the oldest flies to survive and grow into the next generation. In twenty years, he had carefully bred 500 generations of these little flies and doubled their life span.

The task of analyzing the actual genetic mechanisms involved in longevity are complex and require a great deal of specialized knowledge and equipment, but it all began with a simple question and some very common insects (who gave their lives, so to speak, to science).

Once patterns of observation are established, children have the intellectual tools to think about and investigate such things as the differences among animals. How is a dog's or cat's life cycle different from a butterfly's? Which insects eat plant matter and which insects eat animal matter? Can insects taste things? All the questions that children ask are valid. Not all of them are answerable. Good science teaching replaces a dismissive "we don't know" with an encouraging "maybe you'll find out."

Plant Study. Plants make good subjects for investigation because most of them respond very quickly to changes in their environment. The addition of something beneficial to their soil quickly produces a flourishing plant, while the addition of something detrimental results in obvious symptoms of unease or disease. They are also satisfyingly, and very visibly, sensitive to the larger environment. When you vary such elements as temperature, available sunlight, or water supply, the visible results are generally quick and straightforward.

Plants also provide a convenient way to study growth and development. Seeds are readily available through catalogs, from plant nurseries, feed and grain stores, or health food stores. Health food stores often sell seeds for salad sprouting such as mung beans or wheat berries, and these germinate very quickly. When a school system has coordinated years of science study (or when you do science projects at home), plants are useful for demonstrating simple genetics. For instance, sowing pink and blue morning glories one year often produces some seed that will grow into plants producing a rich purple blossom during the next growing season.

The mechanisms of genetics are broadly understood, but the intricacies of how and why are still being discovered. In the elementary years, complex explanations of the process aren't necessary. Simple observations of the transmission of characteristics are enough to stimulate children's curiosity and raise the questions that will be studied later.

THE SCIENTIFIC METHOD PART TWO

The Scientific Method continues. After your child has (1) thought of an idea, (2) researched a topic, and (3) planned an experiment, then:

Do Your Experiment: Party time! This is where you get right down to the nitty gritty of doing the experiment, collection of the data, rolling up your sleeves, and diving in to the science fun. Remember to always follow safety rules!

Collect and Record Data: This is all the information that you're seeking. You'll include all your information in charts, data tables, lab notes, and records of observations.

Come to a Conclusion: Compile the data that you've collected, evaluate the results, answer the question you asked at the beginning, write a law describing what you observed, then . . . collect your Nobel Prize!

—The Wild Goose Co.

Making the Grade

NO OVERKILL

Anything that we encounter at home, we try to turn into a learning experience, but we don't go in for overkill. An example would be going outside and picking up leaves and how to make a picture with them. We try to enhance the creative side of our kids. We also have a computer with lots of software, everything from a drawing program to science, reading, writing, arithmetic. Anything where our kids can learn something and get something more out of it, my husband and I are all for it.

Skeletons and Bones. The skeleton, our bony framework, always fascinates children. It is the most obvious indication of the busy world inside our skin. The lumps and angles of bones are clearly visible just beneath the surface, and a little prodding here and there gives us access to most of our own skeletal structure.

Of course, any time we eat chicken, fish, chops, or ribs, we come into contact with the skeletons of other creatures. Bones tell a detailed story about the kind of creature they come from, about the individual creature, and about what kind of role the bones have in the creature's body.

A bone's function determines its shape and internal structure. The bones of birds are relatively hollow; they have to be as light as possible while still supporting the bird's muscles. A cow's thigh bone, which supports the cow's considerable weight, on the other hand, has a relatively greater massiveness than a bat's. Comparing the neck bones of a giraffe and a human being reveals a great deal about both animals. Finding bones and guessing what they are and what kind of animal they come from is a puzzle that fascinates everyone from 3rd and 4th graders to forensic pathologists.

Essentials of Life. The study of plants and animals and how they live leads to a simple generalization about living organisms; they all share certain common, essential life processes. These essentials are respiration (breathing), nutrition (eating), elimination (getting rid of what the body doesn't use), and reproduction (making more of your kind). These four needs are the same as those needed by life forms that have been recently discovered in the abysmal depths of the sea and deep within the seemingly solid rock of the earth's crust as they are by humans. Not all life forms breathe, eat, excrete, or reproduce in the same way or even with the same materials, but all living things perform these functions.

Web of Life. Humans, plants, and animals are interdependent. Some of the relationships among living things are clear and easy to observe. Although we don't always think of ourselves as being in beneficial relationships with insects, we are. Bees, for instance, are necessary to pollinate the feed crops grown by farmers to support the animals who feed the farmers (and the rest of us). Everywhere you look in the living world you will find relationships among living things.

Sometimes we discover important relationships only when something goes wrong. For instance, some use of chemical fertilizers too close to fresh water can cause a growth of vegetation that cuts off the supply of oxygen to fish, resulting in a source of food being decreased or eliminated entirely. Or it may be that we have imported a plant or animal for some purpose only to discover that it interferes with relationships that we have come to depend on. The kudzu vine and the gypsy moth are examples of such unanticipated results. Each time something like that happens, humans get another lesson in how important it is to know as much as possible about the natural world, since whatever we do in it affects it!

In later grades, students will explore in greater depth more sophisticated ways of looking at these relationships such as predator/prey, parasite/host, and consumer/producer. In the elementary grades, the concept of interrelationships is usually introduced with broad and concrete examples based on common life experiences.

Core Area 2: Physical Science

The story of Sir Isaac Newton and that famous falling apple may or may not be literally true. But true or not, it hits us directly on the head with this simple truth about the learning, teaching, and doing of science: *Physical exploration of the world is where it all begins* (whether you do it under an apple tree, in a classroom, or from the instrumentation room of a particle accelerator).

Science grows and changes much too fast for students to spend time memorizing today's facts, for many of these will be outdated or superseded almost before the textbook ink is dry. The field of nanotribology, for instance, didn't even exist

PETS AND SCIENCE

Getting to know and care for animals—from goldfish to gerbils to golden retrievers—is a great kind of hands-on biology lesson for children. They can learn firsthand about a pet's life cycle, intelligence and behavior, feeding and grooming habits, adaptation, and reproduction.

Before choosing a pet, have your child read about different animals, birds, fish, and other creatures and the care each requires. Be clear about who will be responsible for feeding, exercising (regular walking, if necessary), and clean up (the aquarium, cage, litter box . . .). Having a pet is a great science learning experience, but parents just might end up with much of the responsibility. Be prepared for a mixture of rewarding learning experiences, some heartwarming times, and a lot of work.

SMALL VICTORIES

Parents should build a child's confidence in the home so that when they're in the competitive world, they can be competitive and excel. If parents give their children small victories and tastes of success in the home, then children will be able to recognize those victories in school and keep working hard to reach new levels of achievement. Focus on one small area of learning and say to your child, "Wow, you really did a great job; let's go get some ice cream." Confidence builds on those small, sometimes insignificant moments. But their importance can't be overestimated.

THE WHY FILES

The National Institute for Science Education has a nifty Web site with topics lifted from the headlines. Questions like, "Is there life on Mars?" are addressed in fun, readable essays accompanied by charts and illustrations. Messaging boards and a great science image library make this a site worth exploring with your child: http://whyfiles.news.wisc.edu

before 1990 when Dr. Jacqueline Krim coined the term to describe the study of friction on the atomic level. Today, nanotribology is an entire field of study with researchers, textbooks, journals, and potential practical applications worth billions of dollars.

Elementary-level physical science covers the areas that in higher grades carry the names of *physics* and *chemistry*. For students in grades three and four, the task is to gain fundamental inquiry skills and a wealth of concrete experiences so that they will be adequately prepared for later theoretical work.

Properties of Matter. Picking things out of the blurred background of the everyday for special scrutiny is a starting point for much of science. And *things* are at the heart of this part of physical science. It begins with the study of the materials that we encounter all around us.

Learning about common materials—where they come from and what their properties are—takes place in many ways. Discussions and explorations can begin with wondering whether something is found naturally or is manufactured, whether something occurs as a material all by itself or is a combination of other materials, or whether it is nonliving or the product of a living creature.

In these grades, the properties of water are frequently used as an introduction to the different possible physical states of matter in the child's world. Water changes its physical state over a relatively narrow temperature range allowing solid, liquid, and vapor forms to be created and studied in simple experiments. Observing these changes of physical state and experimenting with them builds classification and inquiry skills as well as a solid science vocabulary.

The next step moves these discussions into the world of experimentation. What floats and what doesn't? If it floats, was it once living like wood or are there nonliving things that float? Can it be scratched or does it scratch other things? Will a magnet stick to it? What happens when you fiddle around with two or more magnets? Does it burn?

Thinking of questions and finding ways to try to answer them is what experimentation is all about.

Forms of Energy. The question "Does it burn?" leads to an important aspect of physical science—heat. What is heat anyway? By taking the temperature of different things, by placing cold things next to hot things and seeing what happens, by experimenting with things that transfer heat and with things that keep heat in, and by noticing that things that give off light may also give off heat, children begin to explore the nature of energy.

Electricity, too, is a common topic in elementary science, where it is especially important to stick with physical experiences and to avoid complex terminology. Studying static electricity, experimentation with bulbs and batteries, and tinkering with simple circuits is delightful and instructive.

"Energy is conserved," is the summation of the First Law of Thermodynamics. At this level, students encounter the physical expression of this law when they talk about the different forms of energy that they know about and when they play with materials and machines that involve the transfer of energy. A windmill converts the energy of the wind into mechanical energy. If the mechanical energy is applied to a turbine, it is converted into electrical energy, which enters a house or school and is converted into the energy of light and heat by the filament of the light bulb.

Properties of Motion. Things move. How do they move? Do they move by themselves? Do they move when other things touch them? What kinds of forces make things move? When children are not in motion themselves, they are often involved with making other things move.

Whether it's sports or household activities, elementary-level students have endless opportunities to set things in motion. Classroom work often involves slightly more controlled experiences of the same kind. Making instruments whose strings vibrate, setting pendulums in motion, working with rubber bands, and manipulating magnets are all science

WE LOVE TINKERING

John R. Pierce, an electrical engineer with an enormous list of accomplishments both as a researcher at the Bell Laboratories, a science educator, and former head of the American Academy for the Advancement of Sciences, expressed it well: "When I was a boy, in the early days of broadcasting, I built crystal and electron tube radio receivers. I loved to tinker with them, even though I didn't fully understand them. Perhaps a sense of wonder and mystery contributed to my fascination." —from *Waves and Messages*, by John R. Pierce (Science Study series, Doubleday, 1956)

CAST DOUBTS!

Here's some great advice for parents when it comes to science education:

- Cut your kids some slack. Don't tell them they have to believe something like Newton's First Law just because it's the "right" way to look at things. There's no better way to turn kids off to learning.

- When you're talking about science concepts with kids, and the concepts don't jive with everyday life, encourage kids to be skeptical. That's what scientists do. Tell them *not* to believe anything unless they're convinced. But make it clear that you don't have to believe in something to understand it. This amounts to an end run around those kids who will claim they don't have to get something right on a test if they don't believe it.

- Use sentences like, "According to Newton's First Law, what should happen here?" That way, you make it clear that the purpose is to understand the concept and how it applies to a situation rather than to believe the concept.

- Show kids that even though it tends to contradict common sense, something like Newton's First Law helps predict a lot of things. In other words, it works. If it didn't work, we wouldn't use it.
    —The Wild Goose Co.

activities that help establish the idea that motion—the hows and whys of things moving—is a wonderful, and important, area for exploration of physical science.

Core Area 3: Earth and Space

Our life-sustaining and relatively comfortable environment is the product of the interaction among the:

- Hot, active bulk of our planet
- Cold, vast reaches of space
- Great radiating energy of our star, the sun

All the familiar landmarks, geographical features, and the meteorological phenomena of our physical environment are shaped by the interaction of these three elements.

Variations in Local Curricula. The eastern coast of North America is regularly visited by the great seasonal storms known as hurricanes, the western coast knows volcanism and earthquakes firsthand, and our continental interior periodically suffers the weather extremes that produce droughts, floods, and tornadoes. Since the regions of North America suffer different examples of the more severe effects of our planet's dynamic processes, you may find that the emphasis in your school's earth science lessons differs from this general presentation. Since children are legitimately concerned with the events that directly affect them, it makes sense to focus their learning around the particular phenomena that directly affect their lives.

Forces that Shape Our Planet. In most areas of science, direct physical experience is the best place to begin. In this core area, however, direct physical experience is not always possible (or desirable). The nature of our planet, the direct effect that its behaviors have on our lives, and commonly accepted knowledge that is the basis for everything from the television weather to classroom discussions mean that a certain amount of teaching and learning will have to be based on our understanding of the most current general theories and on models of geological and meteorological processes.

Until quite recently, most people believed that the surface of Earth, while not always calm, was a fairly stable place. Continents were assumed to have been always more or less the same shape and size and always located pretty much where they are today. In the last few decades, we have realized that this stability is definitely not the case! Our planetary surface has turned out to be more like the skin on the surface of a hot, thick pudding that never completely cools.

Earth's continents are actually plates of cooler solidified material that float on the surface of the earth's more molten mantle layer. Material from deep within constantly wells up along cracks (hidden in the depths of the sea) between enormous continental plates and slowly pushes them apart as new material is added. The movement of our continental plates that this process causes is extraordinarily slow. In North America, we are creeping westward at a pace that can be measured in just centimeters a year. To earth scientists, however, a year is only a wink in time. They see the movements in terms of hundreds of thousands and millions of years. Over the span of geologic time, the motion has been dramatic and has had powerful results.

The resistance that the plates encounter as they push against one another causes the buckling and wrinkling that causes mountain chains to grow. One plate may also override another, pushing it down and under into the deeper regions of the mantle. The pressure, cracking, and sliding that this overriding causes along the edges results in earthquakes and also, scientists now think, much of the earth's volcanic activity.

Forces that Alter Our Planet. Even as continental forces are pushing mountain ranges and volcanic mountains up, other forces are at work wearing them down. Erosion is the name given to this second process. The constant motion of our atmosphere and the constant action of our watery surface environment are both incredibly slow, but amazingly powerful agents of change. The force of the wind and the action of falling rain and running water are the most obvious causes of erosion.

DON'T GIVE UP

Parents need to keep making suggestions to their children. My immediate response to my parents' suggestions was, "No, I don't want to do this." I probably thought all along it was a good idea, but they kept suggesting, and I eventually went along and did things that I later realized were really fun and good for me. So, parents, don't give up. Give kids ideas constantly. Some day, they just might take your ideas and go with them!

NOBODY'S PERFECT

In learning, we have to teach children that we're always going to make mistakes. When we don't get something right on the first try, you're proving what you already know to yourself. When you learn, you may not get it right for awhile, but you continue to strive. In the process, you'll show yourself what you need to know.

LET'S STAY IN TOUCH

To prepare America for the 21st century, we must harness the powerful forces of science and technology to benefit all Americans.

This is the first State of the Union carried live over the Internet. But we have only begun to spread the benefits of a technology revolution that should be the modern birthright of every citizen.

Our effort to connect every classroom is just the beginning. Now, we should connect every hospital to the Internet, so doctors can instantly share data about their patients with the best specialists in the field. And I challenge the private sector to start by connecting every children's hospital as soon as possible, so that a child in bed can stay in touch with school, family and friends. A sick child need no longer be a child alone.
—from the 1997 State of the Union Address, President Clinton

Another eroding force is the action of water as it changes state from liquid to solid. As a liquid, it seeps into rock at the surface, expands as it freezes, and then splits it. As snow, it forms the centuries-deep accumulations that become glaciers. Glaciers, with their hundreds and thousands of feet of heavy ice, can scrub towering mountains into gentle hills.

Water with enough heat changes into vapor. Ground water also percolates deep below the surface as a liquid and then is changed to steam by the interior heat. It can force rock apart or even dissolve it.

Characteristics of Our Planet's Materials. It is with the evidence of the work of erosion that we can bring physical exploration back into the classroom. Rocks, soils, and sand are everywhere and they are perfect objects for all of the skill-building tasks appropriate to the later elementary grades. Rocks can be weighed, sorted, classified, and used in simple experiments.

Rocks come in what seems like a bewildering variety, but they can be sorted into three main categories. Igneous rocks are formed directly from the molten material in the earth's mantle. (Their name comes from the Greek word for fire, just like the word *ignite*.) Sedimentary rocks are formed as layer upon layer of sand, silt, and clay (sediment) settle out of the earth's rivers and seas, where time and pressure compress them into rock. The third kind of rock is rock whose form has been changed. (Its name, *metamorphic*, comes from the Greek *meta* for change and *morphe* for form.) As the earth's crust is pushed and folded under by the movement of the continental plates, layers of sedimentary rock that were once on the surface are squashed and heated. The loose, crumbly sedimentary layers are compressed and melted together to form metamorphic rock. Igneous rocks that are folded back under, then heated and compressed also transform into metamorphic rocks.

Most of us think of sand as the anonymous loose, fine material of beaches and sandcastles. Closer examination (a magnifying glass will do) reveals a fascinating material that is rich in clues to the earth's surface history. Sands can be read in two ways.

First, students can look at what kinds of materials have gone to make up the sand. On some Hawaiian beaches, for instance, minute pieces of basaltic glass give the sand an extraordinary black color. This sand comes from the busy volcanoes that have formed those islands. The glistening white beaches of the Florida keys tell a completely different story. There the sands are largely composed of the shells and fragments of shells of countless small sea creatures. The rivers and lake shores of northern central and eastern North America have sands that are a jumble of different minerals–the legacy of the glaciers that scraped and abraded the region over tens of thousands of years during the ice ages.

The second story that sands can tell involves looking at some other properties. The surface of the grains provides clues as to where and how the sand was formed. Grains with rounded, cloudy surfaces are usually formed by the buffeting action of wind and are characteristic of desert sands. Water-deposited sand is often less abraded and appears more jagged. Water that carries sand drops out its sand particles by weight, with the heavier bits falling to the bottom first. For this reason, water-deposited sands tend to have grains that are similar in size. Desert sands usually have much greater variation.

Unlike sand, soil is a composite material. Examination reveals that soil contains both nonliving matter (grains of sand and small rocks) and living matter (dead or decaying plant and animal material, bits of twigs, leaves, pieces of insects, and worm castings). Soils are as different as the regions in which they are found and provide scientists—young and old—great subjects for close study.

Water Cycle. Life could not exist without water. Even the recently discovered microbes that dwell in the seemingly solid rock miles below the earth's surface depend on the presence of water for their lives. Beyond our need for the basics of life, the essential processes, our familiar

WHAT WOULD YOU DO?

What would you do if you learned that your child was doing poorly in some subject at school? Parents of unsuccessful students try to handle the problem themselves, at home.... Schoolwork then becomes an area of contention in the household, which only interferes with the child's chances of improving.

Parents of successful students, in contrast, mobilize the school on their child's behalf—they "work the system." When they discover that their child is having a problem with a subject or teacher, they begin by phoning the school and setting up an appointment to meet with the child's teacher, guidance counselor, or principal. They express their concern and offer their assistance in solving the problem. If the school suggests certain home exercises that require the parents' participation, parents of successful students cooperate. But they make it clear that they see their role as helping the school to better serve their child, rather than solving the problem themselves.

—from *Beyond the Classroom*, Laurence Steinberg, Ph.D. (Simon & Schuster, 1996)

environment is completely bound up with what is called the *water cycle*.

The cycle itself is relatively simple. Water is changed from its liquid form to its gaseous form by increases in temperature at the earth's surface. The vapor rises until higher altitudes cool it enough to return it to its liquid (or if it gets cold enough, solid) state. Now heavier, it falls or floats back to the earth. If it falls on land, it flows downhill until it is either turned back into water vapor along the way (through evaporation) or it reaches the oceans. As water passes through this cycle, it nourishes crops, fills reservoirs, carves out deep canyons, fills the oceans, and sustains life.

Our Relationship to the Sun and Solar System. The earth is one part of an enormous system of planetary bodies, planetary bits and satellites (natural ones and manufactured ones as well), and debris. All move in orbit around a central star, which we call the sun. Scientists believe that this solar system was formed several billions of years ago and, like all other parts of our known universe, is still in the process of change.

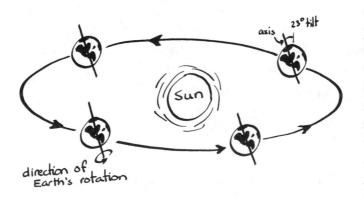

Our solar system is in constant motion. Our planet turns around a central axis once every twenty-four hours (plus a little more) and this spinning in relation to the sun gives us the day and night cycle. At the same time we are moving in an orbit around the sun that takes approximately 365.25 days to complete. (That extra quarter day adds up to the one day we add to our calendar every four years.) During the time of our annual orbit, the tip of our axis brings first the bottom and then the top of our planet slightly closer to the sun. This is what causes our seasons.

The Sun as a Source of Light and Heat. You could think of our sun as an enormous furnace. Staggering, colossal, and unimaginable are words that don't begin to describe the magnitude of the forces at work deep in the core of our star. The sun broadcasts an enormous amount of energy into the area of space surrounding it. We receive only a small portion of the sun's radiation and, for children, only a small portion of this is observable.

Even though the amount of heat and light energy that falls on the surface of our planet is small in relation to the sun's total output, that amount is essential for life, and it is the engine that drives the forces of our oceans and atmosphere. The movement of the winds, the deep and not fully understood currents of the oceans, the process by which plants make food, and the water cycle are all powered by solar radiation. Whether you pick grains of sand, worn from distant mountains, out of your picnic sandwich, or head for cover as a hurricane approaches, or munch on a piece of broccoli, you are experiencing the work of our sun.

Core Area 4: Technology

You could say that the difference between science and technology is a difference of purpose. The purpose of technology is generally considered to be the use of tools and materials and scientific knowledge to solve human problems, whereas the purpose of science is generally considered to be the study of all aspects of the natural world. However, even in the adult world, the distinction between science and technology is not always clear. A computer scientist might be concerned only with the wildest kinds of mathematical theory or she might be concerned with the nuts and bolts, like connectors and wires of network interconnections. More than likely, she is working with both at the same time.

IT'S DIZZYING!

If you have a spare moment, try this little mind game. Lie on the floor with your feet pointing west. Imagine yourself hurtling westward as our globe spins at over 1,000 miles per hour. Once you have that picture in mind, imagine your spinning self and the globe hurtling counterclockwise around the sun at almost 68,000 miles per hour. Of course, the whole solar system itself is spinning along on the outer reaches of an arm of a spiral galaxy, and that galaxy itself is in motion . . . better take a break!

CYBERSCHOOL MAGAZINE

Go to this site and you'll be hit with a variety of educational information. The articles here are fun and different and slightly disorganized, but the real prize is the Surfin' Librarian page, with loads of links to museums, libraries, maps, and education sites on the Web. Check out this cool tool at: http://www.infoshare.ca/csm/index.htm

For elementary and middle school students, the distinction is worth knowing; but since much of the science work in these years is concerned with physical exploration using tools, machines, and the beginnings of scientific concepts, the distinction is not always important except as an introduction to how we put our knowledge to practical use.

Uses of Technology. Two good ways to begin helping children think about technology are by making distinctions between natural and human-made objects and by observing and discussing the ways in which we use machines to shape materials. A third and even better way is to have them work on solving actual problems with simple tools and materials and helping them understand how these simple machines work.

Basic Computer Skills. Many schools place computer instruction in the science curriculum. Practical learning includes simple operation skills and, in some areas, an introduction to keyboarding. Children at this level should also be aware that computers, in spite of the razzle-dazzle, are only machines. They are only as capable as the people who give them their instructions and feed them information.

Famous Inventors and Scientists. The autobiographies of the people whose creativity and persistence have pushed our technology ahead are an inspiring source of information for young scientists. They provide an instructive and (for those who like reading or being read to) relaxing way to gather information about the different and sometimes extraordinary ways in which creative thinking gets done.

Some inventions represent hours and hours of trial-and-error experimentation. Edison's finding the right material for the light bulb filament is an example of such persistence. Other inventions, like the crucial placement of the hole on the sewing machine's needle, for example, come to their creators in an intuitive dream after long periods of frustrating work.

FAMILY PROGRESS

We constantly brainstorm at home about how important the future is for our children, and it's all tied in with how well they're doing. We constantly mention their progress, and they like to hear how much they're accomplishing.

Simple Devices Solve Problems. Planning and making rubber band-powered vehicles, building indestructible egg containers, and constructing load-bearing bridges out of toothpicks are all ways that 3rd and 4th graders can gain experience both with the use of tools and materials and with their own creative, technological powers (and have a great time in the bargain).

Identifying Recyclable and Nonrecyclable Materials. We all benefit from technological advances and we all suffer from the consequences of poorly thought out technology. In the enthusiasm and rush to develop atomic energy into a cheap source of power, for instance, little thought was given to the inevitable waste byproducts and their harmful effects on the environment.

Activities like making paper, building a compost heap, or building a solar-powered toy, all draw upon the various core areas of the science curriculum to explore the use of environmentally less-destructive materials. Learning about the qualities of materials that allow them to be reused is a first step in raising a generation of adults who can think responsibly about all aspects of technological development.

Core Area 5: Health

Thinking about our health requires thinking about our bodies and our environment. Although health is an aspect of science, how schools integrate health education into the elementary curriculum varies. In some school systems, for instance, health programs are defined and taught separately, while in others health topics are covered not as a separate science core area but as a part of other core areas, such as life science.

Health teaching often has less experimentation and exploration than other areas of science. No one wants hands-on experiences with poison ivy! Some health issues make it necessary to provide information and lay down rules. This is even more true where the hazards are unseen, like viruses or the lead in soil and paint, where the risks are great.

DON'T GET SCARED

This is one educational company's philosophy about science education: Scientists spend their lives asking WHY this or that happens. Most people assume that a good scientist will be able to answer a few WHY questions for them.

"Why do things fall to Earth?" Everyone knows it's because of gravity. "Well, what is gravity?" Well, it's the thing that makes stuff fall to earth. Duh! You see, the answer isn't really an answer at all, it just gives a name to something. Now a physicist will give you a different answer. She will talk about a force that acts between all things, and she'll write down a formula that describes how the force behaves. But, why does this force exist?

If you're looking for the "ultimate" answer to your WHY questions, science is the wrong place! Science doesn't give ultimate answers. Try your favorite religion or inspirational source. Why do we bring all this up? Because we believe that if kids understood some of the limitations of science, they may not be so scared of it and may be willing to tackle those limitations head-on to find even more.
—The Wild Goose Co.

BLUE BLOOD

This observation is just a place to begin a discussion. Venous blood returning to the heart without the oxygen it has carried out to the body's cells is darker in color, but the blue is only how the darker blood appears through the wall of the vein and layer of skin.

TALK THE TALK

As a single parent, I have a tendency to talk with my child as another adult. We talk about everything. We're very open with each other. You talk about things and you say things that they might not understand, and they ask you what something means—that's all a big part of education at home.

Inside the Human Body. Children being children, they often encounter one of the principle elements of their circulatory system, blood. It's red, tastes salty, and when exposed to air, dries to a brownish crust. Beginning with these facts, they can go on to learning a little about that extraordinary muscle, the heart. Although the heart is not visible, its action can be easily detected with a paper towel tube or stethoscope or with fingertips placed on the wrist. The observation that blood appears red in a wound, but the visible veins are blue can lead to a discussion of the complete circuit blood makes in the circulatory system and its connection to the respiratory system.

Some people have said that the skin should be considered an organ all by itself. Among its many tasks, it acts as a barrier to harmful organisms and substances, contains thousands of sensors, and regulates body temperature. Skin varies from person to person in color and texture. It is even different on different parts of the body.

An important part of health teaching is helping children to deal with the hazards that they will encounter throughout life. This is an area in which there is less possibility of hands-on work, but in which communication is vital. All children need to be taught to exercise caution about a number of things in their environment. Poison ivy is an example of a hazard that can be recognized. Ultraviolet radiation, on the other hand, cannot even be seen. This kind of radiation needs to be discussed because of the sun's cumulative effect on human skin and the consequences of this damage in later life.

Human Diseases. Learning about the human body can lead directly to learning about the organisms that cause disease and how the body defends against them. The skin, the digestive system, and the immune system all act to protect us. In situations in which they are not sufficient, we have learned to use substances like vaccines to build a defensive system for ourselves.

Some diseases are of short duration and not very serious, like the common cold; and some may be fairly short yet severe, like influenza. Others are of longer duration—tuberculosis, for example. Chronic diseases affect the patient for much longer, usually for life. Diabetes and cerebral palsy are two examples. The first is believed to be the result of a malfunctioning organ system, the second is believed to be the result of birth injury.

Chronic diseases are not usually communicable. You can't catch diabetes from another person. Other diseases are contagious. They are caused by microbes that are spread from person to person. Children should know that there is a lot that they can do to maintain good health and avoid contagious disease. Personal hygiene is always the starting point. The goal is to avoid the agents of infection in the first place.

Some kinds of essential health education are specific to particular regions of North America. Learning about the ticks that carry Rocky Mountain spotted fever and Lyme disease and how to minimize one's exposure are vital in areas where these diseases are a risk. Rabies is another example of how education about how to avoid infection is extremely important.

Beneficial and Harmful Substances. Children need to learn about what is good for our bodies and what is not. Proper nutrition is essential for good health and the prevention of disease. Adequate amounts of good food plus the necessary vitamins and minerals not only ensure growth and energy, but provide the body with the necessary elements to fight off infection, if it does occur.

Children of this age are ready to comprehend all the fine print on the food labels, but the list of principle ingredients is a good place to begin. If sugar or a sugar substitute ranks toward the top, they should beware or, at least, be aware.

There are a number of substances that do not belong in the human diet—drugs, alcohol, and tobacco. Most schools make an effort to educate their students about the harm these can do to the body's different systems.

ACTIVELY INTERESTED

If you have children, it's your responsibility to raise your kids. You send them to school, you pick a school for them to go to that you have looked into, you go in and walk around, you sit in on the classrooms, you talk to the principal, you find out the school's philosophy—if you're not going to take an active interest in your children, how can you expect anyone else to?

A FAST-TALKING TOWN

We must build the second generation of the Internet so our leading universities and national laboratories can communicate at speeds 1,000 times faster than today, to develop new medical treatments, new sources of energy, and new ways of working together.

But we cannot stop there. As the Internet becomes our new town square, a computer in every home—a teacher of all subjects, a connection to all cultures—this will no longer be a dream, but a necessity. And over the next decade, that must be our goal.
—from the 1997 State of the Union Address, President Clinton

ENJOY IT

For students in the early grades, the emphasis should overwhelmingly be on gaining experience with natural and social phenomena and on enjoying science.
—from *BENCHMARKS for Science Literacy*, American Association for the Advancement of Science, Project 2061

GOOD LEARNING

My husband and I fill in for each other a lot with the children's education at home. He travels and is out of town a lot, so even though I'm very tired and have to work 12-hour nursing shifts oftentimes, we both make a lot of effort to make every interaction with our children a learning experience: cooking, cleaning, reading signs and explaining them—everything is a good learning experience.

Core Area 6: Inquiry Skills

All of the topic core areas of science draw upon a basic set of investigative skills. These skills, in their simplest forms, are part of our basic intellectual equipment as curious human beings. The beginning skills that are outlined below are refined and practiced in the elementary years and, if encouraged, grow into the more sophisticated analytic skills needed in high school and college science.

Observation and Description. These skills involve four basic elements:

- Learning appropriate vocabulary for describing the characteristics of objects such as size, shape, weight, temperature, hardness, smell, texture, and color
- Learning appropriate vocabulary for describing such characteristics of events as speed, frequency, repetitiveness, and duration
- Learning to compare and contrast similarities and differences
- Sorting and classifying using many different categories

Planning Investigations. Doing science means purposefully searching for answers to questions. Children in these years begin to learn skills to do that by:

- Planning simple experiments with familiar (and nonhazardous) materials, trying them out, and discussing the results
- Considering whether or not something can be investigated using direct observation
- Beginning to use multiple lines of investigation to solve problems
- Planning and building simple machines to solve technological problems

Tool Use and Measurement. To carry out any investigation or observation, scientists depend upon an ability to quantify; that means measuring accurately. In grades three and four, students:

- Are introduced to measurement systems
- Practice measurement skills using tools such as thermometers, balances, rulers, and tape measures

• Use observation tools that change the scale of investigation such as microscopes, magnifying glasses, and binoculars

Record Keeping. Making notes and communicating what one learns is central to learning about our world as well as solving technological problems. This key skill is developed through:

• Keeping records of experiments and projects
• Using notes, charts, graphs, and illustrations to communicate findings

Building on Blocks of the Concrete

One final, and very concrete, word on the importance of physical experiences in science education. What children do in a hands-on way in these early years lasts a lifetime. When an elementary student mixes dilute food coloring to see what happens and notices all the possible intensities and gradations of color, an image is established that will be recalled later, in high school, college, or at work, when it's necessary to visualize the spread of the entire electromagnetic spectrum. When a child stirs up tap water and olive oil and watches the result, a mental building block is put in place that will support and inform a high school biology discussion of the movement of lipoproteins within the watery interior of a cell. Likewise, doing the Learning Adventure activities with your child will give her a lifetime of enjoyable physical science references each of these experiences fleshes out the words of science and lays a foundation for future discovery.

A PLACE TO SUCCEED

Not only does *SCORE!* give kids a place to make mistakes, we also give them a place to succeed. Many kids don't care about school. They'll get through school as if it's a social thing, and doing well isn't a priority. If they do well in school, they might not get recognized to the extent they are when they're at *SCORE!*. So we're a place where kids can do well and be recognized for their achievements. When they make three months of progress in science or another subject area, they get a big bronze ribbon and their name up on a mountain on the wall—and the whole Center knows that they've finished their goal. It's a really positive place and everyone congratulates them. A child can never get enough positive feedback like that.

What Can We Do at Home?

CHAPTER 12

Learning Adventures— 3rd Grade Language Arts

▶ AMAZING WORD MAZE MAKER

Your child probably receives a list of spelling and vocabulary words to learn each week. His homework is to learn the spelling and meaning of the 20 or so words on each weekly word list. Use this activity to make learning the words fun, as your child turns them into Word Maze Puzzles to challenge you and others in the family.

At a Glance

Grade/Subject: 3rd/Language Arts—Vocabulary
Skills: spelling and vocabulary practice
Materials: graph paper (1/4" or more)
pencil
weekly word list
dictionary (optional)
needle and thread (optional)
Time: 20–30 minutes each week

Getting Ready

Word search grids are commonly used in schools and are available in word puzzle books at the library and bookstore. Look at some together with your child or make up a word search puzzle using family names before you do the activity

```
L  I  N  D  S  A  Y  A  X
D  G  A  O  U  N  E  T  R
M  R  V  G  E  N  N  C  I
O  E  O  C  T  I  B  L  S
N  E  X  B  O  E  C  A  U
E  T  O  P  E  M  R  I  N
Y  I  A  L  E  R  L  R  N
T  N  R  C  A  N  T  I  Y
S  G  N  I  V  L  A  C  M
B  E  Y  H  T  A  C  E  Z
```

with spelling words from school. (Just use the steps below to create a Family Name Maze. Simply use a list of names instead of spelling words. Then challenge your child to find all the names you've put in the grid.)

Help your child follow the directions below to make his first word maze using his weekly spelling list. Soon he will be able to turn his weekly spelling word lists into Amazing Word Mazes on his own.

Step One

Fold a piece of graph paper in half so that it measures 8 1/2" by 5 1/2". Open it and write the first of the words from the spelling word list into a set of adjacent squares on the right side of the graph paper. Words can be written horizontally from left to right, vertically from top down, or at an angle from left to right (going up or going down).

Then write each of the other words into adjacent squares on the same side of the graph paper. Try to make words cross over one another so that a letter in one word is also a letter in another word.

Step Two

Number each word on the list of words. Then make up a clue for each word and write the clues on the left side of the folded graph paper. (A dictionary can give helpful ideas.) Write the number of the word and then its clue. Clues can be a synonym or antonym, a definition, a sentence with the word missing—anything you like. Here are four different clue examples for the word *greeting:*

Hello
Not a farewell
What is said when people meet
The letter began with a polite ____ .

Step Three

Check that all the words on the list are now placed on the grid and that you have made a clue for each one.

Step Four

Finally, fill in the empty boxes around the words using any letters you wish. You don't need to fill the whole page, just as much as you want. When your child finishes making a word maze, he can give it to a friend or family member to try using his clues to find the words he has hidden.

▶ COMMA CATCHER

By making a scrapbook of examples of five special uses of commas, your child can enjoy developing a solid consciousness of these everyday basics of comma use.

At a Glance

Grade/Subject: 3rd/Language Arts—Mechanics and Composition
Skills: using commas to separate in addresses, dates, letter greetings and closings, and direct address
Materials: material you collect from mail that comes to your house
scissors, paper, paste, or tape
colored pencils or markers
Time: 20–30 minutes

Getting Ready

Collect envelopes and cut off and save any parts of letters you receive that include any address, date, greeting, closing, or use of direct address. (Junk mail provides particularly rich resources for this activity.)

Step One

Talk with your child about how commas are needed in writing to help people understand addresses, dates, and direct address. Have him say what town and state he lives in.

BEING BAD CAN BE GOOD

One girl used to get a stomachache or a headache every time she did poorly. She'd want to stop her work immediately when it got hard. So we decided she could have one bad lesson where she HAD to get below 70 percent and she could still get *SCORE!* rewards: shoot a basket and try for *SCORE!* cards. At first she raised her hand and said, "Can I do my bad lesson now?" So, I'd say sure, and told her that she had to purposely get answers wrong to score low. This went on for about a month. Then she grew to just seeing if a lesson was hard, then letting that be her bad lesson.

In four months, we told her that if she got a bad lesson, she wouldn't get to shoot a basket, and she was okay with that. It took six months not to get upset if she did poorly, but her entire attitude changed towards learning with positive reinforcement. Her parents were very supportive and helped their daughter stick with the program.

REFERENCE LIBRARY

Mindscape's *Student Reference Library* combines writing and research resources for students, plus multimedia helps, into one CD: an encyclopedia, dictionary, thesaurus, manual of style, U.S. history guide, quotes, atlas, photos, maps, videos, animations, audio, and a Lycos search feature (hooking up with your Web browser) on the Internet. For younger students, parents and children can explore any subject together. Contact Mindscape at (800) 234-3088.

WHAT'S MORE

Punch the pages for your child to assemble in a notebook where he can continue finding examples to add to each section.

Give your child newspapers and magazines he can cut up to add to his collection.

Have your child write a letter to a relative or friend in which he uses these commas correctly. He might even write to tell about this project.

Point out how we make a little pause between the town and state to make clear that they are the names of two places. Say the date (day, month, year); then ask him where he heard pauses and why they were there.

Give him one of your mail samples and have him find the commas used in the addresses and dates.

Step Two

Talk about the other special places commas appear in the mail—in the greeting and the closing. Point out how these indicate a pause in how we would say those parts of the letter out loud. Talk about how commas are also used to separate the name of a person being directly spoken to. Of course, the greeting is a special example of direct address. If there is no other example in the letter, you can insert your name to show your child how direct address works.

Have your child write each of the five kinds of places for commas on the top of a piece of paper. Encourage him to use whatever words he wants for these headings as long as there is one each for:

- Commas in dates
- Commas in addresses
- Commas in greetings
- Commas in closings
- Commas in direct address

Step Three

Using scissors and paste or tape, your child can cut up the letters and envelopes to put as many examples as possible of each use of commas. Supply extra paper as needed. He can mark each example in color and decorate the pages as well.

▶ COMMERCIAL SUCCESS

Out of every hour of commercial television your family watches, you'll see about 16 minutes of commercial messages (sometimes it seems like more, doesn't it?). How often do you and your kids leave the room or change the channel during those times? Pretty often, you say? Well, here's another way for you to spend those commercial breaks that's fun and informative! The plan is to have your child make his own commercial to play during one of the real ones. And the product that he is going to advertise is a book that he has enjoyed reading recently and that he wants you, the viewer, to read.

At a Glance

Grade/Subject: 3rd/Language Arts—Listening, Speaking, Viewing, Literature
Skills: listening for meaning, speaking with a purpose, note taking
Materials: book your child chooses to read
television
paper and pencil
VCR (optional)
video camera (optional)
Time: several blocks of 10–15 minutes each; 30–45 minutes total

Getting Ready

Do a little research to find out what books your child has read recently so that you can make a suggestion if he can't come up with a title himself. Then think about what show you want to be watching when this special commercial break happens. It's probably best to start with a half-hour show this first time through.

If you tape the show ahead of time, you will give yourself and your child more control of the final production. That

GOOD READS

Try some of these titles for your child to read in preparation for the Commercial Success activity:

Babushka's Doll by Patricia Polacco
Alexander And The Terrible, Horrible, No Good, Very Bay Day by Judith Viorst
We're Going on a Bear Hunt by Michael Rosen

Contact Simon & Schuster Children's Publishing Division at (800) 223-2336 for a catalog of titles; on the Web, visit them at http://www.simonandschuster.com.

way you can stop and start the show to accommodate your child's contribution.

Give a little thought to how you might discuss the purpose and format of commercials with your child before he gets started planning his own.

Step One

Watch a few television commercials together and talk about what you have seen in those specific commercials and in TV commercials in general. Talk about the purpose of commercials—to sell, to convince viewers that what the ad is about is what the viewer wants.

Then talk about how commercials do their selling. Have your child cite examples of how specific ads you've seen have tried to convince viewers to want what they are pushing. The main ideas will probably have to do with the words they use (*new, now, special, fast, cheap, soft*), the images they show (beautiful scenery, red car going fast on a twisty road, cute babies, funny or cuddly animals), music, humor, and emotions such as fear or excitement.

Ask your child to make his own commercial to sell one of his favorite books. Give him one of your reading suggestions if need be. Talk about which TV program he would like to "sponsor" with his commercial. You could decide together, too, if you'd like.

Step Two

Help your child make the general plan for his commercial.

- During what show will you play his ad?
- How long will it be? (Check the length of time devoted to most of the show's commercials.)
- What will you use for the opening line, the attention grabber?
- What are the main points to make about the book (funny, everything you want to know about horses)?
- How will the commercial end (special one-time offer, Read Me!)?

WHAT'S MORE

Videotape your child's commercial if you have a camera.

———

Have the commercial be about a favorite or imaginary product rather than a book.

———

Involve siblings and friends as additional actors in the commercial.

———

Start the process by having your child write a script for the dialogue in the commercial. Or have him make a storyboard (a series of pictures—kind of like a cartoon strip—that shows the storyline of the commercial) before presenting the commercial.

• Are there any drawings or other props needed (show an illustration, the book jacket)?

Plan out some sentences together that cover the information above and have your child write up the ad.

Step Three

Do a dry run. Time the presentation to make sure it will fit between two show segments. Give your child feedback on his delivery. Is he persuasive? Did you hear enough about the book to decide that you might read it? How about his style of dress? What is best to wear to help push the product? Mention anything else you think could enhance the presentation.

Step Four

Prepare for the real thing by gathering all the needed materials or props near you as you sit down to watch the program. When the commercial comes on, you should use the mute button or turn the volume all the way down. Have your child's commercial "air" during the first break in the program. Then repeat it during each subsequent break. There's lots of room in this activity to adjust it to your child's level of fun and interest.

Step Five

Afterwards, discuss which presentation went best and why.

• How effective does your child think his ad was?
• Would it benefit from being "shown" during a different program?
• What difference does repetition of an ad make?

▶ Do You Remember?

When kids find a book that they like, they talk about it (given the chance). You can encourage them to remember their favorite parts, tell about their favorite character, and

CARROT ON A STICK

Television is more like a reward we use with our children. If they get done with their homework or chores, we respect their feelings and personalities and let them pick their own programs to watch. We watch TV with our children, too— and a lot of their shows are funny. We all laugh at them together and even imitate the commercials.

READ A LOT

It's important for children to see their parents reading a lot. My children have been early readers— my two boys both started reading in kindergarten. We live close to a library, so that's our neighborhood hangout. Sometimes I feel that my kids' school homework and assignments prevent them from reading as much as they should.

compare things in it to people, feelings, and events in their own experience. Here's a short activity that helps you get involved in the enjoyment your child can get from recalling a story.

At a Glance

Grade/Subject: 3rd/Language Arts—Reading
Skills: sentence meaning, reasoning, discussing reading material
Materials: books or passages from books that your child has read
pencil and paper or word processor
Time: 15–20 minutes

Getting Ready

If you are not already aware of some of the things your child has enjoyed reading, then start with a little research. You want to find a story or poem (try your home library or your child's school reading book) or an article or other nonfiction piece (from a magazine he likes) that he has read and enjoyed. Take a look at the material in order to use some actual sentences for this activity. Your child's teacher or a sibling may be able to help with identifying your child's reading matter.

Once you've identified a favorite or two, pick several sentences from each and write them—one to a line—on your paper or into your computer. Next, pick a word to leave out of each sentence. Then make an activity page containing each sentence with a blank line where the missing word goes. (Here's where a word processor makes life especially easy since you can use the copy and paste functions.)

If you pick the key words to skip over (like the subjects and verbs), you will find out more about how well your child understood and remembered what he has read. Write the missing words from each activity on a separate piece of paper. Your child can use these words to fill in the blanks.

WHAT'S MORE

Scramble the completed sentences up (you can cut up the paper that you were working on) and have your child put them back in the order that they happened in the story.

Take out more than one word from the longer sentences.

Put several distracters—words that won't fit any of the sentences—in the word list.

Make up sentences that will "test" your child's understanding of the reading material. Leave key words out of each so that your child can flex his comprehension muscles.

Step One

Any time it is convenient—like waiting in line at the store, driving in the car, or washing dishes together—strike up a conversation with your child about one of the reading selections you have chosen. Listen to your child talk about it and get a general feeling for his understanding and recollection of it.

Step Two

Pick a time to sit down together with the activity sheet you made. Tell your child that you have written some sentences from the material he likes to read, but they are each missing a word—and you bet he can figure out what word belongs in the missing spot! Mention that the missing words are available on a separate piece of paper that he can look at if he needs a clue. Let him read each sentence to himself and then write the missing word in each blank. Encourage him to do as many as he can before consulting the clue sheet.

Step Three

When he is finished, have him read each sentence out loud to you as a way of checking his own work; you usually can hear it when words in sentences don't make sense. Help him work out the correct answers if need be. And, of course, if he gets started and then keeps talking about the story, go for it!

Step Four

Invite him to prepare a similar set of Do You Remember? sentences for you to work on. Decide together whether he wants to pick sentences from reading that he likes or from a magazine or book you are reading.

▶ FIND-IT FITNESS

By the time we're adults, using a dictionary has become so routine that we forget that it involves a number of specific skills. The sooner your child views a dictionary as her helpful friend, the better off she'll be in all her schoolwork.

BE A SPORT

Girls and boys both get a lot of support from success in sports, and it's not just a "boy thing." This winter at Lake Tahoe, I went down a black diamond ski run and nearly killed myself, but there were all these 14-year-old girls and younger who were handling it in style and having a great time. Parents should encourage their kids to take up sports because it gives them so much confidence. Some sports offer opportunities for kids to succeed and be strong in something that can eventually give them confidence in academics.

Parents should identify the strengths in their children, and it may not be in sports. If academics or sports isn't their strength, then find out what is and tie that back in to the academics. You can't start out in gymnastics walking back and forth on the floor. Of course not. You work on it and get better in it. You can do the same thing with reading and math. It takes the practice and perseverance to move forward.

WORDS ON WHEELS

My daughter and I like to do spelling words in the morning on the way to school. We make it fun, it passes our half hour to school, and she gets 100% on her spelling tests. She's had fun doing it, and that's the best way we learn together.

Getting comfortable and speedy in using a dictionary is fun when you use it to play games.

Kids are familiar with sports and fitness training. In this activity, your child becomes a "dictionary athlete" by working out with words.

At a Glance

Grade/Subject: 3rd/Language Arts—Study Skills, Vocabulary
Skills: use guide words, pronunciation key, and multiple meanings list in a dictionary
Materials: dictionary
paper and pencil
stopwatch or wristwatch with a second hand
Time: 10–20 minutes for the initial "fitness workout" (plus Steps Three and Four sessions; play as long as you're both motivated)

Getting Ready

Look through your dictionary and familiarize yourself with how it handles pronunciation, guide words, and multiple meanings. Look at Step Three below and select a few words you could use with your child when you first do this activity. Obviously, you want to select words that will interest her and be new to her without being absurdly difficult.

Step One

Before beginning the game, review what your child knows about how to use the dictionary by playing "Can You Find This?" with her. Hand her the dictionary and give her each of the following challenges:

- Can you find a guide word (the bold words at the top of each page to indicate first and last words on the page)?
- Can you find the first word that begins with *c* ?
- Can you find the last guide word for words beginning with *f* ?
- Can you find instructions for pronouncing a word?
- Can you find a word with more than one definition?

You can make up as many such challenges as you wish, just to give your child practice in identifying guide words, pronunciations, and multiple meanings, as well as using alphabetizing. If she has trouble, talk through any problems. Discuss with her how the guide words are used. Have her practice using the pronunciation key. Talk about the different meanings given for some words and try using the word in a sentence for each meaning.

Step Two

Play fair; now it's her chance to make up challenges for you. Making up her own challenges will help her solidify her own grasp of these elements of dictionary use. When she has given you as many "Can You Find This?" challenges as she wants, you are ready for her Find-It Fitness workout.

Step Three

As her fitness coach, select a word from the dictionary that has more than one meaning and make up a sentence that illustrates the meaning you choose. Write the sentence, underline the word in it, hand it to her, and time how long it takes her to find the word in the dictionary. Have her write her time next to the sentence.

Her next task is to figure out which of the meanings provided for the word is the one you chose for your sentence. When she chooses, have her explain why she thinks she's right. Have her pronounce the word and read your sentence aloud.

Step Four

Repeat Step Three's Find-It activity as long as you can maintain interest. When she's feeling proficient, offer to switch roles and let her choose the word, make the sentence, and time you!

Obviously, the more you play, the speedier and more skilled she will become. Encourage her to see how much she can improve her dictionary use time. When words take her longer to find, talk together about the difficulties she has.

WHAT'S MORE

Play Dictionary, the group game in which one player selects a dictionary word, spells it, and pronounces it. Each of the rest of the players defines it as correctly as he or she can or makes up imaginary definitions—lots of laughs here, as well as good vocabulary and dictionary practice.

Play a more elaborate version of Dictionary by having all players write down their made-up dictionary entries for the word chosen. Meanwhile, the person who chose the word writes down the actual entry. Then the word chooser reads everyone's dictionary entry and players vote for which one they think is the real definition. Then another player becomes the word chooser.

FOOD FOR THOUGHT

At a seminar, a speaker expert in social work pointed out that kids who have a solid sense of themselves and are well adjusted to family life come from homes where the family meals are regular and definitely happen more than once a week. The more often the mealtimes are scheduled together with the family, the better. Children are not second priorities.

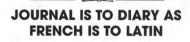

JOURNAL IS TO DIARY AS FRENCH IS TO LATIN

The French word for "day" is *jour*; in Latin it is *dies*. So . . . what does that have to do with keeping a journal or diary?

▶ GET THE JOURNAL HABIT

Around ages seven, eight, and nine, children usually love the idea of keeping a diary. Think of how many attractive blank diaries kids receive during the holiday season! Think of the enthusiasm of New Year's resolutions to write something down every day! Then think of how diary entries dwindle or die by the time February rolls round . . . The trick (and huge reward, of course) is to fill the diary, to have it to look back on—and, as kids soon discover, to be able to draw upon its content for school writing assignments all year long.

Journal writing is essentially a question of just developing a habit. Once the routine is established, keeping to it is easy, and its rewards are so valuable that it can become like distance running—those who do it can't do without it. If you can get your youngster started, he'll thank you for the rest of his life.

At a Glance

Grade/Subject: 3rd/Language Arts—Written Expression
Skills: writing personal narratives, descriptions, poetry, developing ideas, reflecting on feelings in writing
Materials: blank book (preferably one with lines) or word processing program
pocket-sized notepad
Time: 10–20 minutes regularly (daily, or three or four times a week)

Getting Ready

Observe for a week or so how your child uses his time. When might be a convenient time for him to do his journal writing? If you have a word processor and he can use it, consider whether he might prefer to keep his journal electronically instead of in a book. If your child will write in his own book, browse in a book or stationer's store to select a blank book or diary that will be visually appealing to him. Whether he writes in a computer file or in his own personal book, get him a pocket-sized notebook to use for quick jotting when he's away from the computer or his writing time, so that he can refer to it later when he writes his journal entry.

Think about whatever exposure to diaries and personal journals you may have had.
- Have you ever kept a journal?
- Have you read any journals or excerpts from journals?
- Would anyone care if Julius Caesar had not kept a journal? or Richard Nixon? or Anne Frank?
- What are some of the reasons people write in journals?

Consider keeping a journal yourself and buy yourself a blank book that pleases you—or plan to do it on your computer.

Step One

Introduce the idea of keeping a journal to your child. Talk with him about what a journal is, why people write in them, and what kinds of things a person can write about in a journal. Encourage him to realize that not only can *anyone* be a journal writer, but that his own private journal is a place where he can write about *anything* and *everything* he wants to!

If you have written in a journal (especially if you have anything you wrote when you were a child), read him something you wrote.

Present him with the special book you got for his journal (or set up a file with him for using the word processor).

Step Two

Take the next ten minutes or so for him to write an entry. (If you write in your journal at the same time, you will help him by example and companionship.) If he's stuck for an idea, suggest that he write about his thoughts and feelings about keeping a journal or about what you have been

"DON'T BOTHER ME—I'M WRITING."

Let those ten minutes expand if your child is engrossed in his writing. Take your cue from him as to when to stop (or pause) in writing to talk about the experience.

talking about, or simply about "what happened today." Tell him that he should never worry about what he is writing, but should just write and keep writing for ten minutes.

Step Three

After ten minutes, interrupt the writing to talk a little about it. How does it feel? Has writing given him any new ideas? Would he like to draw an illustration in his journal?

Brainstorm together a long list of all the possible things he could write about at some time in his journal. As you brainstorm, have him write the list on the inside back or front cover of his journal.

Brainstorm also all the different kinds of entries he could make—lists (10 best..., top 10 reasons for...), jokes, poems, narrative accounts of true events, stories he makes up, letters to himself or others, drawings, copying in something he's read or heard that he likes or objects to, pros and cons of doing something or making some choice, etc.

Step Four

Point out that what makes journal keeping work best is picking a regular time to do it and sticking to it. Decide together how often he wants to write and what time he'll schedule for it. Plan for a brief time—ten minutes every day won't seem like much to a kid. He may stretch his ten minutes when he really gets into something he wants to write about. And when he is not inspired, giving his journal just its allotted ten minutes won't kill him (or you).

Step Five

Support his every effort with all your heart—even when you don't like what he is writing. Encourage any indication you observe that he has written something he'd like to read to you or show you. But never pry. Stress that the journal is his own private writing place, which he need not show to others. Praise him for sticking with the journal when you are talking to friends and family. In short, keep him aware that you value what he is doing.

WHAT'S MORE

Try a Dialog Journal. This is a special, shared journal in which people take turns writing so that each entry is in response to what the other person wrote. Any combination will work—you and your child, sibling to sibling, friend to friend, etc.

Try a Family Favorite Quotes journal. Each member of the family enters anything that they feel is worth copying into a shared journal. The quotations can just be entered or entered and then commented on by the person who put it in and others that share the journal. This is a great keepsake!

Find out what a ship's log is. Then keep a log of a trip or vacation or of any activity during the day.

And if you can, try journal writing yourself. Then share some of what you write with him. Schedule some of your writing to coincide with his so that you can both be sitting there scribbling together—fellow diarists!

▶ How'd He Do It?

In this variation of the old Tom Swifty joke, you and your child play with seeing how many adverbs you can supply to the verbs of a sentence and how many places you can put them in the sentence. Word play games as simple as this build language flexibility that your child will find valuable throughout life in both speaking and writing. You might call this game "Howdy Dooit?"

At a Glance

Grade / Subject: 3rd/Language Arts—Grammar
Skills: identifying and using adverbs
Materials: none needed (paper and pencil are optional)
Time: 5–10 minutes (at any time, as often as you like)

Getting Ready

Just check with yourself that you understand that words that describe verbs are *adverbs*. Adverbs answer the questions *Where?, When?, Why?,* or *How?* about the action of a sentence. This game is named after "How?"

Step One

Explain how the game "How'd He Do It?" works: You will make up a very simple sentence, such as "We waited." Your child then thinks of as many ways of adding adverbs as she can—but all of them must answer the question *How?* For instance:

He waited patiently.
He waited angrily.
Patiently, he waited.
He waited sadly.

CLIMBING THE FAMILY TREE

Last year we did a family tree writing project. We got to call the kids' grandmas and find out where Great-Great So-and-So was from. We found out there were many similarities between my background and my husband's, and we were able to get out the atlas and see that these people were from Scotland and these people were from England . . . . It was a great lesson in geography and how far away people came from. The stories were so interesting coming from the grandparents. "Well, your great grandmother had fifteen kids!" We both come from large extended families, and finding out about them was something the kids will always remember.

SAMPLE SIMPLE SENTENCES

I waved.
Joel rowed the boat.
The little man ate his lunch.
The bird sang.
The snow fell.

Play "Wendy Dooit?" (Get it? *When'd He Do It?*) This is a version of the game in which all the adverbs answer the question *When?* (*yesterday, often, always*, etc.).

You can expand the game to call for groups of words that describe a verb such as *last night, during recess, with a pencil, before you came,* or *while I was driving.*

Play "Weirdy Dooit?" In this version of the game (You guessed it: *Where'd He Do It?*), all the adverbs must answer the question *Where?* (This version generally requires groups of words such as *at home, down the road, on the table, in the dark*, etc.)

Each of these adverbs describes how he waited. Your child's turn ends when she runs out of ideas or makes a mistake, such as, "He waited sad."

Together, count how many versions she can make. If you are using paper and pencil, jot down each adverb she uses for each sentence. If not, you can count a finger for each one and when she gets to ten, put a mark. In that way, when she's finished, it will be easy to total how many she makes.

Step Two

To reinforce her understanding of adverbs, ask your child to act out some of the sentences and ask questions about the sentences like, "How could you tell?"

If she uses adverbs that describe where or when, tell her that she is right, those are adverbs, just not ones that answer the question "*How'd He Do It?*"

Step Three

Take your turn. Remind your child that now it is her chance to catch you if you make a mistake. (Be ready also to answer her questions about your sentences and to do your share of acting out "how he did it.") Be sure to use *adjectives* occasionally so that she stays on her toes to catch your mistakes.

Step Four

Stop as soon as your child's interest begins to flag. Return to the game as a pleasurable way to pass time, for instance in the doctor's or dentist's waiting room or while doing dishes together.

Vary the rules to play in ways that work best for your child. For instance, you might take turns supplying the *how* adverb for the same sentence until one of you gets stuck or makes a mistake.

▶ IF IT SOUNDS LIKE A POEM . . .

. . . IT *IS* A POEM! A major element of all poetry is its sound—rhythm, rhyme, repetition, and words whose very sounds give us feelings and stir vivid images and memories. All children are capable of creating poetry. Hey, say it didn't sound like poetry when you first heard a little voice saying, "Mama, Mama" or "Dada, Dada."

No one says poetry has to be *great* poetry, but just making poems awakens a person's ability to listen, read, understand, and appreciate poetry better. And your child is no exception. (You, too, will benefit, so join the fun of this activity.)

At a Glance

Grade/Subject: 3rd/Language Arts—Literature and Creative Writing
Skills: using sounds and images to create poems, listening to poetry, and talking about it
Materials: pencil and paper (or a word processor)
book or books of poems
Time: 20 minutes or so once a month

Getting Ready

At the library or bookstore, pick out a book with poems you like and think would appeal to your child. Nonsense poetry (like those of Lewis Carrol or Edward Lear) might be fun to start with; check out Shel Silverstein, Phyllis McGinley, and David McCord.

Read the poems aloud to yourself, listening to them as you do, to find which ones:

• You think your child will like
• Best show ways word sounds are used

Choose a few poems and ask your child for a poetry date; that is, have him choose a time to set aside for enjoying poetry with you.

WHAT'S MORE

Try having poetry dates in a variety of locations—in the park, at the laundromat, in the schoolyard; there are so many places. Even at home, try different places—kitchen, cellar, bathroom.

After three or four poetry dates, publish the poems the two of you have made by having your child write each one out and illustrate it, then staple the sheets together with a cover entitled something like, "Mother and Son (or Daughter)."

HEAR YE, HEAR YE

Poetry uses sound through
• Repetition of sounds
(big bad bear)
• Rhythmic beat of syllables
(upon a white horse)
• Sounds-like words
(*crack, wave, hiss*)
• Rhyme
(June, moon, spoon)

LUCKY PARENTS

Parents are lucky if they're focused on education in the home as an everyday, fun aspect of their lives. Most of the "teachable moments," those special times where things really click for children and they finally understand something, won't usually happen for kids in a formal setting with 38 other school children sitting around. Parents will get to observe those exciting moments in the more informal home setting.

Step One

Talk with your child about his experiences with poetry. Does he know the words to any songs? Can he recite any? Does he remember any nursery rhymes or other bits of poetry? Reach back into your own memory and see what you can offer, too. Come on, you didn't survive being a teenager without learning a song you could recite!

Step Two

Ask your child to close his eyes and listen, listen only, put his whole self into listening. Tell him not to open his eyes until you say, "Open." Read a poem aloud. Take it slowly to give yourself an opportunity to emphasize the sounds and meaning. (If it's very short, read it twice.)

Step Three

Say, "Open," and ask your child about what feelings and thoughts he had from the poem. You might ask:

- What pictures did you see with your eyes closed?
- What could you hear, or smell, or feel?
- What did it make you think about or remember?

Step Four

Try a few more poems the same way. Invite your child to read one if he wants.

Step Five

End up so that both of you are spending as much time as you want writing poems of your own. Use an idea from one of the poems, or pick some object or experience, concentrate on it, and then write a few lines about it.

▶ A REPORT CARD FOR BOOKS

The normal range of reading abilities for children in grade three is usually very wide. Some kids are becoming solid readers, some are just crossing the threshold, and some are forging ahead on their own. For most, grade three is a time for developing confidence, for practicing, and for establishing the habit of reading for pleasure. You can encourage all of these by making reading an activity that you and your child share.

At a Glance

Grade/Subject: 3rd/Language Arts—Reading and Literature
Skills: reading practice, writing
Materials: plentiful source of books—check out the school or local library
several copies of your book report form that you write together
Time: 20–30 minutes to work out a standard report form with your child
about 1/2 hour twice a week for reading (more frequently, if desired)
about 15 minutes weekly to write or dictate the reports

Getting Ready

Talk with your child about books that he likes and books he doesn't like. Think about ways to describe books that would help other kids know what was a good read. Think up a set of questions about books and write them down.

Make a book report form. If your child likes to write, set up questions that he can write answers to. If writing will get in the way of his doing more reading, make up a form like a report card for the book. You and your child can assign letter or number grades for quality of story, interest of characters, illustrations, or whatever else the two of you agree should be noted about a book. You could even set up scales of 1–10 for different aspects of the book. Leave space at the bottom for at least one sentence of general comment. The report can then be photocopied, printed from a computer, or individually created. Make at least five copies to begin with.

Step One

Pick one book each week that the two of you can read together. These books can be exclusively your child's choice or include some you choose that you think he'll enjoy. (You

---

WHAT'S MORE

If your child is an extensive reader, have him record the books he is reading on his own and rate and write about them in the same way.

_____

Bring your reports or booklets with you as you make a shared visit to the library. Use them to help you find more books by the same author or books on similar favorite topics.

_____

Not all children of this age enjoy writing letters, but some are enthusiastic about being pen pals. Book reports, lovingly or wittily decorated, make great additions to any letter (grandparents love them, too).

_____

You and your child can make a booklet collecting batches of the reports along with drawings of favorite scenes from each title, a great art project to do together.

BOOK CHATS

Educators are putting more and more emphasis on talking about books. You don't have to have a college-level discussion, just a plain, old talk about books. At whatever level the conversation takes place, putting books at the center of casual talk gives reading and thinking about what you are reading a legitimate place in your family's life.

could also alternate weeks of choosing the book or work out whatever arrangement seems best for the two of you. Making decisions about what to read is a part of the process.)

Take turns reading the selected book to each other. How much each of you reads can depend on your energy as well as that of your child. Depending upon the demands of the book and your child's reading skills and comfort level, adjust how much each of you reads. The important element is the sharing back and forth of both reading and listening.

Step Two

Schedule a regular time (at a meal?) each week to review what you've been reading. Work with your child to fill in the regular report form that you prepared together. Adjust the level of work to your child's ability and energy. If writing is an obstacle for your child, try having him dictate some of the report. The goal is to develop a pleasurable sharing around reading and thinking about literature.

> The important element is the sharing back and forth of both reading and listening.

After making sure there is a mention of the author and title, be flexible about how your report form is used. Change what is on your report cards to make them work for you, your child, and the books you choose. The goal is to have the evaluation belong to your child, but you could decide together to have you add your thoughts, too, perhaps in a different color.

Step Three

About once a month or every six weeks, look back over your reports together. Talk about what each of you learned about in the books, about your likes and dislikes, and anything that might be added or changed on each book's report. Use this time to compile a summary booklet that contains the reports, along with drawings of favorite scenes or characters from the books.

CHAPTER 13

Learning Adventures—
4th Grade Language Arts

LOSING YOUR COOL?

Parents can sometimes give their children the impression that mistakes are not cool. That only gives a child heavy baggage to carry throughout school, because mistakes will be made every day.

Parents should relax, make mistakes, and not loose their cool. I love to give kids examples from my everyday life. I tell them that I sometimes hit a wall too, I make mistakes, and it's hard. Kids love realizing that adults are faced with the same things they are.

❯ AND THEN, AND THEN, AND THEN

Your child will learn that a major use of the comma is to separate items in a series. When reading the series, the comma gives a visual clue. They alert readers to the presence of a series and they help readers spot the different items in the series more quickly. The commas in a series indicate a slight pause, just as in speaking such slight pauses make hearing a series easier for a listener to understand. Here are some comma practice ideas that will give your child a better grasp of these useful squiggles.

At a Glance

Grade/Subject: 4th/Language Arts—Mechanics
Skills: using commas, writing paragraphs
Materials: pencil and paper
Time: 1/2–1 hour, as often as you like

Getting Ready

If your child is unclear about the rule for using commas in a series, talk it over. Find some examples in books or magazines and study them together.

HOW COME A COMMA?

The punctuation mark that we call the comma began as a musical notation in the Middle Ages when it was known as a *virgule*. It originally looked like our punctuation mark the slash (/)—actually called a *virgule*—and was used to indicate a short pause during the singing of the Mass. All writing was by hand, and over many years the virgule slowly slid down the page until it looked like this (,). We still use those squiggles to show short pauses in a sentence, and we call them commas.

WHAT'S MORE

Rebuses (substituting pictures for words) can be a light-hearted way to practice the use of commas in a series. Your child can make lists of pets, zoo animals, flowers, or sports equipment (or all those gifts in a wish list) and change all of the word elements into pictures. Don't forget the commas!

A series can be a list of things, attributes, or events. We all know the child whose relentless detailing of the day's activities—"and then I did this and then I did that and…"—cries out for commas. The standard practice is to limit this kind of series to three items—this is a custom, though, and not a rule. The items are separated by commas and the last is joined with a conjunction as well. For example, "She whispered, then talked, and then shouted."

Step One

Around birthdays and holidays little lists probably begin to appear around your house. Some may be crumpled up in the pocket of pants in the clothes hamper, some may fall out of school books, and some probably show up on your bathroom mirror. Organizing these lists into paragraphs with complete sentences and the necessary commas can channel random desires into good writing practice.

You might get a groan from your 4th grader at the thought of writing the list as a paragraph, but the idea of getting it into a form that gets your attention and approval will overcome most objections. And there's no problem with topic sentences for these paragraphs. All you need is something compelling like, "I want ten things for my birthday . . . ." Make sure your child gets all the commas in, but don't worry about making sets of three—that comes next. While you're at it, your child can also write up paragraphs detailing gifts to others, people to invite to a party, and food she'd like to serve. Hey, if she's really into it, she could write a paragraph listing the lists.

Step Two

Once your child has written one or more list paragraphs, the next step is to turn them into something more readable. A long recitation of items (no matter how good they all are) makes for tedious reading. Point out that if a writer really wants the reader to pay close attention to everything, she has to make the writing interesting. One good way to make writing more interesting is to break the list down into smaller parts, each of which gets its own attention. "I would like these three books: book A, book B, and book C. Parents with a child who likes sports will find themselves looking for a soccer ball, shin guards, and cleats." And more, more, and more!

Step Three

Writing descriptions of events—whether it's a sports event, a party, or a trip with friends—can provide comma practice in the same way.

If your child loves to describe, but hates to write, you can alter the exercises above by taking dictation. Have her dictate the description to you, and write it down word for word. When the two of you read it over together, it will be very obvious that some editing is necessary to make it a more entertaining narrative. Have your child write a new version. Top it with a topic sentence and season it with the commas it needs to be digestible.

THE READING BRUSH-OFF

The reading that my husband and I like to do—and we read an enormous amount of books—has brushed off onto our son.

▶ BUILD A READING CORNER

One way to encourage your 4th grader to read is to make his own place to keep the books he likes and collects. It doesn't need to be fancy or large—most homes don't have that kind of space. The point is to make your kid's "reading corner" a special place, a private place that you and he have made together. All it really needs is a small bookcase or shelves and something comfortable to curl up in—a soft chair, a beanbag chair, or some squashy cushions. He also needs good light to read by.

At a Glance

Grade/Subject: 4th/Language Arts—Literature
Skills: reading and appreciating different literary genres
Materials: bookshelf (bricks or cement blocks or milk crates
with two wooden shelves work well)
books for a collection
Time: 1/2 hour to set up the space
at least 30–60 minutes weekly to build and use a book collection

Getting Ready

What furnishings do you already have? What other items might be needed in the space? Discuss with your child and other family members whether you will build them, buy them, or find them some other way. A yard sale, flea market, or your own basement might provide a small bookcase that you and your kid can paint or refinish. The same sources may supply the other items the reading corner needs. But just in case, the steps below offer some suggestions for simple bookshelves that you can build together.

Step One

Discuss with your child what kind of "reading corner" space he wants and what kind of space is practical within your home. Will it be in his room? Maybe it can be in a corner of the living room or dining room.

Step Two

Have your kid gather together some favorite books, the ones he wants to put in his own library. This will give you both an idea of the space needed. Talk about providing room for adding books and magazines.

Step Three

Build a bookcase! The one suggested here is the classic "brick and board" bookcase familiar to college students. It's something you can easily build together. Here's how:

- Place a brick at each end of a board to raise the first shelf off the floor.

WHAT'S MORE

Help your child expand his reading horizons. To get beyond the current "in" favorites of his age group, consult newspaper and magazine reviews and recommendations of books for children. Talk to his teacher and the children's librarian.

Think back to reading you enjoyed as a child. Talk to your child about your memories of reading. Get copies of what you enjoyed.

Get your child a subscription to a magazine such as *Cricket,* or look for one that deals with subjects of interest to your child.

- Then stack three or four bricks at each end of the shelf to support a shelf above it.
- Add as many shelves as you need. Simple, sturdy, practical!

Step Four

Once the bookcase is built, help your kid set up his reading corner. Add a chair, a reading lamp, perhaps posters. Remember that this is now your child's private space for enjoying books. (You probably can't give him anything more precious!)

Step Five

The final step is to help your kid build his collection of reading materials that he likes to own and enjoy, that he regards as old friends. You can, for instance, make giving books a family tradition for birthday and holiday presents. You can also encourage your kid to spend his own money—allowance and gifts—on books he really wants to own. Good, but inexpensive books may also be available through school programs, library sales, and other outlets.

▶ Cool, Cooler, Coolest

Of course, kids use adjectives almost from the moment they begin talking; but in grade four, they are expected not only to be able to identify and define adjectives, but also to use them to express comparative and superlative differences. Playfully practicing making the appropriate forms of adjectives helps your child master using adjectives correctly.

At a Glance

Grade/Subject: 4th/Language Arts—Grammar
Skills: identifying and using forms of adjectives correctly
Materials: paper and pencil for scoring and notes (optional)
      paper and pencil or word processor for writing
Time: 10 minutes or more, repeatedly for fun (a good way to pass the time on car drives, in waiting rooms, etc.) about 15 minutes or longer when your child turns sentences into stories

READING MONSTER

When kids see their accomplishment, no matter how small the goal, they get such a kick out of it. Their confidence skyrockets. I set a goal in reading with one boy who hated to read. After working with him a few times and tracking his reading progress, he gained more confidence. His dad now has to remind him to do his math homework because he takes up so much time reading. It's something he loves to do now. I helped to create a little reading monster!

DARE TO COMPARE

A *comparative adjective* describes a noun as having more of some quality than another noun. It expresses a comparison between two nouns.
—The taller sister reached for the cookie jar. (the taller of two sisters)
A *superlative adjective* describes a noun as having more of some quality than two or more other nouns or than any other.
—The tallest tree in the forest was hit by lightning. (Compared to all the other trees in the forest, this one was the tallest.)

Kids enjoy making up new words. Invent adjectives to describe things and then turn them into their comparative and superlative forms. Make a list of them and use them in a sentence.

Encourage the search for incorrect uses of comparative and superlative adjectives, such as the supermarket sign that says "10 items or less" when it means "10 items or fewer (items)."

If your child does well playing "Cool, Cooler, Coolest," you might try "Hotly, More Hotly, Most Hotly." In that version, players have to use adverbs, which can be trickier.

Have fun "series-alizing." Here's how. Take any sentence and dream up ways of putting items in a series into it. Here is an example of puting three (3!) series of words into the previous sentence:
Take any sentence, paragraph, or passage and find a way, trick, or gimmick for putting ideas, items, or other kinds of mischief into it!

Getting Ready

All you need in order to be ready is to know what an adjective is and how to make the comparative and superlative forms of adjectives by adding -er or -est in most cases. Give a little thought also to the special cases like *good, better, best* and *some, more, most*.

Step One

Check out your child's awareness of how to make comparative and superlative adjectives by asking her to tell you how she would change some examples you offer to make them compare two nouns described by the same adjective—and then more than two. Some examples you could offer might be: a cool joke, a black sheep, a happy kid, a strange pet, the pretty flower, a short song, etcetera. (Notice that changing to the superlative generally requires changing *a* to *the*; for the comparative, either *a* or *the* is usually okay. For instance, *a* happier kid, *the* happiest kid.)

Talk with her about what adjectives are used for and how she changes each adjective to make its other two forms.

Step Two

This simple game involves taking turns making up sentences that contain at least one adjective. Here is how it's played: One of you makes up such a sentence; the other person's task is to restate that sentence, changing all the adjectives in it into their comparative form. For instance, you might say, "A *dirty* bear came looking for our *old* garbage." Your child would then say, "A *dirtier* bear came looking for our *older* garbage." The first person must then restate the sentence using superlative adjectives. "The *dirtiest* bear came looking for our *oldest* garbage."

Scoring: Each time that a player makes a mistake and the other person catches it and corrects it, the catcher/corrector gets a point. The first player to get 10 points wins.

Step Three

Have your child either make a note of sentences that she likes as you play, or after playing the game, remember and talk about some of the sentences in preparation for using them to write a story. Then have her make up a story using any of the sentences that she wants. Maybe she can work all of them into a crazy story! (Did that dirtier bear get into the loudest argument with the dirtiest bear over whose garbage was oldest? Or did a bigger and even dirtier bear interrupt with a louder shout?) The main goal in her story should be to try to use as many adjectives as possible in either comparative or superlative form.

▶ FABULOUS FABLES

Fables are stories that people tell in order to illustrate a lesson or moral that they want to teach. You might be familiar with some of the fables (also called parables) that Jesus told, like the story of the Good Samaritan who helped an injured man when others ignored his plight. The Greek slave Aesop was famous for his fables that taught simple truths like "Where there's a will, there's a way." Many of his fables featured familiar animals, such as the race between the tortoise and the hare, which teaches "Slow and steady wins the race." Remember that the moral of the story fits the action of the story but also, and more importantly, can be applied to how we live our lives.

Making up fables is fun, and a great way for your child to develop creativity as well as an understanding that literature presents ideas for people to think about and apply to their own lives.

At a Glance

Grade/Subject: 4th/Language Arts—Literature and Written Expression
Skills: narrative expression, listening, identify theme applying stories to life
Materials: some fables
       your imaginations

WHOOPS!

Some adjectives will stump you because they cannot become comparative or superlative. One example is *every*. Can you think of any others? Adjectives like that are interesting to talk over with your child. Why can't something be *everier* or *everyist!*

SOME MAXIMS AND MORALS

If at first you don't succeed,
try, try, again.
Look before you leap.
Don't throw good money after bad.
Always do your homework.
Helping others helps you too.
A friend in need is a friend indeed.

WHAT'S MORE

Go to the library together to seek out fables from a variety of cultures that your child can bring home to read and to share with the family.

paper and pencil or word processor

Time: 15–30 minutes

additional time, as desired, for your child to write up and present his own fables

Getting Ready

From your library or bookstore, obtain one or more books of fables such as those by Aesop and various cultures—African American, Native American, Norse, Gaelic, Chinese, etcetera.

Select one to use to start the activity, or, if you prefer, make up a fable of your own. In addition, think of a few "morals" or messages that you and your child could start with when discussing ideas for fables. They can range from familiar maxims like "A stitch in time saves nine" and "Look before you leap" to home-grown lessons you want to teach.

Step One

With your child, pick one of the fables you have selected to read together. One of you can read it aloud, or take turns reading parts of it. When you finish, discuss what lesson it illustrates.

- How is that lesson illustrated by the story?
- How might it apply to people's lives?
- What experiences have either of you had that reflect that lesson?
- Do you know any other stories that seem to have the same lesson?

Select and read another fable together and then discuss it the same way. (If your child wishes and time allows, you can read several or plan to repeat this step again on another day.)

WHAT'S MORE

Have your child make a book of family fables by binding together fables that he makes up along with ones that he writes after getting other members of the family to offer suggestions or stories of their own.

Step Two

Talk together about some morals or messages that could be used for making up a fable. Encourage your child's suggestions; offer some of the ones you thought of ahead of time to help him get started, if necessary.

Have him pick a moral (lesson message) that he'd like to try making up a fable for. Talk together about his ideas for his story.

- Will he use animals? If so, what animals and why?
- What will be the setting and situation where something happens?
- What will happen? What might the characters say?
- How will it end, and how will the ending demonstrate the moral of the story?

Step Three

When your child feels ready to write down his fable, he can go off on his own to do so. When he has made his final version, either copied on nice paper or printed from a word processor, he can make illustrations for it.

Step Four

Give your child an occasion for presenting his fable—perhaps at dinner or a family gathering. Maybe he can inspire other family members to offer fables they know or can make up.

❯ FRONT AND REAR SPECIALISTS

Have you ever seen a Volkswagon bug with a customized front end that looks like a Rolls Royce? Somehow that classy up-front treatment seems like a prefix that turns the good old bug into a superbug! Do you suppose a trailer hooked in back would be like a suffix . . .? Enough of this bugginess—let's talk words, not cars. Familiarity with some very common prefixes and suffixes, and knowing how they work, contributes greatly to your child's word power.

WHAT'S MORE

Read a book like *Wind in the Willows* and talk about how each of the animals behaves in ways that reflect human behaviors. Talk about why adults enjoy that book as much as children. What does the story teach about how we behave and what happens as a result? Whom do you know who is like Toad, Ratty, Mole, or Badger?

If your child likes jokes or puns, try making a Funny Fable together, complete with a silly moral. For example, make up a story about the importance of eating dinner with a moral like "Don't play baseball with a blackbird if you want to eat dinner with the king."

At a Glance

Grade/Subject: 4th/Language Arts—Vocabulary
Skills: recognition and use of some common prefixes and suffixes
Materials: newspapers and/or magazines
    2 ballpoint or felt-tip pens—one red and one blue or green
    kitchen timer (or alarm clock)
    pencil and paper or a small pad
    dictionary
Time: about 15 minutes, or as long as your child retains interest

Getting Ready

Commonly the prefixes *re-* and *un-* and the suffixes *-er/-or*, *-y*, and *-ful* are taught at this level. You can check with your child's teacher or textbook to see which affixes are taught. Decide which of the many affixes of English you want to include in your activity. Write down an example of a word for each affix you decide to include. For instance: replay, untie, teacher, actor, sunny, and hopeful.

Step One

Find out what your child knows about affixes by asking him if he can pick out the prefixes in your set of words and then pick out the suffixes. Talk with him about how each prefix and suffix changes the meaning of the word to which it is attached.

Then tell him you have an idea for playing Front and Rear Specialists—seeing how many words each of you can find that use any of the prefixes and suffixes you have been discussing.

Step Two

Explain that each of you will have a page of the newspaper or magazine on which you will search for every example you can find of these prefixes and suffixes. Whenever you find one, you will use your marker to circle it. Set the timer for 5–8 minutes (depending on your judgment of how long your child will concentrate on the game), then choose a page each. Say, "Go!" and you're both off and running.

Step Three

When the timer bings, exchange your pages and examine what the other person found. On a sheet of paper, list all the words that qualified in columns—a column for *re-*, one for *un-*, one for *-er/-or*, one for *-ful*, and one for *-y*, for instance.

Discuss any words that were circled but may not actually contain a prefix or suffix. For instance *unit* or *religion*. One way of checking each word is to see if the *un-* in it means "not" in the word, whether *re-* means "again," etcetera. Use the dictionary to check as needed. If your child seems ready, you can introduce suffixes, like *-ity* turning an adjective like *real* into the noun *reality*.

You can also use this opportunity to talk about how the spelling of some words changes when a prefix or suffix is added. For instance, *fun* becomes *funny*, doubling the *n* when you add *y*, and *taste* drops the *e* to become *tasty*.

▶ GOOD ENOUGH TO FOLLOW

Hooking up a telephone answering machine, baking cookies, or taking a test—whatever the task—being able to follow directions makes all the difference between success and frustration or disappointment. Children who can competently interpret instructions gain real power over their everyday lives *and* their ability to learn. You can help your child develop that kind of confidence through this activity, which can be integrated into many areas of everyday life.

At a Glance

Grade/Subject: 4th/Language Arts—Reading, Listening, and Written Expression
Skills: following directions and giving directions

ALL ABOUT AFFIXES

A *prefix* is a letter or group of letters added to the beginning of a word to affect its meaning.
A *suffix* is a letter or group of letters added to the end of a word to affect its meaning.
An *affix* is either a prefix or suffix— that is, a letter or group of letters added to either end of a word to affect its meaning.

CREATIVE KIDS AND FEEDBACK

It's good to see parents who are aware of what's going on with their children both inside and outside the classroom, their children's social circles, and the personal values of what's important to their kids. Some creative kids aren't getting a lot of positive feedback when it comes time to learning something very literal like a set of math facts, while kids who are much more literal are getting good recognition. It's important to realize kids have different strengths, and parents can help complement what they're getting or missing in school.

LEARNING PLEASURE

In the best of all educational worlds, the activities of school would be of sufficient intrinsic interest to engage students on this basis alone—students would strive to learn because the process of learning was psychologically fulfilling and the resulting sense of mastery was personally rewarding.

We have all had learning experiences in which we felt this way—energized, invigorated, caught up in the sheer pleasure that comes from mastering something challenging and difficult. It is one of the most satisfying feelings there is.

—from *Beyond the Classroom*, Laurence Steinberg, Ph.D. (Simon & Schuster, 1996)

FULL OF BOOKS

In my family, my husband and I read to our children a lot. We go to the library. We try to look for things that they find very interesting and pick them up. We look up programs at the library that they'll find entertaining. And we fill up our home with books.

Materials: cookbook, car manual, TV manual, gardening book, game rules

instructions packaged with cosmetics, cleaning products, tools, etcetera

manuals from any appliance (stove, vacuum cleaner, microwave...)

do-it-yourself features from newspapers or magazines

(in short, as many examples of printed instructions as you can gather)

Time: 10 minutes for step one

5 minutes to hours for Step Two, depending on what your child chooses to do (during which time the extent of your involvement is basically unnecessary and up to you)

10–30 minutes for Step Three, depending on the complexity of the instructions your child decides to write for others

Getting Ready

Gather a number of different examples of printed instructions from around your home. Check your library's choice of "How to" books as well as magazines you can borrow. Assemble a wide variety of styles and kinds of instructions and make at least one of them contain directions for doing something you think your child will enjoy—perhaps making folded paper animals or a kite, building something, cooking something, or assembling or installing something.

Try to think of some time recently when members of your household needed to follow printed directions to do something—perhaps program a VCR or change the bag on the vacuum or follow a recipe. You can use that experience when talking with your child during Step One of the activity.

Step One

Talk with your child about times when she has had to follow directions in order to accomplish some task. What does she remember about such experiences? When following written directions, what does she think can make them easier or harder to understand? When has she run into difficulties following directions?

Look through each of the examples you have gathered and discuss the instructions to be found in them:

- Where are directions found in the various manuals?
- How well does each example help the reader follow through step by step?
- When reading directions, what can a person do to help herself keep from getting confused or lost?

Step Two

Have your child select one set of directions that she is unfamiliar with to follow and then use those directions to carry out the task they are for. Discuss with her the need to read over the instructions before beginning, and make sure that she has all the materials she needs when she begins the task.

Thereafter, provide support to her as you deem necessary, but do not tell her how to do the task. Instead, if she needs help, help her interpret the instructions. Discuss with her what she thinks the instructions are saying, and where and why they confuse her, for instance. Encourage her to rephrase in her own words what the instructions say.

Step Three

Fresh from the success of following written directions to complete a task, your child is ready to see how well she can write directions for others to follow. Have her choose a task that she knows how to do—whether it is how to make something (like valentine cards or a bike tire repair) or how to do something (like recycle trash or give the dog a bath).

Step Four

Your child can give her completed directions to a friend or family member to see how well they help the person carry out the task.

WHAT'S MORE

If your child likes to cook, how about creating a new taste sensation and having her write up a recipe card?

If she enjoys gardening or indoor plants, how about instructions for raising and caring for favorite plants?

Make a scrapbook of examples of instructions in which your child pastes directions she collects; next to each she can write a few words about what is good, bad, or funny about it.

Hold an Instructions Hunt in which your child, perhaps with some friends, searches for (or thinks of) places where instructions lurk (on cake mix boxes, toothpaste tubes . . .).

READING RADIO

When I was a kid, a radio program that read books aloud came on every night at the time when I had to do the dishes. I loved listening and looked forward each night to what was going to happen next. When my sister and I did dishes together, we didn't even fight! Afterwards we talked about what happened in the story that night.

WHAT'S MORE

Joke books, magazines written at your child's level, humor magazines, and fan magazines are part of children's everyday experience. This reading material may not always be your cup of tea, but a little tongue biting is worth the self-control. Relish the sharing and try to remember how it felt when you hadn't already heard some riddle or joke many times.

▶ READING ALOUD

Issues of beginning adolescence, such as embarrassment (parents—oooh!) and independence, begin to appear by the end of grade four and the start of grade five. Take advantage of the opportunities you have now to extend and enrich reading skills and pleasure through shared reading. For most parents, 3rd and 4th grade are probably the last years in which reading aloud with your child is easily initiated; and reading aloud together at this stage can be especially rewarding for all involved.

At a Glance

Grade/Subject: 4th/Language Arts—Reading, Listening
Skills: apply comprehension skills in listening, use appropriate loudness, phrasing, and intonation in spoken language
Materials: books, stories, poems, and magazine articles chosen by you and your child
Time: 10 minutes and up depending on selection and interest (Your goal is to build a routine that leads to repeated bouts of reading aloud together.)

Getting Ready

Select a couple of books you know your child is likely to enjoy. Get advice from a teacher or children's librarian or ask your child what book she's heard about that she'd like to read. You might consider a book from which a popular movie has been made such as *Little Women* or *Aladdin* or *The Incredible Journey.*

If you haven't read aloud to your child for a long time and feel a bit rusty about getting started again, try reading a little of the story aloud on your own, just to see how easy it really is.

Think about the best time of day to set aside 15 minutes or so for reading together on some kind of regular basis.

Step One

Either at the special time you think might become a regular reading time or at some other convenient time to begin this activity, talk with your child about memories you have of hearing stories read aloud. Tell her about cultures in which listening to stories is not only treasured as great entertainment but even the way in which people pass on the tales of their own history. But perhaps best of all, it is a nice way to spend a bit of quiet, relaxed time enjoying something together.

Step Two

Have your child pick one of the two read-aloud books that you got for this activity. Read the first chapter or section of the book aloud to her. Encourage her to close her eyes and just relax as she listens.

Step Three

When you finish reading, encourage your child to talk about her thoughts and feelings about what was read.

- What does she think might happen next? Why?
- Which characters does she like (or dislike) and why?
- What questions does she have about what she heard?
- How is what is in the reading like (or unlike) real life or other things she's read or seen on television?

Step Four

Set up the time for your next read-aloud session. Depending on the level of reading difficulty, plan for your child to take turns with you reading, if she'd like.

Step Five

When you finish reading the first book or story, have your child select the next herself and read it to you (or take turns with you). When that selection is finished, decide together on the next selection and continue in this way taking turns reading aloud on a regular basis.

WHAT'S MORE

Tell your child about the old Victorian custom of reading a scary or mysterious story during the darkest time of the year. Dickens wrote a special story each year particularly for that occasion. His most famous was *A Christmas Carol*. Start the tradition at your house—one chapter a night up until Christmas eve, New Year's eve, or some other date you and your child choose.

Have your child choose a relatively short story or a poetry book or magazine she likes, and invite friends to a Read-Aloud Party. Plan together how to involve all the friends in having turns reading aloud. (Maybe together you can make a special cake in the shape of an open book and paint an icing title on it.)

Have the school or local children's librarian help you locate a play your child would enjoy. Then involve family members or your child's friends in taking the roles and reading the play aloud.

Set aside some time each week for sharing the latest in your child's Word Power pad. For instance, it could be passed around the table at Sunday breakfast. As proud producer of the Spell Checker's Word Power pad, your child could explain the meaning of each new word and then everyone could try to make up new sentences for the new words.

Your child could use the word processor to create a file of his words.

He could try making up a story using as many of his words as possible. Every time he gets more words, he could continue the story to work in the new words.

Make Jumble Words by choosing a lot of different words from the pad, plus lots of other words your child chooses, and writing them on slips of paper. Include all different parts of speech. Shuffle the words and pick them one at a time to use to build Jumble Sentences and Jumble Stories.

▶ SPELL CHECKER'S WORD POWER

Discovering new words to add to one's vocabulary is fun for children and adults alike. If you have a computer and word processor, your child can enjoy using the program's spell checking tool to dig up new words to use in building word power.

At a Glance

Grade/Subject: 4th/Language Arts—Vocabulary and Spelling
Skills: vocabulary development, using a word processor
Materials: any word processor that has a spell check function
        small spiral pad
        dictionary
        colored pencils (optional)
Time: 15 minutes and up, depending on your child's interest; repeatable whenever your child uses the word processor

Getting Ready

Get your child started using a word processor. It can be just at the simplest level of typing in stories or whatever your child wishes. (With minimal help, most children can use standard word processors for personal purposes.)

Step One

Tell your child to relax and just type anything he'd like. It could be an account of something that happened at school, an original story, a letter to grandma, something copied from a favorite book. Stress that he should not worry about how well he spells whenever he begins typing. Computers make fixing mistakes easy later when people polish up their writing.

Step Two

When he finishes typing, show him how to use the program's spell checking function. As soon as it picks up a spelling that it does not recognize, call your child's attention to the suggestions the spell checker offers for substitution. Ask him what each of the words suggested means. Talk about whether any suggestion is what he wants.

Step Three

Have your child write any word suggested that he doesn't know on its own page in his small spiral Spell Checker's Word Power pad. Then help him change the incorrectly spelled word as needed in his writing on the computer.

Step Four

When your child finishes at the computer, use a dictionary to look up the words in his pad together. Talk about them. Pronounce them. Take turns making up sentences for each of them. Have him write the sentence he likes best for each word on its page in his Word Power pad along with his own definition of what the word means. He can draw a picture to go with the sentence on the page opposite the page with the word, its sentence, and its definition.

> To tickle the spell checker to give more words, you can try spoiling some spelling on purpose. Try adding an unexpected letter or dropping or switching letters. "Tiigers and gosts are raelly scarey."

LOOKING IT UP

I recommend encyclopedias, in book form, for the family. It was exciting when my son had a question and first went to the encyclopedia by himself and started reading.

▶ SUPERLATIVE!

The vocabulary of children in the middle grades grows rapidly as they mature and their horizons widen. Games, sports, and social life have their own special words (perhaps not always the ones that we want them to learn!) and many of their favorite activities have interesting and specialized vocabularies. Word play is extensive at this age with lots of puns, riddles, and slang. You can take advantage of your 4th grader's fascination with words in this activity.

Newspaper, movie, and theater advertising is a gold mine for the adjective seeker. The emphasis is on the superlative, and some of the words stretch the English language a bit. Deciphering the hype is fun, however, and spirited discussions of what is and is not good English are the dream of everyone who teaches language arts.

At a Glance

Grade/Subject: 4th/Language Arts—Vocabulary, Reading
Skills: vocabulary development, descriptive words, dictionary use
Materials: newspaper or magazine, entertainment pages
  looseleaf notebook sheets
  stopwatch or timer
  3" × 5" index cards (optional)
  dictionary
Time: 1/2 hour–1 hour

Getting Ready

Collect entertainment sections from several different magazines and newspapers so that you have ads for at least ten different films, plays, or concerts.

Step One

Read through the entertainment ads looking for the superlative adjectives. You can talk about superlatives (words used to describe often exaggerated positive qualities) and make up sentences using the ones you find as you go along. List them on a sheet of paper.

Step Two

Pick out some of the words (probably no more than ten) and look them up in a dictionary. Have your child write them down alphabetically on a sheet of notebook paper along with his version of the definition.

Step Three

Talk a little about each of the words. What is the root of the word? The superlatives in ads are often forms of the comparative (*big, bigger, biggest*). If some of his words are comparatives, ask him what is the root and what are the other comparatives for this particular word? Remember that

---

WHAT'S MORE

Write the words on one side of 3" × 5" cards. Use your imaginations to come up with the exact opposite and write it on the reverse side. You can use these later as the basis for a word guessing game.

Have your child tell you a story, then stop at each description: "The duck was pink. He was the _____ pink!" You pick out a superlative from the notebook list. Then you tell a story and let your child fill in the blanks.

Play a game of "Which One?" You take turns making up a sentence about two or more of something. The person who did not make up the sentence must make a second sentence that correctly uses a comparative or superlative adjective to describe the things. For instance: (1) I chose one of three kittens at the pet shop. (2) I chose the cuddliest kitten. Another: (1) Do you know those two brothers? (2) I met the older brother.

not all words have comparative forms; *exciting* is an example. These words use auxiliary (helper) words like *more, less,* and *most* (*exciting, more exciting, most exciting*). You can have fun playing with these as well.

Step Four

Cut out at least ten ads. Place them upside down in a stack and then each of you draws an equal amount. Use an egg timer or stopwatch to set a time limit and then see who can find the most superlatives.

▶ THE CASE OF THE TROUBLESOME TELEPHONE

Entering in an amusing story situation triggers children's imagination and stimulates their creative exploration of language. By taking on the role of "detective gossip columnist," your child will analyze words and create brief stories.

At a Glance

Grade/Subject: 4th/Language Arts—Composition
Skills: analyzing meanings, writing stories
Materials: journal or word processor
Time: 1/2 hour to 1 hour
repeatedly if desired, for as many weeks as you can sustain interest

Getting Ready

Set up the situation by presenting your child with the following scenario: Times are tough. Detective work is hard. And now, your telephone, your lifeline to tipsters, is acting up! You have the cool head, the nerves of steel, and the immense imagination needed to solve tough cases. But all you hear from your phone are bits and pieces of what anyone says in voices that are unrecognizable. Besides, your telephone line keeps crossing with that of a two-bit gossip columnist, who has disappeared but keeps getting calls!

FRACTURED PHRASES

Try these broken messages for your young detective's defective phone:

. . . secret . . . chick . . . diner . . pig . . under the table . . .
(a surprise party? a sting operation? something else?)

. . . drilled . . . spurted . . . gold . . . wearing a mask . . . help . . .
(an oil well explosion? a gold mine shoot-out? a dentist's office?)

Step One

You can use those broken bits of telephone messages to sort out crimes and gossip stories. Get ready for a call—RRRRing! A hot tip is coming in (as spoken by you, the parent). Speak a few words separated by pauses (or a phone line crackle sound). Have your child write each word. For example:

> . . . left . . . hit . . . after him . . . safe . . . run . . .

Step Two

When your child has all the words, her job is to imagine. What might the telephone tipster been trying to say? (Was that a burglary . . . or a baseball game . . . or what?) Your child then fills in her story in any way that seems to make any sense. She can even try making more than one story from the same set of tips.

Step Three

Encourage your child to make up broken messages of her own. She can get her bits 'n' pieces for stories in lots of ways. And then write stories for them. Here are some ways of getting bits:

- Turn on the TV, then switch stations to gather words or phrases to use.
- Use the radio for broken telephone messages by turning the volume up just a second and then down. She could do this with a friend who writes down what they hear; then together the children can create stories.
- Open a book, dictionary, or magazine to a random page and point to any word. Jot it down; then keep going until you have your list.

CHAPTER 14

Learning Adventures— 3rd Grade Math

DIFFERENT STROKES

Take a relationships problem like, "Mr. Bumblebee is 6 years old and Mr. Fly is 8 years old. His brother is 3 times the age of the other brother." To help your child understand the problem, have three people stand up and act out the relationships. Or do a diagram or draw a picture of the problem together. Or you can show your child how to guess and check: "How would this problem turn out if we threw in a 3 here?" Teach your child how to use these different kinds of strategies to fit his unique learning style—and start to have fun with problem solving!

▶ A Line of Time

Learning to tell time accurately can sometimes be tricky for children. If you suspect your child is reluctant to learn to tell time well, you won't be the first parent —"Gosh, I'm sorry, Mom. I thought the clock said it was only 5:15!" Have fun with this activity, and see if it can help you get your kid to be home on time, to bed on time, up in the morning on time, ready to leave for a dentist appointment on time . . . well, nobody's perfect.

At a Glance

Grade/Subject: 3rd/Math—Time
Skills: learning to tell time to the minute, problem solving
Materials: analog clock (clock with hands)
digital clock
long piece of paper (computer printout paper or several sheets of paper taped together)
pencil and eraser
crayons or colored markers
Time: a couple of minutes each day to record activities
15–45 minutes to draw timeline and illustrate it with pictures

Making the Grade

MAKING PROGRESS

I see kids who are feeling bad because the older sibling does well—or worse, the younger sibling is the star learner—and there are constant comparisons of "Why aren't you more like your brother or sister?" Don't tell your child that he is working below the grade level of his siblings. It doesn't really matter how others do. Focus on each child as an individual and praise each one for his achievements. "You're doing better and better" should be the line of talk rather than "You're not doing as well as your brother." Set individual goals and praise small victories to keep your child progressing positively.

CREATIVE BATHROOM TILING

My husband and I don't encourage a lot of TV watching at our house, but we will encourage anything creative—cooking, woodworking, building clubhouses, tiling our bathroom.

Getting Ready

If possible, locate a timeline to show him how they work, or make a simple one of your own using years instead of hours, perhaps starting with when he was born and other events of interest to him.

Explain to your child that timelines are a good way of recording events and seeing how the events fall over a period of time. Tell him his own timeline in this activity will show the things he does during the day. It will be a long line with the hours of his day written in chronological order on it, and where he will record the things he does.

Step One

Along the bottom of the long paper, draw a horizontal line. At the beginning of the line, write 6:00 A.M., in the middle of the line write 2:00 P.M., and at the end of the line write 10:00 P.M. Give this piece of paper to your child and ask him to fill in the rest of the hours. Make sure he puts in the A.M. and P.M.

Talk together about how to figure out how many hours will pass between the hours of 6:00 A.M. and 2:00 P.M. Decide on a way to mark those hours on the paper so that the same amount of space exists between each hourly mark. (Use a pencil and eraser so your can make adjustments until all the hours fit in evenly.) Similarly mark the hours between 2:00 P.M. and 10:00 P.M. Write "noon" under 12:00.

When the timeline is ready, explore his understanding of time divisions by discussing questions like:

- Where would you put half hours, like 3:30, on this timeline?
- Where would you put 3:45? or 3:15? or 3:10?
- Where would you put 9:20 A.M.? How about 9:20 P.M.?

Step Two

Explain to him that he will be able to record the events of three days on his timeline. For instance, ask him what time he usually gets home from school and then have him point to where on the timeline he would write down his arrival home. Have him practice again by having him look at the time right at the moment and then point to where on the timeline he would write down "Math Stuff with Mom." Do this with both an analog clock and a digital clock to review how to read the hands of the clock. Plan when to start filling in the timeline. The best three days to have him record his activities might be Saturday, Sunday, and Monday in order to provide three different kinds of days of activities.

Step Three

On day one, have your child look at an analog clock when he gets up, eats breakfast, and so forth and, each time, write the time and the activity down on a piece of paper. Then have him check the time he wrote by looking also at a digital clock.

At the end of the day, have him write each activity where it belongs on the timeline. He should then make a second timeline for the next day, or he could write the days in different colors on the same timeline—red for Saturday's activities, blue for Sunday's, and green for Monday's.

Step Four

Time lines are more fun and more visually informative when they are illustrated. Your child can draw pictures above the activities he has recorded or cut illustrations from old magazines. To add visual communication and to reinforce the correct reading of the hands of a clock, have him draw a clock, showing the exact time, next to each recorded activity.

Step Five

When three days have been recorded, discuss together the three timelines his work shows. Compare what it records:

• Which day did he stay up the latest? Get up earliest?
• What day did he do the most activities?
• What did he spend the most time doing?

LISTEN WHILE YOU WORK

Listen to your children. When they're asking you questions, listen to their questions and give them an answer. If they're doing homework, try to find out what they do know, then help to build on that. Sometimes a child will ask a question and an adult will start to explain each and every step, when it might be just the last step they needed help with.

WHAT'S MORE

Use the timelines to work out time problems such as: What time would it be if you got up 23 minutes later, if you ate breakfast 18 minutes earlier, or went to bed ten minutes later?

Create timelines for other members of the family.

Create a timeline of what you and your family did during a school vacation.

LEARNING ADVENTURES

In S*SCORE!*'s Learning Adventures, we provide children with hands-on learning to introduce key concepts in academic subjects. These are one-week seminars, and in that short time we inspire kids and spark their curiosity and desire to study subjects further. That is good advice for parents too. You can provide little learning experiences for your children at home, just to spark their intellectual curiosity.

THE ADULT WORLD

Whenever I set goals with students, I tell them that when I was their age, I wanted to be on the cross-country team in school, and to get good enough, I had to practice and practice. Then I ask them if there's anything like that going on for them. Share something cool from the "adult world" that shows you had to practice to master something or to understand it. Kids love to see adults as people who make mistakes and aren't born perfect.

▶ AND BINGO IS MY NUMBER-O

In this game, nobody wins cash prizes or a box of candy, but your child can win extra math fluency while having fun.

From creating the game elements to playing the game, here's practice in multiplication facts that are essential in building basic math skills.

At a Glance

Grade/Subject: 3rd/Math—Computation
Skills: learning multiplication facts up to 9
Materials: flash cards with multiplication facts up to 9
several squares of cardboard (at least 5" by 5")
ruler (preferably two)
magic markers
pencil and eraser (for making the Bingo grid)
pennies or any other type of Bingo marker
Time: 15 minutes to make Bingo cards
about 10 minutes each Bingo round you play

Getting Ready

Math flash cards can be purchased (see the Resources section for publishers) or easily made at home by writing each multiplication fact from 1×1 up to 9×9 on a 3" by 5" card with a magic marker. For instance, write the equation $3 \times 4 =$ on the front of the card and the 12 on the back of the card. Write the numbers large.

If you make your cards, have your child help. To keep track most easily, start with $1 \times 1 =$, $1 \times 2 =$, $1 \times 3 =$, etc., until you reach $1 \times 9 =$. Continue with $2 \times 2 =$, $2 \times 3 =$, and so forth, until you reach $9 \times 9 =$. You should end with 81 cards. Have your child make the cards for some of the times tables that she finds harder, as well as the ones that are a snap, like the 1s table.

When the flash cards are ready, lay them on a table with all the answers showing.

Step One

Make your first two Bingo cards together. Each of you takes one of the square pieces of cardboard and uses a ruler to draw a grid on it in pencil. Divide the width into five columns by drawing four lines down. Discuss with your child her ideas about how to make all five columns the same width. (Use the eraser until you've got that problem solved.) Then make five equal columns across to create a grid of 25 spaces.

For each space on your Bingo cards, each of you should choose a number from the backs of the flash cards and write it with a magic marker. Pick the numbers randomly, trying to avoid repeating any numbers. Write them in any space until all the spaces in the grid are filled.

Step Two

With your first two Bingo cards created, you are now ready for the game. Explain that winning this Bingo depends on using multiplication facts. Explain that to win, you must be the first person to cover five spaces in a row on your grid. The rows can be horizontal, vertical, or diagonal. To cover a space, each of you looks for a number on your card that is the answer to the multiplication equation asked for on a flash card.

Divide the pennies (or whatever you are using for markers) between you. Gather all the flash cards into one pack and place the pack on the table with the answer side facing DOWN.

Step Three

Read the equation on the top card out loud. You and your child should each calculate the sum individually. Once she feels she knows the correct answer, tell her to look on her Bingo card, and if the number is there, have her place a penny in that space. Meanwhile look on your own card for the answer also. When pennies have been placed (or not, if the answer is not on the Bingo card), put the top card aside and read the next top card aloud. Continue this process until one of you has five in a row.

Step Four

When one of you gets five in a row and calls out, "Bingo!" together check whether it is truly a win by comparing the numbers in the row to the answers in the pile of cards that were used and then set aside. As you go through the flash cards, one of you reads the equation and the answer and the other person checks the row. If some pennies are not correctly placed, discuss the correct answer, remove the penny, and return to finishing the game.

Step Five

When a round is over, return the set-aside flash cards to the pack and shuffle the flash cards to continue playing as long as you both enjoy it. Save the flash cards and Bingo cards so you can play as often as both of you want. Encourage your child to make more Bingo grid cards to provide variety in play and to let friends or other family members join in.

▶ BUILD THE BIGGER NUMBER

It might be hard for you to imagine how you can sit down with your child and practice reading multiple-digit numbers without boring her to tears, but here's an intriguing little game that involves luck, strategy, and a lot of number-building practice.

At a Glance

Grade/Subject: 3rd/Math—Numeration
Skills: reading, writing, and ordering four-digit numbers
Materials: 40 3" × 5" (or 40 playing cards, just ace through 9 and the jacks to stand for 0)
Time: 20–30 minutes, or as long as your child wants to keep playing

Getting Ready

Decide whether you are going to make number cards (index cards work well) or use a modified deck of playing cards for this game. You will use four of these number cards to build each of your numbers. Then make your two sets of place value labels using 3" × 5" index cards or something just about that size. Write one of the place value words—*ones, tens, hundreds,* or *thousands*—horizontally on each of the four cards. You will use these place value cards to label the digits as you build numbers.

With your child, select a flat playing area—the kitchen table is fine—and let the fun begin!

Step One

Explain that the game works like this: You take turns drawing number cards until you each have four number cards, which you arrange into a four-digit number. Each time you draw a card, you must decide whether to put it in the ones, tens, hundreds, or thousands place. The object of the activity is to build a bigger four-digit number than your opponent builds.

Step Two

Sit side-by-side to play. Before you begin, start by laying out your place value labels in the correct order in front of you. Have your child do the same, talking through what she is doing ("The ones go here, and then the tens . . . "); observe carefully to make sure she has the place values in the right order. Sitting next to your child rather than across from her during play means she can see your numbers as well as her own right-side-up.

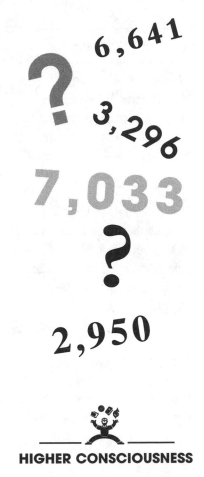

6,641

3,296

7,033

2,950

HIGHER CONSCIOUSNESS

I understand math on a totally different level now, and part of the reason is that I've worked with children so much. Learning the math words again was kind of foreign to me, but then you get it down, the kids learn it with you, and the teaching process makes the information come to life. It's great if parents can teach kids and the parents are open to being taught by their kids. There's an amazing understanding that parents can have in their relearning process— they can discover the "why" of things that they learned when they were children.

Making the Grade

WHAT'S MORE

Provide practice adding thousands by adding up the numbers each of you makes each time and see who gets the highest total in five rounds.

Play the game building five-digit numbers. You can go as high as your child is capable of going. (With your child, make the additional place value cards you need.)

Play the game, but change the rule to try to build the *smallest* four- or five-digit number. In this variation, the penalty point is given to the person whose number is higher.

Get more people to play with you so that you make more numbers each time to read out loud and compare. In this version give a penalty point to each person below (or above) the winner's number.

Before you start the round, name a target number (say 4,500). Then use the numbers you draw to make a number as close to your target as possible (add or subtract numbers to see who's closest).

Shuffle the number cards and place the deck number-side down on the playing surface where both of you can reach it. To demonstrate game play, go first and take the top card, turn it over, and put the card below any of your place value labels. For example, you draw a 6 and place it in the tens column. Keep in mind that you want to build the biggest number you can with your four cards; but once you place a card, you cannot move it.

Step Three

Now it's your child's turn to draw a card and place it below one of her place value labels. Complete the round by taking turns drawing three more cards each and putting each under one of the remaining place value labels. Only one number can go under each label.

At the end of the round, each of you should read your four-digit number out loud and compare the two numbers that you've made. Determine which number is bigger. That person gets one point for the round. The person with the smallest number gets a penalty point for the round. Remember that the person with the fewest points at the end of five rounds wins. Clear the number cards, shuffle the deck, and play again.

Step Four

After a couple rounds, start to discuss your game strategy with your child by asking questions like:

- What have you decided to do with the low numbered cards? Why?
- Where would you put the high numbered cards? Why?
- If I have a five in the thousands place, what number would I need to build a smaller number?

Play as many rounds as you want. When you finish, put the cards somewhere handy so you can easily play some more at any time.

▶ Buzz, Bang, Bop!

Making a game for pairs out of the possibly boring task of learning times tables can be a nice motivation. But stay on your toes (or better–*head*?) because this game really takes some careful ear- and brainwork!

At a Glance

Grade/Subject: 3rd/Math—Computation, Numeration
Skills: multiplication facts up to 9, counting
Materials: none
Time: 15–20 minutes, or as long as your child is interested—play any time you and your child have a little free time together for some lively learning fun

X	0	1	2	3	4	5	6	7	8	9	10
0	0	1	0	0	0	0	0	0	0	0	0
1	0	2	2	3	4	5	6	7	8	9	10
2	0	3	4	6	8	10	12	14	16	18	20
3	0	4	6	9	12	15	18	21	24	27	30
4	0	5	8	12	16	20	24	28	32	36	40
5	0	6	9	15	20	25	30	35	40	45	50
6	0	7	10	18	24	30	36	42	48	54	60
7	0	8	14	21	28	35	42	49	56	63	70
8	0	9	16	24	32	40	48	56	64	72	80
9	0	9	18	27	36	45	54	63	72	81	90
10	0	10	20	30	40	50	60	70	80	90	100

Getting Ready

Ask your child how she likes to practice her times tables. Does her school use flash cards or a chart (a times table grid)? If so, having materials like those around for support might be helpful. Find out how many number families your child can name on the times tables comfortably. Up to 6 × 6? All the way to 10 × 10? Use this information to decide what number you will "buzz" with.

Step One

Start by explaining that the two of you are going to take turns counting (easy enough so far, right?) *but* there are some numbers that *can't* be said. You can't say any "buzz" number—you'll pick a "buzz" in a moment. For example, if the buzz number is 6, then players can't say 6 *or* any of the multiples of 6 (any number in the 6 times table). Any time you come to one of them, you must say *buzz* instead (in this case, 6, 12, 18, 24, and so on).

WHAT'S MORE

Start the game at 100 and count backwards to 1.

Expand the times tables to include higher numbers (12s table, for example).

Invite more people to join in the counting.

BUZZ, BANG, BOP, WRITE

You might have your child write the numbers down as they are said—it helps reinforce the number-multiplication patterns.

WHAT'S MORE

Add a second number that can't be said, a number and its multiples for which players must say *bang*. For example, using 6 and 4, here is how it would sound: 1, 2, 3, buzz, 5, bang, 7, buzz, 9, 10, 11, buzz–bang, 13 . . .

Add a different element. In it, players must say *bop* instead of any number word that contains the NAME of the buzz word. For example, if the buzz number is 3, you would say *bop* instead of "23" (or you could say "20-bop").

Step Two

Decide who will go first. That person gets to pick the buzz number (I pick 4!). Decide how high you will count (up to 50). That person then begins counting by saying, "One."

Take turns saying the next number in the counting order, except for the buzz number family. Here's an example for number 4: 1, 2, 3, buzz, 5, 6, 7, buzz . . . up to 40 (buzz!) for 4×10.

Step Three

Play ends for this round when either of you says a number when you should have said *buzz* or when you reach the highest number in the selected times table. Make a note to use that number again, or check it off as done depending on how well you did.

Now the other person goes first to play again.

▶ COUNTOUT!

This activity may seem extremely easy at first; after all, it's just counting, right? But play a few rounds and then think about what happened. You and your child will discover that you can develop a strategy for guessing and beating this game . . . maybe!

At a Glance

Grade/Subject: 3rd/Math—Problem Solving, Probability
Skills: critical thinking, number sense, probability
Materials: paper and pencil (optional)
Time: 15 minutes, or as long and as often as your child is interested

Getting Ready

No preparation is needed other than deciding how high a number you will start with. You might want to make a number chart (to 50) or a number line if your kid is a stronger visual learner than auditory learner; that is, she does better when she has things to look at while she's learning.

Step One

Explain how the CountOut game works. Here's how: Players start at any number and take turns counting BACKWARDS. Simple enough? Try it. Too simple, right? Well, here's the twist: On each turn, players can choose whether to count down by 3, by 2, or by 1 numbers. For instance, if the game starts at 30, say, the first player has three choices for doing the first countdown: 29-28-27, 29-28, or just 29. The object of the game is to make the countdown end by being the last player, the one who says, "Zero!"

Step Two

Start with a small practice game. Say, "10" as the first number to start this practice game. If you'd like to make sure your child is clear on the way to play, have her tell you all three of her choices for counting backwards, then pick one and take her turn, for instance, "9-8." Let her keep track of the counting on paper if it's easier for her that way.

Then you take your turn. Again, it might be helpful for you to say all three of your counting choices out loud and then pick one to use. Continue taking turns until one of you gets to say, *zero*.

Step Three

Now play another round and have your child pick a CountOut starting number between 10 and 25. Play several times; raise the possible starting number to between 10 and 50, or higher if you wish.

WHAT'S MORE

Try playing CountOut by starting at 0 and picking a countup—not countdown—number you need to reach in order to win.

———

Have a third player join you for playing CountOut. What adjustments in strategy will now help?

———

Play it all on paper. Write the numbers in a grid or number line and take turns crossing out 1, 2, or 3 numbers until zero is left alone!

Making the Grade

MAGIC MOMENTS

Parents shouldn't be giving kids all
the answers when they do
schoolwork together. Kids won't
understand what's going on if this
well-intentioned spoonfeeding
happens on a regular basis. Focus
on providing "teachable moments"
for your child, rather than forcing
the information down. Teachable
moments are times when you can
tell that something new has really
clicked for your child. Maybe she's
struggling with Roman numerals,
then all of a sudden, you know
she gets it!

Step Four

After a few rounds, start to talk about how you both are
choosing numbers. Ask questions like:

- Are you more likely to win if you go first?
- Is it better to start from a higher or lower number?
- Is there any number you have to say, or not say, to win?

Helping your child try to verbalize her strategy makes it
more likely that she can apply it in another round later.

▶ FEE FIE FOE—THREE FRACTS IN A ROW

Here's a variation of the familiar game Tic Tac Toe to help
your child practice equivalent fractions, and have fun trying
to beat you at the same time!

At a Glance

Grade/Subject: 4th/Math—Fractions
Skills: recognizing equivalent fractions
Materials: paper and pencil
1 quarter
8 pennies, 8 nickels (or other distinct counters)
dice

Time: 20–30 minutes

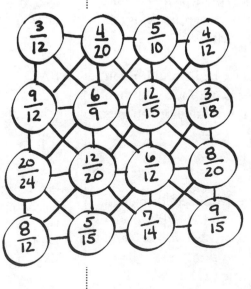

Getting Ready

Make your Fee Fie Foe
gameboard this way: Take the
quarter and trace around it (or do
it freehand if you can draw circles
about that size) 16 times in a 4" ×
4" grid; that is, four across and
four down. Draw a short line
between each circle to connect
them.

Write one of the following
fractions in each of the 16 circles

(any order is fine): 8/20, 7/14, 12/20, 4/12, 4/20, 9/12, 8/12, 12/15, 5/10, 9/15, 6/12, 3/18, 20/24, 5/15, 6/9, 3/12.

Now you are ready to play!

Step One

Do a quick review of proper fractions and equivalent fractions with your child. Need a quick reminder about what they are? Proper fractions have a smaller top number (numerator) than bottom number (denominator), like 1/2, 5/11, or 7/18. Equivalent fractions show the same amount: for instance 2/3, 6/9, and 8/12 are equivalent fractions since all three can be reduced to the fraction 2/3.

After your review, explain how this special version of Tic Tac Toe works. It's really quite simple. Players take turns rolling the dice and forming a proper fraction from the two numbers on top of the two dice. Then they must find an equivalent fraction on the gameboard and cover it with one of the counters. The object of the game is to cover three fractions in a row—vertically, horizontally, or diagonally. The player who first gets three counters in a row wins.

Step Two

To decide who goes first, each of you roll a die. The person with the higher number goes first and rolls the dice to make a proper fraction out of the numbers that come up. If you roll a 4 and a 3, the proper fraction you can make is 3/4 (4/3 is an improper fraction). Then you look at the gameboard and find a fraction that is equivalent to 3/4. You picked 9/12, right? So that's where you put your counter.

Step Three

Now it's your child's turn. He rolls, makes a proper fraction, finds an equivalent, and covers it with his counter. Using paper to write down the fraction and calculate possible equivalents can be helpful.

Watch out—here are special considerations for playing Fee Fie Foe!

WHAT'S MORE

Increase the size of your Fee Fie Foe gameboard and make the game require getting four fracts in a row to win.

Add a little decimal practice to the game by making a game-board with a percent written in each circle (20%, 33 1/3%, 250%) and then include the following extra step in the game: After you roll the dice and make a fraction (proper or improper), you must convert it to an equivalent percent; then find the matching percent on the board and cover it.

FIRM ABOUT HOMEWORK

When our son was in third grade, he one day steadfastly refused to get serious about doing some "grownup" homework early in the year. It took 2+ hours of being firm, but it got done, and he felt relieved, with a sense of conquest.

- There may be more than one equivalent fraction to choose from—look closely, choose carefully!
- If your opponent's counter is already on a fraction that you want to use, you may remove it.
- If either of you rolls doubles, you lose a turn!
- If you make a mistake and put your counter on a fraction that is not equivalent to what shows on the dice, you lose a turn!

Step Four

Alternate taking turns rolling the dice, making fractions, and placing your counters on the game board. The first player to cover three fracts in a row wins.

Then pick up your counters, roll the dice, and play again!

▶ GROOVY GRAPHS

Graphs are a handy way of showing mathematical information in a visual, easy-to-grasp style. In grade three, your child is learning to read both bar graphs and line graphs—a skill useful to her not only in math class but also in science and in social studies. Later on, she'll find that newspapers and news magazines often use graphs to show many different kinds of statistics—from population growth to sales of pop records.

While third-graders are just learning to read graphs, you and your kid may discover in this activity that the best way to get to understand graphs is to make some very simple graphs of your own.

At a Glance

Grade/Subject: 3rd/Math—Graphing
Skills: reading bar graphs and line graphs
Materials: several sheets of squared graph paper
four different colored pencils
ruler
indoor-outdoor thermometer

Time: About 1 hour twice a week while concentrating on this core area

5–10 minutes a day for a week to track the line graph

Getting Ready

Give yourself a quick review of the two basic kinds of graphs that your 3rd grader needs to understand:

- A *bar graph* uses bars of different lengths to show comparisons. These graphs are a dramatic way to show contrasts in amount or number. If you wanted to compare the yearly production of four car makers, for instance, you'd use a graph with four bars.
- A *line graph* most often shows changes in a quantity of something over time. For instance, if you wanted to chart the population of the United States from the year 1790 to the year 2000, you'd use a line graph.

Some line graphs use multiple lines of different colors to show changes in several quantities over the same time span—say, changes in the African American and Hispanic populations of the United States over 100 years. But that's something you might see in *Newsweek* or *U.S. News*, not in third grade!

Step One

To bring the idea of a graph down to earth and close to home, work with your kid to construct a simple bar graph that compares a few familiar, concrete quantities. Point out that a bar graph is just a picture of the different sizes of things—sort of like people of different heights standing in a row next to each other.

The first graph you make together can show the number of kids in the different grades or classes in her school. On one of the sheets of graph paper, set up the two dimensions (see the diagram on the next page).

WHAT'S MORE

Exactly which four classrooms you compare depends on the size and organization of your child's school. For example, you might want to compare all the third grade homerooms, if there are several.

Encourage your child to be aware of graphs in the magazines and other textbooks she reads. Call her attention to ads and other programs on TV that use graphs to illustrate their point.

Charting the temperature with a line graph is typical of the kinds of graphs your child will soon be making and reading in science class. Suggest that she keep track of other natural events with a graph—say, amount of rainfall in a month or changes in height of herself or a sibling.

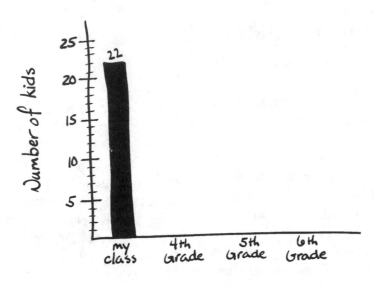

Step Two

Start with your child's own class: "How many kids are there in your class?" Have her use one of the colored pencils to mark a line on the vertical axis beside the number of kids—say, 22. Then use the ruler to draw a bar that extends from the base line label "My Class" up to that 22-kids line. Fill in the bar.

Step Three

To keep this graph simple, you need only compare two or three other classes. Ask your child to guess at the number of students in, say, the fourth-, fifth-, and sixth-grade classes. Knowing the exact number doesn't matter for this graph.

Again, have her mark a line by the number of kids in each of those classes, then draw the bar. For contrast, use different colored pencils for each class.

Step Four

When the three or four bars on the graph have been filled in, check to make sure that your kid can read and interpret the information that she has supplied in making it.

First, make sure that she's clear on what each dimension of the graph stands for: name of class or room (horizontal base line), number of kids in that class (vertical).

Then go on to the first impressions that the bar graph gives.

- Which is the biggest class?
- Which is the smallest?
- Are any classes exactly the same size?

Help your child get the idea that it is easy to get this kind of information quickly by looking at a graph—often quicker than you could get it by comparing the actual numbers.

WHAT'S MORE

Try making neighborhood graphs—do bar and line graphs to show the growth of garden plants (same variety) in different yards, the number of bikes and trikes stored in each garage, the number of adult and kid pairs or blue jeans per household, or the TV viewing hours for each family for a week. Use a different color for each family to make the data really stand out (particularly with the line graphs).

Step Five

In a different take on this activity, set up the basic plan for a line graph that shows temperature changes. To make the point that line graphs generally show change over time, work with your kid to make this graph over a one-week period.

Have your kid write the days of the week along the bottom axis of the graph. Decide together what time of day you'll record the temperature in degrees, and whether you'll use Fahrenheit or Celsius.

Step Six

On the first day of making this graph, have your kid read the temperature on the thermometer and make a dot on the graph above the "day" label and opposite the temperature reading. Continue this process for the week.

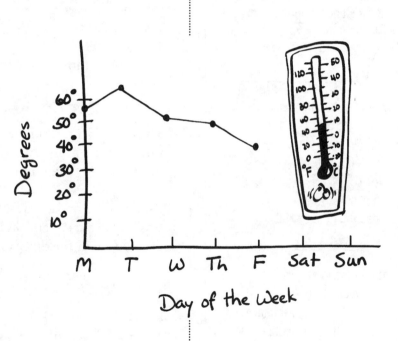

As your kid adds a new dot to the graph, have her draw a line that connects it with the previous day's dot. As with the bar graph, when this graph is finished, check to see that your kid understands how her information went into its making—and how she can get that information back from this (or any) graph.

▶ MAKE A HUNDRED

Get ready for a fast, lively game that uses basic math facts. In this card game, you use your addition and multiplication facts to add numbers to try to reach one hundred. Don't be fooled by how simple the game appears. In fact, it requires a good deal of strategy to progressively add and multiply numbers so that you get to 100 without going over 100.

The activity instructions give you the rules for getting started on the basic game. In "What's More," you'll find some nifty variations on the game. Once you have played Make a Hundred for a while, you might want to make up your own variation. This is the kind of game that can grow more interesting as your child's mathematical skills develop.

At a Glance

Grade/Subject: 3rd/Math—Problem solving, computation
Skills: adding and multiplying one- and two-digit numbers, problem solving
Materials: deck of cards
paper and pencil
Time: 20–30 minutes

Getting Ready

Explain to your child that this game involves adding and multiplying numbers. Make sure she knows the multiplication tables up to 9.

From a deck of 52 cards, take out all the jokers and face cards (jack, queen, and king) and put them aside. You will not need them for this game.

Step One

Shuffle the cards and deal seven to your child and seven to yourself. Tell her to look at her cards and place one on the table face up so that you can see it. Now you choose a card from your hand and play it face up next to the first card. Form either the sum or product of your card and your child's card (ace has a value of 1). You have the choice of either adding or multiplying the two numbers, but keep in mind that the object of the game is to get to 100 without going over it. Write the result on the paper. This value is the start of the running total that together you will keep to play the game.

Step Two

Now it's your child's turn. Tell her to play a card from her hand and form either the sum or product of the values of her card and the card you just played. Add this number to the running total and record the result.

Step Three

You probably get the idea now. Continue taking turns playing a card and forming the sum or product of the values of the current player's card and the previous card. The winner of the hand is the first player who makes the running total closest to 100 without going over it. The first player who wins three hands is the winner of the game.

▶ ON THE AVERAGE . . .

Talk about averages fills our lives, and knowing what averages mean and how averages are arrived at helps your child both listen and think more critically. There are lots of real-world situations that you can use to help give your child practice in calculating this number, from baseball scores to hours of sleep.

People talk about averages a lot in a casual way, but the term has a precise meaning in math, where it's also called the "mean" or "arithmetic mean." To calculate the average, or mean, of a set of quantities, you add them up and then divide that total by the number of quantities or items in the set.

At a Glance

Grade/Subject: 3rd/Math—Statistics and Probability
Skills: calculating averages
Materials: notebook and pencil
pocket calculator
sports section of a newspaper or almanac with past sports statistics
Time: build this calculating activity into real-life situations (whenever and as often as you can)

TESTIMONIAL

SCORE! has been phenomenally great for my children. I really like that kids are being challenged without their being aware of it. The progress that they make continues to be maintained by the program. It's great for parents to know where their child is academically so they can keep challenging them, and *SCORE!* has a record of each child's progress on both a state level and a national level of achievement, which most schools don't have.

CALCULATE AVERAGES

"Could you figure out the average of what we spent on each trip to the store?" (Total expenditures divided by number of trips) "There were 33 peanut butter cookies in that bag, and the four of us have eaten all of them! I had only two. On the average, how many cookies did each of us eat?" (Total number of cookies divided by number of people) "We've really had a lot of snow this month. What do you think the daily average was?" (Total snowfall divided by number of days in the month)

WHAT'S MORE

Figuring averages for a small set of quantities—say three or four whole numbers—is also a good way for your child to practice mental math.

Some sports averages for your kid to find and figure:
- Average winning/losing scores in Rose Bowl games, 1985–1995
- Average age of the U.S. Olympic gymnastic team members
- Average winning times— men, women, wheelchair athletes—for the last five Boston or New York Marathons

---

How about some classroom averages?
- Average heights of boys and girls
- Average weekly hours of homework in each subject
- Average weight of textbooks

Getting Ready

Think of some areas of interest for your child and then make a list of some ideas for what kinds of averages might be calculated related to those areas. This activity and the sidebars suggest quite a few.

Step One

Review with your child how to work out an average by adding up all the items in the set of quantities to be averaged and then dividing that total by the number of items. A good way to do this review is to figure out together the average amount of sleep you or your child got over the past five days. For example, if you slept 6 hours on Monday night, 7 hours on Tuesday, 6 on Wednesday, and 8 on both Thursday and Friday, what was the average amount of sleep you got on those five days? (The total hours, or 35, divided by the number of days = 7 hours.)

Step Two

If your kid likes sports, that's a great starting place for figuring averages. Use statistics from the sports pages or a sports almanac, or draw on his own knowledge and memory. "Who's your town's best basketball player? How would you find out that player's average scoring so far this year?" Work through the averaging process with your kid: Add up all the baskets scored by that player, then divide by the number of games played. "Which are the best soccer teams in your league? What was their average score per game?" "That school seems to have big players on its football team! What do you suppose is the average weight of their players?"

Step Three

Your role in this activity is finding frequent opportunities for your child to practice finding averages, whether calculating them in his head or using a calculator. At the same time, he can come to realize that figuring averages can be useful, providing interesting information and even some fun.

CHAPTER 15

Learning Adventures—
4th Grade Math

SUCCESS WILL HAPPEN

Parents have to begin with what their children really do know. That may seem obvious, but it's not. Some parents have a tendency to jump to the higher level skills and say their child doesn't know them. "You've let me down," is their attitude. Our advice is to start with what your child does know and go from there. "You don't know 5 times 5, but you do know 1 times 5. That's great. Let's work from there." Start with the basics and develop a positive attitude and convey that you really believe in your child. At *SCORE!*, we say, "I totally know you can do this!" and it comes across. Success will happen.

▶ **BUYING POWER**

Elementary level students are familiar with money and understand how it operates on a practical level, but they often need practice working with decimal numbers. We asked a representative 4th grader what was the best thing about money: "Buying stuff" was the reply. And what was the worst thing? "Adding it up." This activity (like life) combines the best and worst of a child's view of handling money, and even makes that worst fun—until realization of the really worst: "Paying bills!"

At a Glance

Grade/Subject: 4th/Math—Money and Decimals
Skills: adding, subtracting decimal numbers
Materials: supermarket (or other) receipts
        mail-order catalogs
        paper and pencil
Time: 1/2–1 hour once a week (more frequently if desired, or needed)

Getting Ready

Instead of steps, this activity offers three kinds of buying power activities. Have your receipts and catalogs available and watch for times when your kid's interest is likely to be piqued, such as upon returning from a shopping trip, when a catalog comes, or when you take time to look at his hobby or collection (or talk about something he'd like to collect or a hobby he'd like to consider).

Buying Power: Cash Count

Put your child's developing skill with decimals to practical use. Here's how.

Supermarket and other everyday shopping receipts are an excellent around-the-house source of decimal number practice material. They have multiple item prices and a subtotal that your child can check himself against (any taxes or discount notations can be ignored if you wish; you can even cross them out).

Begin by having him check off the items bought (and the prices charged) against the receipt as you unload the groceries, hardware items, or whatever. This is also a very practical activity since automated checkout mechanisms do make errors, particularly with multiple items, and this is a math practice activity that can save you money! Then have him check the addition *and* the subtraction to see whether you got the correct change.

Buying Power: Fantasy Funds

Fantasy buying is fun and (almost) satisfying. Since elementary school children are often avid readers of catalogs, take advantage of their interest by having your child add up the prices of all the "Look at this, Mom" items (as another opportunity to practice working with decimal numbers). If you specify an amount—"Imagine you have five dollars to spend on things in this catalog."—your child can work back and forth with addition and subtraction to figure out the best way to allocate his fantasy funds.

Buying Power: Trading Time

Traders' buying and selling offers yet another avenue for highly motivated practice in adding and subtracting

CALCULATORS? NOT!

Calculators are, of course, incredibly useful mathematical tools, but don't use them for these activities. The purpose this time around is to build math skills and comprehension through practice.

WHAT'S MORE

Invite your child to imagine his own office by supplying him with catalogs for furniture, equipment, stationery, and the like. See what he comes up with and what it costs.

decimals. Hobbies and collections also offer opportunities for practice in adding up money. Baseball card fanatics already spend hours pouring over catalogs of cards, and they enjoy the challenge of finding out what their present collection is actually worth. Why not have them add up the "buy price" listings for their cards and compare them with the "sell price" listings (most card catalogs provide both buy and sell price lists).

Of course, Trading Time isn't just for card collectors. Most kids this age are avid collectors of something. So it's easy to ask, what if you owned all of the (fill in this space with the current fad) dolls, horses, or action figures? Followed by questions like:

- What would it have cost you? How would you figure that out?
- How much might you be able to sell each piece for?

▶ CALENDAR RACE

What does a calendar game have to do with math? Lots actually, since this calendar race is a game of strategy; and strategy means that with some careful thought, you or your child can make a plan to win every time!

At a Glance

Grade/Subject: 4th/Math—Problem solving, Probability, Time
Skills: following directions; understanding days and months of the year; predicting outcomes
Materials: calendar and pencil (optional)
Time: 15–20 minutes

Getting Ready

No preparation is needed except perhaps identifying a calendar for easy reference. It might be helpful during the first couple of rounds.

WHAT'S MORE

Any shopping expedition can be turned into a math activity as long as you have your convenient two-legged 4th-grade calculator along. Keep a small notebook and pen or pencil handy for him on these occasions. Supermarkets are filled with places to calculate decimal numbers. What is the difference between the sale price and the actual price? How many sale items would you have to buy in order to save enough to get one free?

PUT MEANING INTO MATH

You can explain something the same way over and over again, and sometimes your child won't understand. You then need to step out of the situation and focus on "How can I relate this better to my child? My child loves soccer, so maybe we'll try this math problem with soccer balls rather than cups of baking flour." Just drawing an analogy from something that means a lot to your child may often be enough to really help.

WHAT'S MORE

Try using holidays or family birthdays for your starting points.

Try going backward on the calendar and be the first one to say January 1.

Step One

Explain how Calendar Race works. Here's how: You and your child take turns naming the dates on the calendar in order. The goal of the game is to be the first one to say December 31! There are just two rules:

- Whatever date you say must be later in the year than the date previously said.
- You may change only the month or the day, never both.

So, if one player starts with March 11, for example, the next player can name a date like June 11 (the eleventh day of any other MONTH) or March 29 (any other DAY in March).

Step Two

Practice Calendar Race. Pick a date like March 23, for instance. To make sure your child knows how to play, have him explain how he can choose his date—by picking any other day between March 24 and March 31 OR the 23rd day in any other month between April and December.

When he has named a date, you take a turn (it might be useful to review out loud your choices before picking a date).

Step Three

Continue taking turns until one of you can say December 31. Talk together about how it went.

- How long did it take?
- Was it hard or easy to get to the end?

Then play another round and have your child pick the starting date.

Step Four

After several rounds, see if you can notice any patterns in your child's actions:

- Does he always change the month or always the date?
- Does he skip large chunks of time or go by little ones?
- Did your child figure out any tricks or strategies?

Talk about how he is picking the numbers:

- Is there any date that must be picked to win? Not picked to win?
- Does it matter if you go first or not?
- What strategy will you try next time?
- If you've done the CountOut activity (in the last chapter), are there any similarities?

Step Five

Play again from time to time in the future. This is a great activity to do "when there's nothing to do." Encourage your child to try to figure out a winning strategy and test it out by playing the game. Thinking, making a plan, and checking whether it works or not is a valuable lesson to learn.

▶ FIBONACCI MAGIC

Numbers have always had a mysterious quality. In ancient Greece, a brotherhood was formed to study numbers and other related subjects, and its findings were considered mysteries that it kept secret.

One surprising group of numbers is called the *Fibonacci numbers*. This number pattern is named after the medieval mathematician Lorenzo Fibonacci, who discovered the mysteries of these numbers. Mathematicians have been studying these numbers for centuries to unearth their many remarkable properties. You and your child will be amazed by the "secrets" that these numbers hold!

WHAT'S MORE

Let a third person join you in your next round of Calendar Race.

If your child likes manipulating materials, make posterboard calendars with markers—one for each month. Arrange the calendars around the room (or in several rooms for even more fun). Players stand by the month each time they pick a date. Moving from calendar to calendar gives a real sense of "racing to December 31st."

GET RIPPED!

Parents and children should count money together. Fractions and decimals can be easily taught by ripping up paper into pieces. I rip up paper into 8 pieces; so how many pieces would I need to get one full piece of paper? What if I had 9 pieces? 1 1/8. By getting children to verbalize and hold something, they learn so much faster. "Do this at home" is what we tell parents at *SCORE!*. You may read to your child at home, but also reinforce math skills.

At a Glance

Grade/Subject: 4th/Math—Computation, Numeration
Skills: practice in adding and multiplying two-digit numbers
Materials: pencil and paper
          calculator (optional)
Time: 20–30 minutes

Getting Ready

Explain to your child that you will be making a special pattern of numbers, and you will be looking for "mysterious properties" in these numbers. Review with your child how to multiply two-digit numbers.

Step One

Write the following number pattern: 1, 1, 2, 3, 5 and ask your child how the number 2 is related to the two numbers before it in the series. Then ask her how the number 3 is related to the two numbers before it.

Now, ask if she can tell you what she thinks the rule may be for how to make this list of numbers. Check her ideas by applying it together to the number 5.

If she doesn't see that each new number in the series is the sum of the previous numbers, write the number 8 next in the series and talk about the numbers together until she figures out the rule.

Step Two

Take turns computing and writing the next nine or ten numbers in the list until you have the numbers 1, 1, 2, 3, 5, 8, 13, 21, 34, 55, 89, 144, 233, 377, and 610.

Step Three

Here's where the mysteries begin. Have your child add the first, third, and fifth numbers (1 + 2 + 5). Is there anything special about the number you get?

WHAT'S MORE

You can make up your own list of Fibonacci numbers. Replace the first two 1's by any same number of your choice (say, 5). Then make the list by adding two consecutive numbers to get the next number in the group. If you use 5, then the first three numbers would be 5, 5, 10. Check whether all the results you have discovered hold for this new list.

You also can explore other properties of Fibonacci numbers. For example, use a calculator to find the quotient of two consecutive Fibonacci numbers, always dividing the larger number by the smaller number. What do you discover?

Then, you add the first, third, fifth, and seventh numbers (1 + 2 + 5 + 13). Talk about what you can see about the number you get.

Ask your child to predict what number you get when you add the first, third, fifth, seventh, and ninth numbers (1 + 2 + 5 + 13 + 34). She can then confirm her guess by adding these numbers.

Step Four

Now for a really bizarre secret . . .

- You begin first. Multiply the seventh number (13) by 11 and add the second number (1). What is special about the number you get?
- Have your child multiply the eighth number (21) by 11 and add the third number (2). Now what's special about the number she gets this time?
- Now you multiply the ninth number (34) by 11 and add the fourth number. Is there anything special about the number you get?
- Ask your child to predict what number she would get if she multiplies the tenth number (55) by 11 and adds the fifth number. Have her check her guess.

▶ FRACTION JACK

It's amazing how "traditional" games like this one can be reworked with new elements to teach math without losing their fun.

At a Glance

Grade/Subject: 4th/Math—Fractions
Skills: addition and subtraction of fractions and mixed numbers
Materials: deck of cards
            paper and pencil
Time: 20–30 minutes (or as long as your child wants to play)

WHAT'S MORE

Try exploring these two other properties:
1. The sum of 10 consecutive Fibonacci numbers is a multiple of 11.
2. For any four consecutive Fibonacci numbers, twice the third number minus the fourth number is always 1.

Take up numbers detective work together. Find other properties of Fibonacci numbers. Your local library can help you research Fibonacci numbers.

Getting Ready

No special preparation is needed, but prior to playing, you might want to check in with your child to see what he knows about adding and subtracting fractions with and without common denominators. The following example can give you a little review and be used for checking out your child's understanding.

Say you are trying to add 2/3 and 4/9. Your denominators are 3 and 9, right? Find the smallest number that both 3 and 9 can be divided into (that number is the least common multiple), in this case, 18. Let's convert 2/3 first. Divide the denominator into 18—that's 6—and multiply by 2 to get the new numerator, 12. So the new equivalent fraction is 12/18. Then do 4/9. Divide 9 into 18 to get 2—and multiply that result by 4 to get 8. So the other fraction is 8/18. Now it's easy to add 12/18 plus 8/18 to get 20/18. Since 18/18 = 1 leaving 2/18 (which reduces to 1/9), in lowest terms, 20/18 = 1 1/9. That's all you need to know to get going on this activity.

Step One

Separate the deck of cards into two packs, one consisting of hearts and diamonds (red cards) and the other of clubs and spades (black cards). Place the two packs face down on the table. In this game, all the face cards (kings, queens, jacks) are wild and may be given any value from 1 to 10. All the other cards have their actual face value.

To start, pick a low number—say 5—to use as your addition target.

Step Two

You can go first to show your child what to do. Draw one card from each pack. Form a fraction by using the numerical value of the black card as the numerator and the value of the red card as the denominator. For example, if you draw a black 5 and red 4, your fraction is 5/4 or 1 1/4 in lowest terms. Write it down. You will be adding several fractions together.

Step Three

Now you go again, drawing two more cards, forming another fraction and bringing it to lowest terms. This time you pick a black 3 and a red jack. Remember that the face cards can be assigned any value you want between 1 and 10—say you choose 4. That makes your fraction 3/4.

Add up the fractions from your two turns. How close is it to your target number, 5? Decide whether you should draw again and form another fraction to add. The goal is to get as close to your target—either above or below it—as possible. When you decide to "stick" and stop drawing, it's your child's turn to draw.

Step Four

Your child goes through the same steps, drawing cards, forming fractions, and adding them together. If he wants to know how close he is to the target 5, you can help him set up the subtraction problem (5 minus his sum).

The "hand" is finished when the second player decides he or she is as close to the target as possible (or when all the cards from both decks are used up). The player who is closest to the target number (in this case, 5), wins that hand. Then play Fraction Jack again!

▶ How Far? How Fast?

Here's an action-oriented math activity for two people that, with a little imagination, lends itself to some intriguing variations.
At a Glance

Grade/Subject: 4th/Math—Graphing
Skills: data collection, plotting a line graph
Materials: ruler (with center groove if possible)
    book (hard cover, 5" × 7" or larger)
    sheets of paper or printer form paper
    marble (more than one, optional)
    4 or more different colored markers
    graphing paper (although plain paper is fine)
    timer, clock, or wristwatch with second hand
Time: 30–45 minutes

WHERE IS YOUR CHILD?

I've heard horror stories of parents who waited for Back to School nights or conferences and were shocked to learn that their children were "*how* far behind in reading?" "They don't know *what?*" Parents need to wake up. Find out what your child is doing in her homework.

If you play an active role in your child's education on a day-to-day basis, and you make that time commitment, you will know where she is struggling and where she's thriving. You won't really have to know from the teacher. You'll be bringing it to the teacher's attention, saying, "I noticed in her homework last week that she's having difficulty with triple-digit addition. Have you found that?" Then the teacher can look through her papers and the two of you can have a conversation about your child.

Getting Ready

Quickly review with your child how a line graph is set up. Note how information is recorded as points on the graph, and then the points are connected by a line formed by joining the points, starting on the left and moving to the right.

In this activity, the information you will use will be the speed of a moving object at several different times. Clear a space about two or three feet square on the floor or on a tabletop to use for setting up a little race track where you can roll some marbles.

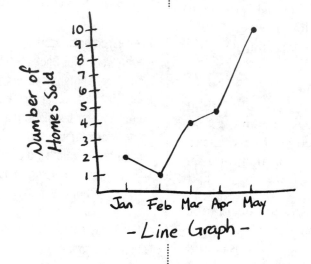

- Line Graph -

Step One

Have your child help you set up the racetrack. Here's how:

- Lay a line of six sheets of paper down to form a long path. If you use separate sheets of paper, smoothly tape the top of each to the bottom of the next sheet.
- Position the book at the beginning of your paper racetrack.
- Rest one end of the ruler on the edge of the book and the other end on the paper track.

Step Two

Prepare for timing:

- Have your child hold a marble at the top of the ruler with one hand and, watching the second hand of a watch or clock, be prepared to start timing as soon as the marble touches the paper.
- Meanwhile, you get ready with the first colored marker to mark the marble's location on the paper track each second as it rolls across the paper.

Start timing the roll:

- As he releases the marble, allowing it to roll down the center groove in the ruler, your child should note the second hand and count aloud the passing of each second until he reaches 4 seconds.
- As each second is announced, you should mark on the paper the position of the marble.

Step Three

After each marble roll, you will have 4 marks (one for each second, right?). Roll the marble several times, so you have several sets of data to use. Change to a different colored marker to make seeing each trial easier.

Measure and record the distance in inches from the end of the ruler to each mark. You might want to put your measurements into a chart like this:

Time in Seconds	Distance in Inches	Speed in Seconds
1	6	
2	20	
3	24	
4	26	

You can use the first two columns (time and distance) to record information for each trial roll. You will fill in the last column (speed in terms of how far a marble goes in how many seconds) after you plot some points and make a line graph.

Step Four

Work together to set up the graph. Label the line along the bottom of the graph "Time in Seconds." Label the lines along the left side of the graph "Distance in Inches."

Plot the points from your marble rolling. You can put several tries on one graph by using solid and dotted lines or by using the different colors.

WHAT'S MORE

Try rolling a smaller or larger marble or a ball. Record and discuss what differences you notice in the distance or speed.

———

Record the distance traveled for times longer than four seconds and see what differences in distance, if any, there might be.

———

Construct a ramp at the other end of your paper path and see how far up a variety of round things can roll. What differences does that make in your line graphs?

———

Try rolling on a few different surfaces like carpet, sandpaper, or glass to see how surface affects the speed or distance.

Step Five

Talk about what the information on the graph means. Can your child tell the following?

- During which time period is the marble moving the fastest? the slowest?
- During which time period does the marble go the farthest distance? the shortest distance?
- What does the steepness of the line graph indicate?
- What does a completely horizontal line mean?

These questions could lead to a general talk with your child about the usefulness of graphs to present information and about factors that affect the information graphs can show.

▶ KALAH

This age-old game of strategy and logic has many variations, many different names, and slightly different rules in different countries. Although Kalah takes just a few minutes to play—the rounds can go quickly—it becomes addictive because of its capacity to stimulate creative mathematical thinking that can lead you and your child to some great discussions about what strategies work the best and why.

At a Glance

Grade/Subject: 4th/Math—Problem solving
Skills: careful observation, logical thinking, planning
Materials: egg carton or other container with 12 cavities
    48 counters (such as beans, buttons, or pennies)
Time: 20–30 minutes, or as long as your child wants to play

Getting Ready

No special preparation is needed other than obtaining your materials—whatever you are using as a container and counters—and choosing where and when to play.

Step One

Explain to your child how the game works. Players start by each placing four counters in each of the six cups on their

MATH'S GREATEST HITS

According to *Newsweek's Computers & the Family* newsmagazine (Fall/Winter 1996), there were quite a few bestselling math computer software titles in 1996, including:

- *Math Blaster: In Search of Spot* (Davidson & Associates) for ages 6 to 12; (800) 545-7677
- *Math Blaster 2: The Secret of the Lost City* (Davidson & Associates) for ages 8 to 13
- *Mathematics* (boxed set by SofSource) for ages 10 to adult; (505) 523-6789
- *Math Heads* (Theatrix Interactive) for ages 10 to 14; (800) 955-TRIX
- *Major League Math* (Sanctuary Woods) for ages 9 to 13; (800) 943-3664

own side of the container. Players will take turns moving the counters around the container, and the object is to capture the most counters. Counters are captured when you drop a final counter into a cup that contains only one or two counters in it.

Step Two

To see how it works, play a sample game as follows. You take the first turn. Pick up all the counters from any one of the six cups on your side. Then, beginning with the cup to the right of the cup that you took the counters from, drop the four that you picked up one at a time into each consecutive cup to the right, moving counterclockwise.

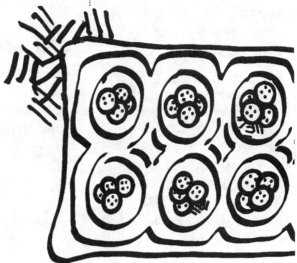

Now it's your child's turn. He picks up all four of the counters in any one of the cups on his side of the container (or five counters, if the cup he chooses now has one of your counters in it) and drops them one at a time into each consecutive cup, again going counterclockwise.

Step Three

Continue to take turns picking up and moving the counters around the container in a counterclockwise direction. After a few moves, you will begin to be able to capture some of the counters from your opponent's cups.

You capture counters whenever the last counter you drop lands on your opponent's side of the container in a cup with only one or two counters in it. (Cups with more than two counters are not captured.) When dropping a counter makes a total of two or three counters in one of your opponent's cups, you pick up the counters in that cup, including the one you just dropped in, and set them aside for counting at the end of the game. You may capture counters only from your opponent's side of the container.

WHAT'S MORE

Add an additional cup to each of your sides, called the Kalah cup. When you are dropping the counters into the cups, you drop one into your own Kalah cup, but not into your opponent's Kalah cup. Once in your Kalah cup, a counter cannot be removed. Each counter in your Kalah cup earns one point. The player with the most counters in his Kalah cup wins.

WHAT'S MORE

By using more than or fewer than 48 counters, you can adjust the length of the playing time. Does it affect your strategy?

Try another age-old strategy game called Nim. You lay out fifteen counters on a playing surface and take turns removing one, two, or three counters. The object of the game is to NOT take the last counter!

KEEP COUNTING

Activities that allow you to help your child develop concepts of quantity and representations of quantity, whether it's with tissue pellets, telephone poles, or Halloween candies, all add to the depth of their numerical knowledge. In later years—when your child comes to working with numbers in different base systems or learning about number theory—he or she will have a set of concrete experiences to draw upon.

Continue playing until one of you has no counters left on your side of the container. Then tally the number of counters you each have captured, plus the number of counters remaining on your opponent's side of the container. The player with the most counters wins.

Step Four

Play as many rounds as you want. Talk about what you are learning in the process of playing. When it's time for supper or bed, or for some other reason you must tear yourself away from playing, put the game pieces somewhere handy so you can easily start up a game at any time.

▶ LET ME COUNT THE WAYS

Successful mastery of number skills is a little like the old joke about the tourist in New York City who asks, "How do you get to Carnegie Hall?" and the New Yorker answers, "Practice, practice, practice."

Helping children to think numerically and providing them with chances to practice working with number facts are two things parents can easily achieve. Many of your child's daily activities have numerical components, and when you find them and play with them together, everyone comes out ahead.

At a Glance

Grade/Subject: 4th/Math—Numeration
Skills: number skills practice
Materials: just about everything—once you start looking!
Time: 1 minute or as long and as often as you and your child have the energy

Getting Ready

No major preparation is required for these activities. All you need is your ability to be alert to the wealth of number experiences in everyday life. Read the steps below as examples. You can use them specifically, or you can extend these suggestions into the unique spaces of your own lives and make up your own.

Let Me Count: In the Bathroom

The children in one family we know use a fluoride mouthwash every night after brushing their teeth. The directions say, "Rinse for one minute," and this family turns that minute into an amusing math lesson. Things started off just by having a parent count to sixty to mark the time. Then the kids counted to sixty by holding up one finger at a time until they reached ten and the parent rolled up a small pellet of bathroom tissue and put it down. Six pellets = six tens = sixty, and you're done.

When everyone got bored with tens, they moved on to fifteens, and so on through all the combinations that make sixty. Using the timer on the kitchen stove, they got a chance to count back down from sixty, and, when that became tedious, they used a three-minute egg timer. This last item wasn't particularly exact (you had to guess when two thirds of the sand had run out before you could start the rinse), but everyone got to work on estimation skills and have a good laugh about the race between the grains of sand and the kitchen clock!

Activities like this, light-hearted, impromptu, and using whatever is at hand, can take the rough edges off boring and repetitive events, and they certainly give new meaning to that traditional parental response, "Just a minute."

Let Me Count: On the Road

You probably have a few road games up your sleeve. Just don't forget they're there; they make wonderful ways to practice number skills.

WHAT'S MORE

Look for more household counting opportunities: How many times can you fold the bedspread (and sheet) in equal halves before you can no longer make a fold? Time the toaster settings—How long to toast on the light, medium, and dark settings? Does the toaster toast the same length of time at a particular setting? Time it on several mornings to see. Compute the average servings of "bits" in your pet's daily dry food ration. Use a food scale to calculate the average weekly dinner serving (including seconds!) for each family member.

Try playground/playing field counting: How long does it take to swing back and forth 100 times? How many times can we make the see-saw go up in a minute? How many times can I toss and catch a ball in a minute? skip rope? hop on one foot?

- How many telephone poles go by in a minute?
- What is the most popular color for cars in regions that you pass through?
- When the road sign says, "ten miles to Euclid," does the odometer agree?

All of these simple activities provide practice in counting and computation. They can be as elaborate or as simple as you wish.

Let Me Count: Halloween

Halloween is the holiday that asks the question, "What are we going to do with all that candy?" To which the mathematically inclined parent could say, "Count it, of course!" To begin with, there's the simple count of how much of everything. Next, comes the question of how much of each kind of candy (and a great opportunity for making a simple graph).

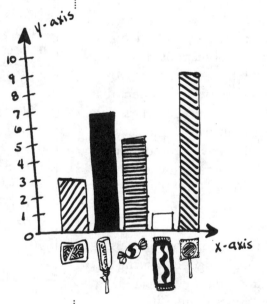

For the ambitious, there is the task of estimating the total number of all the bits of candy that come in packages, boxes, or in regularly divided rolls. Open up a package and count the individual candies, then multiply by the number of packages. Do all the packages have the same amount? Open more and count them up. Raking over the Halloween hoard can easily turn into an argument over who got the most candy, so why not make the most of it mathematically?

▶ MAKING POLYOMINOES

Does your child like puzzles? Many puzzles are based on the arrangement of congruent shapes. One simple but fascinating shape that is found in many games, such as on a checkerboard and in a crossword puzzle, is called a *polyomino*.

Although polyominoes are simple shapes made of squares like the ones shown below, they have surprising characteristics. For example, researchers have discovered that a super computer cannot figure out in a reasonable amount of time whether polyominoes of an arbitrary shape can be fitted together to form a rectangle! In this activity, you will explore some remarkable properties of these unusual critters.

At a Glance

Grade/Subject: 4th/Math—Geometry
Skills: making and identifying congruent figures
Materials: pencil
　　　　several sheets of 4" × 4" graph paper
　　　　ruler
　　　　scissors
Time: 30 minutes

Getting Ready

Explain to your child that you are going to make some shapes called polyominoes using congruent squares. Discuss with him why some of the adjacent figures are polyominoes and why others are not. Make sure that your child understands congruent figures. Review with him the transformations of a figure— that is, a flip, a rotation, and a glide of a figure, such as a rectangle. (Check out the math content in Section II if you feel the need to review it yourself.)

Step One

Draw a square polyomino on the graph paper with a ruler. First, draw a square 1" by 1".

WHAT'S MORE

Try doing Steps Two through Five of this activity again with pentominoes—they are polyominoes made of five congruent squares. Doing this activity with pentominoes can take up a lot of time. For example, there are a lot more basic pentominoes—12 to be exact!

Draw a large rectangle on a piece of graph paper and try to cover it with triominoes. Then try to cover it with tetrominoes.

Try to cover a rectangle with repeating patterns made up of triominoes.

Polyominoes

POLYO-WHAT?!

A polyomino is a shape made up of congruent squares, each of which shares exactly one common side with each adjacent square. Following are two examples of shapes that are polyominoes. Underneath these are two shapes that are not polyominoes because they do not share a common side. The left-hand shape is not a polyomino because it has two squares that meet at a corner. The right-hand shape is not a polyomino because it has a square whose side meets two sides of the adjacent square.

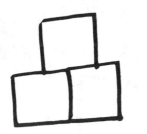

Not polyominoes

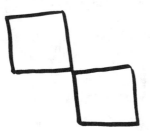

Attach another square of the same size to the first one so that the two squares share a common side completely. Now attach a third square to one of the first two squares so that those two share a side. This three-part polyomino is called a *triomino*.

Step Two

Now ask your child to draw a different triomino using 1" by 1" squares. Have him cut out the triomino and try to fit it on your triomino so that it completely covers it. If he cannot do so, then have him draw a different triomino. When he has found a triomino that covers your triomino, ask him which transformation (flip, rotate, and/or glide) he used to cover your triomino.

Step Three

Next, have your child draw three *tetrominoes*—that is, polyominoes made up of four squares. Meanwhile you also draw three tetrominoes of your own. Then each of you cut out your tetrominoes and try to match congruent tetrominoes. Identify the transformations you used to match tetrominoes.

Step Four

There are five unique tetrominoes. All other tetrominoes can be transformed into one of these basic ones. Work with your child to find as many of the five basic tetrominoes as you can.

Step Five

Find the tetromino that has the smallest perimeter (total outside edge). Ask your child to explain why the perimeter of this tetromino is less than other tetrominoes. Then find which tetrominoes have the largest perimeters!

CHAPTER 16

Learning Adventures—
3rd Grade Science

RED ROVER, RED ROVER

The NASA Mars Pathfinder spacecraft will land on Mars around July 4, 1997, controlled by scientists and engineers 35 million miles away. Mars studies will heat up in your child's science classroom for years to come! See if your child's teacher knows about the "Red Rover, Red Rover" project. Students from classrooms all over the world will build their own Mars-scapes and LEGO space rovers operated via computer software that mimics NASA's control programs. For detailed information you can pass on to your child's teacher, call LEGO Dacta at (800) 362-4308, or visit their Web site at http://www.lego.com/learn.

❯ SCIENCE TOOL KIT

To make doing science with your child a little more special, the two of you can put together a science toolbox (or backpack). It's a convenient way to store science materials so that they're always handy. Since some of the science activities suggested in *Making the Grade* include walks or explorations outside, this is also a good way to carry everything you and she will need.

All of the activities in this book can be done with common, everyday objects. Most of them are in your home right now, and many of them are in the kitchen. In the "At a Glance" section of each activity in this chapter and the next, you will find a list that includes most of the particular materials and simple tools that you will need. You don't have to compile a tool kit, but it does add an official touch and is a good place to begin thinking about the tools of science.

At a Glance

Grade/Subject: 3rd and 4th/Science—All Activities
Skills: being prepared
Materials: lightweight toolbox, fishing box, sweater storage box, or backpack

Making the Grade

SCIENCE THAT COMPUTES

There are many good programs for your home PC that will give kids great science experiences. Here are a few you can start to investigate:

• *Ozzie's World, Deluxe Edition*— Lots of animation, video, and games ranging from simple sorting and matching with Ozzie the sea otter to more involved science experiments, all with tons of replay value. Contact Digital Impact at (800) 775-4232

• *Simpark*—Part of the popular "Sim" software series, this is another engaging, creative way for kids to develop an entire environment/ecosystem, complete with choices for regions and animal and plant species (with great games to help you "Identa-Species"). Contact MAXIS at (800) 33-MAXIS.

• *Devils Canyon*—Be a "Time Blazer," and travel back to the age of the dinos to learn all about fossils and massive reptiles while playing a challenging rescue game. Contact TeraMedia at (800) 818-3990.

(You'll find suggestions for the investigative science materials that you and your child might want to use listed below in Step One.)

Time: You and your child can devote part of an evening to thinking about and gathering the tools and materials.

Getting Ready

Read over the list of suggested equipment for the science tool kit listed under Step One. Don't worry about having everything right away. You can always add things as you go. Can you think of anything else? Are there tools or measuring devices that you use in your work that might be appropriate? Think over the items you use around the house to observe, measure, or record. Are there more things that could be included in our list?

Step One

With your child, read and discuss each of the materials suggested below for her science tool kit. Try to think of other resources she might include for each category. Make any additions or leave anything out as you wish.

Observation Aids: magnifying glass, small compass, pocket manual appropriate to the current activity (optional)

Measuring Materials: ruler, small tape measure, thermometers (outdoor and body, if possible), stopwatch or digital watch with timer function, portable postage meter (0–4 oz) or ingredient scale

Recording Resources: small spiral notebook for note taking, reminders, and doodling (a handy tool, but not necessary if you make your own science notebook as described in the next activity); set of colored pencils; tracing paper, graph paper, pencil, pen

Miscellaneous Matter: a roll of 1/4" or 1/2" masking tape, ball of twine, a few plastic vegetable bags or small earring-sized boxes (just in case there's a good specimen), glue, some rubber bands, eyedropper, a pocket knife

Handy Stuff Too Big to Carry Around: kitchen scale (0–5 lb; if it has metric readings as well, so much the better), a low powered microscope is fun (but not essential for any of the activities), assorted jars and boxes for keeping things that you find

Step Two

Assemble and store the tools and materials for the tool kit. Make a list of things that you don't have, but might want, so that you and she can be on the lookout for them.

Be prepared for your tools and materials collection to grow. As you try different activities, you'll get more ideas about what would be useful. Add them to these lists and to your tool kit.

Step Three

Doing science often involves lots of bits and pieces and sometimes more than the usual amount of clutter. Help your child to return everything to the kit after each use.

A tool kit solves some of the mess and organization problems doing science can spawn, but you'll need a place to keep it. Find a "science place" in your home where your child can keep her tool kit, science books, and the inevitable collections. Making the tools and materials special to being a scientist helps to make your young scientist's tasks special.

▶ SCIENCE NOTEBOOK

A number of activities in this book suggest recording data, keeping pictures, writing up experiments and observations, and making other kinds of entries in a science notebook. Having your child set up a personal notebook dedicated to science activities will not only help him keep track of things, but will also emulate the actual behavior of scientists, who regularly record their work.

FIELD GUIDES

You'll find some recommended field guides in the Resource section at the back of the book. Most public libraries have them available.

MORE SCIENCE THAT COMPUTES

Here are more science software titles to check out:

• *Science Blaster Jr.*—Another popular Blaster title featuring Blasternaut and his dog, Spot, with a test of science knowledge (for ages 4–7). Contact Davidson & Associates at (800) 545-7677.

• *Scholastic's Magic School Bus* series—Based on the popular children's science books and PBS cartoon series, these CD-ROMs explore the earth, the solar system, the ocean, and dinosaurs. Contact Microsoft at (800) 426-9400.

• *Wide World of Animals*—Here's a complete animal encyclopedia, with pictures, articles, audio and video, and minidocumentaries on 700 critters. Contact Creative Wonders at (800) KID-XPRT.

FUTURE FLASH

You can imagine how, years from now, your child will uncover his old science notebook in a box, flip through it, and remember the wonderful walk you had looking for a neighborhood tree or the rainy weekend afternoon that you played together experimenting with static electricity. Maybe at that moment he will be inspired to share this kind of science experience with his own child.

A BIG HEAD START

We already know we should start teaching children before they start school. That's why my budget expands Head Start to one million children by 2002. And, in June, the Vice President and Mrs. Gore will host their annual family conference. This one will focus on the importance of parents' involvement throughout a child's education.
—from the *1997 State of the Union Address*, President Clinton

At a Glance

Grade/Subject: 3rd and 4th/Science—All Activities
Skills: being prepared
Materials: ring bound, loose-leaf notebook
variety of paper—plain, lined, and colored
graph paper with a large grid (4 squares to the inch is a good size)
package or two of section dividers
paper punch
small calendar (8 1/2" × 11" or smaller)
Time: You can spend an evening putting the notebook together; decoration is optional, but fun, and will take a little more time. Some of the items may require a trip to a store.

Getting Ready

Look over the list of materials and see what you may have available around the house. Buy things you need before your child begins making the notebook.

Almost any notebook will do, but because most notebook paper comes in 8 1/2" 3 11", this size is probably the best. A sturdy, loose-leaf notebook with a ring binder will serve all your purposes. If the notebook has pockets, or if you can buy prepunched pocket inserts, you'll have a place to store loose notes and pictures.

A wide variety of papers is always useful. Not all the paper that you might wish to use will come with holes. A standard paper punch will solve that problem. Sheets of drawing paper, oak tag, graph paper, or colored papers can be punched and snapped in when needed.

A calendar that can fit in the notebook's pocket or be three-ring punched is a useful recording instrument. Some of the activities ask you and your child to make periodic visits or observations, and this is a good place to set up the dates and jot down observations. Commercial calendars are free and usually the right size to slip into a standard notebook.

Step One

Have your child load up the notebook with sections of

different paper. The science notebook will evolve as you do different activities, so don't worry too much about what should go where at the start. Talk together about what is put into the notebook and what it could be used for.

Step Two

Decorating and personalizing the notebook is optional, but lots of fun. One way of doing it is for your child to collect magazine and newspaper pictures of "sciency" kinds of things (your child's choice, of course, but your suggestions will help)—animals, flowers, dinosaurs, machines, and spaceships for starters.

He should cut them out and glue them lightly to the front and back covers in any pattern or collage he likes. Then use large pieces of clear, shelf contact paper to laminate over the pictures, front and back. This cover will protect the pictures and the notebook.

Step Three

Have him use one of the section dividers to set up a separate section for science words, perhaps at the end of the notebook. As you do activities together, you will probably encounter specialized words and the names and descriptions of different objects, plants, and animals. New vocabulary can be listed and defined in this section.

Step Four

Section dividers will help your child organize the information that he acquires as the two of you try some of the activities in this chapter and the next. For example, the activity that asks you to make periodic visits to a neighborhood tree could have its own notebook section. Here your child could keep separate pages for each visit, a piece of punched oak tag to stick leaf and seed samples on, the drawing of the tree, and a piece of graph paper on which he draws a neighborhood tree map.

Activities that include any record keeping will have additional suggestions.

CAN YOU IMAGINE?

We help a lot of parents at *SCORE!* with their children's educational problems. Many parents tell me that they have a hard time with their children conceptualizing things. All I tell them is that conceptualization begins with imagination. Have your child imagine something—that's where learning starts. Whether it's taking a break and thinking about how something might be or drawing a diagram on paper with your child, using the imagination to conceptualize a difficult learning task really works.

MOTIVATION AND INTEREST

Parents should be motivators of their children. Also liaisons, talking with their teachers and being the one to express what's happening at home. It's crucial to be a good role model. I always tell my children, "When I was a kid . . .," and they say, "Oh, really?" They appreciate a parent's involvement in their lives and their attention. It's important to show them what the right thing is and what the interesting things in life are.

❯ Bubble or Nothing

Bubbles are the perfect medium for the home scientist. They are fascinating, easy to work with, and (ahhhh) easy to clean up. In higher grades, their properties will be studied in chemistry and the mathematical field of topology. For the elementary-school scientist there is pleasure in making and observing bubbles and satisfaction from investigating the materials used to make them.

At a Glance

Grade/Subject: 3rd/Science—Physical Science
Skills: observing and describing, investigation
Materials: a gallon container and 4 pint-sized plastic containers
dishwashing liquid
bubble blower and/or soda straws
large measuring cup (quart-sized is best, although a standard cup measure and a quart-sized bowl will do)
tablespoon measure
kitchen ingredients such as salt, sugar, and flour
your child's science notebook
Time: 1 hour—can be repeated as often as desired

Getting Ready

Getting ready is part of the excitement in this activity and part of the science practice as well. Fill the gallon container and have your child mix the dish liquid into the water one tablespoon at a time. Both of you can test the mixture after each addition until you agree that it's making good bubbles. Have your child make a note of the amounts of water and dish liquid in his science notebook.

Step One

Blow a bubble or two with a bubble-blowing tool or a straw. Call attention to the size, consistency, and colors of the bubbles. Speculate with your child about what could be added to the mixture to change the quality or quantity of bubbles. What would table salt, or sugar, or flour do if it were mixed in?

YOU'RE IN CONTROL

control: unchanged item to which changed items are compared. In scientific trials or experiments, one way to evaluate results is to have one unchanged, original item that you can use for comparison.

WHAT'S MORE

Try using a whisk or a hand beater to whip up bubbles from the different mixtures in the containers. Make sure you use equal amounts of the bubble liquid for each trial. Compare the amounts of foam.

Different liquids instead of water could also be interesting. Since soda water is already fizzy, does it make better bubbles? What about fruit juices?

Step Two

The investigation: Your child can pour equal amounts of bubble liquid into each of the plastic containers. Set aside one container. This will remain filled with the plain bubble liquid and will act as the *control*.

Step Three

Now your child can pour an experimental ingredient—salt, sugar, cooking oil, or whatever else the two of you have dreamed up—into one of the other smaller bubble-mix containers. Mix gently and then try blowing some bubbles. Have your child note in his science notebook what he added and what happened.

Step Four

Repeat this experimental mixing with the other ingredients and other containers. Record the results for each trial. If he thinks one ingredient really improved the bubbles, encourage him to add more just to see what happens. A chart showing the containers and the ingredients added to each is a nice way to sum up this activity.

▶ GET THE BEAT

All of us are intrigued by collecting and recording information about our bodies—and that goes double for children. Height, weight, and temperature are obvious measurements, but there is something especially interesting and intimate about taking one's own pulse. It's easy to do and provides information that can be used in a variety of ways. It's also a great introduction to the circulatory system.

At a Glance

Grade/Subject: 3rd/Science—Health
Skills: observation, recording information
Materials: 2 fingers
1 body

WHAT'S MORE

Use a stopwatch or stopwatch feature on a wristwatch and a hand beater to see if any mixture produces bubbles faster.

Try other bubble materials. Does your shampoo make better bubbles? What happens if you grate hand soap and stir it into the water?

Can you make a Monster Bubble? Bend a metal coat hanger into a large circle and try dipping it into a batch of the best bubble mix you've concocted. Wave the hanger to make a huge bubble. Do this outside, of course!

BODY BASICS AND BEYOND

For your home PC, explore some of the good titles that can satisfy your child's science curiosity about the human body and health issues, including *BodyWorks* (ages 8 to adult) from The Learning Company (800-227-5609) and *A.D.A.M. the Inside Story* (ages 8 and up) from ADAM Software.

watch or clock with second hand or digital watch with a stopwatch function

your child's science notebook

Time: 10–15 minutes to find the pulses, 5 minutes or less per pulse taking and recording (Use this activity as often as you and your child want.)

Getting Ready

Finding your pulse can be tricky at first, but once you've done it, it's very easy. If you've never tried this before, test it out on yourself first, so that you can be an experienced guide. There are two good locations for the pulse:

• The best place for finding your pulse is the inner (palm) side of your wrist just below the base of the thumb. Use the inner side of the tips of the index and middle fingers.

• The other good spot is on the throat on either side of the windpipe. Two landmark muscles sweep down from the back of the jaw and come together at the base of the throat. Place the fingertips in the middle of the soft triangle made by the windpipe and these muscles. You should find the pulse easily.

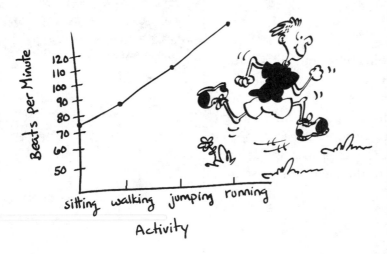

Step One

First teach your child to locate his pulse. A quiet time and away from distractions (such as TV or radio) is best. The pulse is felt rather than heard, but it is subtle, and a peaceful time makes it easier to become aware of it. If your child has a hard time, have him lay his forearm comfortably on a table or his lap, palm up. (Sometimes lying down helps with the location of the neck pulse.)

Have your child experiment on himself and on you. Talk about the pumping action of the heart and how blood is pushed through the arteries and out to the body.

Step Two

Once he can find his own pulse, your child can begin experimenting. Then have him count his pulse while you time 10 seconds. Have him multiply the number of beats by 6. This is his pulse rate per minute.

The 10-second pulse rate isn't as accurate as a longer interval, but it will work well enough for this activity. (If you want to sneak in some math practice, time the pulse for 15 seconds and multiply by 4, or 20 seconds and multiply by 3 and the rate you calculate will be a bit more accurate.)

Step Three

Have your child use his science notebook to jot down the resting pulse rate that he's just taken and then have him run up and down stairs a few times, or skip rope or jump up and down flapping his arms for a minute. Then have him take his pulse again. What has happened? Jot down the new rate.

Step Four

Talk about different things that a person could do to change the speed of his heart.

- What about just slowly walking around? eating? drinking?
- Is pulse rate higher, lower, or the same on a cold day as on a hot day?
- What's your pulse when you wake up?

Have him choose some questions and set up a sheet in the notebook with spaces for entering time and date, pulse rate, and activity.

Step Five

Set up a schedule of observations with your child so that he can make a record of his pulse at regular intervals. He can decide how often and the activities he's interested in testing; you can help remind him (or draw up your own pulse observations). Enter all the data in the notebook and, after a few entries, sit down and talk about it.

WHAT'S MORE

Compare the pulse rates of different family members. Note their ages and what they were doing just before their heart rates were recorded.

Have your child take his own pulse every hour on the hour for a day and see what happens. Help him make a graph placing heart rate on one axis and time of day on the other.

Check it out at the library! There are many grade-appropriate books on the heart, blood, and circulatory system, as well as titles that cover heart disease and cholesterol.

BIGGER ROLES

I think today's schools expect a lot more from parents than ever before, being parent aides, reading helpers, math helpers, and so on. When I was growing up, my mom would bake the cupcakes and drop them off, but today's parents help serve the food and bake them with their kids, getting them involved in the process. Maybe it's because classroom size is so big now, but it seems that more of a role is expected of parents—more field trips, gifts going back and forth, the incentive programs.

▶ HOUSEHOLD ERUPTION!

Volcanoes and earthquakes are sharp and spectacular reminders of an essential geological fact; we dwell on the very thin outer shell of a very active planet. Volcanoes themselves are always a fascinating topic for children. Building a working model of one is a great way to do science together, and seeing the volcano erupt can be a "peak"experience.

Model building is important in science. The volcano model your child makes does not reproduce the actual processes by which magma reaches the surface, but it does present model building as a focus of study. If the two of you choose to extend the project, you can try food coloring or poster paint to color the lava to make a model that roughly reproduces the process of volcanic mountain building as layer upon layer builds up with repeated eruptions.

At a Glance

Grade / Subject: 3rd / Science—Earth and Space
Skills: model building, investigation
Materials: papier-maché—store-bought or homemade mixture
10"–12" square of plywood or stiff corrugated cardboard (two pieces of a pizza box can be glued together)
10 or more pages of standard-sized newspaper
flour, water, household vinegar, baking soda, glue
your child's science notebook
Time: about 1 hour to build a volcano, a few days to let it dry; about 15 minutes each time you do Step Five

Getting Ready

Decide where you want to carry out this activity, which can be a bit messy.

Obtain some commercial papier-maché or use these directions to help your child start her own papier-maché:

- Tear some newspaper into 1- or 2-inch squares.
- Soak the squares in plain, warm water for an hour or so. (Some people soak it overnight.)
- Mix flour and water to make at least 1 quart of a runny paste.

Step One

Wad up some dry pieces of newspaper and arrange them in a cone-shaped pile roughly six inches across and six inches high on the center of the board or cardboard. When you and your child have agreed on the general size and shape, put some of your paste into a smaller bowl and thicken it to use to glue the wadded paper cone to the board.

Step Two

Have your child dip the soaked newspaper squares in the runny paste (so that they are thoroughly covered) and begin laying them, overlapping one another, on the cone of wadded paper. She should continue adding pieces until the papier-maché covering is at least 1/8 inch thick.

As she builds and the newspaper below dampens, she will be able to poke and push to create a realistic volcano shape. Encourage her to add hills, rivers, and other land forms around the volcano.

Step Three

She should use her finger to poke a funnel shaped hole, about 1 inch wide at the top and narrowing down, in the top center of the mountain. This will be the throat of the volcano. It should be about 2 inches deep. Place a couple of small pieces of the paste-covered paper at the bottom of the hole to seal it off.

WHAT'S MORE

Try mixing food coloring, colored ink, or poster paint into the vinegar for a more colorful lava flow. Your child can create several eruptions with different colors. She'll have a model of how volcanic peaks grow over time.

Try stirring in fine sand or flour to produce a thicker lava. What kinds of ingredients and how much to use are up to you and your young geologist. Fine-tuning and mess making may be required.

Hill of Fire (see Resources), an excellent story based on an actual event, tells about the sudden appearance of a volcano in a Mexican family's field.

SELF-ADVOCACY

Let your child make decisions on his own, and if he has problems with his teacher, encourage him to go directly to the teacher and work it out together. A lot of parents, including me, have a natural tendency to intervene in their children's problems, but as children grow up, they'll have to learn to do a lot for themselves. That's the hardest issue for me. There are also times when you have to sense when it's appropriate to go to the classroom teacher with problems and be very open about your concerns.

NURSERY RHYME

"Rock-a-bye baby, on the tree top; When the wind blows, the cradle will rock."

Step Four

Put the damp volcano aside and allow it to dry for two or three days. Your child can return to this activity before the papier-maché has completely finished drying, to paint the volcano with poster paint to make it more realistic.

Step Five

Eruption time! Put about a teaspoonful of baking soda down the throat of the volcano. Then pour a teaspoonful of vinegar in. If this doesn't result in a fully satisfying eruption, try varying the amounts and see what combination works best. Have your child record the ingredients and amounts for the best eruptions in her science notebook.

Talk together about volcanoes. You might ask:

- Is lava really like baking soda and water?
- Why do you think the lava comes out?
- Why is it so hot? What is our planet like inside?

❯ HOW THE WIND BLOWS

Many children are familiar with the old nursery rhyme that teaches some elementary rules of nature—but most students don't know how much wind force affects how much the cradle will rock (or how much bending and weight before the bough will break). Here's an activity that gives your young scientist a way to develop his own measurement tool for describing wind force.

At a Glance

Grade/Subject: 3rd/Science—Earth and Space and Inquiry Skills
Skills: developing a measurement tool, observing, recording
Materials: two paper plates, two paper cups with handles
dowel or other long stick
ruler and magic marker
upholstery tack or small nail
stapler and glue
watch or clock with a second hand
science notebook for recording results

Time: 20 minutes initially—then five minutes a day for as long as you continue

Getting Ready

On windy days, talk with your child about what can be seen (or heard, or felt) that gives some indication of how strong the wind is blowing. Look in the weather section of the newspaper for reports on wind velocity. Do this activity during or after a stormy period when your child's interest in the wind's power is likely to be high. September often carries news of hurricane winds, for instance.

Help your child assemble the materials he'll need for making his wind measuring machine. Then assist him as needed in the following steps.

Step One

Glue two or more paper plates together so that they make a rigid disk. Use the ruler to find the exact center of the disk and poke a small hole through it. Use the ruler to draw lines dividing the disk into four equal sections, each line passing through the center point.

Step Two

Use the magic marker to color one of the cups so that it looks very different from the other three. Staple the handles of each cup on to the disk at one of the four places where your pencil lines meet the edge of the disk. Make sure that all four cups face the same direction around the edge.

Step Three

Stick the tack through the hole and attach the disk to the edge of one end of the dowel. Spin the disk to make sure that the tack is secure but not so tight that the disk does not

BIG BAD WIND!

Hold a *Twister* Party—Rent the popular movie video; play the game; put on the music . . . and do the twist!

spin easily. Plant the dowel in the ground, or in some other way securely place it upright where the wind can blow it. Turn it as needed until it catches the wind and the cups begin turning the disk.

Step Four

Watch the cups turn. Using a clock's second hand, you and your child can take turns counting revolutions per minute, by counting every time the marked cup passes the dowel at the bottom of the turn.

Pick a special time of day, such as *before supper*, to count and record the wind speed. Record the time and the speed. When the wind blows (at any time of the day) is also a good time to go out and clock it. Encourage your child to always write down the date and the time as well as the wind speed.

▶ LEMON POWER

When is a lemon not a lemon? When it's a battery. Well, it's still a lemon and it sure won't make your car run, but making your own electric lemon is fun and teaches kids the basics about how batteries create electric power (however slight). And it offers a tiny taste of the effect of electricity, pointing out the need to practice safety measures.

At a Glance

Grade/Subject: 3rd/Science—Physical Science, Health and Safety
Skills: exploring the nature of electric current (safely)
Materials: a lemon, a paper clip, 6"–8" of copper wire paper, pencil, and colored markers (magazines for cutting up, optional)
Time: 15 minutes for making the battery
(additional time of your child's choosing for making a safety manual comic)

Getting Ready

Assemble your materials. It's more fun if you provide two of everything so that you can create a battery along with your

---

child. You can even experiment with using a small lemon and a large lemon.

Step One

Straighten the paper clip and remove any insulation from around the copper wire.

Stick one end of the paper clip right into one end of the lemon and one end of the copper wire right into the other end of the lemon.

Step Two

Bring the other end of the copper wire close enough to the other end of the paper clip to be able to touch both with your tongue. Touch your tongue to both at the same time.

Discuss what happened. (You will feel a slight tingling sensation on your tongue, caused by the electricity from your lemon.) Ask what would happen if the lemon were bigger and more powerful!

Step Three

Explain that the tongue acts like a switch that turns on the electricity because it completes the electric circuit between the two metals (steel in the paper clip, copper in the wire) and the acid in the lemon. The saliva on your tongue is what makes the "tongue switch" work because water conducts electricity.

Talk together about how this experiment demonstrates why electrical current can be dangerous.

Electrical Hazard

WHAT'S MORE

Have your child do a survey to find out as many ways as possible that people use batteries.

Interview an electrician or other knowledgeable person to learn why special electrical outlets must be used when they are near water.

Try other fruits and vegetables to see how well they work as batteries—grapefruit, lime, tomato, potato . . . .

SHOCKING DEFINITION

conduct: to cause to pass through, transmit

SAFETY FIRST WITH FIRE

Lab safety should be preached whenever kids and adults do lab experiments together. If you're doing any experiments with fire (*not required for any activities in this book*), be extra careful. If your child's clothing accidentally catches on fire and he starts to panic, make sure he knows the three things to do:

• Stop
• Drop
• Roll

Stop whatever you're doing. Drop to the ground or floor. Roll back and forth vigorously to put out the fire.
—The Wild Goose Co.

Step Four

Have your child inventory electrical items in your home. Then talk together about safety precautions that should be observed in using any of them.

Step Five

Have your child make a "Guide to Safe Use of Electricity" in comic book style, drawing examples of dangers and correct placement and use of appliances, lamps, etcetera.

▶ LET IT POUR!

What is more real to children than rain? It has real impact on playing, dressing, tracking dirty boots into the house . . . . Rainfall is measured in inches and is so easily done that young children can get involved in the study of nature, developing the crucial scientific skill of careful measurement and reporting.

At a Glance

Grade/Subject: 3rd/Science—Earth and Space, Inquiry Skills
Skills: observation of weather, measurement
Materials: a can or jar (such as a canning jar) with straight sides and a top that matches the bottom in size
ruler
science notebook, calendar, and a pen
Time: 15 minutes initially—then 5 minutes a day (or a week) for as long as you continue

Getting Ready

Watch a television weather report with your child. Read the weather section of the newspaper together. Talk together about how much rainfall is predicted and how much is reported as having fallen. Ask for your child's ideas about how much rain falls on your home.

Together, assemble the materials your child will need for making your family's home rain gauge.

Step One

Clean the jar or can. Explain that the container will be used to collect rain as it falls and why it is important that the sides of the container be straight from bottom to top and that the top of the container be as wide as the rest of the container.

Step Two

Have your child place the container under the shower and turn on the shower for a minute and then use the ruler to measure how much water has showered into the container. Discuss how water in the shower is similar to (and different from) falling rain.

Step Three

Together, work out a good place to put the container where it will freely receive falling rain, but not get extra water splashed into it. Have your child place it securely so it won't tip (pack sand or some small stones around it).

Have your child prepare her Rain Measuring Report by writing the starting date in her science notebook and marking the calendar.

Step Four

Each day, your child should check the container. If rain has fallen, the ruler should be used to measure the amount. She should record the amount with the date on her report *and* empty the container so it is ready to start gathering the next rainfall.

▶ SHAKE HANDS WITH A TREE

Trees are remarkable organisms. They have been on Earth for millions of years, and they have adapted themselves to an extraordinary range of environments.

In this activity, you can introduce your child to one of your neighborhood trees, observe it with her, find out where it

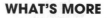

WHAT'S MORE

After recording daily rainfalls, try switching to weekly totals instead by measuring every Saturday morning. Be sure to empty the can after each measurement. Discuss evaporation with your child and how it can effect the accuracy of measuring weekly instead of measuring every day.

———

How much snowfall equals how much rainfall? Let the rain gauge fill with snow, then melt and measure. What's the difference between soft, light snow and heavy snow?

———

Do the Wind Measuring activity and add wind direction to your science notebook rainfall report.

———

Make a monthly bar graph showing the amount of precipitation each day or each week. Compare the graphs from month to month.

———

See if you and your child can tour a TV station's weather center or a local meteorological center (often at airports).

AUTHENTIC SCIENCE ASSESSMENT

The National Science Standards make it pretty clear that the more hands-on and real-world a science teacher's assessments are of your child, the more "authentic" they are. *Authentic assessments* are those that test your child's *understanding* rather than knowledge. Any assessment that requires kids to apply what they know in a new situation, rather than just feed back memorized stuff, is authentic.

Many teachers are having to do a reality check with these standards, however. Hands-on assessments of your child aren't necessarily good by themselves, and they're time-consuming for teachers to create and evaluate. Standardized tests, which use mostly multiple-choice questions, aren't going away any time soon.
—The Wild Goose Co.

came from, learn what kind of a story it has to tell, and make regular visits to observe and record its changes over time.

At a Glance

Grade/Subject: 3rd/Science—Life Science
Materials: crayons or chalk, clear tape
tape measure or string
book on tree identification
science notebook
Time: 1-hour visit (or, preferably, several half-hour visits spread over time)

Getting Ready

Scout around your neighborhood first, maybe on the way home from work or shopping, to locate a variety of trees to choose from. *Deciduous* trees (those that lose their leaves in cold weather), because they show dramatic seasonal changes, are better for this activity than *evergreens.* Even in warm climates, trees go through seasonal variations, even if they do not lose their leaves.

If you plan only one visit, bring the materials with you on the first walk.

Step One

Take a walk around your neighborhood with your child and examine the trees that you find.

Step Two

Have your child pick a tree that appeals to her and then spend some time looking at it more closely. Talk about what she can observe and what thoughts and questions she has about the tree.

• Look at and feel the bark and the leaves.
• How does it smell?
• Compare the tree to nearby buildings, utility poles, or other landmarks and make a guess at how tall it is.
• Does it have many branches?

• What kind of shape does the whole tree have?

If you are not planning to do follow-up visits, include the activities in Step Three during this walk.

Step Three

On another day, return to the tree and have your child bring her science notebook, crayons or chalk, some clear tape, and either a tape measure or a piece of string.

Have your child draw a picture of the tree. Collect a leaf and tape it to a sheet of notebook paper. Take a sheet of paper out, lay it on the bark, and rub over it with a crayon hard enough to record the bark's texture. (She could use several crayons to combine colors and approximate the color of the bark.) If she wishes, have your child give the tree a name. Use the tape measure or string to wrap the trunk and measure its circumference. (You can measure the length of string later with a ruler.) Enter all this information in the science notebook.

Step Four

Using a field guide or reference book on trees, your child can use the materials collected to look up the tree and identify it and to learn more about it. She can enter information in her science notebook such as:

• Facts about her tree's natural history
• Whether it is a native tree or imported
• What parts of the country it grows well in
• Whether there are places it won't grow at all
• What the bark, wood, or vegetation may be used for

Step Five

Plan for regular return visits together at about 1-month to 6-week intervals for the rest of the year. Make a science notebook entry for each visit with the date, all observations, and a picture. Notations should include the weather conditions and everything she can observe about the tree on that visit. This might include the state of the leaves; the

---

WHAT'S MORE

Using the information from the science notebook, your child can make a special booklet devoted entirely to your tree, including a map of the tree's neighborhood.

Try making an inventory of all the trees in your neighborhood. Are the trees native, ornamental, and how did they get there? Your child could collect the same kinds of information, bark, leaves, and story about other trees and add them to the science notebook.

If you are able, plant a tree with your child. Pick out the kind of tree that would do well in the location you choose. Chart its growth and development, and read up on its care and upkeep. Many communities offer tree planting or Arbor Day events that are fun to participate in.

presence of buds, flowers, or seeds; and the presence of any animal life.

Talk together about the effects of weather on the tree. Is there storm damage? Do the leaves turn color or change in any way during a dry spell or seasonal change?

CHAPTER 17

Learning Adventures—
4th Grade Science

LEARNING TOOLS

The notion of purchasing a home computer "for the children" is probably a symptom of the parent's own feelings about computing. In our *SCORE!* Centers, we find that children raised in this era are almost always completely at ease using the computer as a tool for learning, whether or not they have ever had a chance to "interact" with a computer at home.

▶ DIRTOLOGY—PART 1

The soil that we depend on for our food is a rich and complex substance. It's much more than just plain old dirt. Soils are compound materials, made up of both living and nonliving components. The balance of these components is what makes a soil capable of sustaining the growth of the plants we depend on for food.

At a Glance

Grade/Subject: 4th/Science—Life Science
Skills: observation, experimentation
Materials: measuring cup (1 cup)
plastic bags, paper towels
stick-on labels for the bags (or pieces of masking tape)
trowel or large spoon
kitchen scale
magnifying glass
several small plastic drinking cups, or 8 oz. yogurt containers
science notebook
Time: 1 hour for soil collection expedition
1 hour total for activity (this can be spread over several days, if more convenient)

GOOD SPOTS FOR DIRT

Hard-packed soil from a playground path, the soil from a flower bed, and soil from beneath a tree will all have somewhat different characteristics. Even urban areas have a surprising variety of soils. If you are hard pressed, you can find potting soils at many hardware stores or in the flower department of supermarkets.

WHAT'S MORE

Make a map of your soil gathering expedition and mark off the locations where you took samples. Note the human activity that takes place around each of your locations.

Heat up and dry out a cup of each sample on a cookie sheet in an oven, in a toaster oven, or in a skillet. Do any of the soils shrink at all? If you have a fine enough scale, weigh them. Any differences?

Getting Ready

Since this activity involves finding several kinds of soil, devote a few moments beforehand to thinking about different places where you might find some different soils in your neighborhood or yard.

Step One

Make a dirt-finding expedition to gather different kinds of soil with your child. Be prepared to poke about before choosing the samples that you want. Collect samples that are as different as possible from one another.

Select two or more locations with your child, and collect 2 cups of soil from each. Store the soils in separate bags and label them. Write a short description of each location in the notebook. Have your child use a new page for each location. Later, when she's examining the samples more closely, she can make notes for each soil's location page.

Step Two

When you get your soils home, you can set up your dirtological laboratory together. Begin by carefully weighing your soil samples. Measure out an exact cup of each kind (scrape off the top so it's level). Note the weight per cup of each soil on its own page.

Step Three

Spread out a tablespoon of each sample on its own piece of paper towel and take a close look at each. Encourage your child to talk about what she can see about what's in the soil. Then use a magnifying glass or loupe to take an even closer look. Most soils contain bits of sand, organic debris like bits of bark, leaf, and twig, and decomposed (or digested by worms) organic material. Do some soils have more of one kind of stuff in it than another? Have her write up the findings for each soil on its own page in her science notebook.

Step Four

Place a level tablespoon of one kind of soil in a small bowl or on a plate with an equal amount of water. Mix them into runny mud. Pour the mud into the center of another piece of paper towel and let the water soak into the towel. Do the same for each of the other samples.

- Is there a "muddiest" sample?
- Do they stain their pieces of towel differently?
- What's left over after the water soaks away?

Note your findings in the science notebook.

Step Five

Have your child fill the cups with equal amounts of dirt to a little below the top. Pour about 1/2 cup of water slowly into each. Notice how the water soaks in.

- Does it sink in slowly or quickly disappear?
- Does it pool on top and not soak in well?

After the water has been soaked into all of your samples, feel the top layer and notice how wet or dry this is. Note all this information in the notebook on each soil's own page.

Step Six

Draw a magnified picture of the contents of each of the samples on the location pages. As your child draws, you can talk about what's been observed and her ideas about it.

- How do these soils differ?
- How do you think they get that way?
- Which ones would be good for growing seeds in?
- Where can we find out more info on soil?

▶ DIRTOLOGY—PART 2

Farmers depend on the soil for their livelihoods. They crumble bits of it into the wind, smell it, poke at it, and

WHAT'S MORE

It's quite possible that you and your child will encounter a few living things as you poke through some of your dirt samples. Set them aside in a small container with a pinch or two of moist dirt and a couple of leaves. Return them to the outdoors at your convenience. You can talk about respecting life and the role that most of these little animals play in replenishing the soil.

Earthworms can also be added to your potted plants (depending on your feelings about worms)! One of our authors discovered that adding a worm or two made house plants much happier over the dryer and colder months. They happily munch up dead leaves, make the soil richer, and their tunnels keep the soil from packing up.

analyze it with all of their senses. They're interested in the properties of the soil that will produce good crops. You and your child can explore soils in the same way.

Although this activity uses the three soils you and your child researched in the Dirtology 1 activity, you can do it without having done that activity. Just be sure to select your soil samples from several different kinds of locations.

At a Glance

Grade/Subject: 4th/Science—Life Science
Skills: experimentation, record keeping
Materials: soil samples from Dirtology 1 (or gather more)
4 (or more depending on how many samples you have) small plastic or wax paper drinking cups, or 8 oz. yogurt containers
measuring cup (1 cup)
sprouting seeds or beans—only one kind is needed
1–2 cups of sandbox or beach sand
ruler
science notebook
Time: 3–14 days for seed test (explained in Getting Ready)
1 hour for experimental setup
5–10 minutes for regular observations (once a day until sprouts appear, once every three days to follow growth)
1 hour for windup

Getting Ready

Part of doing science is making sure that your experimental materials will work well enough to give you information. Have your child check on the viability of the seeds you select before you begin this activity. Soak a few in water, wrap them in a piece of paper towel, and place them in a cup in a warm location. Check every couple of days to see if they've germinated. This preparation stage also gives you and your child a look at the beginning of the particular plant's early stages and a rough idea of how long it takes the seeds to germinate.

WHAT'S MORE

Try seeds from different plants. In the fall, collect maple flyers, acorns, and other tree seeds and give them a try.

As your seedlings grow, transplant them to a larger pot, and when they grow big enough (weather permitting), transplant them into a garden. Continue to watch them grow and record what you see.

QUICK GROWERS

Radish seeds, mung beans, and wheat berries are all relatively quick germinators. They are available throughout the year in health food stores where they are sold for salad sprouting. Radish seeds are also widely available once gardening time comes around. Other dry beans you buy at the grocery store for eating often do well.

Step One

Have your child fill the cups with the sample soils, one kind in each cup, and fill one cup with plain sand. Soak them thoroughly, and plant three or four of your seeds in each cup. Place the cups in a sunny window.

If it's winter, be careful not to place the cups too close to glass that gets very cold. Heated environments, on the other hand, will dry the soil quickly, so teach your child the fingertip test. Using the tip of an index finger, feel the soil and water often enough to make sure the soil stays moist, but don't water so much that it gets muddy.

Step Two

With your child, make a chart on a page in his science notebook where he will record daily observations starting from the time he plants the seeds. The chart should also allow room for noting the length of seedlings as they grow and the number and size of any leaves that appear.

Step Three

When the seeds have sprouted (poked up and begun sprouting little leaves), it's time to thin the crop. Pull out all but the sturdiest seedling in each container.

Step Four

Continue observations for as long as you and your child can keep the seedlings growing. Once they've sprouted and you've thinned them, daily observations aren't necessary. Pick a convenient interval such as three times a week, and keep a schedule of observations. At each observation, take measurements, talk about what you see, and note any changes you can observe.

• In what ways are all the little plants the same?

> ### WHAT'S MORE
>
> Broccoli, kale, mustard, and brussels sprouts are all members of the same big plant family. Botanists speculate that they were all bred from a few less specialized cousins by early agriculturalists. You might want to try growing seeds from just this family to see what differences you can find as they sprout and flourish.

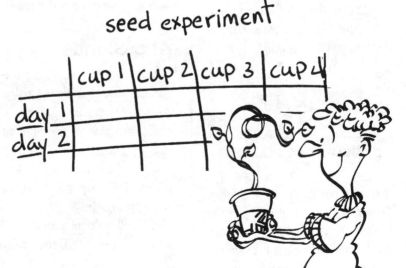

LET KIDS BE KIDS

Education at home has to be done in a way that allows kids to learn at their own pace. They shouldn't be pushed. They should be allowed to develop and learn from where they're most comfortable. Kids keenly pick up on a parent's disappointment, and they really want to please. Some parents may have very high expectations, like "We've been working on this for a month; you should be able to work on this alone by now." Try to leave the "you shoulds" out of the picture entirely. Be sensitive to when children are ready to move ahead and when they need to slow down the learning pace. It's a good idea to have a relaxed pace, and just let kids be kids.

DOUBLE YOUR PLEASURE

Using two colors (the flavors are up to you and your child) will give the model a more dramatic look. Pour the top layer on before the skin has had a chance to form on the bottom layer. There will be some mixing, but don't worry about it. If you or your child is lactose intolerant, or you prefer not to use cow's milk, soy milk may be substituted.

- Do they differ in height, color, or leaf size?
- Are the stalks all the same?

If you conclude that some soils are better than others for sprouting or sustaining plants, note that information in the notebook pages devoted to the different soil locations.

▶ EAT A PLANET

Plate tectonics is the name given to the study of the movement of the earth's continental plates that float as a crust on the hot and more fluid mantle below. Scientists frequently use models to study processes like this that are too dangerous, too large, or too small to study directly.

Students use models to study how things work as well. Usually this is done as an aid to understanding, rather than to make predictions as a scientist might. The skin of a pudding serves as a model of plate tectonics. In this activity, you get to have your model and eat it, too!

At a Glance

Grade/Subject: 4th/Science—Earth and Space
Skills: model making, following directions, eating
Materials: pudding mix (2 boxes of different colored puddings, for more dramatic effect; just remember to use a bigger pan)
2 or more crumbly cookies (graham crackers work well)
about 1/2 cup confectionery sugar (optional: multicolored sugar sprinkles)
8" × 10" baking pan with high sides or an 8" or 9" pie pan
2 spatulas—the bigger the better—and 2 spoons
Time: 1 hour to make, cool, and work with the model (10 minutes or less to eat!)

Getting Ready

Follow the directions on the pudding box and begin making the pudding. While one of you stirs the pudding, the other can grind the cookies up into a coarse powder.

Step One

Pour the pudding into the baking pan or pie pan and sprinkle the confectionery sugar and cookie crumbs across the surface. Try for a uniform spread, but don't worry about it. Set the pudding aside to cool.

Step Two

When a skin has formed, you are ready to begin your earth moving. Use a spatula to work around the outside edges of the pudding and free it from the walls of the pan.

Step Three

Let your child use the spatulas to slowly push the pudding inwards from opposite sides. As the pudding's skin deforms, talk about the creation of mountains and valleys as the continental plates push against one another.

You can use the edge of the spatula or a knife to slide through the pudding to create a few continental plates of your own. See what happens when you work the plates toward one another with the spatulas.

Step Four

Finally, use those two spoons. Eat your planet!

▶ LEAF LOOK

Different plants have different characteristics, and botanists use these characteristics to classify and identify them. You can use soil from a garden or use a commercial potting soil, or even soil you gathered from doing the Dirtology activities earlier in this chapter.

At a Glance

Grade/Subject: 4th/Science—Life Science
Skills: experimentation, observation
Materials: 3 small plastic cups or 8 oz. yogurt containers

WHAT'S MORE

You can make a more elaborate surface model using multicolored sprinkles or other lightweight cake decoration materials to form "land masses" on the earth's surface.

Insert a bendable straw into the pudding and gently blow through it to see if you can simulate the welling up of magma from below the surface. This will work a little better if you try it before the pudding completely cools.

A MEANS, NOT AN END

There is nothing inherently beneficial about "getting your child on the computer," unless this is the best way to provide your child with access to content that you have selected. Children should begin "interacting with computers" when they are capable of working with appropriate content. The computer is not an end in itself, but a relatively neutral medium. It can be used for good or ill, much as a book. The content determines the appropriateness for children, regardless of age.

3 kinds of seeds
about 1 quart of soil
science notebook
Time: 1/2 hour to set the experiment up
five 10-minute observations, every two or three days, for at least a month
1 hour for final observations and record keeping

Getting Ready

Pick three different kinds of seeds. Radishes, beans, and broccoli will give you plants that represent different plant families and distinctively different foliage, but feel free to substitute others.

Step One

Have your child fill the containers with soil, but not all the way up to the rim. Plant several seeds of one variety in one of the containers and pour in enough water to soak them thoroughly. Repeat this with the two other containers, putting a different kind of seed in each. Label each container clearly and note the date on the containers. Set the containers in a sunny location.

Step Two

Make a notebook page for each of the containers with the name of the plant, a picture of the seed that shows its size, and the date you planted it.

Step Three

Check your seeds frequently and keep the soil moist, but not soaked. As the seedlings come up, sprout, and start to show distinct leaves, your child should remove the weakest to thin them down until there is just one plant growing in each container. Have her write in the size, number, and description of each of the seedling's leaves when they first appear. Have her draw pictures, if she likes.

Step Four

Make regular observations and note the appearance of new leaves, the height of the shoot, and any other characteristics that seem noteworthy.

Step Five

When you and your child decide that the plants are well on their way to full growth, she can end this experiment (or transplant the plants outside). Pluck one leaf from each plant and trace it on the appropriate notebook page. Describe the color and texture of each leaf.

- Is it smooth or hairy?
- What is its shape?

Make a page that shows the three leaves together.

- How do they compare?
- How do the plants that they came from compare?
- Which is the biggest?
- Are they all the same color green, or can your child notice differences (for example, lighter, darker)?

▶ ME AND MY SHADOW

Some of the earliest discoveries in science were made by curious people who observed the sun and the changes that occurred as it apparently moved across the sky. One of the most intriguing of those changes is what happens to your shadow as the sun's position changes—long and thin in the morning and evening, but almost invisible beneath your feet at high noon.

Many kids are already intrigued by their shadows. You and your child can use the visible changes in your shadows as a way to observe the changing positions of the sun during the

CAN WE HELP?

Parents need to be right on top of their children's education. If I'm not working in the classroom, or if I'm working on a school project but can't be in the classroom, I talk to my children's teachers and ask if everything is going okay. Is there anything I can do to help?

VIRTUAL EARTH SCI

Look into Pacific Interactive's software title *Bill Nye the Science Guy: Stop the Rock!* (ages 9 and up). Your child will perform experiments in order to save our planet from an off-course comet. This title, and other science greats on today's retail shelves, turn learning into an exciting game. Another Earth Science title to check into: 7th Level's funny and learning-filled primer, *The Universe According to Virgil Reality* (ages 8 and up).

TRUSTING YOUR KIDS

I like parents who feel comfortable letting their children have some independence, some control over what's going on in their lives. Kids are pretty in tune with what's happening for them in school, and they know when things aren't going well. If they have the freedom to say "This is something I'm scared to try," or "This is something I'm good at and want to do more of," without any outside pressure, they'll usually do okay. When kids start to feel there are expectations they have to live up to, things start to get more challenging for them.

day and, if curiosity persists, as the seasons change. These changes make it clear how the earth is moving relative to the sun and the direction in which it is moving.

At a Glance

Grade/Subject: 4th/Science—Earth and Space
Skills: observing relationships between the sun and earth, keeping records
Materials: washable chalk in several colors
a sunny day
Time: 15 minutes, 3 or 4 times a day, once a week for as long as interest continues
To observe seasonal changes, do twice a month for as many weeks as interest continues. Changes are most noticeable in the weeks after the spring and fall equinoxes (March/September).

Getting Ready

The only ingredient you must plan on beforehand is a day with enough sunshine to cast a strong shadow. In order to see dramatic changes, plan to do this "shadow play" no more than once a week. More frequent shadow drawings may not show enough change to keep your child interested.

During the school year, it's best to plan this activity for the weekend, so that you can both be home at observation time.

Step One

With your child, plan a daily schedule to observe your shadows in the sunlight at least three times a day. One of those observation times should be just before or just after noon. With a three-times-a-day schedule, make the other observations at about 8:00 A.M. and 4:00 P.M. With a four-times-a-day schedule, observe your shadows through the day at 9, 12, 3, and 6 o'clock.

Step Two

At the first scheduled morning time, stand together so that your shadows fall on a cement sidewalk or driveway. With the washable chalk, have your child first draw a circle around your feet and then draw the outline of your shadow on the walk. Then take the chalk and draw the outline of his feet and his shadow.

Step Three

At the next scheduled time for the same day, go outside and stand together in the same place as before. Notice how your shadows have moved. Also notice how the shadows have changed shape—growing shorter as you approach noon. Can either of you fit into your old shadow?

Discuss with your child the changes you can see in each of your shadows. Are the shadows longer? Wider? Why have these changes happened? From the direction that your shadows have moved, try to figure out which way the earth has moved relative to the sun.

Draw your new shadows with a different colored chalk. Then speculate with your child as to what changes you will see at the next observation time. What shape will the shadows be? What direction will they have moved?

Step Four

Repeat Step Three through the day. Keep a record of your shadow diagrams and observations. At the end of the day, wash the outlines off the sidewalk so that it will be clear for your next observation *or*, if the sidewalk is on your private property, use a different color of chalk for succeeding observations so that you can keep an actual record of the movement of your shadows.

▶ CAN YOU FLOAT THIS?

Surface tension makes it possible to float surprising things on water—like needles, pins, and paper clips. What else? In this activity, your child's understanding of surface tension will develop along with her curiosity and desire to experiment with possible floaters.

WHAT'S MORE

Make a sundial with a "shadow stick." Mount a stick in a board, check its shadow at one-hour intervals during the day, and draw a line to mark the position of the shadow each time.

If your child makes a sundial, check its accuracy together each hour by consulting a clock. Read about sundials in an encyclopedia. Discuss how it would work year-round.

Make notes or drawings of where and when the sun rises or sets. When does it shine most directly through the windows? How does that position change over time?

At a Glance

Grade/Subject: 4th/Science—Physical Science, Inquiry Skills
Skills: experimentation, surface tension
Materials: large pan or bowl
paper and scissors
sewing needle, pin, paper clip
pencil and paper
science notebook
Time: about 1/2 hour, depending on your child's curiosity and inventiveness

Getting Ready

Talk with your child about what she knows about things that float or sink in water. Ask her whether she thinks it is possible to make something that is heavier than water float on top of the water. Introduce the idea of finding out what happens when you try to float a needle on water. Have the materials you will need handy.

Step One

Have your child fill the pan or bowl with water and try dropping the needle (and then the pin and paper clip) into the water. Ask her to explain what happened and why she thinks it happened.

Step Two

Together cut the paper into squares of about 1 1/2 inches each. Then have her lay a square on the surface of the water and lay the needle on it. Ask her to describe what happens as you watch. Gently press the edges of the paper into the water. (As the paper gets wet, it absorbs the water and sinks, leaving the needle floating.)

Step Three

Have your child use her science notebook or pencil and paper to write a description of what has been done and what happened.

WHAT'S MORE

Ask your child for ideas about how the surface tension might be broken and what would then happen. Try each idea.

Try the experiment anew with fresh, still water in the pan; then add one drop of detergent. Have your child describe and record what happens.

Try the experiment adding oil to the water.

Step Four

Have her try the same experiment with the pin and the paper clip, each time recording her description of what she did and what happened. Encourage her to look for other things to try floating.

Step Five

Explain that the molecules of water on the surface of the water stick so closely together that, under the right conditions, things that won't usually float end up floating.

▶ Nice Salt Ice

If you've driven in icy weather, you've probably appreciated the use of salt on dangerous roads. But have you thought about why it helps? The freezing point of salt water is lower than that of ordinary water. So the salt lowers the freezing point of the water and melts the ice. But why take that on faith? You and your child can experiment with salt and ice and water to see what happens.

At a Glance

Grade/Subject: 4th/Science—Earth and Space, Physical Science, Inquiry Skills
Skills: experimentation, measurement, observation
Materials: 2 freezer-safe containers
freezer thermometer, kitchen timer
measuring cup, measuring teaspoon
water, salt
pencil and paper
Time: 5–10 minutes for setup, then checking every 15 minutes

Getting Ready

Check that your child knows how to read a thermometer. Does he know what is meant by the *freezing point* (32° Fahrenheit or 0° Celsius)?

WET DEFINITION

surface tension: the property of liquids whereby molecules at or near the surface become cohesive, contracting to make a surface resembling an elastic-like membrane or skin

---

HOT DEFINITION

temperature: a measure of how hot or cold something is

Step One

Using his science notebook, have your child record the following preparation for the experiment as he does it.

- Label one freezer container "salt water," and turn the freezer to its coldest setting.
- Put 1 cup of water into each freezer container.
- Mix 2 teaspoons of salt into the container labeled salt water.
- Put both containers in the freezer, write down the time, and set the timer for 15 minutes.

Step Two

After 15 minutes, have your child take both containers out and write down the water temperature in each, along with the time. Reset the timer and keep repeating this process until freezing occurs. You can set the timer for shorter periods if you choose.

Step Three

When one container contains frozen water, your young scientist should write down the time. He should then calculate how long it took to freeze and write it down.

Continue checking and recording the temperature of the water in the other container until it freezes. Then write down the time and calculation of how long that water took to freeze.

Step Four

Encourage him to experiment with other mixtures, each time recording his description of what he did and what happened. Here are some possibilities:

- What happens with twice as much salt in one cup of water?
- How long does cranberry juice take to freeze? milk?

Step Five

Turn your freezer back down to its normal setting.

▶ ONE POTATO, TWO POTATO, CLEAN POTATO

"Don't forget to wash your hands!"—the eternal cry of the parent and the prime directive of personal hygiene. Here is a simple activity that is (almost) guaranteed to get children to the table well scrubbed. It's also a lesson about the microscopic organisms all around us.

At a Glance

Grade/Subject: 4th/Science—Health
Skills: experimentation, observation, hand washing!
Materials: 3 medium-sized potatoes
3 jars or clear plastic containers with lids
pot big enough to boil the potatoes
vegetable peeler or paring knife
spoon or tongs
labels (stick-on type or pieces of masking tape)
magnifying glass (optional)
Time: 20–30 minutes to peel, boil, and prepare the potatoes
1–2 weeks to observe the results (take a look once a day)

Getting Ready

Assemble the materials you need in the kitchen where you and your child do the preparation necessary to set up this experiment. Be sure you have containers with openings big enough for your potatoes to go through (or potatoes small enough to fit through).

WHAT'S MORE

How can you make water "bigger?" Try filling a container (like an empty frozen orange juice can) to the brim with water and setting it in the freezer. After the contents freezes, measure how high the frozen water rises above the brim. Compare it to one filled to the brim with salty water.

TAKE A TREK

The *Ecology Treks* (grades 3 to 9) and *Earth Treks* (grades 4 to 12) software programs involve children in great games, from survival contests to globe-trotting excursions, and offer databases of information, fun facts, and quizzes that can expand your child's understanding of biology, life science, Earth's creatures, world languages and cultures, Earth history, and the natural environment. Contact Sanctuary Woods at (800) 943-3664, or visit them on the Web at www.ah-hah.com

WHAT'S MORE

You can repeat this experiment with other foods. Try pieces of toast (don't boil it; the toasting will do the job) or peeled apples.

Do an experiment to compare a piece of toast, an apple, and a potato—each well handled with dirty hands. Sterilize one sample each and then give each sample the same amount of handling. Does examination over the next few weeks show any differences in results?

Step One

Boil enough water in the pot to cover the three potatoes. Put the spoon or tongs in the boiling water to boil as you prepare the potatoes. Help your child peel the potatoes and put them into boiling water for four or five minutes. The purpose of boiling isn't to cook them, just to sterilize them. They don't have to stay in long.

Step Two

Have your child remove one potato with the sterilized spoon or vegetable tongs. Without touching it, drop it directly into one of the jars. Put the lid or cover on tightly. Label this container, "Boiled, Not Touched."

Remove the next two potatoes and put them on a plate so that they can cool enough to be touched, but don't touch them yet.

Step Three

When they have cooled, have your child pick up one potato and handle it. Pass it back and forth between you, pat it, and roll it about in your hands. If there's anyone else around, have them join in.

When it's been well handled, place it in a second container and close it. Label this one "Boiled, Well Handled."

Step Four

Before anyone touches the third potato, everyone should wash their hands thoroughly. Then have your child repeat what was done with the second potato—that is, pass it around for really thorough handling. When it too has been well handled, have her place this third potato in a container, seal it, and label it "Boiled, Well Handled, Clean Hands."

Step Five

Place all three containers in a place where they can sit undisturbed for a week or two, but *not* in the hot, direct sunlight of a window. If you feel brave, you could set them up in the middle of your kitchen table!

Step Six

For the next two weeks, have your child look closely at the potatoes once a day and make a record of what she sees in her science notebook. Talk over questions like these together:

- Why did we put lids on the containers?
- Why did we boil the potatoes first?
- What does what we see suggest we can conclude about cleanliness? About sterilization?

If you have a magnifying glass, use it to take a closer look.

▶ PICK A COLOR, ANY COLOR

Science and technology use color in many ways. For young scientists the two most important are *identification* (What color is that bird's tail?) and *testing* (aquarium enthusiasts use color when checking the acidity of tank water with litmus paper).

About 30 years ago, color became standard for television broadcasting. The electrical engineers who operated control rooms and did the videotaping had to sit down and have a quick lesson in how to discriminate among colors. This activity will help your young scientist learn to carefully observe color and to develop a color vocabulary.

At a Glance

Grade/Subject: 4th/Science—Inquiry Skills
Skills: observation, science vocabulary development
Materials: color charts such as color chips from paint or hardware stores, hobby shops, or art supply stores
watercolors or colored pencils
watercolor paper (or paper that is a little thicker than writing paper, but is still absorbent)

GREAT IDEA!

This potato activity was originally developed by parents and science educators working together at the St. Louis Science Center, St. Louis, MO. To find out more about science centers and museums in your area, contact ASTC, an association of centers and museums with over 400 member institutions across the world. Their address is listed in the Resource section at the end of this book.

WHAT'S MORE

Traditionally, men and women are never supposed to agree on the blueness or greenness of colors like turquoise, aqua, and sea green. Glue some of your blues and greens (and blue-greens and green-blues) onto cards and make a survey of how different friends or family members describe each color.

small watercolor brush
glue (liquid or in stick form)
magazines with lots of ads
scissors (optional)
science notebook

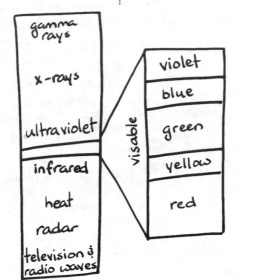

Time: 1 hour or longer, if you really get rolling (This activity can be added to later, if you and your child wish.)

Getting Ready

Visit as many local stores as you can and collect the small, free color charts that are usually available.

You can also cut small rectangles of color from the ads in glossy magazines. Don't worry about having all the colors. Part of this activity will involve providing some colors that your child will make.

Step One

Have a conversation about colors with your child. Pick out objects of different colors in the room around you. Find two or more objects that are of the same general color and move them close together. Are they really the same? What makes them different from one another?

Step Two

Draw a thin, up-and-down line along one side of a sheet of plain notebook paper. From your color chips and charts pick out a blue, a yellow, and a red. Cut them out and lay them on the paper along the line, blue at the bottom of the page, yellow in the middle, and red at the top of the page.

WHAT'S MORE

Colors are sometimes displayed on a wheel. To make your own color wheel, trace around a small saucer or bowl on a second sheet of notebook paper. Lay your six basic colors (this time use violet, green, and orange) around the circle so that they are equally separated B, G, Y, O, R, V (and back to B).

(Optional: If your child is familiar with colors, she can add an orange between red and yellow, and a green between blue and yellow).

The simple way to designate colors is to represent them with the symbols R, O, Y, G, B, I (for indigo), and V (for violet, or use P for purple, if you wish). Label your colors with these letters.

Step Three

Sort through your color chips and charts and begin to add colors that are somewhere in between. Don't stick them down at first because you may change your minds. If your child decides that there is a missing color, use the colored pencils or paints to make color chips that will fill the gaps.

When the two of you feel that you have enough colors, take a close look to see if they seem to be laid out correctly. When your child is happy with the arrangement, help her stick them down.

Step Four

Label the new colors that you've added to your color line. Have your child use the letter designations for all the colors, such as RO for a color that lies between red and orange, or YOY for a color that appears more like a yellow than an orange color.

Sometimes it's hard to figure exactly what a color is. This problem is good because discussing the colors and their properties is the best possible way of learning about them.

Advertisers and manufacturers often try to come up with appealing or exotic names for the colors of their products. If you have magazines with car, clothing, or cosmetic ads, or catalogs, look for some of the exotic names. (Cosmetics are a treasure trove of color words!) Go back to your color line and write in some of these names where they seem to belong.

COLOR MY WORLD

My sisters and I loved coloring together with our wide variety of crayons when we were kids. We made up names for all the colors. As adults, we still refer to a certain green color as "dead green."

WHAT'S MORE

Make a separate sheet of just greens. Arrange them in different ways such as dark green to light green and from blue green to yellow green. Give all your greens names (plain, like Dark Yellow Green, or exotic, like Deep Southern Mint or Lime Green Glimmer). Use these greens to accurately describe the different colors of celery, broccoli, lettuce, or other greens from your refrigerator or the foliage of your household plants.

LEGO GOES FOR LEARNING

Every child loves LEGO™ building systems, but did you know there are many learning kits for science and technology education from LEGO's Dacta division that aren't available in stores? Call (800) 527-8339 for more information!

PICTURE IT

Making good science records doesn't always have to involve writing. Making drawings based on actual observations and creating maps, graphs, and charts to represent data are some important nonverbal methods of record keeping.

Step Five

Have your child put her color line chart into her science notebook and keep it there as a reference for other activities.

▶ PILL BUG WORLD

Worms get all the credit for chewing up the old dead leaves and adding to our topsoil, but they're not doing this great service to our earth all by themselves. A different kind of creature is also hard at work—the pill bug. These fascinating little creatures aren't really bugs. They are a member of a crustacean order called the *isopods,* and they're the distant cousins of lobsters and crabs.

Pill bugs are known by many names: sow bugs, rolly pollies, and wood lice. Although their ancestors were aquatic, they have adapted to life on land and do quite well, thank you—as long as they can find a little moisture. When things get too tough for them, or too dry, they roll up in a ball for protection and water conservation and look like little pills. They're fascinating critters.

At a Glance

Grade/Subject: 4th/Science—Life Science
Skills: observation, animal study/experimentation
Materials: plastic storage box with cover, 8" × 10" or larger (You could try using an old casserole dish with a cover.)
playground or cactus potting sand, or aquarium gravel
pieces of bark, leaves, and twigs
some small stones
6 (preferably more) pill bugs (You can find them under rocks, or use the trap described below to catch them, or you can buy them from some school biological supply houses. Check with your child's teacher.)
1 potato or apple
science notebook
Time: 15–30 minutes to find pill bugs in your neighborhood (or overnight if you are using the vegetable trap)
30 minutes to assemble the pill bugs' habitat; observation

times of varying lengths, according to the kind of experiment your child conducts

Getting Ready

Think about where you can look for the bugs and obtain the ingredients for their new home. Talk with your child about what she may know of these little guys and get her ideas of where to look.

Step One

If you build it, they will come—well, you will be able to bring them to it. First, have your child fill the bottom of her container with sand or aquarium gravel so that it is 1/2 " to 1" deep. Make a little pile of leaves, small stones, and bark scraps on top of the sand in the middle and sprinkle enough water on it to make it moist to your touch.

Step Two

Get some pill bugs. Pill bug hunting is easy in some areas; they live under rocks, leaf piles, and small logs. If they are hard to find, the two of you can build a pill bug trap. Take a potato or an apple and cut out a deep tunnel with an apple corer or a knife. Put this into a likely pill bug environment. This could be under leaves, in a scooped out hollow up against a wall, or even in a damp basement. Leave the trap overnight and collect your pill bugs the next day.

Step Three

Pill bugs seem to like moisture, but good science requires testing. This test will take about half an hour to get started and then an overnight wait to see the results.

To make the test, have your child mix together some leaf litter, bark or twigs, and stones. Divide this mixture in half and place one half in a bowl of water and the other half on a paper towel in a hot, sunny window or on a radiator to dry out for an hour or longer. Then, gather your pill bugs gently (a spoon will help) into a cup. Take their home base material out of the home container and put your dried material at one end and the wet material at the other. Put the cover

---

WHAT'S MORE

Draw some pill bug portraits. A magnifying glass will help, but is not necessary. Cartoons are fine, too. Your child could record the data for the tests of pill bug preferences by drawing a map and marking where each pill bug is when she first takes a look. She should draw a view from the top of the pill bug habitat, first. Then, record all the objects that are present such as the home base, different foods, or whatever she is testing and then draw a little picture for each pill bug where she finds them.

back on and leave overnight. When you look, note where the pill bugs are hanging out. Have your child write up the test and its results in her science notebook.

Step Four

So what does a pill bug like to eat? Again, you can use the habitat you've made as an experimental station. This test takes only a few minutes to set up and the observation takes place the next day.

Place only moist stones in the center for their home base. Make a list of possible foods: For instance, different kinds of vegetables, maybe a bit of tuna fish or cheese, chocolate chips might be worth a try, or anything else your child wants to experiment with. Decide on two items to test, and put one at each end. Cover the habitat and check it the next day.

- Can you tell where the pill bugs have been?
- What kinds of evidence do you see?
- Which food did they prefer?
- Where were they when you opened the container?

Use the science notebook to make notes of what you find. Try again with two other foods. Then try comparing the "winners" of each of the first two tests.

Step Five

What other kinds of things could you and your child find out? Take some time to brainstorm together about possible pill bug likes and dislikes. Grape juice? Onion slices? Ginger ale? Together, think up at least one other experiment and have your child try it and write it up.

Step Six

Have your pill bug research colleague put together a short pill bug booklet. Based on what she has written in her observations, have it tell all about what they like best and how they like to live.

WHAT'S MORE

You can add some earthworms to your habitat and see how they and the pill bugs get along. Do they occupy different places in the habitat? Do they both have the same favorite foods?

Draw pictures and maps to record observations and write up conclusions in the science notebook.

Pill bugs can live from two to five years under good conditions, so they make interesting, low-maintenance pets. Female isopods have one to three broods every year and the infants look just like adults with a much lighter color. Use what you have learned in observing them as your guide to feeding and keeping them moist. If you and your child tire of maintaining your pill bug world, gently return the bugs to their natural habitat.

How Can Our Family "Make the Grade"?

CHAPTER 18

What Should I Do About . . . ?

HOMEWORK

Ah, homework—for some of us it was a chore, and for others a delight. But now we all find ourselves making sure that our children get it done! It's useful to keep in mind the two important functions that homework serves in education.

What we know of the process of long-term learning shows us that information needs to be processed several times for it to become a part of anyone's store of knowledge. Hearing something in the classroom is a first time and, if students don't think about it or use it a second or third time soon after, that first time becomes the *last* time. Homework is an opportunity to make a new piece of learning stick. Homework also helps to make teaching more efficient. When your child makes the effort to be prepared for a class, she and her teacher can then use their time together to expand on the knowledge, share insights, and move into new areas of learning.

How can I be sure my child does her homework?

If only parents could just wave a homework wand! Without it, here are some guidelines that may help homework time be less stressful.

Establish a routine and help your child stick with it. This is likely to require some time from you at the beginning, but it's well worth the effort. Let your child know that you expect that she will do her homework in the same way you expect that she'll eat dinner, participate in sports, or go to bed at a certain hour. Even if you hear the cry, "But I don't have any," sit and spend some time talking about what she did that day at school. (Maybe your child's teacher requires students to keep an assignment notebook—wouldn't that be great!) Encourage her to write in a journal, do a little online research on nights when there isn't a real assignment to do, or do one of the Learning Adventure activities in this book. Your attention and involvement will help your child see that it is part of her day to think about school things at home.

Practice some time management with your child. Look at her other time commitments (sports, music lessons, that favorite and acceptable TV program, other family routines) and help her set out a schedule that she can maintain reasonably. A set time every day is the easiest to remember but may not always be feasible. The point is to have the homework schedule make life easier not harder. Be sure to work in the extra time required for doing long-term research papers and special projects.

Create a study area. Make sure that it has few to no distractions and good lighting (stay outside of earshot of the TV if you can manage it). Going to a space that encourages your child to focus on work is an important part of the routine too. It might be where the computer is (as long as she has room to set out her books or papers and write), or it might be the table after supper is cleared. Keep homework items in a bag or box so they can be easily laid out and then picked up each night.

Make time in your own schedule. Those few moments you spend taking an interest in what your kid is doing, reviewing her progress, or giving a little help where needed make a big difference. (But do resist the temptation to actually do the work for her!) Keeping in touch prevents your child from thinking she is banished to do her homework in solitary confinement. Some work should certainly be done alone, but a lot of problem solving and creative thinking can be done through dialogue. If you care about what she is doing, she'll care more too.

My child's math is way over my head. How can I be helpful?

This isn't an uncommon problem for parents. Some basic school content will always be the same, but emphasis, styles of teaching, and (particularly in the case of science and some areas of mathematics) new discoveries and teaching techniques mean changes in the standard curriculum. There are several things you can do.

- First, remember that you don't have to replace the teacher. What you can most easily provide is a comfortable and supportive environment for your child's homework. This may mean putting a firm hand on the television power switch. It may mean setting aside a space where your child can work quietly and without disturbance. At all times, respect your child's ability and express confidence in him. Reassure him that you will help in whatever way you can.

- Second, if the problems are with understanding specific material or just a general failure to be able to get and follow directions, consult with your child's teacher. Some children find it difficult to ask for help or information in the classroom. Work with the teacher to make it possible for your child to ask.

- Third, use the Learning Adventure activities in this book to turn potentially difficult subject matter into something both fun and understandable.

- Fourth, some communities sponsor call-in homework phone assistance. Others have programs to connect students with mentors or tutors. After-school programs like *SCORE!* provide subject matter remediation and enrichment for the community. Check with your school's principal and with other parents to find out what is available.

- Fifth, ask your child's teacher for suggestions about books, magazines, and other resources that you can use to stimulate an interest in the subject. Try the Resources section in this book for further ideas.

How much should I help my child with her school projects?

All of us know some parents who do most of their children's work. It's really annoying, isn't it, to see a so-called student project that clearly has had lots of parental time and expertise (and sometimes money) expended on it. In most cases, though, the signs of such parental help will probably be just as obvious to the teacher or outside judges as they are to you.

Keep in mind that learning to use her ingenuity and knowledge is the goal of such projects for your child. If you do a major part of the work, she'll learn nothing (except how to manipulate you to do her work!). Of course, you can give advice and suggestions or ask helpful questions that will stimulate her imagination and creativity—if she asks you to. Just make sure that the actual final project, report, or experiment is her own.

How much help should I give my child with grammar and spelling in his written work?

In this situation, you need to walk a fine line between answering your kid's questions and actually taking over what ought to be his practicing of the editing and proofreading steps of the writing process. Encourage him to do as much as he can on his own. Even when you answer a question, try to cast yourself as the last resort. For instance, the first response to, "Mom, how do you spell . . . ?" probably should be, "Have you tried finding it in the dictionary?" or it could be asking him about a spelling guideline. After that, you can give some guidance in finding the word and, finally, help with the actual spelling.

If you're not certain about grammar and usage questions, admit your uncertainty. See if you can look up the rule or explanation together. Turn your rusty skills into a positive opportunity for you both to learn something.

What can I do when my child doesn't do his homework?

While this is a familiar problem, it has many answers—depending mainly on what problems or issues stand between your child and his homework. If he doesn't have a place to work, if his time is taken up with family chores, or if he has a TV in his room, those problems need to be solved first.

If there are no outside reasons or interference, it may be just a question of his developing self-discipline. There should be a definite time set aside for doing whatever homework has been assigned: no TV, no phone calls. Make it clear that the faster the homework gets done, the sooner he can be on the phone or doing something else.

If there's a serious problem, he may try to convince you that he just doesn't have any homework. In most schools today, having no homework is unlikely. Try to find out the truth—from other parents or, if necessary, from the teacher. Then you'll have to impose discipline from the outside.

TECHNOLOGY

Technology is a confusing and difficult area for both parents and educators. Although schools grew in size and complexity from the eighteenth century to the early twentieth century, the basic technology of education—blackboards, books, paper, and simple writing instruments—remained almost the same from decade to decade for almost 250 years.

Suddenly, following the Second World War, school equipment began changing, and they have been changing ever since. Technology like tape recorders, slide projectors, television, photocopiers, and film loop equipment became an increasingly regular part of school apparatus. But these additions were minor compared to the upheaval caused by computers. Today's information technology is so powerful, so full of promise, and so certain to alter how we work, play, and learn that schools and parents alike have to struggle to comprehend its implications.

Two problems stand out for parents and schools. One is trying to understand a technology that is still developing and whose implications for us are still unclear. The other is the enormous expense of this technology. Families and schools face hard economic and educational decisions as computer consumers and users.

How do I decide which computer to buy for my family?

Your decision will involve a combination of research and self-assessment; and unfortunately the answer may not be cut-and-dried for you. But here are the things to consider:

• Who will be using the computer?
• What programs will you want to use now? in the future?

If both you and your children will use the computer, you should consider checking into what your child's school has for hardware and software; kids tend to be pretty flexible when it comes to jumping from one program to another, but continuity is good if you can arrange it. (Many programs today can run on either a Windows™ or Macintosh® computer, so compatibility issues are less important than they used to be.) Depending on what you plan to do with the computer (word processing, telecommunicating), you may need to consider buying add-ons like a printer and a modem. As you consider what computer model to select, try to think ahead to what your computing needs will be a year or so from now. As with any electronic device, today's model may be outdated tomorrow; but if it meets your budget now and can meet your work plans for a couple years, then it is probably the right choice for your family.

How do I pick educational software that is good and that my kids will use?

It's sort of like picking out toys or books or clothes for children—some guesswork, some research, some sense of your child's likes and dislikes, and some luck. And after all that, they may still grow out of it in a year . . . . Given the number of new software titles that appear on store shelves every month, it is a bit daunting to go into a store or open a catalog and know what to buy. In general, your home software library should include a variety of programs (as your budget allows) in several main categories:

- Tools like a word processor (there are some very simple ones for even the youngest kids) and database or spreadsheet programs for older kids
- Creative programs like art, music, and card-making programs
- Academic programs that provide instruction and practice in areas like spelling or math
- Games that result in learning something like words, geography, or historical events (If you look around, you can find many that kids are motivated to play, but aren't the shoot-'em-up kind.)
- Simulation programs and other thinking-skill activity products (they involve kids in decision making, problem solving, anticipating outcomes)

Here are several solid ways to help you make your purchasing decision.

Find out what your kids are using at school. There may be a title that your child particularly enjoys or that the teachers think is great. This is a good opportunity to strengthen the home-school connection.

Talk to other parents. Someone may have done some research that can benefit you. Fellow parents can give you firsthand reports of what their kids are doing with products they have or why they like them. Recommendations from them about what not to buy can be helpful, too.

Subscribe to one of the many family-oriented periodicals with software reviews. New ones come on the newsstands every month (Another choice to make!), and there are a bunch that specialize in home computing software. Reviews and articles are likely to talk about a range of issues like titles that are good for 5 year olds but are also enjoyed by 4th graders and safety tips for letting your kids use your home computer.

Make note of brand names that are usually good. When your kids have a really good time with a particular title, see what else the company makes.

Keep your eyes open for reviews. Software and multimedia reviews appear in lots of places: weekly news magazines, your daily newspaper, flyers that you pick up in a store, on the Internet, and on other online services.

What should I know about the World Wide Web?

To understand the World Wide Web (WWW), we need to start with the Internet, which is an immense linkage of computer networks all over the world. When it started in the 1950s, the Internet was used primarily by the government and universities to conduct and communicate research projects. It displayed only text (words, numbers, symbols) on-screen, and users had to type in commands to do anything. Since then, the Internet network of computers has expanded to include thousands of new users—business people, educators, and families like yours—and in ways that are extremely more friendly and easy to use.

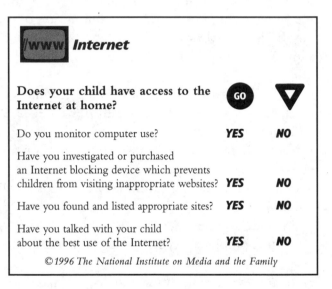

Another major development in the Internet is the way in which you can see and use information on screen. You use one portion of the Internet—called the World Wide Web—by clicking on pictures and images rather than typing in words. Probably because of this ease of use, it is said to be the fastest growing part of the Internet. There were an estimated 30 million users of the Net in 1996, and that figure may double at an annual rate.

Now, thanks to programs called Web browsers (perhaps you've heard of Netscape™ or Internet Explorer™), you see screens that look like the colorful pages of a magazine, but besides text and images these pages also offer sounds and sometimes even video clips. Some of the graphics and text on these pages are highlighted. By clicking on highlighted items, you can jump to other places (sites) in the Web. (Think about the intricate arrangement of a spider's web and the name World Wide Web makes sense.) The first page of any Web site is called its home page—sort of like the contents page of a magazine. The home page usually contains a table of contents for the rest of the site.

Should I let my child have access to the Internet considering some of its bad press?

With some guidance, your child can use the Internet as a very beneficial tool. Our children live in a dynamic, video-oriented age; their daily worlds are filled with videotapes, music videos, cartoons, TV shows, and advertisements. The Internet can merge this video culture with traditional academic learning. Furthermore, it adds interactivity, which is not available in the passive surround of video and TV. To use the Internet, children have to get involved rather than just sit and watch. And their involvement can take place in the form of writing, critical thinking, math, conversation, or research—all with a level of excitement that you seldom see in other learning situations. In the same way that you monitor what TV shows your child watches (or where she goes or what she eats), you can set up guidelines for how and when your child uses your online service. You may also want to look into one of the many new software programs that allow you to restrict access to certain areas of the Internet.

What should I do about how much TV my child watches?

We can't ignore television. We all grew up with it and lived to tell the tale. But the degree to which TV can dominate the development of many children is much greater now than it was when there were fewer programs, channels, and TV sets in a home—and more scruples about what finds its way onto the screen. Sure, TV can be addictive and too many parents use it as a pacifier or baby-sitter, but it is also a powerful tool that can be turned to the advantage of valuable learning. Your challenge, as a parent, is to reduce the role of the television to one of educational support, supplemented with a small dash of recreation. Do not put a TV set in your child's room. Find some programs that are educational—drama, science, history, the arts, or whatever. Watch *with* your child as often as possible and talk together about what you see. If you're not monitoring family TV viewing, your child may be spending too much time with TV. Show that you care about what and how your children learns by setting some serious goals (and examples), and follow through with them.

Should I regulate which TV shows or videos my child watches?

Yes, when possible—in much the same way that you make choices for her about what to eat, what books to read, and what language to use. Young children usually need clear guidance in the choices available to them and there are many lists available in print and online that provide guidelines for age-appropriate viewing. As they progress through elementary school, children can begin to make some of their own decisions well *if* you talk with them about what they are watching, what they think of it, and what alternative things might be as engaging for them as watching TV.

Here are some helpful ways to start such discussions. Ask for your child's ideas on:

- How to choose between two programs
  (If you could watch only *Nick News* or *Goosebumps*, but not both, which would you pick? Why?)
- How to distinguish between reality and fantasy programs

(What did you think when the man jumped out of the window and didn't get hurt? What do you think would happen if someone you know tried it?)
- How commercials influence our behavior
  (Why do you want that toy, cereal, soda . . . ? Where did you hear about it? How do you know whether it is good or not or whether you would actually like it or not?)
- How to set a schedule for viewing
  (Let's pick some shows together for you to watch during your TV hour today. Let's figure out some fun things for you to do when TV time is over.)

Well, then how useful is educational TV?

It's the same for educational television. How much information do we retain from even the most thoughtful educational program that we've seen only once? How many details of Civil War battles, naval engagements in the Second World War, or the great moments in the arts and sciences can you recall that have passed before you on educational television? We watch serious educational programming, but unless we do something with the information, it's almost literally in one ear (and eye) and out the other. We feel briefly edified, but are we *educated* by it? Not unless we spend some follow-up time thinking about it, writing about it, talking about it—and the same goes for our children.

Kids don't learn from television just by watching it, but television can be a part of their learning. When those flickering images are grounded in real-world activities and supportive discussion, learning takes place. The activities don't have to be any more complicated than a discussion of what was seen, but spending time with children to "debrief" their TV viewing takes time and energy on the part of parents and teachers. Adults need to be thoughtful about both the use of television and how much time they are willing to put into making it work as a tool for learning.

Do I have to use videos with my kids, and if so, should we rent, buy, or borrow them?

This is truly one of the personal choices you may make about what happens in your home. It really depends on what you think your kids need or should have at the time. Many families use videos for a variety of reasons:

- To have an alternative to TV programming
- To see a film or show originally broadcast on TV or shown in theaters
- To learn a specific skill or study a specific topic

Use of videos is usually just one option in a range of possible family activities. If you decide to include videos in your family's list of things to do, it's nice to have several options for obtaining them.

You could rent videos to start and then purchase them only if they are ones your kids like to watch a lot and your budget is up to it. You may decide that there are titles you want to invest in for your collection, too—your family classics, in other words.

And don't forget about borrowing them! Most town libraries now have collections that circulate and this is a great (free) way to check out videos (literally!). Libraries are often the best nearby source of nonmovie titles like how-tos and historical or geographic programs.

Is it better to use a dictionary or a computer to look up words?

This is one of those questions that has an "on the one hand/on the other hand" answer. Computer-based dictionaries have some definite advantages. They are fast, usually provide very contemporary examples of usage, often incorporate appealing pictures, and sometimes include an audio component.

Books have their own advantages. They are slower but this also offers advantages. Sometimes it is psychologically important to move at a slower pace. Children should not have to learn (and, in fact, sometimes don't learn) on the run. Books also provide opportunities for peripheral learning—you can't help but encounter other members of a word family and other eye-catching and interesting words on the same page. For younger children, dictionaries in book form are an important way to practice alphabetization skills. And last, but not least, if electricity fails or your computer crashes, you will still be able to find your word!

Finally, the answer to this question really depends on the age of your child and the kind of learning activity she is engaged in. In the younger grades, when basic word skills are being developed, the dictionary is often the best choice. In the later grades, when skills have shifted to story or theme writing and the word is needed for spelling or quick reference, the computer can often offer real advantages.

THE PARENT-SCHOOL PARTNERSHIP

Forty years ago it would not have been unlikely for your 8th grade teacher to look you in the eye (in the way that only 8th grade teachers could) and say, "I remember when your father used to have the same trouble with square roots."

Today, such memories would be almost impossible. Teachers and students have become part of a highly mobile society. Everyone is on the move. Everyone is also working longer and longer, and two-paycheck families or single-parent families are common. Increased mobility and busier families mean extra strains on school and parent relationships, and this makes good communication between parents and teachers extremely important.

Should I worry about expecting too much of my child or when a teacher expects too little?

Children respond to their own expectations of what they can and cannot learn. If they believe they are able to learn something, whether solving equations or riding a bicycle, they usually make real headway. But when they lack confidence, learning eludes them. Children grow in self-confidence as they experience success in learning, just as they lose confidence in the face of repeated failure. Thus teachers and parents need to provide them with challenging but attainable learning tasks and help them experience success.

Research has shown that children's personal expectations are closely linked to what they perceive others think of them. Children, especially many girls, are quick to pick up the expectations of success or failure that others have for them. The positive and negative expectations shown by parents, counselors, principals, and peers affect students' expectations and hence their learning behavior. In addition, we know that parents and teachers who expect a child to succeed tend to more effectively support that child's learning. If you suspect that your child's teacher has low expectations for her, address the problem directly before it becomes a self-fulfilling prophesy. And you and your child's teacher need to bolster your child's enthusiasm for learning—even in a school and youth culture that may not think being smart and working hard is "cool."

How can I make the most of parent-teacher conferences?

Preparation is the key to a good conference. Most teachers will have gathered up marks, thoughts, and examples of your child's work to bring to your conference. If you plan out beforehand what you want to ask about, you'll be able to get the most out of your meeting:

- Ask your child if there is anything she wants you to talk over with her teacher.
- Think about what you want to cover and make a list of questions; then order them to put the most important questions first.
- Check your list frequently during the conference so that if you and the teacher get sidetracked you can be sure to cover what is most important.
- Jot notes during the conference and then take a moment afterwards to fill in the notes enough so that you can follow up on comments and suggestions over the year.
- If there are problems, whether it's homework, classroom behavior, or social issues, ask for specific ways to help your child.
- After the conference, check back in with the teacher on a regular basis.

What can I do to support my child's teacher?

For starters, just keep in mind that teachers are people. We all tote around baggage left over from our own childhood as well as our present anxieties about our children. If feelings take over our relationship with a teacher, it's very hard to communicate anything.

It can be helpful to remember that teaching is an extremely demanding occupation and, considering the expectations we have of the profession, not a very well paid one (compare the starting salaries for the department of sanitation or public transport workers to those for teachers in your community). Classroom teachers are answerable to principals, superintendents, school boards, a large number of ever-changing parents, and their own desires to do the best they can for their students. In most schools, they work steadily, with few breaks and little opportunity to interact with other adults, and then they take work home with them in the evening.

So begin all interactions with a measure of patience. This doesn't mean you should not be firm and persistent, but you'll get off to a more productive start if you assume that you and your child's teacher have the same goal—to do what is best for your child.

Can I help out in my child's class?

Managing a school day is a hard job, and most teachers appreciate the offer of time and help in the classroom. Let the teacher know that you are willing to help in some way, and then let her determine when and how. Teachers have a complex schedule that is usually worked out months in advance, so let the school know when you are available (to accompany a field trip, for example) or if you have a particular skill, occupation, or interest that you would like to share.

If you work at a job in a company that is interested in supporting local schools, find out if your company has any willingness to offer time off to employees who would like to volunteer in a school for a day or half day.

Should I speak up if I disagree with how my child is being taught math, science, art . . . ?

Please do. Education is best conducted as a partnership between parents and schools. We rely on teachers to be skilled at running their classrooms and competent in their fields. That's a fair expectation. Teaching is a profession and most teachers, in addition to their regular work in school, take refresher courses, workshops, and pursue advanced degrees. Education, like other fields, changes, and new ways of presenting material, organizing classrooms, and evaluating students appear regularly. Sometimes these new ways of doing things baffle parents, particularly when they suddenly appear during a homework session at the kitchen table.

Teachers are usually eager to share what they have learned and what they are doing, so if you have questions about what kids are doing in the classroom, teachers are generally glad to meet with you and explain it. In the rare instance when a teacher is not performing up to the standards of the school system, it is important for you and other parents to speak up and work with the school administration to solve the problem.

I've been reading about a better way to teach reading; should I raise this with the school?

Sometimes parents hear of new approaches to teaching that they wish their kid's teachers would try in the classroom. Curriculum research and development is always producing change and, yes, if you hear of something new and potentially useful, bring it up with the school. Don't expect to get instant results, however. A school's investment in materials and staff development time, plus the many hours of work that go into curriculum development on the local school level mean that changes won't take place overnight.

Do some homework. If you have an idea or suggestion, research it as fully as you can before bringing it up with your school. Read more about it, find out the pros and cons, and make a list of reference materials. Presenting a short suggestion accompanied by some literature that the teacher can read and think about at a quieter moment will get you more of a hearing. Some suggestions are more appropriately passed on to the school principal. Topics that involve the whole school and larger social issues, such as public health questions, a "how to deal with bullies" curriculum, or an anti-racism initiative, involve the whole school community rather than the individual classroom.

Should I spend time finding out the details of our school's curriculum?

Absolutely. School conferences and open houses are times when you can ask questions about the specifics of classroom instruction as well as about the curriculum in general. If there isn't time to cover everything, ask your child's teacher for recommended books and periodicals. If enough parents are interested, a school may be willing to arrange an evening devoted to presenting information about curriculum specifics. If individual parents or parents working through a PTA or other parent/school organization offer to set up and arrange the meeting, they will probably be even more willing.

My child's teacher doesn't seem to like my child; what can I do?

Talk with your child's teacher. In almost all cases, and particularly with younger children, apparent slights or injured feelings are the result of misunderstandings. Most teachers have had years of experience with many children and families. They are happy to sift through the problems of communication to find ways to support your child and make him comfortable. In the rare case when a teacher has for some reason taken a dislike to your child, also begin by talking with the teacher. But don't be confrontational. The teacher who dislikes a child and acts upon it is behaving in an unprofessional way, even if unintentional. A gentle nudge may alert the teacher to an awareness of her actions, thereby prompting her to do whatever is necessary to correct the situation. If your effort is not successful, consult the principal, and then if necessary, talk with other parents.

Teachers here are big on "cooperative learning," but my child works best alone. What should I do?

It's a good idea at a parent-teacher conference to bring up any question like this that's troubling you and your child. It's true, there's a lot of emphasis today on cooperative projects that bring together students of varying abilities and skills. And it's also true that some kids—like yours—may be more comfortable with other approaches.

But before dismissing the idea of cooperative learning, take a look at what it's all about. One of the ideas behind cooperative learning is that it's good preparation for the real world, where interpersonal skills and teamwork are often required.

Genuine cooperative learning differs from traditional group projects, though, in the way it involves every member, not just the smartest kid or the strongest leader. The aim in cooperative learning is to develop youngsters' capacity for working as a real team. Most importantly, each member of the group is responsible for a specific part of the overall project or goal. Those goals and ideals mean that cooperative learning may actually be a good experience for a kid like yours, who already knows how to work by herself (an equally valuable gift). At the same time, do bring this issue up at a conference. The teacher who is guiding the cooperative learning activity needs to keep such individual differences in mind when structuring the group and to keep watching for how each child participates and benefits.

My child will miss a week of school because the family has to be out of town. What should I do about this?

Plan ahead! The worst thing to do is to leave without an explanation to your child's teacher and to try to have your child make up missed work when you return.

Before the absence, write a short letter to the school administration explaining the absence; you may also want to call the school office. If your kid is quite mature, have him deliver the letter to school, explain the situation to all his teachers, and get assignments in advance for the time he'll be absent. With a younger child, telephone (or visit) the principal or teacher and explain the situation. Ask for work assignments for the time away. Be prepared to follow up on that issue by meeting with the teacher, if necessary.

While your child is out of school, you may have to be stricter than usual to get your kid to do those assignments—especially if both of you are distracted by outside events. It's helpful to remember that you'll both be happier if he keeps up with his work so as not to fall behind.

SCHOOL SERVICES

It's part of every school's mandate to meet children's physical, social, and intellectual needs. Toward that end, school buildings are being modified for access by students of all mobility levels and are becoming increasingly equipped for a wider range of educational needs and activities. As budgets allow, school staff lists include both the core teachers and the specialists needed to meet students' group and individual needs.

My school wants my daughter to have a Special Ed evaluation. What does that mean?

Typically kids are referred for this type of evaluation when their teacher feels they are not working up to their potential in the classroom or they raise some behavioral issues of concern to the teacher. The purpose of the evaluation is to determine why your child is having difficulties in succeeding at the moment and to identify a plan for helping her to improve her learning performance. Going through this formal evaluation makes it possible for your child to receive services from specialists, if need be—services paid for by the school district.

The exact nature of special education evaluations varies by school system, but here is a description of some of what you might expect. A team of specialists will use a variety of formal and informal measures to get an accurate picture of your child's current educational situation. The team will want to see how she does in her present day-to-day setting as well as on examinations when she is under pressure. They will observe her in the classroom and review her school work—to see how she reads, does math, spells, and writes. There will be psychological tests and a review of medical records, as well as interviews with the teachers and you, the parent.

Throughout the evaluation, the team wants to see whether your child has developed the kind of skills that help her succeed in the classroom, such as:

- How efficiently she uses her eyes and ears
- How quickly she catches on to new ideas and concepts
- How long she can concentrate on a difficult task
- How much she knows about the world around her—neighborhood, family, home, community
- How well she understands the conventions of direction, order, rhythm, and rhyme
- How well developed her speaking and listening language is
- How accurately she understands and remembers spoken directions, explanations, and casual conversations

The most useful information will come from time spent actually working with your daughter to see how she learns most effectively. Figuring out what helps her learn something new—explanations, demonstrations, combining several approaches, repetition, slowing down, or cutting down on distractions—is a key part of making an appropriate educational plan for her.

When the evaluations are completed, you will meet with the team to discuss the results and make a plan. Your daughter may be invited to attend too if being there to speak for herself and to hear about her educational plan is key to the development of an appropriate approach.

What is Attention Deficit Disorder (ADD)?

Everyone can remember a few kids from their school years who never stayed in their seats, talked out of turn, threw spitballs, or turned in sloppy papers. And the teacher may have ignored them or sent them on an occasional trip to the principal's office. So what's all this recent fuss about kids who are hyperactive or have an attention problem? How is "hacking around a little" now considered a *special need*?

Well, we have a little more information to work with now. It is reported that approximately 3–5 percent of all American children—up to 3.5 million—have Attention Deficit Disorder. ADD is a neurologically-based disability (that is, it has to do with the brain). Some researchers believe that ADD is due to altered brain biochemistry. Research has shown that the rate at which the brain uses glucose, its main energy source, is lower in persons with ADD—especially in the portions of the brain that are responsible for paying attention, handwriting, motor control, and inhibition responses.

Since the symptoms of ADD—among them being fidgety, talkative, bossy, and inattentive—are behaviors seen in most children at some point in their lives, the diagnosis and labeling of a child with ADD is often the subject of debate. Some kids who seem jumpy or act out now may simply grow out of it; others may need intervention to learn how to have more control. It is vitally important to put together a complete picture of a child's development and draw from many sources of information before rendering a diagnosis.

School is often where the characteristics of ADD may be more easily recorded, since the school setting requires the very skills that are difficult for kids with ADD—sustained attention to a task, waiting turns, and staying seated.

A child suspected of having ADD should receive a comprehensive evaluation, including medical, psychological, educational, and behavioral components.

Can I ask to meet separately with the special teachers who see my child?

This depends entirely on your local school system's policies and resources. Widespread reluctance to adequately fund education at both the local and national level means that the specialist teachers are frequently overburdened. Many are willing to work with parents, but they feel that their limited time is best spent with the children. If you have a special need, begin first with your child's regular teacher. She or he is in the best position to help get you the information you need. If this is not successful, consult with your school's principal.

How do I know if my child has a learning disability?

A big indicator is when you, as a parent, sense something is amiss. You may notice that your child, who generally seems smart, has no major physical problems, and does very well in some things, just can't cut it in some other basic areas. Your suspicions may be reinforced at parent/teacher conference time when you hear things like: "He's a good kid and does very well in math, but he doesn't apply himself, especially when it has to do with reading or following directions. He should be doing a lot better."

Putting a finger on a learning disability is tricky because there are as many combinations of problems as there are children who have them. But some familiar patterns can be identified. Basically, kids with a learning disability have trouble learning some things, but not all things. They may

- Consume reading material like crazy, but not deal well with even simple social situations; or have great difficulty reading and act out to avoid having to read
- Be completely aware of current events and enjoy talking about them, but be completely frustrated by any attempt to put pen to paper
- Do academic subjects well but not be able to ever follow directions (especially oral ones) or do something that requires physical coordination

Success in school (and in life, for that matter) has to do with making sense of what we see and hear. Think of the brain as a big filing cabinet. If all the information is in neat files and in alphabetical order so we can get to it easily, then reading, writing, computing, and talking is generally pretty problem free. For kids with LD concerns, however, the information is there, but not neatly piled and alphabetized; it takes longer for these kids to figure some things out. One of the goals in providing them with special education services is to help them develop better information-processing skills.

The severity of an LD problem may seem to rise and fall over the years. That's usually because different classroom environments can either amplify what's hard for a child or support what he can do well. People don't generally grow out of a learning disability but rather learn to compensate for a weakness by focusing on the things they are very good at. (Lots of kids with learning disabilities even use their smarts to sidestep doing what's hard for them!)

It's definitely possible to be a student with a learning disability and still be successful. Consider just a few famous examples: Winston Churchill, Albert Einstein, Beethoven, John F. Kennedy, Walt Disney, Whoopi Goldberg—there are lots more. With perseverance, they made it—so can your kid.

SCHOOL PROGRAMS AND CHOICES

It was simpler back then, wasn't it? Kids went to school and parents basically knew what was going on. Things were solid. It felt right. Now you overhear your kids' conversations, get flyers at home, read newspaper articles that talk about alternative classes and magnet schools. You can even choose to attend a school out of your neighborhood!

The school wants to put my daughter into the next higher grade. Is that a good idea?

Moving to a new community or changing schools can present this problem at least as often as having an especially bright child. Regardless of the reason, there are several factors to consider. One important one is your child's social and physical maturity—will it be obvious that she's younger? Might she be teased or bullied as a "baby" by her older and bigger classmates? Will she feel socially different or unprepared? Such problems could outweigh the benefits and cause lasting problems with social relationships.

On the other hand, if she's grown-up enough to fit in and deal with slightly older kids, it could be a good opportunity to challenge her intelligence and avoid her being bored by materials and skill lessons she may have already mastered or learned in her old school.

Sometimes kids at our school make up their own program. Shouldn't the school decide what the kids study?

These types of programs—often called "exploratory"—are one of the many new approaches that try to fit school experiences to each individual kid and his particular needs. Although found in some elementary classrooms, exploratory programs appear most in the middle school years. You know that many kids at this age constantly develop new interests, then just as quickly change their minds and go on to something else. While it may be maddening to parents to watch last week's expensive hobby equipment gathering dust, it's part of the age. The intent of "exploratory" programs is to give kids a safe way to explore a new idea or interest—to test their abilities without much risk of failure.

It's a mistake to view exploratory programs as just fooling around. First, a chance to explore is an important part of growing up. Then, planning and carrying out a project in a safe and noncompetitive atmosphere is another great experience for children, especially adolescents. Since it's the child's own idea, he has no reason not to focus and work hard on it. Projects are usually short-term, and teachers who take part are frequently following their own interests along with your child, too. That means the level of enthusiasm is high, and can generate a real love of learning.

A school providing children this kind of involvement in their own learning choices is quite progressive in encouraging students to generate their own projects to explore individual interests. Such schools and their teachers take on an obligation to make sure that their curricular goals are met overall and that children's choices contribute to those goals. More traditional schools approach this problem in other ways, such as elective courses in the arts and sciences or opportunities for independent study.

What happens if my child works too far ahead of her class in some subjects? Will she be bored?

This can be a problem, particularly in classrooms that adhere closely to a standardized curriculum. When students have already accomplished the classroom goals, they are placed in a difficult position. Going over what they already know is boring, and they may either suffer in silence or get into trouble. Neither of these is a desirable alternative.

This doesn't mean that you should hold back on your child's academic development or that you shouldn't make an effort to extend her education. The best solution is to consult with your child's teacher. Together you can plan learning paths that supplement and extend the standard curriculum without overlapping what the whole class is doing together. Your child can forge ahead at her own pace, explore new material, and continue to be challenged. In the "What's More" sidebars with the Learning Adventure activities in this book, you will find sets of supplemental activities. These extend the skills practice or knowledge base of the activities and are an example of how a single learning activity can encompass a greater depth of learning.

Should I worry that there is less and less physical education in my daughter's school?

Yes, it should be a concern to all parents for two reasons. The most important is the physical well being of your child. Modern children lead increasingly sedentary lives, and this is probably related to the alarming increase in obesity throughout our country. C. Everett Koop, the former U.S. Surgeon General, and other health experts identify obesity as a major health problem and a contributing factor in a number of disease conditions ranging from diabetes to cancer. Removing any opportunity for movement and exercise should be protested by concerned parents. Try to enlist your local public health figures in efforts to maintain physical education programs.

The second (and more academic) reason is that children learn better when study time is broken up by the opportunity to move around and change environments. Japanese schools, often cited as models of intense academic pursuit by some educators, do have longer days and longer school years, but they also build in many more breaks for exercise, relaxation, and organized sports. All work (and sitting at a desk all day) does indeed make Jack a dull boy.

Do extras like art and music take away from my child's real academic work?

The simple fact is that the arts are not just a frilly adjunct to a good education, they are an essential dimension of learning. It means doing art in the same way that you would do science or math. It means spending time on making pictures and performing music. A famous comparative study of European and American schools some years ago highlighted this. French children are systematically given a fairly rigorous course of instruction in drawing in their schools. As a result, all French students at the equivalent level of our high schools are very comfortable using drawing as a way of expressing themselves not just in art, but, for example, in the sciences where they can easily illustrate the view in a microscope or detail the results of a dissection or lay out the workings of a mechanism. Similarly, performing music, aside from the pleasure it gives, develops a sensitivity to mathematical patterns and sequences that is lost to children who are deprived of this opportunity.

For children who learn best through their hands, senses, and movement (read the essay "How Do Children Learn?" in Section I of this book), time spent on instruction in the arts is essential. It doesn't take away from the basics; it makes learning the basics possible for some, and enhances and extends that learning for everyone.

What is this America 2000 plan that people talk about?

The Goals 2000: Educate America Act was signed into law on March 31, 1994. This act serves as an outline for redefining school systems in the United States in an attempt to ensure that all students are prepared for life in the twenty-first century. It targets areas that need to change, particularly in light of the developments in information processing and global connectivity. It talks about changing roles and expectations of teachers, functions of schools, and attitudes and behaviors of students. Here are the eight national goals. The actual document is over 200 pages long, so just highlights are included here:

1. **School Readiness:** By the year 2000, all children in America will start school ready to learn.
2. **School Completion:** By the year 2000, the high school graduation rate will increase to at least 90 percent.
3. **Student Achievement and Citizenship:** By the year 2000, all students will leave grades 4, 8, and 12 having demonstrated competency over challenging subject matter including English, mathematics, science, foreign languages, civics and government, economics, the arts, history, and geography, and every school in America will ensure that all students learn to use their minds well, so they may be prepared for responsible citizenship, further learning, and productive employment in our nation's modern economy.
4. **Teacher Education and Professional Development:** By the year 2000, the Nation's teaching force will have access to programs for the continued improvement of their professional skills and the opportunity to acquire the knowledge and skills needed to instruct and prepare all American students for the next century.
5. **Mathematics and Science:** By the year 2000, U.S. students will be first in the world in mathematics and science achievement.
6. **Adult Literacy and Lifelong Learning:** By the year 2000, every adult American will be literate and will possess the knowledge and skills necessary to compete in a global economy and exercise the rights and responsibilities of citizenship.
7. **Safe, Disciplined, and Alcohol- and Drug-Free Schools:** By the year 2000, every school in the United States will be free of drugs, violence, and the unauthorized presence of

firearms and alcohol and will offer a disciplined environment conducive to learning.

8. **Parental Participation:** By the year 2000, every school will promote partnerships that will increase parental involvement and participation in promoting the social, emotional, and academic growth of children.

In the first two years of the plan, 46 states wrote school improvement plans and were granted Goals 2000 funds. Some states and communities are creating new schools—called *charter schools*—while others are revitalizing existing ones. Community participation in schools is a vital part of local reform efforts. If you are a parent who wants to make an impact in your school system, Goals 2000 may offer an opportunity for you. Check with your local school board to see what is happening in your community.

THE SOCIAL SIDE OF SCHOOL

School is a social setting and, like it or not, social issues play a large part in the success of the learning environment. It is a major challenge for us as parents to be aware of the moods and feelings of our children, and it's one of the challenges that gets more difficult as they mature. Sorting out the normal grumps and bumps from the unusual mood swings that signal a problem isn't easy, but it is important to keep checking. Most children, and probably yours, have days when they are reluctant to go to school, but have these suddenly increased? Has normal play outside of school diminished? Has your child's performance in school inexplicably dropped off? This is an area in which communication between you and your child's teacher will make a tremendous difference.

What should I do when my child is teased?

Differences in size or weight—even wearing glasses—can sometimes be cause for suffering among school children. Whatever the problem, your child needs you to be accepting of his feelings and to give him emotional support. At the same time, let him know that he is a strong and capable person. Bullying and teasing behavior comes from children who are bullied and teased themselves and, although they are the perpetrators rather than the victims, these children are also hurt by situations in which they act out unchecked. This information may not seem immediately helpful to your child, but it is useful to have.

The point is not to minimize the emotional hurt your child receives, but to demystify the menace by putting it into perspective. Make contact with your child's teacher right away. A note or phone call will serve as an alert, and make an appointment to meet as soon as possible. Children can sometimes be cruel, but they can also be very supportive, and a good teacher who catches potentially hurtful situations in the early stages can turn them around. If you notice or hear of things going on before the school does, don't hesitate to speak up.

Should I worry that my kid, an only child, tends to be a loner?

Some of the world's most interesting and creative people have been loners. A lot depends on your definition of "loner." Is your kid simply self-reliant and self-sufficient, and good at being alone and entertaining herself? Many only children develop such valuable traits.

Since there are no other kids in your family, an only child may sometimes feel very much at home among adults. You can help her be more sociable with people her own age simply by facilitating visits to other kids' houses and having friends over. You also can encourage her to take part in activities with kids with similar interests.

On the other hand, some kids—and not just only children—seem to be loners to an extreme degree. If your kid is truly withdrawn and seriously moody or hostile, the situation probably demands stronger interest and intervention, and possibly some outside counseling.

TIME OUTSIDE OF SCHOOL

It has always been true that children receive a good share of their education outside of the schools. In fact, kids are always learning (aren't we all!), so it matters what they are learning during the majority of their time, which is spent away from school.

The quality and quantity of outside educational experiences is directly proportional to parental involvement. The more you put into it, the more they get out of it. Whether it's locating enrichment programs, supporting youth programs, doing a little teaching yourself, or just offering your support for your child's quest for knowledge, you make a tremendous difference.

I don't have much time or money to provide my child with after-school activities. Help!

You're not alone. Many parents have discovered that our schools have less and less to offer in the way of extracurricular activities. Even though they have less and less time, parents are having to do more and more. The Learning Adventure activities in this book have been designed for after-school fun with little or no cost to parents—so there's one place to start!

Other help is available. Established after-school or extended day programs, both commercial and community supported, are becoming more common. Shopping around isn't always possible, but if it is, look for programs that have a specific focus. Programs built around activity—whether it's sports, supplemental education, ethnic identity, the arts, or crafts—tend to be more stimulating and thoughtfully run, than those that are just places for kids to stay. But after-school centers simply designed for kids with nowhere else to go can include aspects of all such activities. And you can encourage these centers to offer more by making suggestions, helping think of places to visit, and the like.

Sometimes just beginning to look for opportunities for your child will help. As you look for programs and activities, people will suggest other resources and, more importantly, you will encounter other parents engaged in the same search. Connecting with other busy parents means you can share resources and information and pool your energy. Connecting can be as simple as talking about your search with other parents at the playground, church, or at a PTA meeting. A note on the local library bulletin board or a message in the school newsletter may be enough to organize other parents around a particular activity.

Is enrolling my child after school to learn our ethnic culture and language asking too much of her?

Being proud of one's heritage is an important component of every person's self-esteem. Programs that support this are excellent supplements to regular schooling. Indeed, given the frequent cutbacks in school arts programs, these can be an important resource for your child's intellectual growth. The experience may even help her do well at school. Whether or not committing her time to such a program serves your child well depends entirely on your assessment of her abilities and needs.

Learning a second language is extremely valuable. Many of us forget how immigrants to North America, including those who've made major contributions on this continent, became bilingual and, not infrequently, trilingual. Having a second language and being intimate with another culture gives your child an educational advantage, particularly if it's also a source of pride.

What kinds of reference books should I get my child?

A quick answer: small ones! Thick atlases, massive encyclopedia sets, and other large reference books look impressive, but the old idea of encompassing all of human knowledge in an expensive shelf of books has gone out the window. Our body of knowledge continues to undergo rapid change (just look at the cartographic scramble when the Soviet Union came apart or the overnight shifts in thinking in the medical and biological sciences). Large atlases, encyclopedias, and other reference books themselves have changed, and most of them are available at the library, in software, or online; many are capable of being rapidly and inexpensively updated on a regular basis.

Dictionaries, almanacs, field guides, and smaller reference books are a different story. These contain information that is more useful on a day-to-day basis, and they are inexpensive, portable, and worth buying. Besides, even if you have a computer-based encyclopedia program, you'll need something if the power goes off!

What books for kids does it make sense to buy?

Sometimes it seems like books for children are a little like their shoes, too expensive and too quickly outgrown. Most of us, however, have a cherished old book or two tucked away in the bottom of a box or bookcase. Good books are treasured—read and reread and worth the investment. That doesn't mean you have to buy every book that comes along. Use the school and public libraries to discover the particular books that will strike your child as wonderful. Read reviews of literature for children in newspapers and magazines. Check out lots of library books and encourage your child to participate in the selection. Not every one will be a hit; but over time, you will find books, authors, and subject matter that both suit and fascinate your child. This can be your guide to the occasional purchase.

If money is tight, think twice about spending money on fad toys. Toy makers and sellers spend vast sums on market research that, at its heart, only creates new ways to exploit children's gullibility and parental guilt. Stroll past any yard sale and add up the amazing amount of money that was spent on yesterday's gotta-have-it toy. And while you're there, check through the children's books—you may find some buys.

Birthdays and holidays are prime occasions for book buying. A gift list of books can add to your home library. Grandparents and relatives often ask for gift suggestions. If they don't, drop them a note with ideas before the holidays or birthdays roll around. This helps them with their gift buying and (sometimes) means you won't be getting that toy that you really don't want in the house! If you have a ready list of books, sharing it with others makes life easier.

How can I find good children's literature?

Check the Sunday papers around the winter holiday times. There are often articles or supplements that provide listings and reviews of what's new and recommended in children's literature. Cut these out and save them for future reference.

When you're in a library, wander around in the periodical section looking for articles on children's books in magazines for parents. Most libraries have bookmarks, pamphlets, or information from the American Library Association on their annual award-winning books (ask for the Caldecott, Newbery, and Coretta Scott King awards). Periodicals as different as *Mothering* and *The Scientific American* have book review sections that occasionally feature children's fiction and nonfiction books.

Subscribe to, or borrow from the library, children's story and special-interest magazines. Authors and illustrators usually do short pieces or excerpts from books for these periodicals. The magazines also make great bedtime and leisure reading for younger children, and you will find many authors whose style or subject matter appeals to your child. You can then go to the library together to search out this author's books.

How can I add to the educational resources in my home?

Start by being selfish. Think about what you would like to learn, and go for it. Even though we are constantly reminded by our children that they mimic us ("Where did you hear that, Sally?" "Dad said it when he dropped the microwave."), we forget that our children are modeling themselves on our good habits as well. Your enthusiasm for learning will be contagious.

First, recycle your own trash for craft and Learning Adventure activities—everything from egg cartons and milk jugs to shoe boxes and junk mail can be used for school and home educational projects.

Second, be a trash picker. You don't have to push a shopping cart down the street, but be alert to the value of other people's castoffs. We know a parent who scans the neighborhood on trash day. When a neighbor of his who coached a hockey team threw out an old goal net, our trash picker turned part of it into a climbing net hung from a tree branch, and part of it became a fantasy spider web for a child's school project on creepy crawlies. Somebody installing lots of carpet? Those long cardboard tubes can turn into alpenhorns, flag poles, and tunnels for rolling balls (and don't forget your hamster's love of tubes!). Some towns have a transfer station (today's incarnation of the town dump) where castoffs are set aside to look for new owners.

Be an advanced trash picker. A manufacturer of file folders and envelopes produces enormous amounts of cut ends and defects. These go straight to the shredder unless an alert parent or teacher gets there first, and the company is more than happy to get the good will that comes from giving away a treasure in paper. Offices are treasure troves of discarded memo and computer paper, envelopes, folders, and catalogs. The same is true for any small manufacturing concern that produces useful (to someone) waste material. Small electronic parts, metal stampings, bits of brightly colored plastic, and pieces of wood are all much better off as parts of collages, dioramas, and science or construction projects than they are as landfill.

How can I keep my child's education going during summer vacation?

Of course, you'll obviously find lots of great ideas in the Learning Adventure activities in this book! Once school is out, you can involve the whole family in some of them. Take time also to play board games such as Scrabble™ or Monopoly™ as a family. Monopoly, for example, is a subtle way of being sure your kid practices math skills as the banker or the rent-collecting proprietor of Atlantic Avenue and the Water Works. Scrabble challenges everyone's word knowledge.

When summer's here, you'll want to look at the outdoor resources in your community. Some city park systems or schools have summer programs that focus on nature study and the outdoors, augmenting your kid's science knowledge. Nature experiences are usually a part of camp life too. Summer projects can offer practice in both math and science. Carpentry projects, for instance, require careful measuring. Building a rabbit cage, remodeling projects, or redecorating involve measuring, figuring square footage, estimating costs, and other math challenges. To keep up your kid's interest in language arts, turn to your local library. It may have a summer reading program or, for younger children, story and reading hours. Look for free or low-cost summer theaters, which often present Shakespeare and other theater classics. Even without special programs, your kid can learn to revel in the summer joys of reading at the beach or in a hammock.

Without money for expensive camps or trips, how can family vacations provide an outdoor learning experience?

Imagination and good planning can be more valuable than lots of money in making a nature-oriented vacation trip something your family will all remember and learn from. If you want to be outdoors, look into nearby state or national parks with campgrounds, and check into park ranger or park board programs that emphasize science and nature. Depending on your locality, these range from short walking tours along a local river to extensive hands-on programs for both kids and adults. On your own, you don't have to wait for a long vacation—spend a Sunday morning or afternoon picnicking in a local forest preserve. Take short trips to nearby zoos or natural wonders such as caves, waterfalls, fossil beds, and rock formations.

For full-fledged vacations, investigate working farms and ranches that welcome guests in exchange for help or small fees. Or investigate the moderately priced family-oriented vacations run by groups such as the National Wildlife Federation.

Our family has a rare chance to spend two weeks in Europe. Should my child miss that much school or stay home?

Travel can be a marvelous educational experience for the whole family. If your child is a good or average student, the benefits of a valuable overseas experience probably outweigh the possible difficulties. Be sure to discuss the trip with your kid's teachers and the administration in advance, though. Trying to keep up a regular schedule of homework assignments while traveling is probably not realistic, but you or he might ask for special assignments geared to the trip—perhaps keeping a journal and a special written or oral report when he returns. There should be an understanding about makeup work and missed tests, too.

But what if your kid is having trouble in school? That makes the decision harder, especially if there are friends or relatives with whom he could conveniently stay and not miss school. Discuss the question with his teachers and—depending on his age—with him. Then balance all the factors in making your decision.

When special opportunities arise, you, your child, and the school need to work together to make tough decisions. On other occasions, though, it's usually wisest to try to arrange trips and vacations so your child misses as little school as possible—no matter how good a student he is.

CHAPTER 19

What Resources Should I Use?

Here's our nonexhaustive list of resources in print, on disc, and online. They cover various areas, including math, science, language arts, and parenting issues. A good starting place!

PARENTING

Books and Newsletters

All Kinds of Minds, by Mel Levine (Cambridge and Toronto: Educators Publishing Service, 1993). A sympathetic, light-hearted, and extremely intelligent presentation of learning abilities, learning disorders, and other learning issues.

Beyond the Classroom: Why School Reform Has Failed and What Parents Need to Do, by Laurence Steinberg (New York: Simon & Schuster, 1996). Discusses authoritative parenting and the home environment, the power of peers, ethnicity, and more.

Child Safety on the Internet, by the Staff of Classroom Connect with Vince Distefano (Lancaster, PA: Classroom Connect, Prentice Hall, 1997). A guide to protecting children from accessing inappropriate material on the Internet; includes "Kid Safe" Internet sites.

Dr. Gruber's Essential Guide to Test Taking for Kids, by Gary R. Gruber (New York: William Morrow and Co., 1986). Teaches kids early in the game the critical-thinking skills and test-taking strategies that will help them when it comes time to take elementary tests.

Education on the Internet: A Hands-On Book of Ideas, Resources, Projects, and Advice, by Jill H. Ellsworth (New York: Macmillan Publishing USA, 1996). A great way for parents to tune in to good material on the Net.

Helping Your Child Succeed in School: A Guide for Parents of 4 to 14 Year Olds, by Michael H. Popkin, et al. (Atlanta: Active Parenting Publishers, 1995). Fun, supportive, and creative ways to help your children learn, including working with the school system.

Parents' Choice
P.O. Box 185
Newton, MA 02168
(617) 965-5913
Quarterly newsletter that reviews books, toys, audiotapes, videotapes, catalogs and more.

Playing Smart: A Parent's Guide to Enriching, Offbeat Learning Activities for Ages 4–14, by Susan K. Perry (Minneapolis: Free Spirit Publishing, 1990). Hundreds of ideas for educating and entertaining kids while cultivating their creativity.

Positive Coaching: Building Character and Self-Esteem through Sports, by Jim Thompson (Portola Valley, CA: Warde Publishers). Designed to be a helpful philosophical aid for any adult who works with kids. Features 50 motivational stories that can be used to develop strong communication skills.

Quantum Learning, by Bobbi DePorter with Mike Hernacki (New York: Dell Publishing, 1992). Written for students, teachers, and parents, *Quantum Learning* helps students of all ages develop a personal learning style and a positive attitude toward learning new skills.

Super Fun for One: 366 Solo Activities for Kids, by Patricia Gordon and Reed C. Snow (Kansas City, Missouri: Andrews and McMeel, 1996). Activities that require minimal materials and preparation time, organized in segments of 5, 15, 30, or 60 minutes.

The Parents' Answer Book, by Gerald Deskin and Greg Steckler (Minneapolis: Fairview Press, 1995). User-friendly, comprehensive resource for child and adolescent development questions.

The Problem Solver: Activities for Learning Problem-Solving Strategies, by Shirley Hoogeboom and Judy Goodnow (Mountainview, CA: Creative Publications, 1987).

Why It's Great to Be a Girl: 50 Eye-Opening Things You Can Tell Your Daughter to Increase her Pride in Being Female, by Jacqueline Shannon (New York: Warner Books, 1994). The title says it all.

Catalogs

Active Parenting Publishers
810 Franklin Court, Suite B
Marietta, GA 30067
(800) 825-0060
Books, videos, games, and programs for workshops to help parents build academic success and overall parenting skills.

Fairview Press
2450 Riverside Avenue South
Minneapolis, MN 55454
(800) 544-8207
http://www.press.fairview.org
Fairview Press publishes books on family activities and a variety of family- and community-related issues.

Free Spirit Publishing
400 First Avenue North, Suite 616
Minneapolis, MN 55401-1724
(800) 735-7323
Books, posters, and a host of products to build children's and teen's self-esteem, assist with homework, and help confront difficult topics.

National PTA Catalog
135 S. LaSalle St., Dept. 1860
Chicago, IL 60674-1860
http://www.pta.org
Resources for educators and parents on family involvement, child safety, and local PTA activities.

Internet Sites

Association of Science-Technology Centers
http://www.astc.org/astc/
ASTC is a nonprofit organization of science centers and related institutions, including zoos, nature centers, aquaria, planetariums and space theaters, and natural history and children's museums. ASTC's membership includes nearly 400 science museums in 40 countries.

Children's Literature Web Guide
http://www.ucalgary.ca/~dkbrown/index.html
Lists of juvenile bestsellers and great links.

Classroom Connect on the 'Net
http://www.classroom.net
Classroom Connect's Web site helps educators and students to locate and use the best K–12 educational resources the Internet has to offer. Includes its own search engine and a resource section.

Computer Curriculum Corporation
http://www.cccnet.com
A leading publisher of comprehensive curriculum-based educational software.

EdWeb Home Page
http://edweb.gsn.org
Find online educational resources around the world, learn about trends in education policy and information infrastructure development, and examine success stories of computers in the classroom.

ERIC—Educational Resources Information Center
http://www.accesseric.org/
A vast clearinghouse of educational issues and links, plus a search engine.

Family Planet
http://family.go.com
An online magazine about education, legislation, health, and child-rearing issues, with advice and reviews of kids' products.

Global SchoolNet Foundation
http://www.gsn.org
Resources and links pertinent to integrating the Internet into K–12 classrooms.

International Registry of K–12 Schools on the Web
http://web66.coled.umn.edu/schools.html
Links to school Web pages throughout the world.

National Center for Fathering
http://www.fathers.com
Resources for dads, including articles from *Today's Father* magazine, parenting tips, and humor.

The National Institute on Media and the Family
http://www.mediaandthefamily.org
Children's Impact Statements for the family on TV shows, movies, and video games.

National PTA
http://www.pta.org
The site for family involvement in education, for parents and educators.

Newsweek's Parent's Guide
http://www.newsweekparentsguide.com
Comprehensive guide to children's software. *Newsweek* writers rate software and send the best to committees of parents, kids, and teachers for additional review. All titles receive report cards, and the most notable get in-depth parent's guide reviews.

Parent Soup
http://www.parentsoup.com
Online support and information on parenting, plus homework help.

Parenting Q&A
http://www.parenting-qa.com
A searchable database of parenting issues, with answers from experts in child development and behavior.

ParentsPlace.com
http://www.parentsplace.com/
A grab bag of information on parenting.

ParentTime
http://www.pathfinder.com/ParentTime/homepage/homepage.all.html
Chat and info on parenting, personalized for your child's age and interests.

Educational/Creativity

Tools and Supplies

Carson-Dellosa Publishing Company, Inc.
P.O. Box 35665
Greensboro, NC 27425-5665
(910) 632-0084
Includes rubber stamps, easels, manipulatives, etc.

Learning Forum
1725 South Coast Hwy.
Oceanside, CA 92054-5319
(800) 28-LEARN
Books, videos, audios, music, summer camps, and tools for ensuring student success and learning fun.

LANGUAGE ARTS

Books and Magazines

Exploring Cultures Through Literature (Greensboro, NC: Carson-Dellosa). Thirty-seven literary works are used as the basis for studying cultural diversity. Includes a wide range of peoples and traditions.

New Moon: The Magazine for Girls and Their Dreams
P.O. Box 3587, Duluth, MN 55803
(800) 381-4743
Written by and for girls, this magazine contains creative writing and artwork from girls worldwide.

Totally Private and Personal: Journaling Ideas for Girls and Young Women, by Jessica Wilber (Minneapolis: Free Spirit Publishing, 1996). A 14-year-old writer gives an inside look at how keeping a journal can help young writers explore feelings and sort out issues pertinent to preteens and teens.

The Young Person's Guide to Becoming a Writer, by Janet E. Grant (Minneapolis: Free Spirit Publishing, 1996). Tips for young writers on developing a personal writing style and getting work published.

Making the Grade

Catalogs

Educational Software Catalog
Sanctuary Woods
2228 S. El Camino Real #223
San Mateo, CA 94403
(800) 943-3664
http://www.sanctuary.com
A catalog of educational and entertaining language arts, social studies, math, science, and ESL software for kids of all ages.

Great Source Education Group
A Houghton Mifflin Company
181 Ballardvale Street
Wilmington, MA 01887
(800) 289-4490
http://www.greatsource.com
Intended for in-school use but handy for home-based learning as well, this catalog includes language arts and mathematics for students grades K–12.

Ideal School Supply Company
(800) 323-5131
Basic Facts Bingo and other games and resources for reading, spelling, language arts, and science.

Simon & Schuster Children's Publishing Division
(800) 223-2336
http://www.simonandschuster.com

Software

Great Word Adventure
7th Level
(800) 884-8863
Mac and Windows CD-ROM
Games that teach word recognition, categorization, alphabetization, rhymes, and more.

Kid Phonics 2
Davidson & Associates
(800) 545-7677
Mac, Windows, and Windows 95 CD-ROM
Designed to help kids ages six through nine sound out more than 350 words and understand the uses of prefixes and suffixes.

Read, Write & Type
The Learning Company
(800) 852-2255

Mac and Windows CD-ROM
Animated adventures and sound games teach reading, phonics, and keyboarding skills.

Schoolhouse Rock: Grammar Rock
Creative Wonders
(800) 543-9778
Mac, Windows, and Windows 95 CD-ROM
Cartoons and games teach grammar basics.

Word Munchers Deluxe
MECC/Softkey
(800) 227-5609
Mac, Windows 3.1, and Windows 95 CD-ROM
Over 6,000 words in five difficulty levels (grades 1–5) in a game with 3-D graphics.

Internet Sites

Children's Literature Web Guide
http://www.ucalgary.ca/~dkbrown/index.html
This site, designed for parents and teachers, archives children's literature on the Web.

CyberKids
http://www.mtlake.com/cyberkids/
A quarterly online 'zine by and for kids ages 7-16.

Just for Kids who Love Books
http://www.geocities.com/~abrown/
Kids can find out about their favorite authors, titles, and series.

Kid's Crambo
http://www.primenet.com/~hodges/kids_crambo.html
Kids can make up their own rhymes and wacky word definitions at this fun site.

KidPub
http://www.kidpub.org/kidpub
Stories written by kids and by language arts classes around the world.

KidZone
http://www.mckinley.com
Magellan's site has lots and lots of book-related links to explore.

Math

Books

Coupon Math (Greensboro, NC: Carson-Dellosa). Using manufacturer "cents off" coupons, students engage in sorting, matching, logic, problem solving, probability, and more.

Eyewitness Books: Money, by Joe Crib (New York, NY: Knopf, 1990). Great info about the history of money.

Math Wizardry for Kids, by Margaret Kenda and Phyllis S. Williams (Happauge, NY: Barron's Educational Series, Inc., 1995). Puzzles, games, and projects for kids ages 8–12.

Mega-Math (Greensboro, NC: Carson-Dellosa). Reproducible pages on basic operations, fractions, measurements, decimals, geometry, and more.

Problem Solving and Measurement (Greensboro, NC: Carson-Dellosa). Examines length, capacity, mass, temperature, and time through use and creation of tables, graphs, and patterns.

Manipulatives

Holey Cards
3817 No. Pulaski
Chicago, Il 60641
(312) 588-5761
Kids have two minutes to get math fact questions right. Use the cards over and over again until the two-minute goal is reached. Multiplication, subtraction, and addition cards available.

Catalogs

Creative Publications
5623 W. 115th Street
Worth, IL 60482-9931
(800) 357-MATH
Books, manipulatives, and teacher resources to help teach everything from counting to algebra.

Dacta
The Educational Division of the LEGO Group
555 Taylor Road
Enfield, CT 06083-1600

(800) 527-8339
http://www.lego.com/learn
Science, technology, and math kits for constructing simple machines, gears, levers, etcetera, out of LEGOs.

Educational Software Catalog
Sanctuary Woods
2228 S. El Camino Real #223
San Mateo, CA 94403
(800) 943-3664
http://www.sanctuary.com
A catalog of educational and entertaining language arts, social studies, math science, and ESL software for kids.

MPH Catalog
P.O. Box 1125
Fairfield, CT 06432
Deck of 52 cards, all marked differently from 1 to 25. Fun card games for learning addition, subtraction, division, and multiplication.

Simon & Schuster Children's Publishing Division
(800) 223-2336
http://www.simonandschuster.com
A complete line of educational books for children.

Software

The Fennels Figure Math
McGraw-Hill Home Interactive
(800) 937-4663
Windows CD-ROM
The Fennels are hosting a house full of guests (from throughout history) and need help feeding them. Learn how to convert weights, use a thermometer, read a map, and more.

Infinity City
Headbone Interactive
(800) 267-4709
Mac and Windows CD-ROM
Bunji the frog takes kids through a construction site and demonstrates how math functions in everyday use.

Interactive Math Journey
The Learning Company
(800) 852-2255
Mac and Windows CD-ROM
Early math skills are taught through a journey through ten math lands.

Math Ace
Sanctuary Woods
(800) 943-3664
Mac and Windows diskette and CD-ROM
For kids grades 3–12, this popular program teaches math in a visual context and lets students practice at their own level.

Math Workshop
Broderbund
(800) 521-6263
Mac and Windows CD-ROM
Seven games teach spatial concepts, equivalencies, fractions, shapes, and math basics.

Mighty Math Calculating Crew
Edmark
P.O. Box 97201
Redmond, WA 98073
(206) 556-7552
Mac and Windows CD-ROM
Cartoon superheroes need help dealing with their finances. Use simple addition through geometry to help save the universe.

Pajama Sam in No Need to Hide When It's Dark Outside
Humongous Entertainment
16932 Woodinville-Redmond NE
Woodinville, WA 98072
(206) 486-9258
Mac and Windows
An interactive adventure in which Pajama Sam, afraid of the dark, goes forth to capture darkness. Children must help Sam solve problems along the way.

Snootz Math Trek
Theatrix
(800) 955-8749
Mac and Windows CD-ROM
Solve math and logic problems while having an intergalactic adventure.

Internet Sites

Dr. Math
http://forum.swarthmore.edu/dr.math/dr-math.html
Swarthmore College math students act as "math doctors" and answer students' math questions from all over the world. E-mailed questions and answers are gathered into an archive, organized by grade level and topic. Includes search function.

The Math Forum
http://forum.swarthmore.edu
This site covers simple and advanced mathematics, offering help to both students and teachers.

Mathematics Resource Page
http://www.deakin.edu.au
Math links for teachers and students.

MathMagic
http://forum.swarthmore.edu/mathmagic
MathMagic provides strong motivation for students to use computer technology while increasing problem-solving and communications skills. MathMagic posts challenges in each of four grade categories to trigger each registered team to pair up with another team and engage in a problem-solving dialogue.

Mega Mathematics
http://www.c3.lanl.gov/mega-math/welcome.html
Advanced mathematical concepts are explained here for elementary school children.

SAMI: Science and Math Initiatives
http://www.learner.org/k12/sami
A clearinghouse of information for science and math teachers, but appropriate for home learning as well.

SCIENCE

Books and Magazines

Amazing Poisonous Animals, by Alexandra Parsons (Knopf, 1990). Looks at the world of poisonous animals, including close-up photos.

Amazing Frogs and Toads, by Barry Clarke (Knopf, 1990). Examines frogs and toads of all kinds; with full-color photographs.

Animalearn, The Magazine for Kids Who Love Animals
801 Old York Rd. #204
Jenkintown, PA 19046-1685
(215) 887-0816
Stories, interviews, fun facts, games, and puzzles for kids and parents who "care about the earth and the critters who live here."

Build with Beakman: Bacteria Farm (Andrews and McMeel, 1996). Fun with fungi is the focus of this book and kit (including petri dishes and other supplies). Beakman, of television's *Beakman's World*, is the host.

Experimenting with Inventions, by Robert Gardner (New York: Franklin Watts, 1990).

Girls and Young Women Inventing: 20 True Stories About Inventors Plus How You Can Be One Yourself, by Frances A. Karnes and Suzanne M. Bean (Minneapolis: Free Spirit Publishing, 1995). Inspiration for girls who love science and inventing.

Hill of Fire, by Thomas P. Lewis (Harpercrest, 1987). Tells the story of the eruption of Paricutín, a Mexican volcano, and how it affected the people living nearby.

Linking Science with Literature (Greensboro, NC: Carson-Dellosa). Weaves various science activities around 51 selections from children's literature.

Night Sky, by Carole Stott (London: Dorling Kindersley, 1993). This *Eyewitness Explorer* book is a pocket-sized field guide packed with projects and information on how to identify the constellations.

Science by the Season (Greensboro, NC: Carson-Dellosa). Seasonal experiments and outdoor activities, including sprouting seeds and constructing a sundial, teach about the natural world.

Science Wizardry for Kids, by Margaret Kenda and Phyllis S. Williams (Happauge, NY: Barron's Educational Series, Inc., 1995). Magic tricks, projects, and experiments for kids age 8–12 make science fun.

Seeing Stars: A Book and Poster About the Constellations, by Barabara Seiger (Price Stern Sloan, 1993). Facts and stories about the 35 most familiar constellations. Also includes full-color poster of the constellations, plus 400 glow-in-the-dark stickers to add to it.

The Ultimate Book of Cross Sections (Dorling Kindersley, 1996). Examines the inner workings of vehicles and other machines.

Zero to Einstein in 60, by B. K. Hixson (Salt Lake City: The Wild Goose Company, 1989). Billed as "60 experiments guaranteed to cure science nincompoopitis," this fun book contains experiments for teachers and parents of children 8 and up.

Catalogs

Carolina Biological Supply Company
2700 York Road
Burlington, NC 27215-3398
(800) 334-5551
http://www.carosci.com/index.html
Great general science resource, as well as selling manipulatives in quantities as small as twelve.

Dacta
The Educational Division of the LEGO Group
555 Taylor Road
Enfield, CT 06083-1600
(800) 527-8339
http://www.lego.com/learn
Science, technology, and math kits for constructing simple machines, gears, levers, etcetera, out of LEGOs.

MindWare
2720 Patton Road
Roseville, MN 55113
(800) 999-0398
A catalog that contains puzzles, games, and books intended to "tap the other 90 percent of your brain," MindWare products help kids and parents develop math, science, and reasoning skills.

Simon & Schuster Children's Publishing Division
(800) 223-2336
http://www.simonandschuster.com
A complete line of educational books for children.

The Wild Goose Co.
375 Whitney Avenue
Salt Lake City, UT 84115
(800) 373-1498
Kits, books, and science equipment and accessories for teachers and students for wacky and fun science experiments. Includes the Newton's Apple Science Kit series. and fun kits like *Slime Chemistry.*

Software

Microsoft Dinosaurs
Microsoft
(800) 426-9400
Mac and Windows CD-ROM
Guided tours, plus an atlas, timeline, and index of dinosaurs.

Making the Grade

Microsoft Explorapedia: World of Nature
Microsoft
(800) 426-9400
Windows CD-ROM
Thaddeus "Tad" Pole and his frogship guide kids through the natural world, with games and projects to do both on and off the computer.

The Multimedia Bug Book
Swfte International/Expert Software
(800) 759-2562
Mac and Windows CD-ROM
An interactive field guide to crawlies.

Scholastic's The Magic School Bus Series
Microsoft
(800) 426-9400
Mac and Windows CD-ROM
Take the Magic Bus and learn about space, the ocean, and the human body.

Internet Sites

Ask An Expert
http://njnie.dl.stevens-tech.edu/curriculum/aska.html
Send your science, technology, or math questions to these experts!

Dinosaurs dinosaurs dinosaurs!
http://www.DinoDon.com
Offers a dinosaur dictionary, dino art, and a different guest paleontologist every month who answers kids' questions.

Liberty Science Center
http://www.lsc.org/
Homepage of this cool science museum.
MayaQuest 98
http://www.mecc.com/Maya/More/html
Learn more about the ancient Maya civilization with a group of explorers in Central America.

NASA Homepage
http://www.nasa.gov/
Exciting photos and lots of great space links.

National Institute for Science Education's Why Files
http://www. whyfiles.news.wisc.edu
Explains the "science behind the news" for children, teachers, and parents.

Nye Labs Online
http://nyelabs.kcts.org/
Public Television's Science Guy, here is Bill Nye's homepage, complete with online experiments and a "Demo of the Day."

Yahooligans!
http://www.yahooligans.com
Yahoo's kids' directory.

The Yuckiest Site on the Internet
http://www.nj.com/yucky/index.html
Yuck! All about cockroaches, courtesy of New Jersey's Liberty Science Center.

About

KAPLAN

Educational Centers

Kaplan Educational Centers is one of the nation's leading providers of premier education and career services. Kaplan is a wholly owned subsidiary of The Washington Post Company.

TEST PREPARATION & ADMISSIONS

Kaplan's nationally recognized test prep courses cover more than 20 standardized tests, including secondary school, college and graduate school entrance exams and foreign language and professional licensing exams. In addition, Kaplan offers private tutoring and comprehensive, one-to-one admissions and application advice for students applying to graduate programs. Kaplan also provides information and guidance on the financial aid process.

SCORE! EDUCATIONAL CENTERS

SCORE! after-school learning centers help K-8 students build confidence, academic and goal-setting skills in a motivating, sports-oriented environment. Its cutting-edge, interactive curriculum continually assesses and adapts to each child's academic needs and learning style. Enthusiastic Academic Coaches serve as positive role models, creating a high-energy atmosphere where learning is exciting and fun. SCORE! Prep provides in-home, one-on-one tutoring for high school academic subjects and standardized tests.

KAPLAN LEARNING SERVICES

Kaplan Learning Services provides customized assessment, education and professional development programs to K-12 schools and universities.

KAPLAN INTERNATIONAL PROGRAMS

Kaplan services international students and professionals in the U.S. through a series of intensive English language and test preparation programs. These programs are offered at Kaplan City Centers and four new campus-based centers in California, Washington and New York via Kaplan/LCP International Institute. Kaplan and Kaplan/LCP offer specialized services to sponsors including placement at top American universities, fellowship management, academic monitoring and reporting, and financial administration.

KAPLAN PUBLISHING

Kaplan Publishing produces books, software and online services. Kaplan Books, a joint imprint with Simon & Schuster, publishes titles in test preparation, admissions, education, career development and life skills; Kaplan and Newsweek jointly publish guides on getting into college, finding the right career, and helping your child succeed in school. Through an alliance with Knowledge Adventure, Kaplan publishes educational software for the K-12 retail and school markets.

KAPLAN PROFESSIONAL

Kaplan Professional provides recruitment and training services for corporate clients and individuals seeking to advance their careers. Member units include Kaplan Professional Career Services, the largest career fair provider in North America; Perfect Access/CRN, which delivers software education and consultation for law firms and businesses; HireSystems, which provides web-based hiring solutions; and Kaplan Professional Call Center Services, a total provider of services for the call center industry.

DISTANCE LEARNING DIVISION

Kaplan's distance learning programs include Concord School of Law, the nation's first online law school; and National Institute of Paralegal Arts and Sciences, a leading provider of degrees and certificates in paralegal studies and legal nurse consulting.

COMMUNITY OUTREACH

Kaplan provides educational resources to thousands of financially disadvantaged students annually, working closely with educational institutions, not-for-profit groups, government agencies and other grass roots organizations on a variety of national and local support programs. Kaplan enriches local communities by employing high school, college and graduate students, creating valuable work experiences for vast numbers of young people each year.

Want more information about our services, products or the nearest Kaplan center?

 Call our nationwide toll-free numbers:

1-800-KAP-TEST for information on our courses, private tutoring and admissions consulting

1-800-KAP-ITEM for information on our books and software

1-888-KAP-LOAN* for information on student loans

 Connect with us in cyberspace:

On AOL, keyword: kaplan
On the World Wide Web, go to: www.kaplan.com
Via e-mail: info@kaplan.com

 Write to:

Kaplan Educational Centers
888 Seventh Avenue
New York, NY 10106

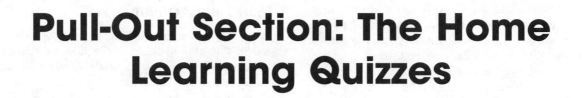

Pull-Out Section: The Home Learning Quizzes

Your child learns in a unique way. In fact, all children vary greatly in learning style, level of maturity, individual personality, and how they learn on any given day. This is why single standardized tests administered across a grade level are not always accurate indicators of what academic skills your child has mastered. What these tests *can* indicate are possible problem areas or concepts that your child may need further practice to understand *and* material your child has not yet been introduced to in school.

Your Child's Quizzes

As a bonus, we've added our pull-out *Making the Grade* Kids' Home Learning Quizzes (the last eight pages of this section) to help you and your child locate possible problem areas or gaps in learning in language arts, math, and science. The questions cover material that your child *might* have encountered in 3rd and 4th grade. Each quiz starts with 3rd grade work and progresses to 4th grade items (an equal number from each grade level).

After your child quizzes herself, use the grade- and subject-specific Learning Adventure activities in *Making the Grade* to help her practice and hone skills in particular subjects. The quizzes are not meant to serve as definitive tests of your child's intelligence or an indication of subject mastery; they serve only as a supplement to the Learning Adventure activities to help you and your child spend more time on specific activities that correspond to problem areas or brand new material. Keep the home learning focus on having fun and "serving the learning in welcome helpings"; never pressure your child to "score high" or "learn on command."

Your Quiz

The first eight pages of this section are for parents only. They contain your *Making the Grade* Parents' Home Learning Quiz, explanations for the quiz, and the answer key for the kids' quizzes. Taking the parents' quiz will help you identify possible gaps in your own knowledge and awareness of your child's growth and educational development. Like the subject-specific quizzes for your child, the parents' assessment is not an all-encompassing evaluation of your parenting or home education skills; just take the assessment to acquaint yourself with the latest educational and development issues. As with the kids' quizzes, there is no emphasis on how you score. Approach it as another level on which to discover something new or reinforce previous learnings.

Using the Quizzes

Your Parents' Home Learning Quiz is self-explanatory. Take it on your own, at your convenience. It's a little more complicated with the Kids' Home Learning Quizzes, but you can be sure that there is no *right* way for your child to take them. Take all the quizzes in a row, or take one quiz one day and save the others for different occasions. Your child can quiz himself—like taking a fun activity break with *BrainQuest*™—or you and your child can take the quizzes together for an exercise in finding out how much you *both* know about 3rd and 4th grade subjects. Photocopy his pull-out quiz pages and time each section. Compare notes and answers when you finish.

Making the Grade

Have your child use a pencil to fill in the answer bubbles and make scratch-note calculations; provide an eraser to change answers. Also discuss the purpose of the last two answer bubbles. One oval (e) will indicate to both of you that a question covers skills your child hasn't learned in school yet; your child can mark this oval without selecting an answer (there's no point taking time to guess). The last bubble (f) signals that a certain question covers previously learned material that is still difficult for your child; this can be marked along with one of the answer choices to the question.

Here are some specific ideas for sitting down with your child after taking the quizzes:

- Praise your child's correct answers on the quizzes, and have him show you how he made his calculations or worked through the steps that led to the correct answer.

- If your child chose an incorrect answer *and* didn't indicate that the material was difficult, go through the answer with him and try to clear up any confusion with the skills covered. An appropriate Learning Adventure activity can clarify skills and reinforce learning.

- If your child scored correctly *and* indicated difficulty with the material, celebrate the correct answer and bolster your child's confidence! Perhaps your child is ready to tackle new material in a particular subject matter; use a Learning Adventure activity to introduce the new skills in an informal, enjoyable way.

- If your child indicates that a question covers new material not yet taught in school, you have the future option of introducing the new skills through a Learning Adventure activity—if and when your child is ready and open to the new material.

- You might want to review the quizzes with your child's teacher to verify the responses, learn when new skills will be covered, and work together to develop a plan of action to bolster weaknesses and fill in learning gaps.

USING THE ACTIVITIES

Work with your child on the Learning Adventure activities in this book. Pace the flow of activities from day to day, week to week. Never push the learning, but develop a natural pacing that meets your schedule and reinforces your belief in fostering learning at home. As you do an activity with your child, observe her progress. On-the-spot observations of a specific activity might even tell you more about what's really going on than the quizzes. And you will be giving your child the attention, support, and encouragement that enhances any learning activity.

Build a picture of your child's learning style. Everyone learns in a unique way. Determine your child's learning style(s) by noting what goes on as she works on an activity. Does she learn more easily by *reading* the material or by *listening* to you as you direct the activity? Does she become more enthusiastic when drawing and performing other *hands-on* activities? Noting these subtleties can help you better suit the activities to your child's strength, as well as work on the weaker learning styles.

Assess what your child knows. Evaluation does not depend on tests alone. Observe your child working on an activity and assess how well he understands and handles information. Are there basic concepts that he needs to work on? In a math activity, does your child grasp the main idea but have trouble with the process, the basic math calculations? Does he write creatively but have trouble with quotation marks and punctuation? It's not necessary to grade the work or point out the deficiencies; just use these notes to select the activities, resources, and ways of supporting your child that will build competence and confidence.

LEARNING TIPS FOR HOME

The *Making the Grade* Parents' Home Learning Quiz concludes with evaluations and suggestions to help you become even more knowledgeable and aware of your child's education and development. In addition, be aware of just three simple guidelines—Be Alert, Be Patient, and Be Positive—to establish a successful learning environment in your home.

Be Alert. There was once a master of the martial art t'ai chi who was so adept, a sparrow landing on his upraised arm was unable to fly off. The art of this master was neither speed nor strength, it was awareness. He was so alert that as soon as the sparrow crouched to take flight, he sense it and lowered his arm just enough to interrupt the sparrow's upward spring. The goal of education is, of course, just the opposite. We want to encourage the upward spring of our young sparrows.

The technique, however, is the same. Being alert at the end of a long day is easier than you think. Being alert is really only enhanced relaxation. Just remind yourself, once in a while, to relax and be open to your child.

Watch for subtle cues. Children communicate with their bodies. Closely watch your child at work. Is she slouched over or poised and energetic, calm or fidgety, morose or happy? Is she easily distracted or attentive? Facial expressions and tone of voice are also key clues.

Allow for emotional needs. Some children tell their parents what is going well and what isn't, but many won't. Sometimes your child's issues surface at home in ways that have nothing to do with your home life. Tensions surrounding your child's friends and school often surface indirectly at home. Emotions will probably spring to the surface during some of the activities.

Tears may erupt over a broken pencil tip, or a sulk develop over a misunderstood word in a reading assignment. These reactions may often be much stronger than the situation warrants. Don't let these moments defeat either of you. Children generally feel safer about showing their feelings to their parents than they do to their teachers. They feel safer at home, and it's good that they do, but it sometimes makes your job a little harder. The trick, and it works most of the time, is to accept the feelings, acknowledge the hurt, and weather the emotional release. And *weather* is the key word. The storm passes, the sun comes out, and then, in most cases, you'll be able to move on. For the times when this doesn't work, heed the advice of the Kenny Rogers song, "know when to hold 'em and know when to fold 'em." There will always be another time to try a Learning Adventure activity.

Note lack of interest. Your child may show signs of boredom, whether physical or verbal. These are important to watch for, but they can be ambiguous. Boredom can mean a task is too hard; it can be your child's way of reacting to an activity that asks too much. But boredom can also mean that an activity is too easy. Figure out what your child is really communicating; don't react to the sometimes irritating signs of boredom itself.

Note signs of interest. One child's enthusiasm may be communicated with an exuberant, "Look at these earthworms!" Another may react with increased concentration and silence as she focuses on a task that excites her. Indications of interest are just as important as signs of boredom in helping you determine where to go next, whether or not to repeat an activity or move on to harder skills, etc.

Be Patient. We all feel the pressure to achieve. It's there and it's real, but it doesn't belong in home learning situations. Communicating this pressure to children while they're engaged in academic work usually doesn't do much for the learning process. This doesn't mean that hard work and the desire to successfully learn something aren't important. They certainly are. However, external tensions, particularly those brought in from the adult world, can interfere with learning. The more you can relax and be your child's guide and supporter, the more successful you both will be.

Adjust to your child. Take your time doing the activities and pace yourself to allow your child to take his time. Each of us has his own style and pace for learning. Adjust the rate to which you start new activities to your child's natural pace. Remember that there are day-to-day events such as head colds, late evenings the night before, or the anticipation of birthday parties that affect your child's concentration and energy. Longer-range maturational changes also alter behavior and ability. Read (or browse through again) the essay on development in Section I.

Focus on individual learning tasks. Enjoy each moment of learning with your child and don't worry about what is next or where it's all headed. The Learning Adventure activities are meant to function as building blocks. Each activity should give your child a taste of success—which you can both celebrate!

Making the Grade

Be patient with yourself. No teacher or parent gets it right every time. Learn from any mistake, and don't let it derail you. You care enough to spend time on your child's education, so give yourself a pat on the back—and then figure out what to do differently next time.

Be Positive. Each step in learning is important and deserves praise. The old "ruler on the knuckles" technique produced children who couldn't wait to get out of school. Help your child get the most out of staying in school and develop a lifetime love of learning.

Positive doesn't always equal fun. Some things are just plain old hard work. For some children, mastering the frustratingly inconsistent spelling of English is a chore. Others find it difficult to calculate sets of math facts such as the times tables. Effortless spelling and ease of computation will come, but the process is sometimes hard going. You can acknowledge this truth and yet regard the work in a positive light. The rewards are real. As different skills are mastered successfully, hard work and practice will pay off.

Use praise that works for both of you. Although children need positive reinforcement, they are able to see through transparent praise. Kids are the best spotters of what is phony. Specific praise for achievements, on the other hand, always works. Statements like, "You did that math problem very well" and "That graph explains things so that I can understand" are more useful than a general pat on the head because they tell your child that you have paid attention to what she has done. If things aren't going well, that problem also needs to be acknowledged and, just like the praise, put in concrete terms. Focus on the positive (even in the problem) and draw upon that to tackle what might not be going well.

SIMON SAYS

These recommended books for 3rd and 4th graders will help your child "make the grade":

MATH
Twelve Snails to One Lizard: A Tale of Mischief and Measurement by Susan Hightower
Math in the Bath (And Other Fun Places Too) by Sara Atherlay
Pigs in The Pantry: Fun With Math and Cooking by Amy Axelrod

SCIENCE
Outside and Inside You by Sandra Markle
Yuck! A Big Book of Little Horrors by Robert Snedden
Macmillan Children's Guide To Endangered Animals by Roger Few
Backyard Safaris: 52 Year-Round Science Adventures by Phyllis S. Busch

WRITING
The Days Before Now: An Autobiographical Note by Margaret Wise Brown
Dear Peter Rabbit by Alma Flor Ada
My Grandmother's Journey by John Cech
Dear Willie Rudd by Libba Moore Gray

READING
I'm in Charge of Celebrations by Byrd Baylor
The Dancing Granny by Ashley Bryan
We're Going on a Bear Hunt by Michael Rosen

These books can be found at your local bookstore or from Simon & Schuster Children's Publishing Division at (800) 223-2336. For a catalog of titles write: Simon and Schuster Children's Marketing, 1230 Avenue of the Americas, New York, NY 10020.

Parents' Home Learning Quiz

How much do you know right now about your child's growth and educational development? Test your knowledge and awareness.

Directions: Mark Y (yes) or N (no) for each statement below, as it applies to you.

Ⓨ Ⓝ **(a)** I praise my child—even for small achievements.

Ⓨ Ⓝ **(b)** Doing well on weekly assignments is fine, but I think my child's test scores and grades are what really count.

Ⓨ Ⓝ **(c)** I talk to my child about school at least twice a week.

Ⓨ Ⓝ **(d)** I meet my child's teacher(s) fewer than three times a year.

Ⓨ Ⓝ **(e)** I do not feel adequately prepared to help my child with homework.

Ⓨ Ⓝ **(f)** I attend my child's school-related programs most of the time.

Ⓨ Ⓝ **(g)** My child watches more than three hours of television per day.

Ⓨ Ⓝ **(h)** If I learned that my child had stolen something from someone, I would first want to know why and then discuss a plan for repayment.

Ⓨ Ⓝ **(i)** If I learned that my child was doing poorly in a particular subject at school, I'd handle the problem myself rather than go through school channels.

Ⓨ Ⓝ **(j)** I believe that my child's problems at school can be readily detected at home.

Ⓨ Ⓝ **(k)** I could easily describe my child's performance in school.

Ⓨ Ⓝ **(l)** I sometimes feel guilty about not providing more enriching experiences for my child.

Ⓨ Ⓝ **(m)** There have been incidents involving violence, harassment, or drug use at my child's school.

Ⓨ Ⓝ **(n)** I am a single parent.

EXPLANATIONS: PARENTS' HOME LEARNING QUIZ

That was relatively painless! Here's an explanation of the yes and no responses for each statement:

(a) *I praise my child—even for small achievements.* If you chose *yes,* good for you! Even acknowledging small hurdles and achievements helps your child maintain a positive attitude about learning. Try coming up with creative, fun expressions of pride and celebration instead of giving him gifts or monetary rewards. A special meal you plan and cook together, an outing, going to the movies, playing one-on-one sports, or just hanging out together are rewards your child will appreciate. Spending some private time together works well, especially in families with several children.

(b) *Doing well on weekly assignments is fine, but I think my child's test scores and grades are what really count.* If you said *yes* to this statement, you're half right (the first part is positive). If your child practices solid learning skills and study habits, the good scores and grades will come in due course, and she will develop excellent skills for a lifetime of learning. Use test scores and grades as feedback to help your family focus on successes and problem areas, but also give your child praise for plugging away on those weekly assignments. Emphasizing the *whole* learning process is the right message to send to your child.

(c) *I talk to my child about school at least twice a week.* Great, if this applies to you! It's important that parents make their interest in education clear to their children. This is especially necessary given a recent survey by Dr. Laurence Steinberg, co-author of *Beyond the Classroom: Why School Reform Has Failed and What Parents Need to Do* (Simon & Schuster, 1996), which found that 72 percent of students aged ten to thirteen said they would prefer to talk more often to their parents about their homework, while only 40 percent of parents believe they are not attentive enough to their children's education. This discrepancy suggests that children would open up more about school-related issues or difficulties if they were given the opportunity to do so by their parents.

(d) *I meet my child's teacher(s) fewer than three times a year.* Meeting with your child's teachers has more educational value than you may be aware of. By offering insights about your child's home life and social habits, you help the teacher gain a fuller understanding of your child. You are also conveying to the teacher your interest in your child's education, and your willingness to collaborate to further his learning progress.

(e) *I do not feel adequately prepared to help my child with homework.* Even if you said *yes* to this, there are many ways to support your child's education, and all of them require only your energy and enthusiasm for learning. If you have a little time and willingness, you can use your feelings of inadequacy as motivation to learn with your child and test your skills together. In doing so, you'll be teaching your child an important lesson: Don't hesitate to undertake something that you might not do well. As a fellow student, you'll also be more sympathetic to your child's struggles, and he will appreciate the interest and attention. If time and other responsibilities do not allow for these sessions, you can still serve as your child's cheering section and keep in touch with his teacher.

(f) *I attend my child's school-related programs most of the time.* If you answered *yes* to this, good! Parents who attend school functions—extracurricular activities, teacher conferences, and "back to school" nights—are indicating that school is important to them and that, by extension, it should be equally important to their children. When parents don't get involved in some capacity with their child's activities, intended or not, they're sending a strong message that they're not interested. Make the time; your effort will not go unnoticed by your child.

(g) *My child watches more than three hours of television per day.* Educators generally agree that watching too much television can affect a child's emotional makeup. Without supervision, children will be disturbed by particular types of programs or news pieces, depending on their maturity level. TV is also a passive activity. Monitor your child's viewing habits. Watch TV with your child and carefully screen programs. Some TV shows have sound information and entertainment content, but try to offer more active ways to spend free time with the family (like after-school or community-based programs).

(h) *If I learned that my child had stolen something from someone, I would first want to know why and then discuss* *a plan for repayment.* That's the way to go. By encouraging your child to come up with his own plan for restitution (for example, saving money through odd jobs and allowance to pay off what he stole), you're also making him face the consequences of his actions. This will go a long way toward helping him become more autonomous while taking responsibility for the theft. Your child's stealing might be a warning sign. It could be that this is merely the first time your child has been caught; repeated offenses could be indications of a larger problem, like drug abuse or extreme peer pressure. On the other hand, your child may be trying to get your attention or test your limits and see how much he can get away with. Monitor your child for a while, just to be sure. Don't feel as though you've done something to cause this behavior or that you've failed as a parent. Children naturally test rules. Provide direction and be a positive disciplinary force. Other reactions:

Punitive punishment Any action that emphasizes your anger rather than the issues at hand teaches children to behave by intimidation rather than by education. Help your child develop a sense of responsibility and autonomy, and obedient behavior should follow.

Light reprimand Parents who treat this matter lightly run the risk of conveying to their children that their behavior is not entirely inappropriate. When parents fail to discipline their children in proportion to the seriousness of an offense, kids may fail to develop a sense of value and responsibility. Instead of standing by idly, help your child see the larger picture and take responsibility for his behavior.

(i) *If I learned that my child was doing poorly in a particular subject at school, I'd handle the problem myself rather than go through school channels.* The problem with trying to tackle these difficulties at home is most children are taught subjects differently from how their parents learned, and this can make helping out more difficult. When a child doesn't understand a concept *or* a parent's explanation of it, no amount of increased study time is going to help. Try meeting with teachers and counselors and discussing ways in which the *school* can help. You do your child the service of getting involved in her education, and you do teachers and counselors a service by conveying you have faith in their abilities. Set up an appointment with a teacher or counselor. Discuss how they can better serve your child, and offer your assistance. Exploring other strategies . . .

Punishment You could punish your child for his lack of diligence, but that makes parents believe that their child's performance will improve. In reality, punishment may help a child understand how important schoolwork is to his parents, but it will not help the child understand the material itself. Instead of alienating the child through punishment, parents should try to affect the learning process itself by getting involved, speaking and collaborating with teachers to isolate problem areas, and supporting their child's efforts.

Doing nothing You've never heard of your child having such problems before, so you're content to just let the kid tackle it on her own. Be careful! There are any number of reasons your child's performance decreased: learning problems, increased social calendars, needing reading glasses, drug abuse, or emotional trauma (to name a few). Observe your child for indications of change, and arrange to speak with teachers.

(j) *I believe that my child's problems at school can be readily detected at home.* Parenthood is probably the most difficult job—you deal with every aspect of your child, including emotions that are either revealed or hidden. You can't expect yourself to know everything your child is feeling, thinking, and experiencing. What you can do is observe your child and pick up on warning signs. Look for changes, and discuss them openly and calmly. Your child may not know how to approach you with difficulties she may be experiencing, so reassure her of your love and support. Emphasize that if she has done something wrong or been hurt or confused, you want to know about it regardless of how it will make you feel.

(k) *I could easily describe my child's performance in school.* Good job if you said *yes* to this one! The concern that enough parents don't demonstrate an interest in their child's performance in school is warranted. According to a study published by Dr. Laurence Steinberg, co-author of *Beyond the Classroom: Why School Reform Has Failed and What Parents Need to Do* (Simon & Schuster, 1996), nearly one-third of students believe their parents have no idea how they're doing in school, one-sixth don't think their parents care whether they earn good grades in school, and more than half say they could bring home grades of C or worse without upsetting their parents. Regardless of whether these assessments pertain to you and your child, the fact that so many students believe them is an indication that both parents and children need to break some communication barriers.

(l) *I sometimes feel guilty about not providing more enriching experiences for my child.* Parents often feel guilty when they can't afford to spend enough money on their children's needs or take the time necessary to do all the things they'd like with their children. Instead of pressuring yourself, investigate the variety of quality, inexpensive opportunities offered in your community, namely after-school and community-based programs in art, music, dance, and sports. By encouraging your child to participate in these activities, you can engage him in worthwhile, rewarding experiences without having to expend energy or money that you don't have. Consider letting your child know that your family must prioritize purchases; by comfortably discussing your financial situation, you stand a better chance of raising a child who is more conscious of and responsible about money matters.

(m) *There have been incidents involving violence, harassment, or drug use at my child's school.* It's sad if you had to answer *yes* to this statement. There's really no way to shield your child from being aware of these incidents, but you can stop your child from experiencing them directly by stunting their innocent curiosity with cold hard *facts*. If you need to get informed yourself, check out the resources listed in the back of *Making the Grade* or check out your local library. Don't wait for schools to teach your child about these issues. Schools may address them, but schools are not administrators of social service—they are administrators of curriculum-based education. A parent is the only reliable resource a child has on these and other developmental issues. Please make yourself available!

(n) *I am a single parent.* Single parenthood can prove to be an extremely hectic lifestyle. Time is a rare commodity, and single parents find they must budget it wisely just to complete day-to-day responsibilities. Under these circumstances, you may not be able to spend as much time with your child as you would like. But even two-parent families experience time crunches and hectic lifestyles. Whether you're a single parent or not, allow your child to handle some of the responsibilities, preferably those that could be finished faster with two individuals. This way, you and your child can talk and bond while you work. Hopefully, handing over some of the responsibilities will also free up some time that you can spend with your child in more entertaining and educational activities. Try preparing in advance so you can attend meetings with your child's teachers and school programs in which your child is participating. And don't feel guilty for putting your child to work; by letting your child help you out, you're actually teaching good values and responsibility. Success at school and success at home—that's what "making the grade" is all about!

FOR PARENTS ONLY: ANSWERS TO THE KIDS' HOME LEARNING QUIZZES

Language Arts

1. (b)	12. (b)
2. (d)	13. (d)
3. (c)	14. (a)
4. (d)	15. (c)
5. (a)	16. (b)
6. (a)	17. (c)
7. (b)	18. (a)
8. (d)	19. (a)
9. (c)	20. (b)
10. (d)	21. (d)
11. (a)	

Math

1. (c)	11. (b)
2. (d)	12. (a)
3. (a)	13. (c)
4. (b)	14. (a)
5. (d)	15. (c)
6. (c)	16. (b)
7. (a)	17. (d)
8. (d)	18. (c)
9. (c)	19. (c)
10. (b)	20. (c)

Science

1. (b)	9. (a)
2. (d)	10. nervous
3. (a)	11. circulatory
4. (b)	12. urinary
5. (b)	13. respiratory
6. (b)	14. (b)
7. (d)	15. (b)
8. (c)	16. (d)

Kids' Home Learning Quizzes

Language Arts See how many questions you can get right! Follow the directions for each question. Read everything carefully before filling in one answer bubble. Fill in the (e) bubble if you haven't been taught something in the question. Fill in the (f) if you've learned this already in school, but it's still hard for you.

Question 1: Select the *simple subject* of the sentence, and fill in the matching answer bubble.

1. At <u>dawn</u>, <u>sunlight</u> <u>comes</u> through my bedroom <u>window</u>.
    - (a) dawn
    - (b) sunlight
    - (c) comes
    - (d) window
    (e) We haven't studied this in school yet.
    (f) We've studied this, but it's still hard for me.
    ⓐ ⓑ ⓒ ⓓ ⓔ ⓕ

Question 2: Select the simple predicate of the sentence, and fill in the matching answer bubble.

2. After a long <u>wait</u> at the <u>restaurant</u>, our <u>waiter</u> finally <u>seated</u> us.
    - (a) wait
    - (b) restaurant
    - (c) waiter
    - (d) seated
    (e) We haven't studied this in school yet.
    (f) We've studied this but it's still hard for me.
    ⓐ ⓑ ⓒ ⓓ ⓔ ⓕ

Questions 3–4: Select the response in which commas are used properly, and fill in the matching answer bubble.

3. (a) 101, Hudson Road
    (b) Sarah Lisa and Philip
    (c) Sincerely Yours, Tracy Chang
    (d) riding my bike reading, and teasing my sister
    (e) We haven't studied this in school yet.
    (f) We've studied this, but it's still hard for me.
    ⓐ ⓑ ⓒ ⓓ ⓔ ⓕ

4. (a) On August, 31 1988
    (b) in, Philadelphia Pennsylvania
    (c) Dear, Juan,
    (d) fencing, dancing, and soccer
    (e) We haven't studied this in school yet.
    (f) We've studied this, but it's still hard for me.
    ⓐ ⓑ ⓒ ⓓ ⓔ ⓕ

Questions 5–7: Select the answer that best completes the sentence, and fill in the matching answer bubble.

5. My mother _____ me shopping next weekend.
    - (a) will take
    - (b) takes with
    - (c) took
    - (d) taken
    (e) We haven't studied this in school yet.
    (f) We've studied this, but it's still hard for me.
    ⓐ ⓑ ⓒ ⓓ ⓔ ⓕ

6. Does this scarf belong to _____ or Jesse?
    - (a) you
    - (b) yourself
    - (c) yours
    - (d) your
    (e) We haven't studied this in school yet.
    (f) We've studied this, but it's still hard for me.
    ⓐ ⓑ ⓒ ⓓ ⓔ ⓕ

7. Which of the three coats is _____?
    - (a) more warm
    - (b) warmest
    - (c) most warm
    - (d) warmer
    (e) We haven't studied this in school yet.
    (f) We've studied this, but it's still hard for me.
    ⓐ ⓑ ⓒ ⓓ ⓔ ⓕ

8. Reorder the following sentences to make the best paragraph.

1. The tomatoes were watered first because they were shriveling up in the heat.

2. Getting hot themselves, the girls went inside for a glass of lemonade.

3. Regina and Mai were watering the garden.

4. Next, Regina took care of the plum tree, her favorite plant in the whole garden.

(a) 1-3-2-4
(b) 3-4-1-2
(c) 2-4-3-1
(d) 3-1-4-2

(e) We haven't studied this in school yet.
(f) We've studied this, but it's still hard for me.

ⓐ ⓑ ⓒ ⓓ ⓔ ⓕ

9. Choose the sentence that fits in best with the paragraph.

Cats are intelligent animals. They're very perceptive: they can see in the dark, and they have very sharp hearing. _____ They also know to refuse cat food that they don't like!

(a) Baby lions are very cute, but watch out for their mothers!
(b) Cats come in all sorts of colors and breed, just like dogs.
(c) When they sit still, it looks like they are deep in thought.
(d) The mythological sphinx is half human, half lion.

(e) We haven't studied this in school yet.
(f) We've studied this, but it's still hard for me.

ⓐ ⓑ ⓒ ⓓ ⓔ ⓕ

Questions 10–11: Read each sentence carefully. Find the sentence that uses correct punctuation and capitalization, and fill in the matching answer bubble.

10. (a) Libbys family owns a cabin in ogunquit maine.
(b) On fridays, Libby watches a movie at southwyck cinemas with her friends!
(c) When shes not, Libby likes riding her horse, cherub.
(d) Libby says she wouldn't dream of living anywhere else.

(e) We haven't studied this in school yet.
(f) We've studied this, but it's still hard for me.

ⓐ ⓑ ⓒ ⓓ ⓔ ⓕ

11. (a) Joel brought in his puppy, Spike, to show his class.
(b) At Joel's command Spike rolled over caught a frisbee and licked Joel's face.
(c) All the kid's were so happy they clapped for spike.
(d) Joel said, It took my dad six month's to teach him those tricks.

(e) We haven't studied this in school yet.
(f) We've studied this, but it's still hard for me.

ⓐ ⓑ ⓒ ⓓ ⓔ ⓕ

Questions 12–13: Read the first two sentences. Then find the sentence that combines them into one sentence without changing their meanings, and fill in the matching answer bubble.

12. Mark just bought a new car.
The car is red.

(a) The red car Mark just bought.
(b) Mark just bought a new red car.
(c) Mark's new red car he just bought.
(d) Mark just bought a car and it is red.

(e) We haven't studied this in school yet.
(f) We've studied this, but it's still hard for me.

ⓐ ⓑ ⓒ ⓓ ⓔ ⓕ

13. Maggie went shopping yesterday.
Jeffrey went shopping yesterday.

(a) Maggie went shopping yesterday and Jeffrey too.
(b) Maggie and Jeffrey yesterday shopped.
(c) Shopping yesterday were Maggie and Jeffrey.
(d) Maggie and Jeffrey went shopping yesterday.

(e) We haven't studied this in school yet.
(f) We've studied this, but it's still hard for me.

ⓐ ⓑ ⓒ ⓓ ⓔ ⓕ

Questions 14–15: Find the sentence in which the underlined word is misspelled for how it is used, and fill in the matching answer bubble.

14. (a) Cary has <u>groan</u> two inches.
(b) Jeremy is <u>bored</u>.
(c) That is a tight <u>knot</u>.
(d) She has been <u>busy</u>.

(e) We haven't studied this in school yet.
(f) We've studied this, but it's still hard for me.

ⓐ ⓑ ⓒ ⓓ ⓔ ⓕ

15. (a) Peter is the oldest <u>son</u>.
     (b) Prison <u>cells</u> are usually small.
     (c) You look <u>pail</u>.
     (d) A sunset is a pretty <u>scene</u>.
(e) We haven't studied this in school yet.
(f) We've studied this, but it's still hard for me.

ⓐ ⓑ ⓒ ⓓ ⓔ ⓕ

Questions 16–18: Read each question carefully. Pick the right answer, and fill in the matching answer bubble.

16. If you want to find the meaning of the word *amendment*, you should look in _____.
     (a) an encyclopedia
     (b) a dictionary
     (c) a thesaurus
     (d) an owner's manual
(e) We haven't studied this in school yet.
(f) We've studied this, but it's still hard for me.

ⓐ ⓑ ⓒ ⓓ ⓔ ⓕ

17. If you want to find another word for *amendment*, you should look in _____.
     (a) an encyclopedia
     (b) a dictionary
     (c) a thesaurus
     (d) an owner's manual
(e) We haven't studied this in school yet.
(f) We've studied this, but it's still hard for me.

ⓐ ⓑ ⓒ ⓓ ⓔ ⓕ

18. If you want to find a description of the constitutional amendments, you should look in _____.
     (a) an encyclopedia
     (b) a dictionary
     (c) a thesaurus
     (d) an owner's manual
(e) We haven't studied this in school yet.
(f) We've studied this, but it's still hard for me.

ⓐ ⓑ ⓒ ⓓ ⓔ ⓕ

Questions 19–21: Use the following dictionary entries to answer each question.

shine (shin) *v.* 1. To give off light. 2. To excel in an activity. 3. To be obvious or apparent.

ship (ship) *n.* 1. A sailing vessel. 2. An aircraft or spacecraft.

shirr (shur) *v.* 1. To gather (cloth) into rows by stitching. 2. To cook (eggs) by baking until set.

shish ke•bab *n.* a dish containing pieces of seasoned meat and vegetables that are roasted on skewers.

19. Which of the following could shine?
     (a) the sun
     (b) coffee
     (c) meat
     (d) carpet
(e) We haven't studied this in school yet.
(f) We've studied this, but it's still hard for me.

ⓐ ⓑ ⓒ ⓓ ⓔ ⓕ

20. When you gather cloth into rows and stitch, you are _____ it.
     (a) shipping
     (b) shirring
     (c) shaking
     (d) shifting
(e) We haven't studied this in school yet.
(f) We've studied this, but it's still hard for me.

ⓐ ⓑ ⓒ ⓓ ⓔ ⓕ

21. Which of the following words is spelled correctly?
     (a) shir
     (b) shish kebob
     (c) shipp
     (d) shine
(e) We haven't studied this in school yet.
(f) We've studied this, but it's still hard for me.

ⓐ ⓑ ⓒ ⓓ ⓔ ⓕ

You're done! Now look up the answers and see how many questions you got right.

Making the Grade

Math See how many questions you can get right! Keep some scratch paper handy if you need extra space to work out the problems. Read everything carefully and "do the math" before filling in one answer bubble. Fill in the (e) bubble if you haven't been taught something in the question. Fill in the (f) if you've learned this already in school, but it's still hard for you.

1. What adds up to 52?
   (a) 2 tens and 5 ones
   (b) 52 tens
   (c) 5 tens and 2 ones
   (d) 1 tens and 5 ones
   (e) We haven't studied this in school yet.
   (f) We've studied this, but it's still hard for me.
   ⓐ ⓑ ⓒ ⓓ ⓔ ⓕ

2. What is the number for 5 hundred and 6 ones?
   (a) 5,006
   (b) 56
   (c) 5,600
   (d) 506
   (e) We haven't studied this in school yet.
   (f) We've studied this, but it's still hard for me.
   ⓐ ⓑ ⓒ ⓓ ⓔ ⓕ

3. Which of the following statements is true?
   (a) 543 > 453
   (b) 435 < 345
   (c) 345 > 354
   (d) 534 < 533
   (e) We haven't studied this in school yet.
   (f) We've studied this, but it's still hard for me.
   ⓐ ⓑ ⓒ ⓓ ⓔ ⓕ

4. What does 3 mean in 5,378?
   (a) 3,000
   (b) 300
   (c) 30
   (d) 3
   (e) We haven't studied this in school yet.
   (f) We've studied this, but it's still hard for me.
   ⓐ ⓑ ⓒ ⓓ ⓔ ⓕ

5. Pick the next number in this sequence: 21, 28, 35, _____.
   (a) 41
   (b) 52
   (c) 46
   (d) 42
   (e) We've studied this, but I don't understand it.
   (f) We haven't studied this in school yet.
   ⓐ ⓑ ⓒ ⓓ ⓔ ⓕ

6. Which number has the most value?
   (a) 1.10
   (b) .110
   (c) 10.10
   (d) .010
   (e) We haven't studied this in school yet.
   (f) We've studied this, but it's still hard for me.
   ⓐ ⓑ ⓒ ⓓ ⓔ ⓕ

7. Which fraction is greater than 1/4?
   (a) 1/3
   (b) 1/8
   (c) 2/12
   (d) 3/13
   (e) We haven't studied this in school yet.
   (f) We've studied this, but it's still hard for me.
   ⓐ ⓑ ⓒ ⓓ ⓔ ⓕ

8. What fraction of the figure above is shaded?
   (a) 4/1
   (b) 1/3
   (c) 3/4
   (d) 1/4
   (e) We haven't studied this in school yet.
   (f) We've studied this, but it's still hard for me.
   ⓐ ⓑ ⓒ ⓓ ⓔ ⓕ

9. Solve the following equation: 26 − 17 = _____.
   (a) 43
   (b) 11
   (c) 9
   (d) 7
   (e) We haven't studied this in school yet.
   (f) We've studied this, but it's still hard for me.
   ⓐ ⓑ ⓒ ⓓ ⓔ ⓕ

10. Solve the following: 27/3 = _____.
    (a) 243
    (b) 9
    (c) 6
    (d) 12
(e) We haven't studied this in school yet.
(f) We've studied this, but it's still hard for me.
        ⓐ ⓑ ⓒ ⓓ ⓔ ⓕ

11. Solve the following: 741 + 37 = _____.
    (a) 796
    (b) 778
    (c) 787
    (d) 717
(e) We haven't studied this in school yet.
(f) We've studied this, but it's still hard for me.
        ⓐ ⓑ ⓒ ⓓ ⓔ ⓕ

12. Solve the following: 461 − 229 = _____.
    (a) 232
    (b) 222
    (c) 321
    (d) 248
(e) We've studied this, but I don't understand it.
(f) We haven't studied this in school yet.
        ⓐ ⓑ ⓒ ⓓ ⓔ ⓕ

13. Solve the following: 4 3/4 + 6 3/4 = _____.
    (a) 10 6/8
    (b) 10 1/2
    (c) 11 1/2
    (d) 11 6/4
(e) We haven't studied this in school yet.
(f) We've studied this, but it's still hard for me.
        ⓐ ⓑ ⓒ ⓓ ⓔ ⓕ

14. Solve the following: $16.47 + $2.29 = _____.
    (a) $18.76
    (b) $19.76
    (c) $18.16
    (d) $19.16
(e) We haven't studied this in school yet.
(f) We've studied this, but it's still hard for me.
        ⓐ ⓑ ⓒ ⓓ ⓔ ⓕ

15. Chocolate Blockheads sell for $.89 a pack. How much would it cost to buy three packs?
    (a) $2.47
    (b) $2.77
    (c) $2.67
    (d) $3.77
(e) We haven't studied this in school yet.
(f) We've studied this, but it's still hard for me.
        ⓐ ⓑ ⓒ ⓓ ⓔ ⓕ

16. Which of the following shapes is a pentagon?

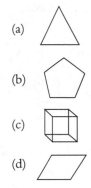

(a)

(b)

(c)

(d)

(e) We haven't studied this in school yet.
(f) We've studied this, but it's still hard for me.
        ⓐ ⓑ ⓒ ⓓ ⓔ ⓕ

17. Marie and her mother went shopping at 11 A.M. They came home four hours later. Which clock shows what time it was when they got home?

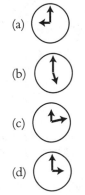

(a)

(b)

(c)

(d)

(e) We haven't studied this in school yet.
(f) We've studied this, but it's still hard for me.
        ⓐ ⓑ ⓒ ⓓ ⓔ ⓕ

Making the Grade

The graph below shows how many children in each grade take the bus to Shadow Valley Elementary School each day. Use the graph to answer questions 18–20.

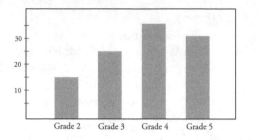

18. How many third graders take the school bus every day?
    (a) 27
    (b) 15
    (c) 25
    (d) 34
(e) We haven't studied this in school yet.
(f) We've studied this, but it's still hard for me.

ⓐ ⓑ ⓒ ⓓ ⓔ ⓕ

19. How many more students in grade 4 take the school bus than in grade 3?
    (a) 9
    (b) 22
    (c) 10
    (d) 29
(e) We haven't studied this in school yet.
(f) We've studied this, but it's still hard for me.

20. In which grade do the most students ride the bus to school?
    (a) 2
    (b) 3
    (c) 4
    (d) 5
(e) We haven't studied this in school yet.
(f) We've studied this, but it's still hard for me.

ⓐ ⓑ ⓒ ⓓ ⓔ ⓕ

You're done! Now look up the answers and see how many questions you got right.

Science See how many questions you can get right! Follow the directions for each question. Read everything carefully before filling in one answer bubble. Fill in the (e) bubble if you haven't been taught something in the question. Fill in the (f) if you've learned this already in school, but it's still hard for you.

Use the chart below to answer questions 1–3.

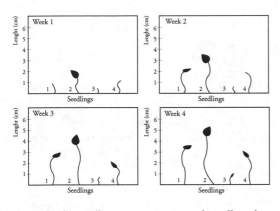

1. Which seedling was consistently taller than the others each week?
   (a) 1
   (b) 2
   (c) 3
   (d) 4
(e) We haven't studied this in school yet.
(f) We've studied this, but it's still hard for me.
ⓐ ⓑ ⓒ ⓓ ⓔ ⓕ

2. Which of the following would not explain why seedling 3 grew so little?
   (a) It did not get enough light.
   (b) It did not get enough water.
   (c) The seed was planted in sand.
   (d) The seed dropped on the floor before it was planted.
(e) We haven't studied this in school yet.
(f) We've studied this, but it's still hard for me.
ⓐ ⓑ ⓒ ⓓ ⓔ ⓕ

3. How tall is the shortest seedling at four weeks?
   (a) 1 cm
   (b) 3 cm
   (c) 1.5 cm
   (d) .5 cm
(e) We haven't studied this in school yet.
(f) We've studied this, but it's still hard for me.
ⓐ ⓑ ⓒ ⓓ ⓔ ⓕ

4. What is photosynthesis?
   (a) The chemical used to develop camera film.
   (b) A process in which plants use solar energy to make food from carbon dioxide.
   (c) The tendency of a plant to move toward or away from a light source.
   (d) A technique used to fuse two photographs into one.
(e) We haven't studied this in school yet.
(f) We've studied this, but it's still hard for me.
ⓐ ⓑ ⓒ ⓓ ⓔ ⓕ

5. Which of the following items will not float?
   (a) a person
   (b) a pen
   (c) a corked bottle
   (d) a balloon
(e) We haven't studied this in school yet.
(f) We've studied this, but it's still hard for me.
ⓐ ⓑ ⓒ ⓓ ⓔ ⓕ

6. About how long does it take Earth to orbit once around the sun?
   (a) 12 hours
   (b) one year
   (c) 24 hours
   (d) 30 days
(e) We haven't studied this in school yet.
(f) We've studied this, but it's still hard for me.
ⓐ ⓑ ⓒ ⓓ ⓔ ⓕ

7. Which of the following is not a terrestrial planet, or one of the four closest to the Sun?
   (a) Venus
   (b) Mars
   (c) Mercury
   (d) Jupiter
(e) We haven't studied this in school yet.
(f) We've studied this, but it's still hard for me.
ⓐ ⓑ ⓒ ⓓ ⓔ ⓕ

Making the Grade

8. Who invented the electric light bulb?
   (a) John Ray
   (b) Albert Einstein
   (c) Thomas Edison
   (d) James Watt
   (e) We haven't studied this in school yet.
   (f) We've studied this, but it's still hard for me.

   ⓐ ⓑ ⓒ ⓓ ⓔ ⓕ

9. The crust, mantle, and core are all parts of
   _____.
   (a) the earth's structure
   (b) Saturn's atmosphere
   (c) a volcano's layers
   (d) the Sun's center
   (e) We haven't studied this in school yet.
   (f) We've studied this, but it's still hard for me.

   ⓐ ⓑ ⓒ ⓓ ⓔ ⓕ

Questions 10–13: Draw a line from the body part on the left to its matching bodily system on the right. If you haven't studied this in school yet, fill in the (e) bubble. If you have studied this in school but it's still hard for you, fill in (f).

10. spine   respiratory

11. blood vessels   nervous

12. kidneys   urinary

13. lung   circulatory

(e) We haven't studied this in school yet.
(f) We've studied this, but it's still hard for me.

   ⓔ ⓕ

14. Which of the following practices does not belong in a proper health regimen?
    (a) exercise
    (b) smoking
    (c) balanced diet
    (d) hygiene
(e) We haven't studied this in school yet.
(f) We've studied this, but it's still hard for me.

   ⓐ ⓑ ⓒ ⓓ ⓔ ⓕ

15. A communicable disease is one that _____.
    (a) you can get only if someone talks to you
    (b) is contagious
    (c) you can't get from someone else
    (d) grows in the throat
(e) We haven't studied this in school yet.
(f) We've studied this, but it's still hard for me.

   ⓐ ⓑ ⓒ ⓓ ⓔ ⓕ

16. Which of the following is not a source of pollution?
    (a) smoke
    (b) garbage
    (c) volcanoes
    (d) rivers
(e) We haven't studied this in school yet.
(f) We've studied this, but it's still hard for me.

   ⓐ ⓑ ⓒ ⓓ ⓔ ⓕ

You're done! Now look up the answers and see how many questions you got right.

How Did We Do? Grade Us.

Thank you for choosing a Kaplan book. Your comments and suggestions are very useful to us. Please answer the following questions to assist us in our continued development of high-quality resources to meet your needs.

The Kaplan book I read was: _____

My name is: _____

My address is: _____

_____

My e-mail address is: _____

What overall grade would you give this book? Ⓐ Ⓑ Ⓒ Ⓓ Ⓕ

How relevant was the information to your goals? Ⓐ Ⓑ Ⓒ Ⓓ Ⓕ

How comprehensive was the information in this book? Ⓐ Ⓑ Ⓒ Ⓓ Ⓕ

How accurate was the information in this book? Ⓐ Ⓑ Ⓒ Ⓓ Ⓕ

How easy was the book to use? Ⓐ Ⓑ Ⓒ Ⓓ Ⓕ

How appealing was the book's design? Ⓐ Ⓑ Ⓒ Ⓓ Ⓕ

What were the book's strong points? _____

How could this book be improved? _____

Is there anything that we left out that you wanted to know more about?

Would you recommend this book to others? ☐ YES   ☐ NO

Other comments: _____

_____

_____

Do we have permission to quote you? ☐ YES   ☐ NO

Thank you for your help. Please tear out this page and mail it to:

Dave Chipps, Managing Editor
Kaplan Educational Centers
888 Seventh Avenue
New York, NY 10106

Or, you can answer these questions online at www.kaplan.com/talkback.

Thanks!

SIXTY · YEARS · OF
KAPLAN
60
BUILDING · FUTURES